Asian Feminisms and Youth Activism

Asian Feminisms and Youth Activism

Focus on India and Pakistan

Edited By
Nilanjana Paul
Namita Goswami
Sailaja Nandigama
Gowri Parameswaran
Fawzia Afzal-Khan

This is a joint publication of the Journal of International Women's Studies and Wagadu Press.

ISBN: 978-1-952356-02-5

To order additional copies of this book, contact
Wagadu
www.wagadu.org

About the Editors

Nilanjana Paul is an Assistant Professor of South Asian and World History at The University of Texas Rio Grande Valley. She is the author of *Bengal Muslims and Colonial Education, 1854-1947: A Study of Curriculum, Educational Institutions, and Communal Politics* published by Routledge in 2022. Her articles have appeared in *South Asia Research* and *Journal of History*. She has received several awards including the Humanities Texas Grant and Louise Gloeckner M.D. Research Fellowship from Drexel University for her work.

Namita Goswami is Professor of Philosophy at Indiana State University. She works in continental philosophy as well as postcolonial, critical race, feminist, and queer theory. She has published in a wide range of journals such as *Hypatia, SIGNS, Angelaki, Journal of Speculative Philosophy, Contemporary Aesthetics,* and *Critical Philosophy of Race* and in edited volumes such as *Rethinking Facticity* (edited by Eric Nelson and François Raffoul), *Asian and Feminist Philosophies in Dialogue: Liberating Traditions* (edited by Ashby Butnor and Jen McWeeny), *Phenomenology, Embodiment, and Race* (edited by Emily Lee) and *Constructing the Nation: A Race and Nationalism Reader* (edited by Mariana Ortega and Linda Martin Alcoff). She is the author of *Subjects that Matter: Philosophy, Feminism, and Postcolonial Theory* (SUNY Press, 2019) and co-editor of *Why Race and Gender Still Matter: An Intersectional Approach* (Cambridge University Press: Pickering & Chatto, 2014). She is currently completing a book on Gayatri Spivak.

Sailaja Nandigama is an Associate Professor at the Humanities and Social Sciences department of Birla Institute of Technology and Science (BITS), Rajasthan, India. She completed her PhD in Development Studies in 2009, from the International Institute of Social Studies, the Netherlands with a Netherlands government fellowship (NFP Fellow), and worked in the University of Sheffield, UK and the Wageningen University and Research Centre (WUR), the Netherlands as a Post-Doctoral researcher before joining at the Birla Institute of Technology and Science (BITS), Pilani, Rajasthan, India in 2014. Her research interests include human and environmental systems, climate change, gender studies, feminist political ecology, social justice and policy issues. At present she is actively engaged as an Associate Editor with the interdisciplinary Journal of Environmental Studies and Sciences (JESS), published by Springer Nature, and is also part of the Editorial Board of the Journal of International Women's

Studies (JIWS) USA.

Gowri Parameswaran is Professor and Chair of Educational Studies and Leadership at the State University of New York at New Paltz. She obtained her MA and PhD in Cognitive/Educational Psychology from Rutgers University. Her research explorations center on gender, socioeconomic status and culture and their impact on children and adult cognition both in the USA and in India. She is the co-editor of an introductory text for Women's Studies – Women: Images and Reality published by McGraw- Hill. She has also published books and articles on diversity and inclusion in education. In recent years she has written theoretical articles critiquing the historical assumptions around developmental psychology and how to teach about topics such as the privileging of the Global North over the Global South. Email: paramesg@newpaltz.edu.

Fawzia Afzal-Khan is Professor of English, a University Distinguished Scholar (2009-10), and former Director of the Women and Gender Studies Program at Montclair State University, NJ (2009-2015). In addition to having published numerous scholarly and journalistic essays, poems, plays and a memoir *Lahore with Love: Growing Up With Girlfriends Pakistani Style* (Syracuse University Press, 2010), she has authored three books of scholarly criticism, *Cultural Imperialism: Genre and Ideology in the Indo-English Novel* (Penn State Press 1993), *A Critical Stage: The Role of Secular Alternative Theatre in Pakistan* (Seagull Press, 2005), and *Siren Song: Understanding Pakistan Through its Women Singers* (OUP: 2020), and edited two scholarly anthologies, *The PreOccupation of Postcolonial Studies* (Duke University Press, 2000), and *Shattering the Stereotypes: Muslim Women Speak* Out (Interlink Books 2005 . She maintains a blog called www.travelingfeminista.com and her website can be accessed at www.fawziaafzalkhan.com.

About the Executive Editors

Dr. Diana J. Fox is Interim University Director, Institute for Gender and Development Studies-Regional Co ordinating Office, The University of the West Indies. She is a cultural anthropologist, decolonial feminist scholar-activist, and documentary film producer. She is Professor of Anthropology at Bridgewater State University in Massachusetts, USA, where she has taught since 2000.

Dr. Mechthild Nagel is Professor of Philosophy at the State University of New York, Cortland. She is the founder and Editor-in-Chief of *Wagadu: A Journal of Transnational Women's and Gender Studies* and the Director of the Center for Ethics, Peace, and Social Justice.

Dr. Bekeh Ukelina is an Associate Professor of History and Africana Studies at the State University of New York. He is the Director of the Center for Gender and Intercultural Studies and the Managing Editor of *Wagadu: A Journal of Transnational Women's and Gender Studies.*

Table of Contents

CHAPTER 1

Introduction:

South Asian Feminisms and Youth Activism: Focus on India and Pakistan

Nilanjana Paul[1], Namita Goswami[2], Sailaja Nandigama[3], Gowri Parameswaran[4], Fawzia Afzal-Khan[5]

Introduction

These are turbulent times for the many countries that form the Global South. South Asian nation-states are no exception; the last half century has ushered in liberalization of economies, forced structural adjustments, climate chaos, criminalization of indigenous and lower caste populations, and rapid technological changes. All these forces have resulted in massive upheavals often manifested in political, economic, and social crises. Experts observe that in times of instability, the most marginalized groups, already the target of social violence, are disproportionately subjected to enormous stress, anxiety, and insecurity. In South Asia, women, as one such group that faces multiple intersectional oppressions depending on class, caste, religious locations, etc. have been active participants on the frontlines of struggles for social justice and equity. In the new era of hardened nationalism and militarism, they have also been the targets of violence and brutality. Challenging and complicating the national security analytic that drives most area studies approaches to South Asian knowledge production, this special issue centers transnational feminist work that can help us read various social justice movements unfolding across South Asia through a "queer optic"[6] that aims to decolonize the normative narratives of nation, gender, class, sexuality, ethnicity, and religion, among others. In being alert to the complex shifts in our understandings of these lived embodiments of sexed categories, we have included interventions by women from varying backgrounds and selected essays reflecting women's many lived realities: as mothers, daughters, wives, lovers, and activists across different backgrounds, as they take on the acute challenges of forging coalitional alliances to assert agency in public and private spaces.

As a result of our methodological imperative of "queer optics" that decolonize normative narratives, we foreground how local, small-scale public pedagogies not only reverberate far beyond their regional inflections but rupture entrenched oppositions between the local (the non-west) and the global (the west). If postcolonial critique excavates the historicity of civilizing missions deemed necessary for progress and development, then the queer optics proffered in this volume suggest that the analytic horizons assumed as always already tangential to dominant forms of knowledge production may in fact convey and uphold precisely those governing circuits of exchange that must be sundered. It is this complicity, continuity, and mutual implication that moves us away from conflating privileged material practices of self-perpetuation and self-elaboration with effective—and affective---rebellion towards an analytic horizon wherein we map our perilous, fleeting, and cacophonous quotidian realities as disclosures of a language of kinship, coalition-building, and liberation.

The essays in this collection thus reflect the many ways in which women are not just victims of state (and familial) apparatuses of power across South Asia but have also organized and fought back against heteropatriarchal class and caste oppressions, while supporting their communities against the precarity of our neoliberal times. The Humanities and Social Science methodological approaches that frame the essays that follow represent interdisciplinary mappings of women's rights broadly construed, as these intersect with environmental and ecological interventions, land rights, LGBTQI+ identities and concerns, as well as hitherto unforeseen regressive trends regarding the mobilization/weaponization of religion and masculinist nationalisms in a neoliberal world order. As our edited collection demonstrates, our contemporary moment connects colonial and postcolonial realities in South Asia, showing how these historical eras are deeply intertwined and co-implicated in the resultant inequities spawned by neoliberal globalization, reflecting what the late Nawal el Saadawi dubbed, the patriarchal class system.

Section 1: Historical Groundings

Historically, the construction of "veiled" and "enslaved" South Asian women has fired the imagination of colonial rulers; they condemned Indian religions as well as customs regarding women and focused on "civilizing" the Indian population. However, India has always had a rich tradition of indigenous feminist struggles that gained momentum with Indian independence movements. Concurrently, by the middle to the late nineteenth century, a small group of missionaries and British feminists understood the exploitative nature of British colonial exploitation and allied with Indian women's aspirations for equity, with the former committed to the education and rights of all Indian women (Forbes, 1996 & Jayawardena, 1996). In that context, the authors in the first section examine a wide range of topics including how missionary education influenced Indian women's fight for their rights by both challenging colonial rule as well as patriarchal customs. Women themselves came forward to articulate their ideas in terms of education, communicated their right to work outside homes and local communities, and formed organizations that addressed their needs. Despite obstacles, the struggle for women's rights continued after independence in 1947 and was extended beyond domestic and employment rights. For example, women participated in grassroot level environmental protests like the Chipko movement and developed new frameworks to think about sustainable communities (Jain, 1984). Overall, these essays provide an overview of the history of the various strands of women's coalitional struggles from pre-independence to modern India.

Nilanjana Paul tussles with the complexities of the roles that Christian nuns played in both helping empower women in the public sphere and representing an imperial power whose main aim was exploiting a colonized country. Just like many western missionaries, British women came to the sub-continent often with the intent of "emancipating" the local population, especially women. The Loreto nuns, however, were an exception in that they also challenged the traditional church hierarchy and became allies to Indian women in their quest for advancement. While the nuns set up convents to educate children from wealthy European families, they also built schools and colleges where Indian students of diverse backgrounds enrolled. Throughout this endeavor, the nuns' efforts were opposed by the upper echelons of the church hierarchy. The educational spaces offered by the Loreto nuns provided an opportunity for women to mingle and educate each other in their many differences. In their later years in India, the nuns were instrumental in opening institutions of higher education. Through their institutions, the nuns remained committed to both social justice and women's emancipation. For over more than a century, educational institutions run by Loreto nuns helped empower women through forging alliances across class, caste, and religious lines.

Shoba Rajgopal critiques the genealogical primacy granted to western feminists by using the occasion of the centenary celebration of the 19th Amendment in the United States (2020) to affirm a first wave feminist legacy in India that predates western feminist intellectual landmarks such as Simone De Beauvoir's *The Second Sex* (1949), or Mary Wollstonecraft's *A Vindication of the Rights of Women* (1791). Tarabai Shinde, Lakshmi N. Menon, Dakshayini Velayudhan, Begum Aizaz Rasul, Madam Bhikaji Cama, Sarojini Naidu, among others, created a radical and intersectional revolutionary feminism that not only included the battle against British colonialism and Christian proselytization in its activism but also represented diversity of caste, class, religion, region, and politics. Rajgopal details how India's first wave feminists advocated for property rights, education, secularism, social welfare, and suffrage and participated in the writing of India's constitution. Rajgopal's return to this feminist archive undermines the very basis of the "civilizing mission"—the ostensible liberation of native women from the barbaric violence perpetrated by native men.

Gowri Parameswaran traces the post-independence history of ecological movements led by women in India. She highlights the rich diversity of backgrounds and frameworks that these grassroots movements adopted. Many of the early efforts were not to protect the environment primarily but were rooted in the material needs of the women who were doing the organizing. The Chipko movement, for instance, was an attempt to safeguard the forests that were under threat due to mining. The grassroots organizers had to confront Indian state power head on, and they did so through their intimate connections to family and community. When ecofeminism as a guiding paradigm was adopted by pioneers like Vandana Shiva, India had already had a half century of ecological movements led by women. With the increasing liberalization of the Indian economy in the 1990s, there was a pervasive assumption that economic development requires a sacrifice of ecological goals. Today, a new generation of ecofeminists challenge that notion by pointing to the direct impact that ecological destruction has had on the health and the wellbeing of individuals and communities. They call for Eco socialism, an environmentalism of the poor centering an equitable redistribution of resources as the only path to stop ecological destruction.

Section 2: Violence and Precarity Through Queer Optics

Our examination of South Asia through a queer optic does not decolonize normative narratives through reconstituting India and Pakistan as Queer Nations, a figuration that reinforces western narratives of modernity and consumer-based neoliberal notions of citizenship. Given the absolute triumph of capital, the disarming of labour power, and the conflation of moneyed interests with democratic norms, reimagining agency requires "spatial, temporal, and corporeal convergences, implosions, and rearrangements" (Puar, "Assemblages" 121). As political and social infrastructures are inexorably appropriated for profit maximization and institutional self-preservation, queerness does not simply manifest an identitarian analytic or rallying cry. Rather, a queer optic discerns and maps those extremely hard-won relationalities that subvert teleological trajectories of queerness. In this rendition, the politics of visibility that "outs" the hitherto latent or covert in fact presuppose precisely what must be painstakingly forged in the transnational annexation of "life" itself: those fragile and momentary affinities that form the very substance of a coalitional politics.

Valorizations of the vanguard, revolutionary, or transparent, therefore, often confuse the (re) fashioning of a patent or trademark with the actual (often maddeningly glacial) struggle for change. The authors in this section, therefore, primarily, challenge how understating and thereby discounting the diversity, dissonances, multiplicities, and multifariousness of the lives that are being actively erased and/or reified ironically depoliticizes queerness and results in stagnant liberatory practices stuck in an endless dialectic of exclusion vs. inclusion that leaves the hegemonic place of this encounter unmarked. Contra such stale forms of theory and activism, the queer optics adopted by the authors in this section not only attempt to shift regulatory frames of disciplining and normalization that congeal queerness as a diagnosis and/or corrective of technologies of power, but also yield the historicity that unproblematically posits public self-expression as civil disobedience.

Anhiti Patnaik focuses on digital feminisms by formulating a cripqueer notion of futurity that subverts capitalist fetishization of efficiency, productivity, and expansion, which disproportionately affected women during the lockdowns precipitated by COVID-19 in India. These lockdowns manifest a biopolitics that results in techno precarity, a population of temporary workers denied the most basic means of survival. Statist biometric surveillance and patriarchal nationalism exacerbated already chronic deprivations to further expose these populations to death and decrepitude. Patnaik suggests that algorithmic scales of efficiency, productivity, and expansion, manifest, for example, in the number of shares and likes one receives, create forms of cultural and socioeconomic capital that renders temporary workers permanently disabled. She demonstrates how cripqueer resistance to exploitation and invisibility allows us to determine the mutual imbrication of gender, class, caste, sexuality, and ability in producing pliant, hyper-objectified labour.

Satnauka Banerjee's queer optics attempt a synthesis of transnational digital feminism through capturing the emerging hashtag movements and their real-life reverberations. Along with providing a global overview of recent feminist online campaigns, she focuses on Indian feminist activist discourse in historical and contemporary context, a queering of neoliberal forms of subjectivity and agency that explicitly addresses rural women. Using a qualitative approach, she explores online spaces, such as social media and webpages, that initiate discourses and conversations about various women's issues to build a transnational network that can augment activism from various social groups seeking justice. She underscores that the existing digital divide often holds non-urban women back from asserting their rights and voices and acts as a significant factor in marginalizing women in terms of class, caste, and sexuality. Consequently, she calls for making the transnational feminist activism in online spaces more diverse, inclusive, decentralised, and democratic, aiming at collective emancipation.

Taking Gayatri Spivak's well-known use of literature as facilitating an "uncoercive rearrangement of desires," **Aakanksha Singh**'s reflections venture beyond conventional understandings of queerness to proffer disparate queer subjectivities. Although Deepa Mehta's 1996 film Fire is credited as the catalyst for Pride movements against neoliberal Hindu fundamentalism, Singh enjoins the synonymity of queerness with visibility. Even as queer publics must necessarily reconstitute civil society through progressive legislation, nonheteronormative desires nonetheless find expression only in making themselves visible. Contesting specular logics that equate liberation with being "out," Singh suggests that demanding an appreciable exteriority from queer subjects, particularly through social media, parades, protests, etc., reduces queerness to flamboyant performativity. Such an identity's shallowness restricts the heterogenous force of queer subjectivities that make their presence felt precisely through their quiet resistance.

Namita Goswami also takes Gayatri Spivak as her point of departure by reading Saadat Hasan Manto's short story, "Thanda Gosht" (1950), through Spivak's concept of "originary queerness." Manto's synecdoche ("cold meat") for an unnamed, abducted, and raped female corpse captures the brutality visited upon women's bodies during the partition of India and Pakistan in 1947. Instead of focusing on the story's subaltern victim, however, Goswami argues that "Thanda Gosht's" female protagonist, Kulwant Kaur, by way of her repeated question about this subaltern—who she *is*, (re)figures reproductive heteronormativity as a process of unknowing. Her lover Ishar Singh's peculiar affective idiom, when describing his necrophilic encounter by way of a response, dockets the teleological futurity of Nation itself as (visiting) "burre ki ma ka ghar" (बुरे की माँ के घर; the house of Bad's mother).

Section 3: Women, Labor, Activism

Women organizing together and adopting a collective outlook towards empowering their everyday lives and livelihoods is the theme of this section. The papers highlight the agency of women as well as their collective participation in challenging mainstream discourses around professions such as agriculture and pastoralism, which are considered masculinist. The recently concluded farmers' protest opposing the farm laws of 2020 in India is taken as a reference point by Chakrabarti to reflect on the fascist, masculinist tendencies of the state in favor of the corporatization of Indian agriculture. These hegemonic suppressions have been successfully challenged through collective action from women farmers across various intersectional identities. At the same time, these collective protests by women farmers have also highlighted the strong and undeniable presence of female farmers in an otherwise male dominant sector. In the same spirit, Malhotra et.al., foreground collective community-based actions and divisions of labor taken up by Gaddi pastoralist women. Their observations offer an alternative worldview on women's role and their collective exercise of agency in ensuring the continuity of pastoral livelihoods. These two papers revisit mainstream narratives around farming and pastoralism and document the presence of alternative forms of representations by women that most often get sidelined.

Paromita Chakrabarti presents a critical outlook on neoliberal forms of governance and the hegemonic oppression of dissent. Focusing on the large-scale participation of women in the farmers protest across multiple caste, class, occupational, and religious divides, she asserts that the composition and dynamics of collective resistance in contemporary Indian democratic society have become symbols of solidarity and intersectional dissent. The farmers' protests has brought to the fore women's role in mass mobilisations, especially in the context of the corporatization of agri-businesses. Women farmers have successfully challenged this masculinist control of the state, as well as conventional notions of male dominance in the farming sector, through their participation in big numbers at the Delhi borders. Chakrabarti concludes that women's participation in this protest has tremendous significance for the larger women's movement for justice, equality, and rights and can pose a challenge to the return of the "Strong State" because women's collective expression of agency in the face of excessive fascism might rekindle democratic spirits.

In **Aayushi Malhotra, Sailaja Nandigama and Kumar Sankar Bhattacharya's** exploration of women's role in pastoral communities, the authors peel back commonly held perceptions about pastoral work being a masculine venture. Through a survey of literature and using specific cases, the authors establish that women play a significant role in the day to day economic and social activities related to a pastoral livelihood. Given the dearth of studies in this field, the authors use a gendered framework to make women's agency evident—in their roles as herder, trader, knowledge bearer, and healer. With the men in the community often being away with the herd, women have the space to exert their influence within their social context. Though pastoral work is organized in a patriarchal manner, women use their situated knowledge to bring about positive change that benefits their families and communities. In times of precarity, women in these communities organize across caste and religious lines and engage in political activism. At a time when the Indian government is on a mission to "sedenterize" migratory communities, women's voices in the community are especially important to ensure justice.

Section 4: Challenging National/Religious Myths through Literature, Film, Music, Theatre

Protest movements have always integrated indigenous cultural forms in their expression and South Asia is no exception. In recent years, as religious fanaticism and militant heteropatriarchal nationalism have risen in the region, communities targeted by violence have expressed their outrage and garnered public support by utilizing traditional art and mythological narratives. Women's rights activists have engaged in reinterpreting age-old stories from new perspectives, forcing the public to engage with tough issues seriously. At the same time, art forms relegated to the margins of society have been reinvigorated and centered by a new generation of artists who problematize protest itself; they raise important questions around issues of caste oppression and religion through the lens of folk art. The essays in this section challenge what we understand as "old" and "new" by either appropriating art forms available only to the beneficiaries of neoliberalism or by demystifying age-old myths and ancient hatreds as represented in various mediums.

Shruti Chakrabarty tackles feminist revisionary mythmaking through one of India's most overdetermined female figures, Sita in the Hindu epic the *Ramayana*. As the epitome of female virtue, Sita's presence in the epic paradoxically serves to reinforce her absence. Chakrabarty contends that Samhita Arni's graphic narrative *Sita's Ramayana*, complemented by *patachitra* or scroll painting by Moyna Chitrakar, a female artist from rural West Bengal, undermines androcentric interpretations of the epic. Arni and Chitrakar challenge Brahmanical orthodoxy through folk art forms reminiscent of a sixteenth century retelling called *Chandrabati Ramayan* by Chandrabati, the first women poet of Bengal. These ballads, sung by rural women of Bengal and Bangladesh, upend Ram's canonical deification and demystify the storied grandeur of the battle between Ayodhya and Lanka by rendering them secondary to Sita's suffering and resilience. As such, Sita represents the quotidian travails of common women rather than idealized wifehood.

Pramila Venkateswaran engages with the performances of rap, *gaana*, and street theater (*koothu*) in Tamil Nadu by young Dalit men and women and their effort to change the narrative of caste oppression. Youth activists perform protest songs in the genre of rap and song, using elements of slam poetry and rap from African American artists and blend them with local musical innovations. Through youth rappers, such as Arivu and Isaivani's performances, Venkateswaran examines the reasons for their popularity and how they reflect on both current and historical caste and gender injustices. Lastly, these performances demonstrate the integration of cultural expressions as a medium of protest and throw a spotlight on Dalit feminist activism and the future of Dalit people

Shreerekha Pillai Subramanian features the entrenched cinematic responses in India to social justice movements, touching upon the lives of an inter-faith couple and their children. She points to director N. Padmakumar's *A Billion Colour Story's* lack of an explicit gaze on a Hindu-led political hegemony, and the excesses of violence performed by the nation-state and its Hindutva brigade against its minoritized "Muslim" and othered subjects. She highlights the film's usage of a black and white binary that effortlessly presents the image of a nation of teeming diversity and its border-crossing love from a child's point of view while also contextualizing the film within a neoliberal economic hegemonic system that works in tandem with a regressive Hindutva agenda.

Section 5: Pakistani Feminisms in Neoliberal Contexts

In our penultimate section, **Naila Sahar**, **Afiya Sheherbano Zia**, and **Fawzia Afzal-Khan's** essays provide a roadmap of some key issues that are germane to artistic, activist as well as scholarly concerns within the realm of Pakistani and Pakistani-diasporic feminist theory and praxis. Given the heavily India-centric focus of this issue--a result not by design but default, due to India's role as the South Asian regional hegemonic power-- it is unsurprising that most of our submissions reflected this regional imbalance of voices. We therefore felt it appropriate to conclude with a focus on Pakistani feminists and feminisms that are situated in, and reflective of, local and global contexts, and which have now had a long history of dealing with the impact of various fundamentalisms on women's and minorities' rights. The required negotiation between the scylla and charbydis of Islamism vs. Islamophobia places Pakistani feminist movement at the center of issues engulfing South Asia currently. This is particularly the case now with India's government promoting a Hindutva brand of nationalism, that has profoundly serious implications for minorities and women's rights within India, similar to what unfolded across the border in neighboring Pakistan under the extremist Islamist policies put in place by the late General Zia ul Haq during the 1980s. To date, state policies and laws enacted in the name of religion in Pakistan, continue to exercise detrimental ramifications on the country's ideology and consequently, on its citizens' lives and rights. India, as the region's dominant power, with a far greater population than any of its other South Asian neighbors including Pakistan, has much to learn from the unraveling of the latter, if it is to avoid a similar fate which could have far more regressive repercussions not just for India but the entire subcontinent, especially on women, religious minorities, and LGBTQ identified populations spanning the region.

Naila Sahar's essay alerts us to some of these regressive consequences faced by two Pakistani women, one an activist and the other an artist, who shot (pun unintended!) to worldwide fame when the former, a young teenager named Malala Yousafzai was shot by the Taliban but survived and went on to win the Nobel Peace Prize for her advocacy of girls' education, and the latter, a female filmmaker named Sharmeen Obeid-Chinoy, made a documentary film about the crime of acid-throwing on women that won her an Oscar for best documentary feature. Sahar's exploration of the g/local contexts of nationalism, local patriarchy, and western liberal feminisms in service to imperialist hegemonic agendas, which shape the representational frameworks within which these cultural workers' scripts circulate and gain currency, points to the double-bind in which such discourses are caught, thereby limiting the reception of its protagonists to an either/or dichotomy: national s/heroes, or native informant apologists for western imperialist feminist agendas.

Afiya Shehrbano Zia's examination of the fraught field of Pakistani feminist activism notes both the importance, yet also the inefficacy, of a cultural politics disarticulated with the political goals of (secular) feminist-identified policy platforms. Thus, she argues that, whilst Pakistan's annual Aurat March (Women's March) demonstrations have seen thousands of women (and their male allies) take to the streets in major cities since 2018 to protest a g/local patriarchal culture of sexual harassment (tied to bodily shame, a notion that pietist Islamic discourses, like most patriarchies, endorse), and that such interventions do indeed signify "a milestone in the culture of feminist protest," the potential power of such protests to enhance rights-based activism has been compromised. One reason for this weakness is that the organizers of Aurat March, comprised of younger millennials, failed to heed advice from senior activists of the Pakistani feminist movement, "to connect protest marches on sexual freedoms and violence with women's bodily, health, and labour rights." In lieu of chalking out a "stable ideological vision" that could help reform state institutions and governmental policies on women's rights by "developing strategic engagement with political parties and laws," this younger generation of feminist activists has run afoul of the religious establishment and conservative politicians; even some older-generation liberal progressives and feminists were made uncomfortable by the Aurat Marchers' use of sexually explicit and provocative slogans deemed inappropriate/culturally insensitive in a Muslim society. Because of their decontextualized approach to sexual politics in Pakistan, that opens itself up to charges of "foreign influences" in the absence of broad-based coalitional work that could link sexual politics to longstanding feminist rights-based demands for access to health, education, employment, and fair wages, the net effect of the Aurat March phenomenon has been Pakistani postmodern feminism's performative failure to engage the neoliberal state in reverting to a progressive, secular, rights-based model, and away from the pietist politics enabled by the man-military-mullah nexus.

Fawzia Afzal-Khan's essay is the broadest of the three in terms of both its transnational and its transdisciplinary purview. Several issues discussed in the other two Pakistan-focused essays are brought into a shared analytic space under a materialist rubric, establishing the need to link various discursive formations to economics as a precondition for decolonial feminist movements. Thus, concerns adumbrated by Sahar regarding the "double-bind" of discursive formations that feminist activist and artistic interventions within Pakistan's body politic find themselves ensnared in, which are critiqued as an insufficient politics through Afiya Zia's analysis of the culturalist limitations of Aurat March demonstrations across Pakistani cities, and which are issues germane to cultural and political activism, are linked to a broader transnational economic heuristic. Her intervention concludes the section (and the special issue), by elaborating affinities between the nexus of neoliberal/ rentier capitalism, religious extremism, and patriarchy as coeval fundamentalist ideologies, which, when seen in g/locally interconnected ways, provide the tools for a properly materialist intersectional analysis of women's and human rights.

It is our hope that this collection of essays exemplifies the heterogeneous praxes being employed by women from India and Pakistan as they bridge both discursive and rights-based conceptual terrain, thereby enabling us to (re)envision and (re)enact solidarities for progressive social change in South Asia and beyond. These intersectional feminisms offer alternative forms of historical temporization and spatialization and manifest the unpredictable ramifications of collective agency against the confluence of patriarchy, communalism, and capitalism.

ENDNOTES

1 Nilanjana Paul is an Assistant Professor of South Asian and World History at The University of Texas Rio Grande Valley. She is the author of *Bengal Muslims and Colonial Education, 1854-1947: A Study of Curriculum, Educational Institutions, and Communal Politics* published by Routledge in 2022. Her articles have appeared in *South Asia Research* and *Journal of History*. She has received several awards including the Humanities Texas Grant and Louise Gloeckner M.D. Research Fellowship from Drexel University for her work.

2 Namita Goswami is Professor of Philosophy at Indiana State University. She works in continental philosophy as well as postcolonial, critical race, feminist, and queer theory. She has published in a wide range of journals such as *Hypatia, SIGNS, Angelaki, Journal of Speculative Philosophy, Contemporary Aesthetics,* and *Critical Philosophy of Race* and in edited volumes such as *Rethinking Facticity* (edited by Eric Nelson and François Raffoul), *Asian and Feminist Philosophies in Dialogue: Liberating Traditions* (edited by Ashby Butnor and Jen McWeeny), *Phenomenology, Embodiment, and Race* (edited by Emily Lee) and *Constructing the Nation: A Race and Nationalism Reader* (edited by Mariana Ortega and Linda Martin Alcoff). She is the author of *Subjects that Matter: Philosophy, Feminism, and Postcolonial Theory* (SUNY Press, 2019) and co-editor of *Why Race and Gender Still Matter: An Intersectional Approach* (Cambridge University Press: Pickering & Chatto, 2014). She is currently completing a book on Gayatri Spivak.

3 Sailaja Nandigama is an Associate Professor at the Humanities and Social Sciences department of Birla Institute of Technology and Science (BITS), Rajasthan, India. She completed her PhD in Development Studies in 2009, from the International Institute of Social Studies, the Netherlands with a Netherlands government fellowship (NFP Fellow), and worked in the University of Sheffield, UK and the Wageningen University and Research Centre (WUR), the Netherlands as a Post-Doctoral researcher before joining at the Birla Institute of Technology and Science (BITS), Pilani, Rajasthan, India in 2014. Her research interests include human and environmental systems, climate change, gender studies, feminist political ecology, social justice and policy issues. At present she is actively engaged as an Associate Editor with the interdisciplinary Journal of Environmental Studies and Sciences (JESS), published by Springer Nature, and is also part of the Editorial Board of the Journal of International Women's Studies (JIWS) USA.

4 Gowri Parameswaran is Professor and Chair of Educational Studies and Leadership at the State University of New York at New Paltz. She obtained her MA and PhD in Cognitive/Educational Psychology from Rutgers University. Her research explorations center on gender, socioeconomic status and culture and their

impact on children and adult cognition both in the USA and in India. She is the co-editor of an introductory text for Women's Studies – Women: Images and Reality published by McGraw- Hill. She has also published books and articles on diversity and inclusion in education. In recent years she has written theoretical articles critiquing the historical assumptions around developmental psychology and how to teach about topics such as the privileging of the Global North over the Global South. Email: paramesg@newpaltz.edu.

5 Fawzia Afzal-Khan is Professor of English, a University Distinguished Scholar (2009-10), and former Director of the Women and Gender Studies Program at Montclair State University, NJ (2009-2015). In addition to having published numerous scholarly and journalistic essays, poems, plays and a memoir *Lahore with Love: Growing Up With Girlfriends Pakistani Style* (Syracuse University Press, 2010), she has authored three books of scholarly criticism, *Cultural Imperialism: Genre and Ideology in the Indo-English Novel* (Penn State Press 1993), *A Critical Stage: The Role of Secular Alternative Theatre in Pakistan* (Seagull Press, 2005), and *Siren Song: Understanding Pakistan Through its Women Singers* (OUP: 2020), and edited two scholarly anthologies, *The PreOccupation of Postcolonial Studies* (Duke University Press, 2000), and *Shattering the Stereotypes: Muslim Women Speak* Out (Interlink Books 2005 . She maintains a blog called www.travelingfeminista.com and her website can be accessed at www.fawziaafzalkhan.com.

6 We borrow this term from Gayatri Gopinath's book, *Unruly Visions: The Aesthetic Practices of Queer Diaspora*. Duke University Press, 2020.

CHAPTER 2

The Indian Mission of the Institute of Blessed Virgin Mary (IBVM) Nuns: Convents, Curriculum, and Indian Women

Nilanjana Paul [1]

ABSTRACT

This study focuses on the Indian mission of IBVM nuns, and the role played by them in the spread of female education in India. While acknowledging that missionaries were part of the imperial process, this study analyzes the work of Catholic nuns in India, their convents, and curriculum to show how their work advanced women's educational opportunities in India. In the process the study examines how Catholic nuns resisted the dominating attitude of the Catholic Church in India. The last section of the article examines how Christian influence under missionaries not only prepared good mothers and wives but also trained Indian women to defy tradition and become economically independent. By evaluating both the contributions and the limitations of the work of IBVM nuns this article shows the complex nature of their work under colonial rule, their confrontations with the Christian patriarchs and efforts to fight for the rights of colonized women.

Introduction

Great Britain had the largest colonial empire in the world with a diversity of imperial practices. In the case of India, the British government abolished the indigenous institutions and replaced them with new ruling institutions and bureaucracies that were maintained with the help of Indian and chartered company agents. This colonial framework allowed Western women in India to engage in a variety of roles.[2] Antoinette Burton argued that British liberal feminists in India promoted themselves as saviors of Indian women. Feminist newspapers in Britain represented Indian women as enslaved thus, justifying the responsibility of British women saving their Indian sisters. Burton argued that after World War I, British feminists recognized Indian women's contribution to the independence movement. Nonetheless, it would be an exaggeration to say that the war radically changed British women's perception of Indian women or that prewar perceptions evaporated after the international conflict subsided. Like Burton, Indrani Sen explored the participation of missionaries in the "civilizing mission" but also documented their anxieties about the gendered division of their colonial home.[3] Kumari Jayawardane steps out of the dominant image of British women or missionaries in India being arrogant or involved in Christianizing the "savage" Indian population and evaluated the role of a wide variety of Western women in India who were speaking a "different voice" despite colonial rule. In that context, she used the example of Loreto nuns who did not restrict themselves to the narrow objectives of Christianizing Indian women but feminized Christianity, increased educational opportunities for Indian women and challenged the male supremacy of the Catholic Church in India.[4]

This essay builds on Jayawardena's work to study the role of a small group of Irish Catholic nuns who came to India with a genuine concern for improving the educational status of women in India. Mary Ward (1585-1645), born in England to a wealthy Catholic family, was condemned by the Roman Church for educating women in England. In 1609 she founded the Institute of Blessed Virgin Mary (henceforth IBVM), which was a congregation of nuns that travelled to different parts of Europe to educate women and children. Mary Ward saw empowering women through education as a means of renewing the suppressed Catholic faith in England. The Indian Mission of IBVM began when Mother Frances Teresa Ball (henceforth Teresa Ball), Superior of the Irish Branch of IBVM, which was referred to as 'Loreto' in Rathfarnham, responded to an appeal from the Vicar Apostolic of Calcutta in 1841, by sending a group of twelve nuns and postulants under the leadership of Mother Mary Delphine Hart (1818 -1889) (hereafter Delphine Hart) to educate Catholic girls.[5] The main goal of Loreto education was a 'school for all classes, schools to suit all pockets, even the empty ones!'[6] An analysis of their missionary work and expansion of convents in India shows how they transcended racial and gender barriers to provide modern western education to Eurasian and Indian women within a restrictive and colonial structure. While missionaries were referred to as 'agents of imperialism,' this case study shows that Loreto nuns were not overtly trying to convert, through their curriculum they advanced women's position in Indian society by increasing educational opportunities for them. The leadership roles of these nuns provided an agency to Indian women who either individually or collectively, made efforts to improve the disadvantaged status of their sex. In short, Loreto nuns combined the roles of being missionaries, reformers opposing male hierarchy of the Catholic Church and feminist allies for Indian women within the colonial framework.[7]

The final section of this paper examines the impact of missionary education on Indian women. To traditional Hindu families, access to female education was a colonial onslaught on the very essence of Hinduism and Indianness. Tanika Sarkar translated Rasasundari's autobiography, *Amar Jiban* (My Life), where she self-taught herself and kept it secret as her traditional Hindu family opposed female education.[8] Liberal Hindu, Muslim and Parsi families wanted educated wives and allowed missionaries to educate their daughters and wives without bringing Christianity home. However, missionaries preferred institutional education as it allowed them to civilize Indian women. Nevertheless, there were shifts in attitudes and policies of some missionaries towards Indian women. They were concerned about Indian women, their rights and were anxious to make changes. Both Padma Anagol and Claire Midgely argued that Indian women educated at convents and missionary schools or those who converted to Christianity challenged the roles prescribed for women by Hinduism and were engaged with the gendered critique of Hinduism. They built homes for widows and prostitutes and were influenced by a sense of equality in Christianity that did not destroy women's individual liberty.[9] Based on institutional records of Loreto Convents, reports of Director of Public Instruction (DPI) and *Palm Leaves*, this study shows that education at Loreto convents was not always synonymous with conversion. While it is difficult to separate missionary schools from the larger imperial process of converting indigenous people, Loreto convents produced the educated Indian women who opposed caste discrimination and organized resistance against the structures of oppression that denied women their rights.

East India Company and IBVM nuns in Calcutta

The Charter Act of 1813 renewed East India Company's (henceforth EIC) privilege for trade and had two extraordinary clauses. First, Company's responsibility for educating Indians and second, it permitted missionaries to proselytize in India. The act envisaged the establishment of schools and colleges, but East India Company spent most of their money on higher education and educating wealthy classes. They believed that knowledge would descend from this class to those at the bottom of the society. Hence, mass education was left to the missionaries. Church Missionary Society of the evangelical Clapham sect was the first group to start schools. However, Company officials were worried about Protestant missionaries as they wanted to convert heathen minds. In contrast, Jesuits and Catholic nuns who opened schools for all castes and classes in an around the country were welcomed by the Company.[10]

By the time the EIC officials arrived in India, Catholics were already part of the Indian scene. They seemed less threatening to the company in comparison to Protestant missionaries, who were in India to proselytize the population. Catholic missionaries converted Protestants instead of Hindus and Muslims. Catholics believed that Protestants were heretics whereas pagans like Hindus who lived in good faith would not go to hell. Next, EIC appointed Catholic missionaries as part-time chaplains to Catholic soldiers since forty percent of British troops in India were Irish Catholics. Thus, EIC welcomed Roman Catholics missionaries during the first half of the nineteenth century.[11]

In Bengal, Vicar Apostolic, Father Robert St. Leger S.J. and his band of English, Irish, and French Jesuits came to Calcutta in 1834. Over the next six years, they traveled throughout Bengal, Bihar, and Orissa, where they baptized, established churches, and set up St. Xavier's School for Catholic boys in Calcutta. It was at the initiative of Father Chadwick of St. Xavier's that the idea of a Catholic school for girls was first proposed. In 1840, Dr. Bakhaus, a military chaplain of Hazaribagh, was traveling to Rome when he requested Ursuline nuns to set up Catholic girls' school in India, but they declined as they were busy setting up a convent in South Carolina. Dr. Murray, the Archbishop of Dublin, encouraged Bakhaus to present his case to Teresa Ball. After negotiations, Dr. Bakhaus was able to convince Ball to send Loreto nuns to India. In Calcutta, Loreto nuns lived in the country house of Governor Henry Vansittart that extended from Chowringhee to Park Street in Central Calcutta. Initially, Jesuit fathers helped the nuns adjust with the circumstances, though nuns opposed the supremacy of the Jesuits as discussed later. In the heyday of EIC rule, the company welcomed Roman Catholic missionaries and its administrators, allowed Jesuits to promote education at all levels, including female education.[12]

After reaching India, Delphine Hart had to cope with the task of setting up the convent in Calcutta, educate girls in slum areas, and deal with the rising tension between the Loreto Order and Archbishop Monseignor Carew, who wanted to keep the nuns under his control. Despite hardships, Hart started Loreto House Calcutta on January 10, 1842, with sixty students. Loreto House was in the garden house of Chief Justice, Sir Elijah Impey on Middleton Row. Initially, Loreto House included Catholic girls from affluent Eurasian families. Overtime, the convent included girls from Indian families.[13]

In the summer of 1842, Bishop Carew wanted to set up a Loreto Convent at Chandanagore, which was a French Colony in Bengal. The French settlement had a population of thirty thousand of which about one thousand were Catholics. Hart was doubtful as she did not have enough Loreto nuns to look after the convent. However, she finally gave into the request of the bishop and sent three nuns to Loreto Convent Chandanagore, which started on August 1, 1842, inside the old Capuchin monastery. The convent included poor children and orphans and lasted for five years. In 1847, the nuns established Loreto Entally, in the heart of Calcutta, where the orphans were transferred, and the old monastery, which housed Loreto Chandanagore was taken over by the Sisters of St.Joseph Cluny. Along with a convent at Chandanagore, Archbishop Carew wanted to start a convent at Srerampore, which had a Catholic mission since early Portuguese days but did not have a chaplain. The convent at Srerampore started in 1845 with Mother Alexia Egan (hereafter Alexia Egan) as the Mother Superior. It included students who could not pay the fees of Loreto House and day scholars from the military families in Barrackpore. However, within two years, the school was transferred to Loreto Entally.[14] The figures in the table below reflect the enrollment of students at Loreto convents in the early nineteenth century.

Table 1: Number of students at Loreto Convents in Bengal in 1846

Name of the Institution	Number of students
Loreto Convent Chandernagore	74
Loreto House Calcutta	50
Loreto Convent Srerampore	24
Loreto Convent Chittagong	100

Source: Loreto South Asia Province Archive, "Irish Annals: On the Indian Province," Beginnings, 1846.

Over, the course of three years, IBVM nuns worked alongside the Jesuits, traveled to different parts of Bengal, and worked in slums. They established three boarding schools, two orphanages and three days schools in an around Calcutta. Most of the convents were established in areas, which had a large Catholic population to cater to the needs of Catholic girls. In short, they took active interests in education and social work. EIC did not have problems with Loreto nuns or their convents, which included women from all classes of the population. In the second half of the nineteenth century, as the support for female education increased, Loreto convents and orphanages spread all over India. Loreto nuns reached out to more Indian families and educated their daughters at their convents. They introduced western values and ways of living and were part of the modernizing process, which was essential for their success. However, Loreto nuns in India had to fight many battles against the domination of the Catholic Church, which was a complex web of ecclesiastical patriarchy based on conflicting pontifical and diocesan territorialities.[15]

Conflict with the Male Hierarchy of the Catholic Church

In Ireland, IBVM nuns lived under the authority of the Archbishop of Dublin. Teresa Ball had to fight the male dominance of local Catholic bishops to establish a central government for the Irish convents. The convents in India did not share the same benefits as Rathfarnham. This was mainly because of the growing estrangement between Teresa Ball and Vicar Apostolic of Bengal. In India, Hart had to set up schools, teach, look after other nuns, and attend charity calls either in slums or in hospitals. However, the bigger issue was the tension between the Loreto Order and Archbishop of Calcutta, Monseignor Carew. He was described as 'domineering' with 'absolute or authoritarian'[16] tendencies. He wanted to keep the nuns under his control. Hart resisted many of the intrusions including the effort by Carew to move Loreto House somewhere else. Moreover, the Archbishop intervened in the internal working of the convent. She fought back and ensured that education of girls in Bengal was not interrupted. Nevertheless, the atmosphere was oppressive, and Hart gave up her position to Mother Joseph Hogan (hereafter Joseph Hogan) who was her assistant. Later, Hart became the Chief Superior of Loreto Convents in and around Calcutta from 1855 to 1881.[17]

Joseph Hogan also had to struggle against Bishop Carew to secure Loreto House for the nuns who came to India in 1844. In 1845, Carew insisted that Loreto nuns undertake the running of the women's section of the Medical College in Calcutta and train Indian students in Western medicine. Loreto nuns specialized in teaching for which the demand increased as the convents multiplied. Hogan opposed Carew's demands, particularly, the two-year contract for nuns to serve in hospitals where they could not talk about their religion to the patients or be critical of the health care system in India. Moreover, the contracts were developed without consulting Hogan. When she appealed to the Pope, the Archbishop stepped down, but Hogan was removed from the position of Mother Superior of Loreto House. Mother Mary Xaveria MacDonnell (hereafter Xaveria MacDonnell) was appointed as Mother Superior. However, the tension between MacDonnell and the Archbishop continued over whether the nuns should work at hospitals or educate women. In the meantime, the Loreto Order wanted to remove their nuns from the control of the Archbishop. In the end, MacDonnell stayed on and expanded her educational work to different parts of India.[18]

Though the Loreto nuns were conformist within the colonial framework, they had to constantly fight against the male chauvinism and authoritarian attitudes of the church hierarchies. Jayawardane called them "independent" unmarried women who broke the image of white women being involved just in conversion. In opposite, they stepped into the male world of work and were aware of the problems faced by local women. They fought for their right to head schools, travel and above all to be respected and accepted as single women in the evangelical culture, which subordinated women and focused on women's domestic roles.[19] Through the convents, Loreto nuns created spaces that exposed Indian women to modern education. Hindu and Muslim students learned to respect different religions and were also involved in social service at orphanages. In limited ways, Loreto nuns expanded educational opportunities for Indian women and contributed to their emancipation.[20]

Expansion of Loreto Convents in India

The Charles Wood Despatch of 1854 promoted English education and the system of grants in aid (subsidies) favored missionary schools as English was necessary to secure a lucrative profession under colonial rule. However, it did little to change the female learning space in India.The Despatch of 1860 advanced female education to strengthen English middle-class norms, which moved women from traditional Indian education to a colonial classroom. This allowed missionaries and other Western philanthropic groups to spread western education among Indian women and train them to become teachers and school inspectors.[21]

Mother Mary Colmcille the author of *First the Blade: History of IBVM (Loreto) in India 1841-1962* indicated that after the Revolt of 1857, there was further expansion of Loreto Convents outside of Bengal. Railways increased connectivity, which helped nuns to travel outside Calcutta to start three new convents in the 1870s: Loreto Lucknow (1872), Loreto Hazaribagh (1874) and Loreto Asansol (1877). Loreto Lucknow had students from upper middle-class military and landlord families. Initially, in 1872, nuns were afraid of their security as the story of Kanpur massacre was still popular among the Western and Anglo-Indian population.[22] Hence, the colonial government gave them temporary accommodation near the cantonment area. Later, Loreto Lucknow was housed on the property owned by the Nawab of Oudh for seven years. Over time, Loreto Lucknow acquired their own property that had over eleven hundred students.[23]

At Loreto Convent Hazaribagh located in the Chota Nagpur Plateau, nuns were involved in evangelistic, educational, medical, and pastoral work. Hazaribagh had over two hundred Catholics as well as seventy Anglo-Indian and Irish soldiers. The Jesuits sent military chaplains to cater to needs of Irish soldiers. This motivated Hart to open a convent at Hazaribagh, which was referred to as the 'Priory' and consisted of *adivasi* (tribal) students. The colonial government provided permanent rent-free land to the convent. Students were provided with basic education in English and needlework. However, the convent closed after an outbreak of diphtheria that killed many nuns including Delphine Hart.[24]

Finally, Loreto Asansol was about one hundred kilometers from Calcutta. The industrial town of Asansol had a large Catholic Eurasian population who worked for the railways. The convent started with five sisters and thirty-five Eurasian girls. The railway company gave the land and the colonial government helped in the construction of buildings. The low fees of the convent helped in educating girls from lower middle class Eurasian families. By the 1890s Loreto Asansol expanded their network to include Hindu and Muslim girls.[25]

The 1880s marked a new era in the history of the Loreto order. Loreto in India was united with the Mother House of the Irish Branch Institute. This step gave nuns the freedom from control of the Jesuits and ensured the regular exchange of nuns between Ireland and India. The Indian Education Commission (Hunter's Commission) in 1882 recommended more support for female education. Subsequently, Loreto nuns established two more convents at Ranchi (1890) and Simla (1892). Loreto Convent Simla was one of the prestigious institutions for female education in India. All six students from Loreto Simla who appeared for Cambridge School Leaving Examination passed with high grades. In contrast, Loreto Ranchi was started by Mother Gonzaga Joynt (hereafter Gonzaga Joynt) and Archbishop Goethals admitted tribal girls. They received basic education in English, Hindi, music, sewing, and gardening.[26]

EIC allowed Jesuits and Catholic nuns to start schools and convents as it did not impact the working of the government. After the revolt of 1857, the British Raj justified the expansion of Loreto convents as part of the philanthropic project and not a conscious effort to improve women's access to education. To the Loreto nuns, the expansion of the Loreto venture allowed them to remain committed to female education after the British lost interest in their education project with limited decentralization started by the Morley-Minto reforms of 1909. Loreto nuns established Loreto College in Calcutta on February 2, 1912, with ten students, which was affiliated with Calcutta University in 1913, for Intermediate of Arts (henceforth I.A.) with Licentiate in Teaching. Initially, the college included Indian students who wanted to improve their educational standards and secure a college degree. Overtime, India Office Records on European schools indicate gradual increase in enrollment a few years after its establishment with some fluctuations during the inter-war period. The table below confirms it.[27]

Table 2: Enrollment of students at Loreto College

1917-18	314
1918-19	287
1919-20	315
1920-21	306

British Library (Hereafter BL), Annual Report on European Education in Bengal 1917-18 to 1920-21, IOR /V/24/4437.

Loreto College followed a high standard of education. For example, *Report on Public Instruction in Bengal for 1925-26* indicates that in 1925-26 Loreto College sent nine students for I.A. exams and all were successful. Moreover, the college was one of the two institutions in Calcutta that trained teachers as the colonial government did not have a teacher training college for women. Teachers from Loreto College were employed in primary schools and lower classes of secondary schools.[28]

In terms of financial support, Loreto nuns maintained their relative separateness from the colonial state. For example, *the Report on Public Instruction in Bengal* indicated that in 1937-38, Bengal had just two government colleges for women's higher education, Bethune College in Calcutta, and Eden Intermediate College in Dacca. Loreto College received just 500 rupees from Provincial Revenues and the rest 17,720 rupees from private sources for its maintenance. Even Dr. W.A. Jenkins in his *Report upon Girls' and Women's Education in Bengal* acknowledged that the colonial government provided no accommodation for students from Loreto College. However, these obstacles did not discourage Loreto nuns from educating local women. They hired European Catholic religious women as teaching staff to run their convents. These teachers required just living expenses, could deliver instruction of a standard that would please parents. After First World War, these women constituted forty-six percent of the entire teaching staff at Loreto convents and provided quality Western education to Indian and Eurasian girls.[29]

Deirdre Raftery argues that Loreto nuns depended on donations for building the convents, which included classroom, dormitories, and chapels. She refers to the nuns as transnational figures as they worked to establish convents for female education in different parts of the world. However, Raftery does not highlight the limitations of their work. As a private order, Loreto convents worked within the colonial framework to advance women's education in India. Despite financial disengagement with the colonial state, Loreto nuns invited British officers on Sports Day and Prize Distribution ceremonies. Furthermore, the colonial government gave the medal of *Kaisar-i-Hind* to Gonzaga Joynt for her contributions to women's education. In short, while conforming to colonial rule, Loreto nuns fought many battles against the structures of oppression in India to advance educational opportunities for local women. They may not have intended to produce feminist students but were instrumental in advancing female emancipation.[30] In that context, a survey of the curricula will highlight how education at Loreto convents generated a feminist consciousness among colonized women who opposed discriminatory traditional beliefs, fought for their rights, and wanted to change women's position in society.

Loreto education

Through the convents, Loreto nuns stressed neatness, cleanliness, obedience, and modesty. They encouraged specific behavioral patterns such as eating together with girls from all castes, races, and socio-economic backgrounds. Another break with the tradition was in the age of marriage. Indian girls at Loreto convents remained unmarried till the age of seventeen or eighteen. Students' broke caste taboos and followed a western model of education. Loreto nuns did not restrict themselves to just teaching music and sewing but advanced local women's emancipation by combining education with piety.[31]

English was the most important language taught at Loreto schools. Major emphasis was placed on the study of English Literature where students read plays written by Shakespeare. Freny Tehsildar, a student of Loreto Tara Hall in Simla, in an essay titled, 'My opinion on Our English Course,' published in *Palm Lives* in 1936 indicated that they studied *King Lear* for English literature. Many students found it difficult because they had not seen the play or were generally disinterested in plays. At Loreto College, the study of English Honours at the bachelor's level started in 1927. In 1929 Chitra Majumdar was the first Bengali student to secure first class in English from the college. All the successful students of English honors from Loreto College pursued university education. The decision to promote the study of English language and literature was prompted by the idea that the knowledge of English would help to secure higher education and professional careers under colonial rule.[32]

Along with English, students of Loreto convents and the College studied Bengali, Hindi, Sanskrit, and Urdu. This was predominantly because Cambridge Examination Syndicate agreed to accept modern Indian languages instead of French and Latin. Students studied Hindi or Urdu as their second language at Loreto Lucknow and Hindi for a long time was the medium of instruction at Loreto Ranchi. At the B.A. level, Zakiah Ahmed and Razia Ahmed studied Persian Honours with Urdu minor at Loreto College. They secured First Class in the B.A. Examination. Moreover, the introduction of Indian languages in the curriculum allowed Loreto Convents to attract students from Hindu, Muslim, and tribal families. Indian students were exposed to both Western and Indian literature.[33]

From 1880s onwards, there was shift in the curriculum of Loreto Convents to meet the demands for higher education. Science education became popular among women. Loreto Teachers College, which was part of Loreto College, introduced intermediary courses in Science and Mathematics and qualifying studies for medical education. Beyond the narrow limits of Catholic education, nuns at Loreto schools prepared Eurasian and Indian middle-class women for professional careers when opportunities for science education were extremely limited for women in India.[34]

Music, Needlework, Cookery, and Physical Exercise were also part of the curriculum at Loreto Schools. Students prepared for music examinations conducted by Trinity College of Music and examiners like Doctor Creser and Mr. St. George were sent from London to conduct practical examinations. In 1928, six students from Loreto Lucknow appeared for the Royal Academy music examination and all of them were successful with one gaining distinction. Romola Lahiry better known as Sister Stella, joined Loreto College as a staff in 1946 and guided Loreto teams for success in basketball tournaments. Hence, modern education at Loreto convents included the study of domestic management, music, and sports.[35]

Girls at Loreto convents were exposed to modern western education, which was the main goal of IBVM nuns. Outside academics, school magazine *Palm Leaves,* gave women a space to express their opinions on a variety of issues and develop a social network where they demanded rights and freedom for women. For example, Lotika Ghose, daughter of Indian leader Manmohon Ghose, from Loreto House was extremely critical of the Hindu household and the position of women in it. In 'A Scene from Hindu Home,' published in *Palm Leaves* in 1920, she indicated how cruelly Hindu widows were treated at homes and that young Indian women were eager to receive education. Loreto nuns did not challenge the foundations of colonial rule but provided good secondary education that allowed women to enter new professions like teaching and law. They trained teachers at Loreto College since Government of Bengal provided most support to training male teachers. In short, Loreto nuns combined the roles of superintendents and matriarchs, which would become a tradition for missionary schools and colleges in India. In limited ways, the convents introduced reform programs that uplifted women's position in India. Subsequently, these young Indian women defied early marriage and broke away from conventional beliefs like caste and religious prejudices. They struggled for greater equality between men and women.[36]

Westernized Indian women or feminists

Manjula Ray who was admitted to Loreto House in 1931 and later became a senior judge of the Calcutta High Court, praised the secular character of her school, which included students from different classes, castes, and religions. To quote Manjula Ray, 'My school where through the years I befriended young girls of different castes, creeds, and religions and was never adversely conscious of the diversity amongst us, in language, food habits, culture or religion, and later in life was quite at a loss to understand why the Nation was required to be torn apart?'[37] Similarly, Meena Hasan who attended Loreto House in the 1940s praised

European nuns for maintaining a secular atmosphere at school. Professor Ratnabali Chatterjee in an interview indicated that during her school days at Loreto House, she had the opportunity to interact with girls from Armenian, Jewish, Muslim, and Parsi backgrounds. This was also the case at other convents like Loreto Darjeeling and Shillong in the 1930s and 1940s, where they provided higher education to Nepali, Bhutanese, Garo, and Khasi girls. Loreto College in Calcutta included Muslim girls at a time when many prominent educational institutions for women in Bengal discriminated against minority women. Finally, I interviewed Professor Fawzia Afzal Khan on her experience of studying at the Convent of Jesus and Mary in Lahore Pakistan. She appreciated the secular environment and diversity of cultures at her school and indicated that nuns never made any effort to convert non-Christian students.[38]

Table 3: Hindu and Muslim students at Loreto College

Year	Hindus	Muslims
1936-37	22	3
1937-38	21	6
1938-39	28	12

Source: (Compiled by the author) BL, Report on Public Instruction in Bengal 1935-36 to 1947-48, IOR/V/989.

The above examples indicate that Christian education and influence at Loreto convents produced not just good wives but also educated Indian women. They acknowledged that they benefited from missionary education, which helped them to see the world in a different light. Indian students at Loreto schools preferred a more secular atmosphere in school and opposed Hindu vilification of women. This was a departure from the dominant Hindu revivalist discourse, which blamed Muslims for the decline of women's position in India. This 'break with the past'[39] allowed educated Indian women from Loreto convents to oppose hegemonic ideologies of the conservative Indian nationalists and British officials. These educated and emancipated Indian women forged links with the West, pursued welfare programs for the improving the lives of downtrodden women and redefined their relationship between Hinduism and Christianity to secure dignity and self-respect in society.[40]

Through education at Loreto convents, the 'new Indian woman' broke the image of western educated women being luxurious and caring little about their families. Rather, advancement in communication (print media, vernacular press) helped these women to articulate their needs, insecurities, and challenge patriarchal traditions. They communicated with women outside their own religious communities, had professional careers, and expressed their views on gender equality and religious freedom in school magazines and newspapers like the *Palm Leaves* and *The Statesman,* respectively. Women learned to cross the boundaries of home and inspired successive generations to seek education. Even after independence, Loreto Convents had a wider relevance to the progress of female education in India.[41]

Conclusion

Scholars have argued that missionaries viewed colonized women as subjects upon which the liberating reform project depended. They wanted to transform the Indian family system according to the principles of British middle-class structure where they defended western superiority and the imperial agenda. While acknowledging the imperial aspect of their work, this essay evaluates the various dimensions of their work in India. Loreto nuns stepped out of homes, educated local women, raised consciousness about women's issues, and ventured into hostile territories. They introduced some cultural trends of Western Europe like classics, music, and art within India but also encouraged the revival of local arts and crafts and the teaching of vernacular literature. Indian students from these convents secured high scores in foreign examinations and were geared towards graduate studies. Furthermore, the convents in India had Hindu, Muslim, Christian, and tribal women at a time when there was very little scope for minority women's education. At orphanages like Loreto Entally and Ranchi, girls received education that helped them to secure employment. Thus, with limited resources, Loreto nuns made strong efforts to educate Indian women and advance their emancipation.[42]

Overall, Loreto nuns established a network of convents across the British Empire where they transcended racial divides and cultural differences to provide education to colonized women and helped them strive for economic independence. For example, they educated Kenyan women at Loreto Mosongari (1921) and Loreto Limaru (1936). Both institutions were praised for their contributions to female education. Written from a feminist perspective, this article shows how Catholic Loreto nuns influenced the movement towards women's rights in India, which included the right to study, work, travel abroad, and respect for independent women even within the constraints of colonial rule. Indian women under the influence of Christian education opposed caste system, miseries of widowhood and patriarchy.[43] To quote Jayawardena, 'It is not surprising that many South Asian feminists were products of mission schools and convents.'[44]

REFERENCES

1. Allender, Tim. *Learning Femininity in Colonial India, 1820-1932.* Manchester: Manchester University Press, 2016.
2. Amin, Sonia. *The World of Muslim Women in Colonial Bengal, 1876-1939* (Leiden: E.J.Brill, 1996.
3. Anagol, Padma. *The Emergence of Feminism in India, 1850-1920.* Burlington: Ashgate Publishing Company, 2005.
4. Ballhatchet, Kenneth. *Caste, Class and Catholicism in India 1789-1914.* Surrey: Curzon Press, 1998.

5. Burton, Antoinette. *Burdens of History: British Feminists, Indian Women and Imperial Culture, 1865-1915.* Chapel Hill: The University of North Carolina Press, 1994.
6. Chaudhuri, Nupur and Margaret Strobel. Eds., *Western Women and Imperialism: Complicity and Resistance.* Bloomington: Indiana University Press, 1992.
7. Colmcille, Mother, Mary. *First the Blade: History of IBVM (Loreto) in India 1841-1962.* Calcutta: Firma K.I.Mukhopadhyay, 1968.
8. Dasgupta, Aditi. *Change and Continuity: English Studies in Loreto College 1912-2012.* Calcutta: Salesian College Publication 2016.
9. Foley, Tadhg and Maureen O'Connor. *Ireland and India: Colonies, Culture and Empire.* Dublin: Irish Academic Press, 2006.
10. Forbes, Geraldine. *Women in Modern India.* Cambridge: Cambridge University Press, 1996.
11. Jayawardane, Kumari. *The White Woman's Other Burden: Western Women and South Asia During British Rule.* New York: Routledge, 1995.
12. Kerkkhoff, Kathinka. *Save Ourselves and the Girls! Girlhood in Calcutta Under the Raj.* Rotterdam: University of Amsterdam, 1995.
13. Majee, Shantanu., eds. *Women and Education in India: A Representative Study.* Kolkata: Jogamaya Devi College, 2020.
14. Malekandathik, Pius, Joy Pachuau, and Tanika Sarkar. *Christianity in Indian History: Issues of Culture, Power and Knowledge.* New Delhi: Primus Books, 2016.
15. Midgley, Clare. *Feminism and Empire: Women Activists in Imperial Britain, 1790-1865.* Oxon: Routledge, 2007.
16. Nalini, Marthal. 'Gender Dynamics of Missionary Work in India: Isabella Thoburn-A Case Study," *Journal of International Women's Studies* v. 7 n. 4 (May 2006).
17. O'Brien, Stephanie. *Towards Life in Its Fullness: A Story of Loreto (IBVM) in Eastern Africa.* Nairobi: Paulines Publications Africa, 2015.
18. Procida, Mary. *Married to the Empire: Gender, Politics and Imperialism in India 1883 -1947.* Manchester: Manchester University Press, 2002.
19. Raftery, Deirdre. Convents as Transnational Education Spaces in the Long Nineteenth Century. *Espacio, Tiempo y Educación,* v.7, n.2 (2020).
20. Roy, Madhumita Roy. "Englishing" India, Reinstituting Class and Social Privilege, *Social Text,* v.39 (Summer 1994).
21. Sarkar, Tanika. *Hindu Wife Hindu Nation: Community Religion and Cultural Nationalism.* Bloomington: Indiana University Press, 2001.
22. Sen, Indrani. *Gendered Transactions: The White Woman in Colonial India c.1820-1930.* Cheshire: Manchester University Press, 2017.

ENDNOTES

1 Nilanjana Paul is an Assistant Professor of South Asian and World History at The University of Texas Rio Grande Valley. She is the author of *Bengal Muslims and Colonial Education, 1854-1947: A Study of Curriculum, Educational Institutions, and Communal Politics* published by Routledge in 2022. Her articles have appeared in *South Asia Research* and *Journal of History*. She has received several awards including the Humanities Texas Grant and Louise Gloeckner M.D. Research Fellowship for her work. Email: nilanjana.paul@utrgv.edu.

2 Nupur Chaudhuri and Margaret Strobel, "Introduction," in *Western Women and Imperialism: Complicity and Resistance* ed. Nupur Chaudhuri and Margaret Strobel (Bloomington: Indiana University Press, 1992), 1-6.

3 Antoinette Burton, *Burdens of History: British Feminists, Indian Women and Imperial Culture, 1865-1915* (Chapel Hill: The University of North Carolina Press, 1994); 98-9 & 208-9; Indrani Sen, *Gendered Transactions: The White Woman in Colonial India c.1820-1930* (Cheshire: Manchester University Press, 2017), 1-19.

4 Kumari Jayawardena, *The White Woman's Other Burden: Western Women and South Asia During British Rule* (New York: Routledge, 1995), 21-51.

5 Aditi Dasgupta *Change and Continuity: English Studies in Loreto College 1912-2012* (Calcutta: Salesian College Publication 2016), 1-12; The Spirit of Loreto,' *The Statesman*, January 21, 1985.

6 Mother Mary Colmcille, *First the Blade: History of IBVM (Loreto) in India 1841-1962* (Calcutta: Firma K.I. Mukhopadhyay, 1968), 24.

7 Jayawardena, *The White Woman's Other Burden*, 8-10; The idea that Loreto nuns could combine the roles of cultural missionaries, maternal imperialists and be feminist allies builds on Barbara N. Ramusack's work on British women activists in India. See Barbara N. Ramusack, British Women Activists in India," in *Western Women and Imperialism: Complicity and Resistance*, 117-36.

8 Tanika Sarkar, *Hindu Wife Hindu Nation: Community Religion and Cultural Nationalism* (Bloomington: Indiana University Press, 2001), 95-98; Tanika Sarkar, "Forward," in *Talking of Power: Early Writings of Bengali Women from the Mid-Nineteenth Century to the Beginning of the Twentieth Century* eds. Malini Bhattacharya and Abhijit Sen (Kolkata: Stree, 2003), x-xi.

9 Padma Anagol, *The Emergence of Feminism in India, 1850-1920* (Burlington: Ashgate Publishing Company, 2005), 19-55; Clare Midgely, *Feminism and Empire: Women Activists in Imperial Britain, 1790-1865* (Oxon: Routledge, 2007), 92-122.

10 Kenneth Ballhatchet, *Caste, Class and Catholicism in India 1789-1914* (Surrey: Curzon Press, 1998), 13-22; Collin Parsons, "A new religion? Literary study and elementary education in India and Ireland in the nineteenth century," in *Ireland and India: Colonies, Culture and Empire*. Eds. Tadhg Foley and Maureen O'Connor (Dublin: Irish Academic Press, 2006), 28-9.

11 Ballhatchet, *Caste, Class and Catholicism in India*, 14-5.

12 Colmcille, *First the Blade*, 21-8.

13 Colmcille, *First the Blade*, 24-5; Jayawardane, *The White Woman's Other Burden*, 44-5.

14 Colmcille, *First the Blade*, 24-8.

15 Jayawardena, *The White Woman's Other Burden*, 42-3; Tim Allender, *Learning Femininity in Colonial India, 1820-1932* (Manchester: Manchester University Press, 2016), 274-8.

16 Jayawardena, *The White Woman's Other Burden*, 44.

17 Ibid., 44-5.

18 Colmcille, *First the Blade*, 41-3.

19 Jayawardena, *The White Woman's Other Burden*, 9-10.

20 Ibid., 46-7.

21 Geraldine Forbes, *Women in Modern India* (Cambridge: Cambridge University Press, 1996), 36-44; Allender, *Learning Femininity in Colonial India*, 87-8 & 93-4.

22 For more information on the Kanpur massacre and the glorification of English women slaughtered as martyrs see Mary Procida, *Married to the Empire: Gender, Politics and Imperialism in India 1883 -1947* (Manchester: Manchester University Press, 2002), 111-32.

23 Colmcille, *First the Blade,* 127-31.

24 Colmcille, *First the Blade,* 127-37; Sangeeta Dasgupta, "From 'Heathen Aboriginals' to Christian Tribes": Locating the Oraons in Missionary Writings on Chotanagpur," in *Christianity in Indian History: Issues of Culture, Power and Knowledge,*' eds. Pius Malekandathil, Joy Pachuau, and Tanika Sarkar (New Delhi: Primus Books, 2016), 3915-4098.

25 Allender, *Learning Femininity in Colonial India,* 278-9; Colmcille, *First the Blade,* 138-41.

26 Colmcille, *First the Blade,* 142-59; Forbes, *Women in Modern India,* 44-5.

27 Jayawardena, *The White Woman's Other Burden,* 46; Colmcille, *First the Blade,* 162-3; Allender, *Learning Femininity in Colonial India,* 273-8.

28 West Bengal State Archives (Hereafter WBSA), Education Department, *Proceedings of the Government of Bengal for the Quarter Ending September 1927,* Proceedings No: 8, File No: Edn 8 R-1 (3), September 1927; British Library (Hereafter BL), *Report on Public Instruction in Bengal 1938-39,* IOR/V/24/989; Allender, *Learning Femininity in Colonial India,* 271-2.

29 BL, *Report on Public Instruction in Bengal 1937-38,* IOR/V/24/989; W. A. *Jenkins, Report upon Girls' and Women's Education in Bengal,* IOR/V/27/860/26; Allender, *Learning Femininity in Colonial India,* 275-6.

30 Jayawardena, *The White Woman's Other Burden,* 46-7; Allender, *Learning Femininity in Colonial India,* 278-9; Deirdre Raftery, Convents as Transnational Education Spaces in the Long Nineteenth Century. *Espacio, Tiempo y Educación,* v.7, n.2 (2020), 193-205.

31 Jayawardena, *The White Woman's Other Burden,* 37-8.

32 Madhumita Roy, "Englishing" India, Reinstituting Class and Social Privilege, *Social Text,* v.39 (Summer 1994), 83-109; Dasgupta, *Change and Continuity,* 42-55.

33 Dasgupta, *Change and Continuity,* 49-54; BL, *Annual Report on European Education in Bengal for the year 1917-1918* IOR/V/24/4437.

34 Dasgupta, *Change and Continuity,* 42-5; Jayawardane, *The White Woman's Other Burden,* 42.

35 Dasgupta, *Change and Continuity,* 27-8 & 56 -7; 'Loreto Convent High School Lucknow,' *Palm Leaves from Loreto in India,* 1928, 90.

36 Forbes, *The New Cambridge History of India,* 28-9; Jayawardena, *The White Woman's Other Burden,* 9-10; Marthal Nalini, 'Gender Dynamics of Missionary Work in India: Isabella Thoburn-A Case Study," *Journal of International Women's Studies* v. 7 n. 4 (May 2006), 266-86; A Scene from Hindu Home,' *Palm Leaves from Loreto in India,* 1920, 24-5.

37 *Loreto House Calcutta, 1842-1992* (Calcutta: Eureka Publicity Service, 1992).

38 Interview with Professor Ratnabali Chatterjee, 29th July 2019; For more information on Muslim women's education see Sonia Amin, *The World of Muslim Women in Colonial Bengal, 1876-1939* (Leiden: E.J.Brill, 1996); Colmcille, *First the Blade,* 158-9; *Loreto House Calcutta;* Interview with Professor Fawzia Afzal Khan, 1st March 2022.

39 Anagol, *The Emergence of Feminism in India,* 35.

40 Ibid., 30-7.

41 Aditi Dasgupta, 'A Missionary Initiative: The Foundation of Loreto College,' in *Women and Education in India: A Representative Study,* eds., Shantanu Majee (Kolkata: Jogamaya Devi College, 2020), 105-7; Dasgupta, *Change and Continuity,* 56-7; Kathinka Kerkhoff, *Save Ourselves and the Girls! Girlhood in Calcutta Under the Raj* (Rotterdam: University of Amsterdam, 1995), 41-2; Forbes, *The New Cambridge History of India:* 60-2.

42 Jayawardena, *The White Woman's Other Burden,* 26-7; Stephanie O'Brien, *Towards Life in Its Fullness: A Story of Loreto (IBVM) in Eastern Africa* (Nairobi: Paulines Publications Africa, 2015), 50-1.

43 O'Brien, *Towards Life in Its Fullness,* 40-3.

44 Jayawardena, *The White Woman's Other Burden,* 26.

CHAPTER 3

"Fiery Sparks of Change": A Comparison between First Wave Feminists of India and the U.S.

Shoba Sharad Rajgopal[1]

ABSTRACT

The celebration of the centenary of the 19th Amendment in 2020 has seen the resurgence of interest in the struggles of the Suffragette/Suffragist movement. This article examines the representation of first wave feminism in the developing world, with a focus on the Indian Subcontinent, from a postcolonial feminist perspective. As such, it critiques the colonialist perspective regarding women's movements of resistance in the developing world and links it to the critique of racism within the women's movements in the West. It discusses early feminists from India such as Tarabai Shinde whose spirited exposé of the double standards women were subjected to appeared almost a century before Simone De Beauvoir's landmark analysis and compares their movement to that of the suffragettes in the West. It argues too that, contrary to much of mainstream representation, Dalit feminism is a part not just of the current era of feminism but also of the first wave in India.

Introduction

> "I am most anxious to enlist everyone who can speak or write to join in checking this mad, wicked folly of "women's rights" with all its attendant horrors, on which her poor feeble sex is bent, forgetting every sense of womanly feelings and propriety"(Queen Victoria, 1870, quoted in Chernock, 2019).
>
> "She is headstrong, mannish, and full of the perfervid spirit that espouses lost causes" (M.E. Watts, Dewan of Travancore, to C.W.E. Cotton, Agent of Governor of Madras, 1929, quoted in Devika, 2019).

I have juxtaposed the two quotes above, one from the reigning monarch of the British Empire which at the time encompassed India, the other from the *Dewan* or Prime Minister of one of the Kingdoms of the erstwhile British Raj, today a part of the southern state of Kerala. The key point both have in common is that the desire of certain misguided women to fight for their rights is against the norm, even "mannish," in that it is against the sanctioned norms of civilized (British) society. The quote from the Dewan expressed his disdain for the "headstrong" young woman, Lakshmi N. Menon who would eventually become one of the foremost politicians of her era, joining the cabinet of India's first Prime Minister as a Minister of State and leading one of the nation's famous women's organizations, the All-India Women's Conference. However, the quote from the British monarch implies not just a disdain for the suffragettes but even a fear, so much so that she would appeal to others to aid her in addressing the vexing problem caused by the threat. For, despite serving as Head of State in Britain from 1837 to 1901, Queen Victoria held traditional views about separate spheres for men and women and opposed women voting and running for public office. Any opposition to this norm needed to be stamped out as not just mad but wicked, and one whose folly appeared to threaten the crown. This being the case, it is interesting to look back at this tumultuous era and unravel the attitudes towards the demands of this movement in both parts of the world and examine it through a postcolonial feminist lens.

The celebration of the centenary of the 19th Amendment in 2020 has seen a resurgence of interest in the struggles of the Suffragettes/Suffragists in both the US and the UK. In Britain, the statue of the famous suffragette Emmeline Pankhurst erected in Manchester in 2018 illustrates this point. Sculptor Hazel Reeves had chosen to portray Pankhurst standing on a chair as she rallied a crowd. Helen Pankhurst, the great suffragette's great-granddaughter, was among those who unveiled the statue on Friday, 100 years to the day after women got the vote for the first time in the UK (Pidd, 2018). Likewise, in the US it was the veteran suffragettes who started the ball rolling who have been honored with a statue in Central Park, NYC. But the feminist movement has come under much criticism in recent years, due to the marginalization of the role of women of color in the narratives on the movement. The story behind the first statue of suffragettes to grace Central Park is a case in point. That the statue is the first of actual women from U.S history is problematic, considering that the location has 23 statues of men, but the second is that it is the first to commemorate the warriors of women's suffrage in the United States, and it has taken a century for that to happen. It features three women, Elizabeth Cady Stanton, pen in hand, holding the Declaration of Sentiments, with Susan B. Antony and Sojourner Truth gazing intently at her. Truth is represented making a point to which her white sisters are keenly listening. But what many are unaware of is the fact that Truth was not in the original design, which only featured Elizabeth Cady Stanton and Susan B. Anthony, but following accusations of whitewashing, it was changed. That was when the sculptor Meredith Bergman added the imposing figure of the African American suffragette who had shocked audiences back in the day with her passionate denunciation of racism in her acclaimed speech, "Ain't I a woman?"[2] The fact that this happened at this moment in time in the 21st century is disappointing, considering that women of color had mounted a critique of western feminism for over a century, pointing out its marginalization of the contributions of women of color in the movement. It is all the more disturbing considering that women of color made up a large part of the first wave, contrary to how the media have represented it, as numerous organizations of women of color, predominantly African American, but also Native American, Asian American and Latina women had added to the diversity of the movement.

Why then did history continue to represent white women as the main figures of the first wave? Alas, instead of learning from their mistake, they repeated it with the second wave too, leading feminists of color to form their own organizations. It is a critique that has been leveled by various scholars over the past half a century, Anzaldua (1981), hooks (1984), et al. Indeed, Black women recognize that historically, white women have been no less racist than white men, as seen in the women's branches of the KKK in the American South (Freedman, 2002). What is worse is that this innate racism is seen even in some renowned feminists of the second wave, such as Susan Brownmiller and Shulamith Firestone whose writings hark back to the old myth of the Black rapist disseminated in the Reconstruction era (Davis, 1981). As such, the famed sisterhood of struggle appears to have been more of a myth than a reality. This narrowly defined feminism led some feminists of the 1980s and 90s to resist defining themselves with the term 'feminist,' with Alice Walker's famous coinage of the term "womanist" for a Black feminist, stating, womanist is to feminist as purple is to lavender (Walker, 1983). This had been the case in many countries of the developing world as well in previous decades where we note a general hesitation by many women's rights activists to use the 'F-word.' Even while claiming that there is "No turning back," historian Estelle Freedman acknowledges that right from its origins through the social upheavals of the 1960s, the word 'feminist' had remained a pejorative term among most progressive reformers, suffragists, and socialists around the world. At the time universal adult suffrage was extended to women, few politically engaged women called themselves feminists. Within the international women's movement, participants debated whether the term humanist rather than feminist best applied to them (Freedman, 2002). Madhu Kishwar, the founding editor of one of India's famous women's rights journals, *Manushi*, is one of many, as she states in her landmark essay 'Why I Do Not Call Myself a Feminist' (Kishwar, 1999).

It is only today, in the 21st century that the term 'feminist" is being embraced once more, as women of color demand their due as fellow warriors in the struggle, with the term intersectional feminist coined by Kimberlé Williams Crenshaw (1989). But this has not been an easy process, for, as Donna Haraway points out ironically, white western feminists had to "be forced kicking and screaming to notice" the non-innocence of the category 'women,' and that it was the critiques and analyses of different non-white feminists in the west that forced this 'discovery' upon us (Gedalof, 1999:7). It is important for me to name the perspective from which I construct my analysis, and that is as a postcolonial feminist theorist from the developing world who has been writing and teaching for over two decades in the U.S.As such, it has come to my notice that when people speak of feminism and the first wave of feminism, they mean the feminisms of the Global North as they do not seem to realize there are other branches of feminism in other parts of the world too. In fact, to quote the eminent Native American feminist Paula Gunn Allen, some feminisms may even predate western feminism (Gunn Allen, 1986). The question is, do we only recognize feminism when it resembles the societies that we are familiar with, namely those of the Occident? Much critical writing by feminist scholars from the Global South has been tokenized in Western academia, with anthologies on feminist theories still being dominated by western issues, even if they claim to give 'multicultural' or 'global' perspectives on women's studies. The implication is that there is uniformity or even agreement on what feminism means in these very diverse cultures of the world. Western feminism has therefore been subjected to much criticism from Postcolonial and Third World feminists, who resist the transcending of differences it entails and demand that feminists pay close attention to the intersections of gender, race, class, ethnicity, and nation pertaining to their locations (Mohanty, 1991). What is needed today is the re-examination of the early days of feminist history by considering it from different perspectives. Scholars have already begun "queering" the history of the suffrage movement by deconstructing the dominant narrative that has focused on the stories of elite, white, upper-class suffragists (Rouse, 2020). I hope to add to this through my own analysis here of this complex movement in the developing world, through the study of powerful feminist activists and writers who defied the narrow gender norms of their own era.

This essay examines the representation of first wave feminism with the focus on the Indian Subcontinent, using the work of feminist theorists from those regions. Moreover, in addition to those theorists it uses activists whose work is not usually taken as falling within the ambit of feminism such as Dr. B.R Ambedkar and E.V Ramasamy, better known as Periyar, the founder of the Dravidian Movement in Tamilnadu. Gender has been a central issue in India since the colonial encounter, with a deep focus on women's struggles, much of which was perceived by the colonial powers as evidence of the regressive nature of their culture. Much of what we know about other parts of the world and their cultures and histories are those of scholars or travelers from the Occident. Their studies are colored therefore by their own perspectives, with their own assumptions and prejudices. Edward Said had pointed this out in his landmark work on Orientalism, "Orientalism was ultimately a political vision of reality whose structure promoted the difference between the familiar (Europe, the West, "us"), and the strange (the Orient, the East, "them.") (Said, 1978: 43). In Geraldine Forbes's essay on Indian feminism, published in an early issue of the *Women's Studies International Forum,* she cites Miriam Schneir in her trenchant condemnation of Indian society of the 19th century, which mirrors that of many other western scholars, politicians, and writers, Winston Churchill, et al, who used the supposed lack of development and civilization prevalent in the Subcontinent as the rationale to continue to deny them independence. "No feminist works emerged from behind the Hindu *purdah* or out of the Moslem harems; centuries of slavery do not provide a fertile soil for intellectual development or expression" (Shneir, 1972, p. xiv).

Indeed, Schneir justified the focus on the western feminist tradition wherein only one version of feminism is deemed accurate. Forbes condemns Schneir's Eurocentric perspective stating that, on the contrary, feminism did exist in India in the early 20th century, even though the word was not used until decades later, and Indian women did write and speak about women's conditions, and formed organizations to secure desired changes, which eventually had an impact on the institutions of their society. Moreover, like their Western sisters, they had much success in the areas of suffrage, education, and legal and civil rights (Forbes, 1982). Yet they have had to brave criticism that they are a product of western capitalism, based on a foreign culture of no relevance to women in the Third World. This salvo has been rejected by Maitrayee Chaudhuri, who states that ideas about women's rights and gender construction have always been debated in India, albeit differently (Chaudhuri, 2005). Ania Loomba has asserted that while feminism in South Asia was born partly out of the revolutionary zeal of the anticolonial freedom movement, it did not emerge as a force of radical change (Loomba and Lukose, 2005). Kumari Jayawardene from Sri Lanka has pointed out in her landmark book on Third World feminism that they do not operate from a point of direct resistance and immediate demands but tend to opt for gradual changes that result from their collaboration with male counterparts to improve the living standards of their communities. They have instead joined hands with nationalist resistance against colonialism and imperialism, with their main driving force being the burning desire to liberate subjugated and oppressed people (Jayawardene, 1986).

I add a caveat here to Jayawardene's point. How can the key imperative of a movement that has as its central credo the desire to liberate oppressed people especially in that era of revolution not be considered radical? The organizations that emerged in India in the early 20th century, namely, the Women's Indian Association (1917), the National Council of Women (1925), and the All-India Women's Conference (1927) had a sociopolitical agenda that incorporated a comprehensive reform of personal laws that included the contentious issues of child marriage and widow remarriage. How were these not radical in an era when women had very few rights at all, be it in the West or the East? Indeed, few Indian women revolutionaries were even mentioned in the histories compiled by most western historians. Thus, we have Madam Bhikaji Cama, a Parsi revolutionary from India who was exiled to Paris where she co-founded the Paris Indian Society. Together with other notable members of the movement for Indian sovereignty living in exile, Cama wrote, published and distributed revolutionary literature for the movement, including *Bande Mataram* (founded in response to the British ban on the patriotic poem) and later *Madan's Talwar* (in response to the execution of Madan Lal Dhingra). Albeit banned in India and Britain, she managed to send the weekly magazines to Indian revolutionaries (Bhola, 2016), but she is hardly even mentioned in mainstream analyses of the women's rights movement in India.

In this sense I would caution that concepts of radicalism and revolutionary be examined keeping in mind the era when they rose. The early feminists were also concerned with issues that are not usually perceived as part of much of the mainstream feminist agenda in the West, such as the impact of racism and colonization on gender relations. This is still the case with indigenous feminists within Western settler societies who advocate self-determination and cultural survival as their key issues (Gunn Allen, 1986; Trask, 1993). In fact, these activists consider what they call "white feminism" as a facet of imperialism, as it imposes the western perspective while failing to recognize the adverse effects of imperialism and colonialism on indigenous and/or conquered peoples (Herr, 2014).

"Imperial feminism" and "the White Woman's Burden"

The women's movement in India can be divided into two distinct phases, the pre-independence era and the post-independence era, the focus of this article being the former. In the pre-independence era, the Women's Movement began as a social reform movement in which western Enlightenment ideals of liberty, equality and fraternity were imbibed by the Indian educated elite through the study of English and the contact with the West. This era of the early nineteenth century saw the emergence of various socio-religious reform movements in India, such as movements of caste reform, and the struggle for women's empowerment, through an outright ban on all traditions that held them back. This was also the era described by Antoinette Burton as 'Imperial Feminism' on the part of British feminists who expressed a concern for the desperate state of their Indian sisters. According to Burton, Victorian and Edwardian feminists such as Josephine Butler, Millicent Garrett Fawcett, and Mary Carpenter believed that the native women of colonial India constituted a special white woman's burden, adding to the concept popularized by Rudyard Kipling of the white man's burden. Burton asserts that British feminists relied on images of an enslaved and primitive Oriental womanhood desperately in need of liberation at the hands of their emancipated British sisters. She argues that this unquestioning acceptance of Britain's imperial status and of Anglo-Saxon racial superiority created a set of imperial feminist ideologies, the legacy of which must be recognized and understood by contemporary feminists (Burton, 1994).

Interestingly, Black British scholars, Pratibha Parmar and Valeri Amos use the term imperial feminism to describe modern western liberal feminists as well. "The 'herstory' which white women use to trace the roots of women's oppression.... is an imperial history rooted in the prejudices of colonial and neo-colonial periods, a 'herstory' which suffers the same form of historical amnesia of white male historians, by ignoring the fundamental ways in which white women have benefited from the oppression of Black people" (Amos and Parmar, 2001:19).In her analysis of the writings of British women fiction writers of the Victorian era, Shampa Roy quotes a British missionary, Miss Hewlett, who, when asked what the biggest impediment was to progress in India, responded, "We would have to reply, the position of the women. They are socially degraded, treated as animals of a lower order than man, excluded from society and kept in grossest ignorance" (Roy, 2010: 61). Interestingly, the British women did not seem to link this degraded condition of women in the colonized world with their own condition in their own country, where they had very few rights themselves. In fact, that was the crux of first wave feminism in many of the western nations, an issue that appears to have been forgotten by these zealous Christian missionaries, out to save the benighted heathen. In fact, most of them supported the colonial enterprise, using the woman condition to justify it. Interestingly, this rationale of the white man's burden to rescue his brown sisters in the Middle East can be seen even in fairly recent times in the so-called War on Terror that was unleashed upon Afghanistan and Iraq by the Bush administration and its allies.

Back in the 19th century, the women's question was translated into a social reform movement which focused on rooting out social evils, partly in response to charges of Oriental barbarity by the colonial rulers. The social reform movement had its own paradox: on the one hand there was a preoccupation with western ideas to emulate, assimilate or reject; on the other hand, there was also the element of revivalism or a need to reassert and reinforce a cultural identity distinct from the British colonizers. Besides seeking reforms through legislation, education was seen as an important means of changing women's situation. There were periods of reluctance on the part of colonial rulers in intervening on debates regarding entrenched traditions for fear of reprisal, such as the abolition of *sati* in 1829, or raising the Age of Consent for Women in the 1890s, the second causing so much unrest that it led to the British government to rapidly backtrack in order to acquiesce to conservative sections of the native elite and abandon all attempts to initiate further social reform legislation in India until the child marriage restraint act of 1929 (Roy, 2010). Indeed, as Mary E. John points out, the contradictory colonial context created the discourses of modernity while simultaneously reinforcing tradition where it suited the colonial state to do so. The British law in fact deprived women of their right to inheritance, recognized even in religious law. On the issue of women's suffrage, Congress party leader Sarojini Naidu had already led a delegation of activists to request equal female suffrage in the next elections. She had utilized a tone of appeasement even with her own party, arguing that women voters and leaders would not usurp male authority, and that all Indians would be inspired by their nationalism and maternalism. Despite this mild tone, the British had still refused to grant women the right to vote and stand for elections on the same terms as men. This then was the contradictory stance of the British government, one that was replete with contradictions and manipulations, perhaps even more so than their prior efforts to justify their civilizing mission through the regulation of social reform (John, 2000).

It is interesting to note that many of the early Indian supporters of women's rights were men, unlike the situation in the West, where the suffragists were mainly women, except for a few powerful male allies like Frederick Douglass, Henry Stanton, John Stuart Mill, et al. Indeed, Raja Ram Mohan Roy is recognized as one of the early feminists and makers of modern India who historian Ramachandra Guha describes as "The first Liberal" for his principled stance on women's rights. Roy had argued that *sati* was not supported by the Hindu scriptures and had been added only vested interests and was nothing less than murder. Roy's efforts led to the abolition of the practice under Governor-General William Cavendish-Bentinck in 1829 (Guha, 2011). Similarly, Ishwar Chandra Vidyasagar's crusade for the improvement in condition of widows, supported by luminaries such as Nobel laureate Rabindranath Tagore, led to the Widow Remarriage Act of 1856. Tagore had in fact submitted a memorandum to the Legislative Council for the removal of legal disabilities of remarried Hindu widows and the establishment of girl's schools in every suburb of Calcutta. Keshav Chandra Sen was instrumental in getting the Native Marriage Act passed in 1872, which forbade child marriage and polygamy, and encouraged both widow marriage and inter-caste marriages for those who declared that they did not belong to any recognized faith. Jyotiba Phule along with his wife Savitribai Phule spearheaded the movement towards ending caste- and gender-based discrimination and the emancipation from patriarchal social mores. Muslim theologians of the era too such as Maulana Abul Kalam Azad, who later went on to become India's first Minister of Education, supported women's education as integral to a liberated postcolonial nation.

Dalit and Anti-colonial Feminist Activism of the Pre-Independence Era

Among the most powerful male voices of the early 20th century was that of EV Ramaswamy, known as *Periyar* (a sobriquet of respect in Tamil, for "great elder"), a philosopher and activist from Tamilnadu who founded the Self-Respect and Dravidar Kazhagam movements in 1925. Periyar vehemently condemned *Pennadimai* (slavery of woman) and *Pen Izhivu* (degradation of a woman) and pointed out that men were responsible for keeping women as decorated animals. He floated the idea that adorning women with costly dress and jewels is not better than giving them education, knowledge, and self-respect (Sithadharanan and Thirumal, 2018). He denounced patriarchy and its role in preventing women from having reproductive rights in no uncertain terms, a topic that continues to be highly contentious in the U.S today. This was in 1942 when feminists struggled to convince their nations of the importance of contraception, which was finally legalized in the U.S only in 1936. Periyar's vision of the empowerment of women was codified into law by Dr. B.R Ambedkar, the country's first Law Minister.

However, barring notable exceptions, most academic literature including anthologies on Ambedkar and Ambedkarism ignore the contributions of the great Dalit scholar and statesman who dominated Indian political discourse in the 20th century to the cause of women's rights. One of the most important contributions of Dr. Ambedkar in relation to the elevation of the status of women in India was his initiative to draft and introduce the Hindu Code Bill in the Constituent Assembly on 24th February1949. Being India's first Law Minister and Chairman of the Drafting Committee of the Constituent Assembly, he thought it appropriate to liberate women from the bondage of slavery by reforming the Hindu social laws codified by Manu (Kumar, 2016). The Hindu Code Bill attempted to put an end to a variety of marriage systems prevailing in India and legalized only monogamous marriages and sought to confer on women the right to property as well. It is important to mention here that once again, this is a point that first wave feminists in the West had fought for as well, as prior to their activism, women across Europe and the U.S lost their property at the time of marriage.

In all these cases, we have powerful male voices raised to defend women's rights, and it worked to get their issues recognized, much as the powerful voice of Frederick Douglass helped get the attention of society in the US to recognize the demands articulated in "The Declaration of Sentiments" penned by Elizabeth Cady Stanton and Lucretia Mott at the Seneca Falls Convention. But what of the voices of Indian women, were they only represented by either the supposedly benign colonialist patriarchy or the Indian nationalist patriarchy? This is precisely why Spivak's article "Can the Subaltern Speak?" in response to the 1829 banning of *sati* by the British colonial powers in India is important, with her trenchant observation of the role played by white men in saving brown women from brown men (Spivak, 1989). British Indian history texts state that the British colonial authorities passed an act in 1829 prohibiting and abolishing the act of widow burning, condemning it as an inhumane crime against women. The British colonizers are thus collectively represented as the protectors, the saviors of Indian women from an oppressively patriarchal Hindu society. Moreover, by representing *sati* as a barbaric Oriental tradition, the British were able to justify imperialism as a civilizing mission, or in French territories as their "mission *civilisatrice"* in which white colonial administrators believed that they were rescuing Indian women from the reprehensible practices of a traditional Hindu patriarchal society.

This is extremely problematic, not because sati was not a horrific custom, because it definitely was, even if it was not as widely practiced across the country as claimed by the colonial authorities, but because it was not just the British government and western liberal feminists but even many Indian first wave feminists who opposed it, starting with Ram Mohan Roy, whose strong support for the ban is what gave the British administration the courage to go ahead with the ban (Guha, 2011). Further, it was not just certain wise and compassionate Indian male social reformers who opposed it, but many determined and courageous women too and it is disturbing that their resistance was not considered important enough to be noted by British historians of the era. Indeed, it is this representation of women's activism of the first wave in India as passive and subdued that feminist historiography calls into question (Sangari and Vaid, 1989), by focusing on women's collective responses to injustice. Kalpana Kannabiran focuses on the various unregistered incidents that defined women's resistance, giving it, for the first time, the image of insurgency and revolution. While many narratives of Hinduism in the colonial period focus on men's efforts at social and religious reform, Tarabai Shinde and other authors show that there was a growing subculture of resistance which was fashioned and nurtured by women, rarely spoken about, but radical and spontaneous (Kannabiran, 2009). Shinde herself has also been featured in Ramachandra Guha's work as one of "the makers of modern India," and described as a "subaltern feminist" for her spirited attacks on patriarchy. Her spirited exposé of the double standards that women were subjected to appeared almost a century before Simone De Beauvoir's *The Second Sex (1949)*, one of the key feminist tracts for western feminist discourse. *Titled Stree Purush Tulana* (A Comparison Between Men and Women) in Marathi, Shinde's work was penned in response to the unfair treatment of women and religious prejudice that permeated society. Published in 1882, it strikes one of the earliest notes of revolt, a defining moment in the paradigm of feminist insurgency as the first Indian feminist who minutely points out male hypocrisy and women's secondary status in Indian society. Her essay was written in response to the article published in *Pune Vaibhav* which was based on the immorality of widows (Kale, 2014). Moreover, it bears a remarkable similarity to Mary Wollstonecraft's pathbreaking work, *A Vindication of the Rights of Women* (1791), which tears into the many ways in which patriarchy ground women underfoot.

From all this we can see that from the end of the nineteenth century, in the years before independence, the two main issues women's rights activists took up were political rights and the reform of personal laws. This is the time when women started forming their own organizations first at the local and then at the national level. The early 20th century was the period that saw the birth of three major organizations: Women's India Association (WIA), National Council of Women in India (NCWI) and All India Women's Conference (AIWC). All three organizations were formed between 1917 and 1927 after World War I, with the sole objective of involving women in civic and public life and the promotion of social, civil, moral and educational welfare of women and children (Forbes, 2000). Foremost of these was the WIA and the women's journal, *Stri-Dharma,* whose title meant the sphere of women. The journal was launched by Margaret Cousins, an Irish suffragist who moved to India in 1915, and Dr. Muthulakshmi Reddy, who would later go on to serve as the editor of the magazine and the first woman legislator in British India. *Stri-Dharma* would serve as the platform of discussion for the women's movement in India. Comparable to western women's movements in its use of feminist terminology, the journal was published from January 1918 until August 1936 (Broome, 2012). Another important organization founded in this era was the *Bharat Stree Mahamandal,* the Great Circle of Indian Women, a semi-revolutionary group with branches across the Indian subcontinent, one of the very first of its kind. Its founder, Saraladevi Choudhurani hoped that this fledgling organization would help develop a sisterhood that could supply energetic Indian women ready to work to improve the status of women in their nation (Forbes, 1982).

During this period the struggle against colonial rule intensified and Mohandas Karamchand Gandhi legitimized and expanded Indian women's public activities by initiating them into the non-violent civil disobedience movement against the British colonizers. In the decades that followed, women showed active participation in freedom movement paving the way for some women only organizations. When Gandhi came on the political scene, he could draw in a large number of women to the political arena by giving a very broad meaning of *swaraj and* helping them find dignity in public life and a new place in the national mainstream. His views on many issues installed a new confidence among women and a consciousness that they could fight against oppression, even if he held some very regressive ideas on sexuality. As a result of his support and encouragement, many women joined the civil disobedience movement during the thirties. Interestingly, Gandhi's appeal went beyond 'respectable' women to even women who mainstream Indian society looked at askance, such as *devadasis,* who were seen as degraded sex workers. But Gandhi did not disdain them and spurn their determination to join the cause, an extraordinary perspective for an Indian politician of that era but welcomed them into the struggle. Despite this contagion of the movement through the presence of the devadasis, middle class women from respectable families were able to join the nationalist movement with the approval of their families. Nor was Gandhi the only politician to do so, for Netaji Subhash Chandra Bose too decided on inviting women volunteers to join the freedom struggle. Bose believed in overthrowing the colonial regime through armed resistance, and the women who joined his movement such as the renowned Captain Lakshmi Swaminathan served in the "Rani Jhansi Regiment" named after the woman considered infamous by the British colonizers, namely the warrior Queen Rani Lakshmi Bai of Jhansi.

A remarkable feature of politics in the nascent Indian nation state is that women occupied key roles in it. Sarojini Naidu was elected the President of the Congress Party, while Vijaylakshmi Pandit, Lakshmi N. Menon and others occupied key roles in the government of the newly independent republic of India. If we compare this to the U.S one must note the stark difference as not even one woman's name is associated with the Declaration of Independence whereas many women were involved in the very framing of the Indian Constitution, along with their male allies, Dr. Ambedkar, Prime Minister Jawaharlal Nehru and others. In fact, it is interesting to note the intersectional nature of the group of women involved with writing the Constitution and joining the government of the newly independent nation of India. They came from different classes, religions, and castes and different parts of the country too, from princesses like Rajkumari Amrit Kaur and middle-class women like Ammu Swaminathan and Sarojini Naidu to working class women like Dakshayini Velayudhan, the first Dalit woman to be elected to the Constituent Assembly, and Begum Aizaz Rasul, the only Muslim woman member of the Constituent Assembly, who went on the become Minister for Social Welfare and Minorities. Sarojini Naidu was the first Indian woman to be elected president of the *Indian National Congress,* which is tantamount to a major political party in the US nominating a woman as its leader in the early 20th century. This is laudable considering that women in the US only won suffrage in 1920, and that too after a protracted battle against the US government for over 70 years. In India, on the contrary, Sarojini Naidu was appointed a state Governor soon after independence, serving as the Governor of United Provinces in Agra and Oudh from 1947 to 1949. A few years later in 1953 Vijayalakshmi Pandit, the sister of the first PM, became the first woman and the first Asian to be elected president of the *U.N General Assembly.* These women occupied key positions in the government at a time when women in much of the West were struggling to get a voice in the public sphere, let alone become state Governors.

Despite this fact, the early Indian feminists were strongly aware of the need for women to fight for their own rights instead of relying on the protection of male led governments. A women's journal of the 1920s from the southern state of Kerala states this in no uncertain terms.

> "The work of intrepid struggle and sound bargaining to secure legitimate rights is the responsibility of women themselves. Any complacency on their part, induced by the hope that the government - which has displayed its conservatism in all affairs - will concede their rights and authority in full recognition of justice, and the mood of these times, would be most foolish. In all the countries of the world, women have won their freedom and rights only through agitation.... Open your eyes to the realities of the world, ascertain your needs, recognize your rights, and move to secure them."
>
> *(Editorial, Vanitakusumam 1927-28, Devika, 2019).*

First wave feminists in India played important roles in the public sphere, laying the groundwork for women's suffrage. In the time period of 1915-1918 Sarojini Naidu traveled to different regions in India to lecture on women's rights, social welfare of women and nationalism, much as Susan B. Antony and Sojourner Truth did in their time in the U.S. But they did not stop with that. These early Indian feminists even challenged the very foundations of the postcolonial nation state as in 1928, when the women of the All-India Women's Conference (AIWC) demanded 'new *sastras*' (new scriptures) in response to the founder of the Hindu Mahasabha Madan Mohan Malaviya's assertion that the age of marriage could not be raised due to the diktats of Hindu scriptures. This moment anticipated by several decades the demand of feminist historians not just for new histories but for a reinvention of the historical archive (Nair, 1996). It also connects to the rise of Dalit feminist activism of more recent times, and the links to the critiques of the doctrine of the great law giver of ancient India, Manu, namely the *Manusmriti* by India's first Law Minister, Dr. B.R Ambedkar. The late scholar Gail Omvedt clarifies that Ambedkar states that *Manusmriti* postulates that women are not worth being liberated and indeed have no right to enjoy freedom. One of the popular verses expresses that as a child, the woman should be protected by the father, in youth by her husband and in old age by her son; in short, she should not be independent at any point of time. Thus, *Manusmriti* remains a powerful symbol of Brahmanical patriarchy, and it is incorrect to consider the burning of the *Manusmriti* as symbolically important only for Dalits, as it is equally important for women. Further, recognizing *Manusmriti Dahan Divas* (the Day of Burning of Manusmriti) as the *Bharatiya Stree Mukti Divas* (Indian Women's Liberation Day), underlines the special links between gender, caste and patriarchy within India and South Asia in general (Omvedt, 2003).

However, it is curious that, even in India, we do not learn in our schools and colleges that 25th December 1927 is commemorated in Dalit feminist circles as Indian Women's Liberation Day, as that was the date when the Dalit leader, along with hundreds of his followers, gathered at Mahad in Maharashtra, and burned a copy of the *Manusmriti* (Rege, 2013: 45). *Manusmriti* or *Manuwadi* as it is popularly known, remains a highly contested term in India today, being the ideology legalized by Manu, the lawgiver of ancient India, due to its widely cited sexism and racism. It is interesting to note that the proposal to celebrate this date as *Bharatiya Stree Mukti Divas* (BSM) or Indian Women's Liberation Day was forwarded by Dalit women activists who argued that Ambedkar's writings on women's empowerment had been neglected by political groups across the nation due to the Brahminical patriarchal hegemony within them. The eminent sociologist Sharmila Rege whose work focused primarily on the interrelatedness of casteism and patriarchy has pointed out that Dalit feminists emphasize Brahminical hegemony as the chief cause of the enslavement of women and *Manusmriti* as its legitimizing force.As such, the burning of the *Manusmriti* document is a significant symbolic act aimed at ending the interlinked slavery of both Dalits and women (Rege, 2013). The fact that this call has not been taken up by much of the mainstream feminist movement in India is a sad reflection on the caste divide within the movement which has only been increasing in recent times with the rise of the Far Right.

Among the most famous of the early feminists of India were the remarkable Maharashtrian activists Savitri Bai Phule and Pandita Ramabai Saraswati, both of whom campaigned for women's education and against both sexism and casteism, and Dr. Muthulakshmi Reddy. I shall focus on Pandita Ramabai and Dr. Muthulakshmi Reddy as both women overcame remarkable obstacles of caste and creed in their crusade for women's empowerment, and moreover, charted these paths on their own, whereas the few Indian women who were active in social reform in that era did so only with the encouragement or, at least, the permission of their husbands. The *New York Times* in fact features her in an important article, "Overlooked No More: Pandita Ramabai, Indian Scholar, Feminist and Educator," acknowledging, *"Since 1851, obituaries in The New York Times have been dominated by white men, we're adding the stories of remarkable people whose deaths went unreported in The Times" (Khan, 2018). This is a long overdue acknowledgement, as these new* Obituaries focus on non-white people who have been largely overlooked in the western mainstream media. Historian Uma Chakravarti describes her in her biography, *Rewriting History: The Life and Times of Pandita Ramabai,* as the most controversial Indian woman of her times (Chakravarti, 1998). She was the rare woman who had learned Sanskrit, the ancient Hindu liturgical language reserved for Brahmin men, as well as the rare Brahmin to marry out of caste, and the rare widow who remained in public view, defying customs; as well as the rare Indian upper caste woman to decide on her own, to convert to Christianity, which in fact led to a lot of anger from her upper caste Hindu community. Pandita Ramabai was in fact given the very title of "Pandita" (scholar) due to her exceptional erudition and knowledge of Sanskrit texts, acquired from her unusual upbringing, her itinerant parents who dwelt in the forests of Maharashtra. Her most important published work, *The High Caste Hindu Woman,* was written in English in the United States in 1887, when she was 29. It focused on the plight of Hindu widows — she called widowhood "the worst and most dreaded period of a high-caste woman's life" (Khan, 2018). It is important to note here that women from the upper castes and classes were often subjected to even greater prohibitions than those from the lower castes with regard to widowhood. Brahmin widows were banned from remarrying and considered cursed, they were required to shave their heads, wear drab, coarse clothes and subsist on meager food. Ramabai returned to India in 1889, and using the proceeds from her book and lectures, raised funds to open the *Sharada Sadan* (Home of Learning) center in 1889 in Bombay, offering widowed women a refuge where they could study and learn skills like gardening, carpentry and sewing.

First wave Indian feminists belonged to all castes and religions and classes, from the highest caste of the country to the lowest. Thus, the opposite end of the spectrum from Pandita Ramabai was Dr. Muthulakshmi Reddy, who overcame her status as the daughter of a *devadasi* or temple concubine to become the first woman to graduate from Medical College in 1907 and eventually became one of the most famous oncologists of her time, as well as a famous legislator and feminist. Her home state of Tamilnadu commemorated her 133rd birthday by declaring her date of birth, July 19th as Hospital Day. She was closely associated with the All-India Women's Conference and the Women's India Association and helped bring about legislation to abolish polygamy as well as child marriage and the *devadasi* system. Dr. Reddy pointed out that the devadasi system was ostensibly about the dedication of women to temple deities, tasked with passing on the baton of the art of dance to the next generation, but that they were often subjected to exploitation by upper caste men who used them as concubines and were trapped in the system. Dr. Reddy brought about the passage of the 1930 bill for the prevention of dedication of young girls as Devadasis by the Madras Presidency on 5 December 1947, but the mindset of traditional society was yet to change, even among the elite. At an event held to honor her, the speaker commended her work for her "fallen sisters", or devadasis. Her powerful rebuke is legendary. "How dare you call them fallen sisters? Female chastity is impossible without male chastity. The men who exploited them were older and should be held responsible." (Devika, 2020).

The courage and determination of these early Indian feminists must be respected, especially at a time when the nascent movement for women's empowerment in both the personal and the political spheres was yet in its infancy. They had also dared to expose the flaws of their own society at a time when their own communities were deeply conscious of how they were perceived in the West and how that could be used against their independence. Their success lies in their courage in articulating their problems, but in a manner that would enable their own communities to support their endeavors while preventing their western counterparts from using the information gleaned to attack them. Yet another problem these early feminists faced was, how to represent their societies with their own indigenous cultures, their histories and literatures, as worthy of being studied in comparison with those from other parts of the developed world. For feminism means different things in different parts of the world, and even in different classes and castes of the same country, as in the Indian context, and one uniform does not fit all its myriad cultures. In this sense indeed, it makes more sense to refer to feminisms, thereby celebrating its richness and diversity, rather than to one over-arching umbrella of feminism, which is taken in the hegemonic sense as the norm. As the late great feminist Kamla Bhasin puts it in her eloquent turn of phrase, *"Hum Bharat ki Nari hain, Phulnahin, Chingarihain!"* (We are the women of India. We are not flowers but sparks of change!) (Rajgopal, 2021). It is this multi-faceted face of feminism across the world that we must acknowledge and celebrate, rather than a narrow focus on the feminisms of the Global North during the centenary commemoration of women's suffrage.

REFERENCES

Ambedkar, B.R. 2013. In Rege, S (Ed.) *Against the madness of Manu: B.R Ambedkar's writings on Brahmanical patriarchy.* New Delhi: Nayana Publishing Pvt. Ltd.

Anzaldua, G. and Moraga, C. 1981. Eds. *This Bridge called my back: Writings by radical women of color.*New York: Kitchen table: Women of color press.

Bhola, R. 2016. *The Life and Times of Madam BhikajiCama.*Prabhat Prakashan. New Delhi.

Broome, S. 2012. "*Stri-Dharma*: Voice of the Indian Women's Rights Movement 1928-1936." Thesis, Georgia State University, 2012. https://scholarworks.gsu.edu/history_theses/57

Burton, A.N. 1994. *Burdens of History: British Feminists, Indian Women, and Imperial Culture, 1865-1915.* Chapel Hill: University of North Carolina Press.

Chaudhuri, M. 2005. (Ed.), *Feminism in India.* New Delhi: Zed Books.

Chernock, A. 2019. *The Right to Rule and the Rights of Women: Queen Victoria and the Women's Movement.* Cambridge University Press.

Crenshaw, Kimberle, 1989. "Demarginalizing the Intersection of Race and Sex: A Black Feminist Critique of Antidiscrimination Doctrine, Feminist Theory and Antiracist Politics," *University of Chicago Legal Forum*: Vol. 1989, Article 8.

Davis, A. 1981. *Women, race and class,* New York: Random House.

De Beauvoir, Simone. 1949. *The Second Sex.* H M Parshley. Harmondsworth, Middlesex, U.K. : Penguin Books, *1949.*

Devika, J. 2019. "Discovering the First Generation of Feminists in Kerala," *The Wire.*

Devika, VR, 2020. "Remembering Muthulakshmi Reddy, doctor and feminist who led the battle against India's caste-based misogyny," *First Post.com*

Forbes, 1982. "Caged Tigers: First wave feminists in India," *Women's Studies International Forum,* Volume 5, Number 6. Oxford: Pergamon Press, p. 525-536.

Forbes, 1996. *Women in modern India.* Cambridge, UK: Cambridge University Press.

Freedman, E. 2002. *No Turning Back: The History of Feminism and the Future of Women.* New York: Random House Publishing Group.

Ganesh, K. 2019. "Dr. Muthulakshmi Reddi: A Powerful Face of Nationalist Feminism," *The Wire.*

Gedalof, I. 1999. *Against purity: Rethinking identity with India and Western feminisms.* London: Routledge.

Guha, R. 2011. *Makers of modern India.* New York: Belknap Press.

Herr, R. 2014. "Reclaiming Third World Feminism: Or why Transnational Feminism needs Third World Feminism," *Meridians: Feminism, Race, Transnationalism* 12 (1). hooks, b. 1984. *Feminist theory: From margin to center.* Boston: South End Press.

Jayawardene, K. 1986. *Feminism and nationalism in the third world.* London: Zed Press.

John, Mary. E, 2000. "Alternate Modernities? Reservations and Women's Movement in 20th century India," *Economic and Political Weekly*, October 28.

Kale, M. 2014. "Tarabai Shinde's 'A Comparison of Men and Women': A Milestone in Indian Feminism," *Research Scholar*, Volume 2, Issue 2.

Kannabiran, K. 2016. "Women's Lifeworlds and the Idea of Feminist Insurgency." In *Vents d'Est, vents d'Ouest: Mouvements de femmes et féminismesanticoloniaux*. Geneva: Graduate Institute Publications.

Khan, A. 2018. "Overlooked no more: Pandita Ramabai, Indian Scholar, Feminist and Educator," *The New York Times*, New York City, November 2018.

https://www.nytimes.com/2018/11/14/obituaries/pandita-ramabai-overlooked.html

Kishwar, M. 1991. "Why I do not call myself a feminist", *Manushi*, No. 61, 2-8.

Loomba, A. and Lukose, R.A. (Eds.) 2012. *South Asian Feminisms*. Durham: Duke University Press.

Nair, Janaki. 1996. *Women and Law in Colonial India: A Social History*. Bangalore: National Law School of India University.

Omvedt, G. 2003. "Interviews: Why Celebrate 25th December as *BharatiyaStree Mukti Din*," in S. Rege (Ed.)

Parmar, P. and Amos, V. 2001. "Challenging Imperial Feminism," in Kum-kumBhavnani, Ed., *Feminism and race.* Oxford, U.K: Oxford University Press.

Pidd, 2018. "Thousands welcome Emmeline Pankhurst statue in Manchester," *The Guardian*.

Rajgopal, 2021. "Remembering Kamla Bhasin, feminist icon of India," *Ms. Magazine*. October 2021.

Rege, S. 2013. *The madness of Manu: B.R Ambedkar's writings on Brahmanical patriarchy.* New Delhi: Navayana publications.

Rouse, W. "The Very Queer History of the Suffrage Movement," *Ms. Magazine*, 2020.

Roy, S. 2010. "A miserable sham: Flora Annie Steel's short fictions and the question of Indian women's reform." *Feminist Review,* p. 55-74. Hampshire, UK: Palgrave Macmillan.

Said, E. 1978. *Orientalism.* New York: Pantheon Books.

Sangari, K. and Vaid, S. (Eds.) 1989. *Recasting Women: Essays in Colonial History*, New Delhi: Kali for Women.

Shinde, T. 1994. "A Comparison of Men and Women: An Essay to Show Who's Really Wicked and Immoral, Women or Men." In *Tarabai Shinde and the Critique of Gender Relations in Colonial India*, R. O'Hanlon. p. 73-134. New Delhi: Oxford University Press.

Sithadharanan. K and Thirumal, J. 2020. "Periyar's views on empowerment of women through classified venture: A study, "*Journal of Management Research and Analysis* (JMRA), Volume 05 Issue 03, September 2018, Pages: 105-108.

Spivak, G.C. 1993. "Can the Subaltern Speak?" in *Colonial Discourse and Post-Colonial Theory: A Reader*, Eds. Patrick Williams and Laura Chrisman (Hemel Hempstead: Harvester, 1993), p.93.

Tharu, J. Susie and Lalita, K, (Eds.). 1991.*Women Writing in India: 600 B.C. to the early 20th century* New York: The Feminist Press.

Trask, H.K. 1993. *From a Native Daughter: Colonialism and Sovereignty in Hawai'i.* Honolulu: University of Hawai'i Press.

Walker, A. 1983. *In search of our mother's gardens*, New York: Harcourt, Brace, Jovanovich.

ENDNOTES

1 Dr. Shoba Sharad Rajgopal is Professor of International Feminist Studies, in the Department of Ethnic & Gender Studies at Westfield State University in Massachusetts, where she teaches courses on Gender, Race, and Sexuality. Her doctorate is in Media Studies from the University of Colorado, Boulder. Prior to her arrival in the United States, she worked for seven years as a broadcast journalist for the Indian TV networks based in Bombay (Mumbai), India, and has also done in-depth news reports for CNN International. Her journalistic work focused on the struggles of women and indigenous people in the postcolonial nation-state. Her work continues to be published widely, in academic journals as well as newspapers such as *The Times of India* and feminist and Asian news sites such as *Ms. Magazine* and *American Kahaani* in the U.S.

2 The whitewashing permeates the well-known version of Sojourner Truth's speech as well. See the comparison of two speeches, ..."one transcribed by Marius Robinson, a journalist, who was in the audience at the Woman's Rights Convention in Akron, Ohio on May 29, 1851. And Gage's version is on the right, written 12 years later and published in 1863, The full text of each version follows the synopsis below so you can see the differences line by line. I have highlighted overt similarities between the two versions. While Frances Gage changed most of Sojourner's words and falsely attributed a southern slave dialect to Sojourner's 1863 version, it is clear the origin of Gage's speech comes from Sojourner's original 1851 speech." See the comparison between the two speeches here as documentation: https://www.thesojournertruthproject.com/compare-the-speeches/.

CHAPTER 4

A History of Ecofeminist-Socialist Resistance to Eco-crisis in India

Gowri Parameswaran[1]

ABSTRACT

This article traces the history of women's environmental activism in India after independence. The earliest organizing efforts came from women from indigenous communities who wanted to collectively push back against government and private encroachments into communal lands. From the 1970s to the late 1980s, ecofeminism became a dominant paradigm to analyze and respond to environmental issues globally. Indian feminists adapted the model to analyzing ecological issues locally while also pushing back against its essentialism and its blindness to social and economic inequities. Indian eco(feminist) socialists demanded a centering of the voices of the most vulnerable communities in environmental movements. In the 1990s, the economic liberalization of India slowed the energy of women organizing around ecological issues. Even as the country became increasingly polluted and prone to disasters related to climate change, there was very little public discussion on ecological justice, in fact, middle-class environmentalism began to dominate the public space. Today, there is an urgent need for an ecological paradigm that centers social justice, in other words, a revival of an environmentalism of the poor. The alternative is an unsustainable, unlivable world.

Introduction: Post-Independence Indian Environmentalism

Since the early years of British colonialism, Indian leaders have written about the horrors of unmitigated industrial expansion. This phenomenon picked up strength in the first few decades of the 1900s (Guha, 1997; 2014). For instance, Mohanlal Karamchand Gandhi wrote about the evils of industrial development, especially one that mimicked European growth and that exhibited little regard for the many species and other human communities that inhabited the land already scarred through centuries of colonization. His protégé Meera Behn proclaimed that the path for India was in rejecting the unsustainable models of development exhibited by the nations of the Global North; instead, it lay in charting its own path that focused on meeting the needs of the local population without destroying the environment (Gupta, 1993). After India's independence she was given forest lands to manage in a sustainable fashion by the Uttar Pradesh government. She led the newly independent Indian government's push to establish sustainable agriculture and livestock farming in the foothills of the Himalayas. She was one of the first of a long line of women who played a crucial role in connecting women's wellbeing with environmental health (Kumar, 2002). Today Meera Behn is featured in the list of women who played a pioneering role in the field of forestry. Presaging the modern environmental movement, she wrote:

> "You cannot separate economic problems from human ones......Look at what is happening now: wrong cultivation, mechanization in villages causing unemployment and hopeless disorientation... But to stop the death of the forest, for example, would require a bold reorientation by the central Government: the decision to put financial advantages at the bottom and protection of trees and soil at the top". (Sereny, 1982, page 70)

After independence in 1947, India resembled most of the early postcolonial nations in attempting to shake off the yoke of centuries of colonial oppression. In its zeal to advance industrially, its leaders attempted to mimic European and North American models of economic growth, subsuming environmental issues to focus on national economic concerns (Maudsley, 1998). In the west however, the large-scale negative impacts of massive industrialization, insensitive to ecological ruptures, was becoming evident. One of the earliest texts to explore the issue of the grave dangers posed by environmental destruction was *Silent Spring* by Rachel Carson published in 1962. Carson's book accused the pesticide industry of hiding the long-term devastating impact that pesticides have on human life and habitat. While Carson did not argue for outright banning of many of these pesticides, her scientific observations inspired early environmentalists to collectively organize to push back against policies with the potential for negative ecological impacts (Carson, 2002).

The Rise of Ecofeminism in the Global North

Ecofeminism as a framework to understand and respond to the crisis of the Anthropocene arose in the 1970s, as part of the radical traditions for justice in the United States (Gaard, 2010; Gaard, 2017; Salleh, 2017). While communities around the world were already organizing against the ill-effects of rampant environmental degradation, ecofeminism offered a novel way to explore exploitation. With the rise of the civil rights movements in the 1960s and 70s, feminists began to be increasingly concerned with the connections between war, corporatism, environmental destruction, and gendered oppression. A new generation of activists began to call for the dismantling of patriarchy to address ecological destruction. Collectively, these resistance movements began to be self-labelled as ecofeminist, with the connections between class, gender, race/caste, and the ecology being centered for analysis (Estévez-Saá, & Lorenzo-Modia, 2018). The term itself was coined by Francoise de' Eaubonne (1974). While there were grassroots protests environment destruction before her, she articulated a new theory that made an explicit connection between feminism and environmental justice:

> "Practically everybody knows that today the two most immediate threats to survival are overpopulation and the destruction of our resources; fewer recognize the complete responsibility of the male system, in so far as it is male (and not capitalistic or socialistic) in these two dangers;" (Gates, 1977, page 9)

The first ecofeminist conference was held in Amherst, Massachusetts in 1980. Over the next several decades, the importance of the ecofeminist movement was highlighted by the rapid pace of profit-driven technological advancement and its accompanying destruction of ecologies everywhere – new forms of genetically modified crops fueled by the rise of terminator seeds, new instruments of war, increasingly potent pesticides and insecticides, vast amounts of waste products piling up and polluting the air, earth, and water where people live (Warren, 2000; Zakarriya, 2020). When women activists explored these new powerful technologies with the potential to alter the world, they repeatedly observed that it was intimately tied to patriarchy, war and safeguarding the enormous profits of corporations (Gaard, 2010; Warren, 2000). The first generation of ecofeminists concluded that oppression of nature and exploitation of women went hand in hand. Feminists at the conference declared that environmental matters were feminist issues (Gaard, 1993). One of the conference participants Patsy Hallen declared:

> "Ecofeminism proposes that the domination of women and the domination of nature are not only intimately connected but mutually reinforcing". (Jenkins, 1995)

The emphasis of ecofeminism on exploring the domination of nature and women by patriarchy, led to new ways of unpacking the processes through which the domination takes place. One of the fundamental splits that ecofeminists point to is that of humans and nature. In modern capitalist societies, humans are equated with men while nature is equated with women. Thus, both nature and women are robbed of their creative and life-giving force and treated as objects from whom value can be extracted. This according to ecofeminism has had a terrible consequence in terms of ecological destruction and irreversible climate change (Shiva & Mies, 2014). For ecofeminists, to ensure a sustainable future for the earth and its inhabitants, it is important to repair the split between humans and nature, man and woman which can only be done by stopping the molding of nature for profit and exploitation (Warren, Warren & Erkal, 1997).

Over the next few decades ecofeminism branched off into several sub-movements, the different branches reflecting the various feminisms that the movements were embedded within. The liberal ecofeminists who typically tended to come from communities of privilege emphasized reform and increased regulations to address environmental issues (Cuomo, 1992). Ecofeminists of the liberal persuasion believed that while there were looming social, health and economic issues tied to ecological damage, the solution was not fundamental economic transformations but introduction of new rules and policies that addressed specific ecological problems. Radical ecofeminists on the other hand, proclaimed that women had always had a much more intimate relationship with nature as compared to men and called for a strengthening of these intrinsic bonds (Warren, Warren & Erkal, 1997). Radical ecofeminists denied that science and reason were useful tools to ameliorate the threat of ecological destruction and demanded a movement to empower women. The most recent group and perhaps most impactful group of ecofeminists were socialists and they criticized feminisms that highlighted women's special relationship with nature as being essentialist and unhelpful in analyzing the factors that contribute to ecological destruction. Eco (feminist) socialists argued for centering exploitation within capitalism in analyzing environmental destruction. Ecofeminist-socialists argued that capitalism relegated to men, all the productive activities of the economy and relegated to women, the social reproductive activities of society, thereby creating a split that made the maintenance of the system unsustainable (Finlan, 2021). Carolyn Merchant, an early eco socialist argued:

> "In investigating the roots of our current environmental dilemma, and its connections to science, technology and the economy, we must re-examine the formation of a world-view and a science that by reconceptualizing reality as a machine rather than a living organism, sanctioned the domination of both nature and women...decentralized, non-hierarchical forms of organization, recycling of wastes, simpler forms of living involving less polluting forms of soft technology and labor intensive rather than capital intensive are possibilities only now beginning to be explored" (Merchant, 1990, page 9).

Thus, the ideas that unify ecofeminist thought is the belief that organizing and empowering women is key to bringing about a change in government policies regarding ecological destruction. According to ecofeminists and eco-socialists, one key step to reversing environmental catastrophe is the abolition of gendered hierarchies and the organizing and empowering of women for a sustainable world.

Critiques Against Ecofeminism from the Global South

The rising popularity of ecofeminism as a movement was accompanied by critiques against the framework and its roots in the countries of the Global North. South Asian women formed the front line of this critique; they pointed to ecofeminism as a framework that was blind to local context and the intersections of class, caste, and geography (Agarwal, 1998; Rao, 2012). The critics point to how the notion that somehow women are closer to nature than men, simply reifies traditional stereotypes of women as having mystical animal-like qualities and does little to further analysis in this area. These images of women also portray women as being identical across cultural contexts with little regard to differences in status. Thus, the actual impacts of environmental destruction on women are obfuscated and smoothed over without accounting for privilege based on the social locations of women in different contexts. The Ecosocialist strain of feminism found popularity in the countries of the Global South. It centers capitalist patriarchy in its framework for exploring oppression. In India, through the 70s to the 90s, eco(feminist) socialism became the dominant paradigm for feminists to analyze and organize for reversing ecological decay which in turn manifested itself in community distress (Nanda, 1997; 2018).

Ecofeminism and Ecosocialism in India

India has always felt itself vulnerable to changes in global climate systems. The long seacoasts make it vulnerable to the rise in sea levels. Over the last few decades, parts of South Asia have endured desertification while other regions continue to experience yearly floods that have drowned out communities. Since Indian independence, food and water insecurity has become increasingly common with only a few glacially fed rivers that the country depends on. Indian women have repeatedly faced the brunt of these negative ecological stresses. As a result, they have historically taken a remarkably active leadership role operating within a traditional system in resistance movements demanding environmental justice (Agarwal, 1998). In fact, women's role in giving birth to children and their role as protectors of 'nature' assumed a natural connection in myth and reality. Generations of women have reached into mythological archetypes and traditional practices to establish their credibility as protectors of nature (Suresh, 2021; Tøllefsen, 2011). For instance, an early pioneer of forest preservation Saalumarada Thimmakka, is reported to have said that she started planting trees after she was spurned for not having children. Today, the 106-year-old Thimmakka is hailed as the mother of trees (Beevi, 2018).

The Chipko Movement

Early in the struggle women's role as ecological leaders in fishing regions and in forest communities was to simply preserve the resources that were sustaining local communities. Some of the pioneering women environmentalists predated the proper articulation and global spread of ecofeminism as a framework even though today they have been adopted by feminists as part of their historical lore. One such major landmark movement was the 'Chipko movement' which began in the Garhwal region in the Himalayas. The local indigenous community relied on gathering and subsistence farming. In the 1970s, the Indian government began to lease parcels of this land to contractors to feed the nation's need for construction materials. There was little consultation with the local community and the governmental actions led to deforestation, consequent floods, and a huge financial stress on the local communities. Indigenous protests were ignored by the forest department which continued to award trees to a company making sporting goods. The women of the community who felt this negative change the most, decided to take matters into their own hands and hug the trees that were allotted for cutting until the loggers departed. They were led by a local woman leader, Gaura Devi. While none of the participants in the protest identified as an ecofeminist and they were mostly concerned about their own sustainability as a community and less by the larger environmental implications of their actions, the 'Chipko Movement' inspired environmental justice activists globally and provided a model for future resistance within India (Sen, 2020; Sharma, 2021). Gaura Devi's words reflect the very essence of the ecofeminist centering of women's capacities to protect our natural world.

> The forest nurtures us like a mother; you will only be able to use your axes on it, but you have to use them first on us.
>
> *(Chopra, 2019)*

While the Chipko movement is the most well-known resistance endeavor led by women in that period in India, there were several other environmental movements throughout India in the 1970s and into the 1980s. The Indian government had embarked on a massive development and industrialization push that forced the most vulnerable communities into unsustainable spaces and out of the lands that they had lived on for centuries (Swain, 1997). There was conflict over community resources such as land, rivers, seacoasts, and forests between government favored private interests and the communities themselves. In that respect, much of the early environmental organizing in India happened among the poorest and the most marginalized communities, unlike in the west where the middle-class formed the prominent leadership within environmental movements (Gadgil & Guha, 1994). Most of the Indian ecological struggles post-independence, involved the very survival of these vulnerable communities. After the success of the Chipko movement, in 1980, a department of environment was established by the government of Indira Gandhi and there was talk of returning control of local resources to local governing bodies (Sharma, 2021).

The Narmada Bachao Andolan

In the 1980s one significant environmental struggle that raised serious doubts about the miracles promised by runaway economic development and its consequences was the *Narmada Bachao Andolan (Save the Narmada Struggle)*. After the Indian independence from the British, the successive congress governments emphasized the importance of introducing large industrial projects to address the problem of the underdevelopment of India. As part of this push, the resources of the state were galvanized to ensure adequate electricity to fuel the massive growth that was needed to sustain the population (Rana, Sati, Sundriyal, Doval, & Juyal, 2007). The framework used to guide this work was technocratic and local communities were rarely consulted before beginning massive projects, whether mining, hydroelectric power generation or setting up of nuclear plants. In fact, the overt policy of the government was that communities would have to make sacrifices for national progress (Gadgil & Guha, 1993)

One of the rivers targeted for a series of dam projects was the river Narmada; it flowed through several states. After some consultation, the Indian government decided to build several dams of varying heights through the river's meandering path. However, there were government reports circulating that predicted long negative environmental impacts as of the result of the dams under construction and the river being diverted at several points. In fact, the environmental impact report spelled out that it would have a disastrous consequence for local communities along the river's path. Medha Patkar, who was a faculty member of a prestigious university in Mumbai at that time was alerted to the problem and began organizing local communities to resist the dam project from going forth without further review and consultation (Dwivedi, 1997; Narula, 2009).

Patkar and her fellow resistance organizers began following the money for the dam projects and realized that much of it had been sanctioned by the World Bank without a thorough review of the ecological impacts of the project. The *Narmada Bachao Andolan* did not fashion itself as an environmental movement, but it was guided by critiques that questioned the imposition of development projects that did not come from below. Their method of resistance was borrowed from the non-violent freedom struggles advocated by Gandhi and involved galvanizing the consciousness of local communities along the Narmada, to stand up for their rights to their lands through civil disobedience (Rao, 2012). Even as communities were pushed out by the governmental project and arable lands flooded, people stood in the rising waters until they were forcibly removed. It was one of the most electrifying struggles for an inclusive democracy and it garnered the attention of environmental activists and writers like Arundhati Roy who wrote a powerful essay explaining how big dams are antithetical to inclusive growth (Dube, 2017).

Throughout the 1970s and the 1980s, Patkar and others like her continued to work on other areas of environmental justice under the umbrella organization, the *National Alliance of People's Movements*. The founders of the organization realized that the ecological distress that communities were facing was a winning issue in collectively organizing people to address unequal runaway development that only benefited the rich and the wealthy (Passantino, 2017). While the *Narmada Bachao Andolan* had only mixed success in stopping the damming of Narmada, the struggle itself had come upon a formula for both grassroots mobilization and getting international attention on the extremely deleterious impact of big development projects that did not include the voices of the local communities who were affected. The World Bank itself pulled out of the project after the launch of the struggle and the organization was subjected to increased scrutiny regarding its international aid policies (Chaplin, 1996).

Vandana Shiva and Seed Democracy

Internationally, environmentalism in India is synonymous today with the name of Vandana Shiva; she is perhaps the only person in this list of female environmental activists who brands herself as an ecofeminist (Shiva & Mies, 2014). She rose to fame in the late 1980s with her critical writings on the new biotechnological innovations and bioengineering products introduced by some of the major pharmaceutical corporate entities based in the countries of the Global North. The green revolution had just been touted a success in Punjab and the countries of the Global South were told that the future of their countries and their capacity to feed their population lay in implementing large-scale technological changes in agriculture (Salleh, 1991; 2017).

Shiva asserted and continues to assert, more than her other Indian environmental compatriots, that western science is to be rejected because of the violence inherent in its practice. She asserts that it has brought nothing but destruction to the Global South while enriching a few corporations located in the Global North (Vandana & Maria, 1993). She argues for an environmental movement rooted in our inalienable connections to nature, and the tradition of spirituality that has sustained the continent for a millennium (Lorentzen & Eaton, 2002). For her, biotechnology invariably leads to an assault on the integrity of local communities since these technologies only work on large-scale implementation. They are highly capital intensive, consequently resulting in monoculture crop production and a rapid deterioration of the soil. Thus, introducing these profit-driven changes would lead to increasing concentration of wealth in the hands of a few producers and a move away from food production to cash crops. For her, the assault on biodiversity was nothing but a sustained attack on women and their place in agricultural communities (Shiva, 2016). In her later writings she moved away from a traditional ecofeminist stand to outlining a more socialist framework for pushing back against destructive technology. In this connection, she also argued for slowing down the globalization of production and distribution, especially of agricultural products (Shiva, 2008). She has spearheaded several lawsuits against corporations like Monsanto and NGOs such as the Bill and Melinda Gates Foundation in their efforts to patent traditional Indian herbs and seeds. Her most noteworthy achievement was in seed diversity preservation and what she calls, *seed democracy*. Her *Navdanya Foundation* is involved in storing indigenous Indian seeds thereby preserving their diversity for centuries to come (Shiva, 2004).

It is hard to categorize Shiva's politics as purely one of ecofeminism; while she does connect environmental degradation to women's exploitation, she also writes fervently against European models of development. She reaches back to Indian traditional texts to historicize the meaning of the current environmental struggle to India's long tradition of revering nature. She draws inspiration in traditional Sanskrit scriptural writings regarding concepts such as wholeness and integrity as opposed to rationalist science that dissects and splits identities. This has led to criticism against her work by Indian ecofeminists who lean towards a more socialist class analysis of the ecological issues in India today. They detect in her writings, little discussion about historical social and economic inequities and their connections to ecocide (Kilby & Scholtz, 2011). While she writes fervently about the incursion of neocolonialism in Indian agriculture, she does not address the long history of the caste system and other forms of landlord oppression in India. She glorifies agriculture as an occupation but does little analysis on the factors that do not allow most Indian women to own their land for cultivation and keeps most agricultural communities impoverished and therefore vulnerable to corporate abuse (Hall, 1994; Orias & Caputi, 2013; Shu-Lan, 2001).

As many Marxist economists point out, while Shiva rails against the west, she ignores local power relationships that leave the vast numbers of Dalits, Adivasis and other minoritized groups with little power in a hierarchical society (Sur, 2018; Wallis, 2008). In most of India, women are deprived of primary rights to land and the technology that makes land productive. Shiva makes a claim that women are more likely to use natural resources for sustenance than for cash. However, new research with foraging communities and agricultural communities point to the fallacy of the assumption. Recent research also substantiates that woman can act in both negative and positive ways in preserving the environment (Caito, 2012).

In conclusion, the years after independence were marked by protests that reflected social inequities rooted in gender, caste, class, and traditional hierarchies. Activists were guided by their conviction that capital intensive growth was essentially unequal and did not lead to a sustainable nation. Much of the ecological resistance was over the government takeover of agricultural lands or commonly owned forests, to pave the way for large development projects such as dams or mines. For many of the people involved in the struggle, the conflicts were related to their material well-being and basic sustenance as opposed to larger ideas of preserving forests and rivers or cleaning up the air.

International Movement for Environmental Justice in Bhopal

One major exception to the rule was the people's protest movement against Dow Chemical in Bhopal. In 1984, on the night of the 2nd of December, a gas leak by a company owned by Union Carbide (now sold to Dow Chemical Inc.) led to the toxic exposure of over 500,000 people and with hundreds of thousands more having the potential to be injured. It was the largest industrial accident at that time in the world. The disaster brought new awareness of the dangers posed by unbridled development fueled by greed. The Bhopal disaster inspired one of the largest movements of justice that is still ongoing as of the writing of this paper (Sarangi, 2002; Zavetoski, 2009).

Women were again at the helm in terms of organizing for justice for the people affected by the tragedy. Rashida Bee and Champa Devi Shukla, two of the women whose family was affected by the gas leak led several decades long activism to force Union Carbide and later Dow Chemical to clean up the affected areas as well as to adequately compensate the families of victims of the negligence. They organized mostly lower class, lower caste, uneducated women into a powerful force that continually reminded the world of the grave injustice done to the community. Over the two and a half decades that they had been at the helm, the women resorted to continual hunger strikes and rallies both in India and in other places where Dow Chemical offices were located (Bisht 2018). As their protests moved to the countries of the Global North, it drew local workers and activists, many of whom were also survivors of poisonous chemicals let out by large agricultural chemical companies. For instance, in Midland Texas, 300 local residents signed on to the lawsuit against Dow for the contamination of their community by dioxin (Armiero & Sedrez, 2014). The two women, one a Muslim and the other a Hindu, received the Goldman Prize for Environmental Justice in 2004, 20 years after the accident.

The success of the Bhopal justice movement lay less in the theorizing of larger environmental issues than the immediate connection that the activists felt to the health of the soil and air in Bhopal as well as larger concerns regarding the welfare of the inhabitants, both present and the future. In her speech after receiving the Goldman prize, Rashida Bee pointed to how being a mother made her a powerful activist:

> "We know that not just in Bhopal, but mothers everywhere in the world carry poisonous chemicals in their breasts. Bhopal is simply the most visible example of corporate crime against humanity...we are not flowers to be thrown at the altar of corporate profit, but we are the women of Bhopal, dancing flames committed to dispelling darkness." (Bee, 2004)

In her words are echoes of the ecofeminism of Vandana Shiva and the socialist principles espoused by Megha Patkar. Throughout the 1980s and into the early 1990s much of the environmental activism of women was interwoven into a critique of capitalism and the inequities baked into Indian society. While for all these feminist activists, ecological concerns were important, it was couched within a larger critique of profit making under capitalism that looked at the earth as dead material that was to be exploited, just as it objectifies women. Several of these women had been active in the nascent labor movement in post-independence India and believed that the environmental question was inseparable from issues of caste, class, and gender equity.

Environmentalism in the Era of Neoliberalism

The 1990s were a time of rapid liberalization of the Indian economy. Economic growth took off at a dizzying speed. Along with this growth, came the inevitable destruction of local ecologies. Many of the trade barriers and investment restrictions that had been in place since independence were removed. This was not accompanied by regulatory mechanisms to ensure that appropriate environmental and labor practices were followed. The Indian government's choice of which industries to liberalize was based purely on economic considerations and environmental impacts were not considered as important (Badami, 2005). While there were environmental control agencies that have been in existence since the 1970s in India, they have little teeth in implementing anti-pollution measures. As a result, the 1990s saw a huge shift to highly polluting capital-intensive industries from less polluting ones prior to the liberalization (Gamper-Rabindran & Guha, 2004). Between 2008 and 2020, there were 318 million Indian women who have become internal climate migrants (Jain, 2021)

The calls for more regulations and studies on the environmental impacts of this massive growth was dismissed by successive governments as anti-development, and anti-nationalist (Badra, 2013; Kaur, 2021). In many cases, the environmental impact statements were written by developers themselves. The consequences for the most vulnerable communities that lay in the path of these projects was disastrous. Unlike during the years after independence, the Indian middle class and intelligentsia remained oblivious to the environmental injustices perpetrated in the name of development (Veron, 2006). While there were pockets of protests mostly organized by the communities most affected, they garnered little attention by the media which had by now become almost completely privatized or were merely the mouthpieces of one of the political parties. The capitalist class of the country, drunk with the possibility of India becoming a world industrial powerhouse, left no room for dissent. In fact, the biggest polluting industry representatives injected themselves into the government to prevent any meaningful legislation from being enforced (Pillai, 2019). As Ramachandra Guha laments:

> "India today is an environmental basket-case; marked by polluted skies, dead rivers, falling water-tables, ever-increasing amounts of untreated wastes, disappearing forests. Meanwhile, tribal and peasant communities continue to be pushed off their lands through destructive and carelessly conceived projects."
>
> *(Guha, 2013, pp. 2)*

Amidst this rather depressing survey of the environmental movement (or the lack of) in India, a new generation of women scientists committed to social justice have been spearheading the push to more government action. Sunita Narain is perhaps the most well-known among them. During her own growth as a researcher, she was convinced that to tackle the looming massive ecological problems in the country, local democracy was an indispensable tool. She reasoned that local communities knew better than large policy making bodies, where vital resources such as water is garnered, how resources are used, and what are the constraints to developing natural resources in a sustainable way. She was instrumental through the research done by her institute, the *Center for Science and Environment,* in exposing the high levels of pesticides in soft drinks like Coke and Pepsi in India (The Economic Times, 2006).

In recent years she has called for a movement that she titles, *The Environmentalism of the Poor* as opposed to the prevailing *Environmentalism of the Rich* (Martinez-Alier, 2014). For her, a sustainable world cannot be achieved without empowering the most vulnerable communities and engaging in participatory democracy when thinking about resource allocation (Narain, 2013). Like Vandana Shiva, she leans on the long tradition of sustainable community development in India; she points to rain and other forms of resource harvesting, seed preservation, sustainable forest use, irrigation systems that are communally shared, as having a long history, before unbridled development became an unquestionable practice in modern India (Narain, 2008). Narain calls for a total restructuring of cities to allow for spatial and economic mobility. She rails against the model of development that emphasizes unsustainable growth while believing the ill-effects of runaway city growth can be cleaned up and rectified after (Kayastha, 2007).

Most recently, Narain has been taking up the challenge of formulating solutions to the global problem of climate change. The Indian women ecological leaders of an earlier generation were mainly focused on the sustainability of specific communities located in specific spaces. Narain represents a new group of leaders from the Global South that are pushing back against the new colonialism that are laying the solutions for climate change on the backs of the poorest countries in the world. She argues that countries of the Global North, especially the US, have contributed the most to global greenhouse gas emissions since the industrial age began (Narain, 2013). For instance, from the 1950 to 2o2o, the US has contributed more than 28% of the global emissions of CO^2. Therefore, the countries of the Global North have an environmental debt that they owe to the countries that they had colonized for over four centuries. Narain calls for that debt to be redeemed (Narain, Ghosh, Saxena, Parikh & Soni, 2015).

The history of the environment movement in India demonstrates that throughout its post-independence period women have played a significant role in pushing back against environmentally destructive policies and have carved new frameworks that have inspired ecological movements in other parts of the world. In recent years there has been a dramatic rise in transnational women's groups collaborating on the twin goals of environmental health with women's empowerment (Ignatow, 2007). The result has been a spectacular collaboration within and across the countries of the region to ensure women's voices are heard in environmental policy discussions. Many of these organizations have adopted a socialist feminist approach to viewing and addressing climate change and its accompanying negative impacts (Harcourt, 2013).

There has been a tectonic shift in the strength and assertiveness of the new feminist environmental movements in South Asia. Participants are increasingly from diverse backgrounds and represent diverse interests. The leaders of these movements are often digital natives and use the tools of technology to communicate their desires and goals to a wider audience with ease.

The Gaps in Current Environmentalism in India

Despite this new-found awareness among some in the environmental movement, there has really been no recent galvanizing of any community around an ecological issue that can be identified as a new framework to understand the post-industrial phase of environmentalism (Benabou 2021). India in the last two decades has faced a continuous onslaught of environmental disasters that should have provided the impetus to a cohesive national movement but, there is little debate or discussion about frameworks to understand these events. Popular media portrays environmental disasters as incidental or because of corruption by whichever party oversaw the disaster. Over the last few years, the monsoons have gotten either irregular and/or intense, parts of the country are in a cycle of flood and drought, there is massive deforestation, and the cities routinely figure in the most polluted list in the world. And yet, there is little public discourse that connects class, gender, caste, and the Anthropocene (Benabou, 2021).

Guha (1997) has identified the environmentalism of the Indian middle class as disjointed and insufficient. It might help make a splash to save tigers or other endangered species of rare fauna and flora, but it does little to help the country in a sustainable direction. Much of the urban elite think of ecological issues as specific problems to be mitigated so that they can continue with their lives with minimal disruption (Narain, 2013). As has been pointed out by ecofeminist leaders of the past, unless questions of violence and inequities are addressed, India will continue to hurtle towards a terrifying future of dead land and water and unbreathable air that kills children way before their time (Maudsley, Mehra and Beazley, 2009).

In addition to the problems of an environmentalism that centers the concerns of those who are privileged in India, activists are today so busy countering the many assaults on their civil liberties that they have ceded the question of a healthy environment to the media where the problem is rarely understood as one of justice (Frazier, 2018). There are internal conflicts and ambiguities that have remained unresolved as the region faces an urgent climate crisis that demands immediate action. Some environmental groups, especially those whose membership is rooted in religious tradition or non-normative identities and sexualities often feel marginalized and unheard within the larger ecological movement (Alley, 2019). The more powerful or visible groups often are in cities and are composed of middle-class educated women, leaving out the voices of working class and rural women. While the impact of climate change and ecological destruction disproportionately is felt by working class women, their needs are not calculated in high level negotiations on sustainability (Karpouzoglou, Marshall & Mehta, 2018; Kotkin, 2020).

In addition, while women's groups are successful in turning out many women for specific marches and demonstrations, there is a lull in day-to-day action. When there are everyday actions included in the movement, they often consist of individually driven activities such as planting trees or an advertising push to encourage recycling rather than challenging the state to implement environmentally sustainable laws (Frazier, 2018). For any day to be successful, there is a need to incorporate short-term and long-term goals, specific strategies, and mass mobilization towards these goals. It involves sustained communication across differences – religion, class, region, and identities.

To that end, there have been transnational gatherings of women from the Global South including India before, during, and after the 26th gathering of the United Nations Climate Change Conference (COP 26). While there was even a day devoted to analyzing the impact of climate change on women, women themselves have been underrepresented at the official negotiations of the participating governments (Shankar, 2021). In fact, the fossil fuel lobby was one of the largest delegate groups in COP 26, larger than any other country at the meeting; this does not bode well for climate action. There is an urgent need for a new ecofeminist, eco socialist movement that centers the voices of the poor, the marginalized and the frontline communities that are most vulnerable to climate change.

REFERENCES

Agarwal, B. (1998). Environmental management, equity and ecofeminism: Debating India's experience.Carson, R. (2002). *Silent spring*. Houghton Mifflin Harcourt.

Alley, K. D. (2019). River goddesses, personhood and rights of nature: implications for spiritual ecology. *Religions, 10*(9), 502.

Armiero, M., & Sedrez, L. (Eds.). (2014). *A History of Environmentalism: Local Struggles, Global Histories*. A&C Black.

Badami, M. G. (2005). Transport and urban air pollution in India. *Environmental Management, 36*(2), 195-204.

Bhadra, M. (2013). Fighting nuclear energy, fighting for India's democracy. *Science as Culture, 22*(2), 238-246.

Bee, S. (2004). Talk given at the presentation of the Goldman Prize for Environmental Justice. Retrieved from https://www.youtube.com/watch?v=l8PqMPRG8Rs&t=104s (minute 2:55).

Benabou, S. (2021). Carbon Forests at the Margins of the State: The Politics of Indigenous Sovereignty and Market Environmentalism in the North-eastern Hills of India. *Journal of South Asian Development*, 09731741211059052.

Beevi, S. S. (2018). Role of Ecofeminism in Environmental Protection. *Economics, 6*(S1), 78-81.

Bisht, P. (2018). Social movements and the scaling of memory and justice in Bhopal. *Contemporary South Asia, 26*(1), 18-33.

Carson, R. (2002). The Silent Spring. Houghton-Mifflin Publishers: New York

Caito, A. (2012). Vandana Shiva: Stolen harvest: the hijacking of the global food supply. *Agriculture and Human Values, 29*(3), 433-434.

Chaplin, S. E. (1996). The role of the World Bank in India's Narmada valley project. *South Asia: Journal of South Asian Studies, 19*(2), 105-132.

Chopra, J. (2019). Forty-five years of Chipko which brought Uttarakhand region into global focus. The Pioneer. Retrieved on December 1 from https://www.dailypioneer.com/2019/state-editions/forty-five-years-of-chipko-which-brought-uttarakhand-region-into-global-focus.html

Cuomo, C. J. (1992). Unravelling the problems in ecofeminism. *Environmental Ethics, 14*(4), 351-363.

Dwivedi, R. (1997). People's movements in environmental politics: a critical analysis of the Narmada Bachao Andolan in India. *ISS Working Paper Series/General Series, 242*, 1-49.

Dube, R. (2017). Ecofeminism and the telegenics of celebrity in documentary film: the case of Aradhana Seth's Dam/Age (2003) and the Narmada Bachao Andolan. In *Women and Nature?* (pp. 185-204). Routledge.

Estévez-Saá, M., & Lorenzo-Modia, M. J. (2018). The ethics and aesthetics of eco-caring: contemporary debates on ecofeminism (s).

Finlan, P. (2021). The science turned upside down: Carolyn Merchant's vision of nature 40 years later. Public Books.

Frazier, C. (2018). " Grow what you eat, eat what you grow": urban agriculture as middle-class intervention in India. *Journal of Political Ecology, 25*(1), 221-238.

Gates, B. T. (1996) The roots of ecofemism. Interdisciplinary studies in literature and environment. Volume 3 (1). Pages 7- 16.

Gaard, G. (2010). *Ecofeminism*. Temple University Press.

Gaard, G. (2017). *Critical ecofeminism*. Lexington Books.

Gadgil, M., & Guha, R. (1994). Ecological conflicts and the environmental movement in India. *Development and change, 25*(1), 101-136.

Gamper-Rabindran, S., & Jha, S. (2004). Environmental impact of India's trade liberalization. *Available at SSRN 574161.*

Guha, R. (1997). The authoritarian biologist and the arrogance of anti-humanism. Ecologist, 27(1), 14.

Guha, R. (2013). The past and present of Indian environmentalism. The Hindu retrieved on November 30th from https://www.thehindu.com/opinion/lead/the-past-present-of-indian-environmentalism/article4551665.ece

Gupta, Krishna Murti (14 August 1993). "Mira Behn: A friend of nature". India Environment Portal.

Hall, J. K. (1994). *Ecofeminism and geography: the case of Vandana Shiva and Chipko* (Doctoral dissertation, Virginia Tech).

Harcourt, W. (2013). Transnational feminist engagement with 2010+ activisms. *Development and Change, 44*(3), 621-637.

Ignatow, G. (2007). *Transnational identity politics and the environment.* Lexington books.

Jain, S. (2021). Why COP26 stakes are so high for Indian women. Christian Science Monitor,

Jha & Gamper-Rabindran (2004) Environmental Impacts of India's Trade Liberalization. Retrieved on Nov 30th from https://www.gtap.agecon.purdue.edu/resources/download/1690.pdf.

Jenkins, M. (1995). View of the Piano and the tragedy of possession: an ecofeminist perspective. Retrieved on December 1 from http://trumpeter.athabascau.ca/index.php/trumpet/article/view/295/436

Karpouzoglou, T., Marshall, F., & Mehta, L. (2018). Towards a peri-urban political ecology of water quality decline. *Land Use Policy, 70,* 485-493.

Kaur, R. (2021). Nuclear necropower: The engineering of death conditions around a nuclear power plant in south India. *Political Geography, 85,* 102315.

Kayastha, S. L. (2007). Sunita Narain: A resolute environmentalist. *National Geographical Journal of India,* 53(1&2), 129-138.

Kilby, C., & Scholz, S. J. (2011). The impact of globalization on women–Testing Vandana Shiva's critique of development. *Villanova School of Business Economics Working Paper, 15.*

Kotkin, J. (2020). *The coming of neo-feudalism: A warning to the global middle class.* Encounter Books.

Kumar, R. (2002). The History of Doing. An illustrated account of movements of women's rights and feminism in India, 1800-1990. Kali for Women: New Delhi, India. ISBN: 978-8185107769

Lorentzen, L. A., & Eaton, H. (2002). Ecofeminism: an overview. In *The Forum on Religion and Ecology at Yale.*

Martinez-Alier, J. (2014). The environmentalism of the poor. *Geoforum, 54,* 239-241.

Mawdsley, E., Mehra, D., & Beazley, K. (2009). Nature lovers, picnickers and bourgeois environmentalism. *Economic and Political Weekly,* 49-59.

Merchant, C. (1990). Women, ecology and the scientific revolution. Harper: San Fransisco.

Nanda, M. (1997). History is what hurts: A materialist feminist perspective on the green revolution and its ecofeminist critics. *Materialist feminism: A reader in class, difference, and women's lives,* 364-94.

Nanda, S. S. (2018). Women and Natural Resource Management: A Conceptual Analysis. *National Geographical Journal of India,* 111.

Narain, S. (2008). Learning from the environmentalism of the poor. *Arena Magazine (Fitzroy, Vic),* (97), 24-29.

Narain, S. (2013). Environmentalism of the Poor vs. Environmentalism of the Rich. *Wrigley lecture series. School of Sustainability, Arizona State University, Tempe, AZ, March, 27.*

Narain, S., Ghosh, P., Saxena, N. C., Parikh, J., & Soni, P. (2015). *Climate change: perspectives from India* (No. id: 7941).

Narula, S. (2009). The story of Narmada Bachao Andolan: Human rights in the global economy and the struggle against the World Bank. *HUMAN RIGHTS ADVOCACY STORIES, Deena R. Hurwitz, Margaret L. Satterthwaite, Douglas B. Ford, eds., West,* 08-62.

Orias, D., & Caputi, J. (2013). Monoculture & mono-woman: An ecofeminist critique. *FAU Undergraduate Research Journal, 2*(1), 1-1.

Passantino, E. (2017). *Ecofeminism in India: from the Chipko Movement to the Case of Narmada Valley Development Project* (Bachelor's thesis, Università Ca'Foscari Venezia).

Pillai, P. (2019). Coal mining and ecological fragility: Questioning development, questioning growth. In *Women Speak Nation* (pp. 214-221). Routledge India.

Rao, M. (2012). Ecofeminism at the crossroads in India: A review. *Dep, 20*(12), 124-142.

Salleh, A. (1991). Staying Alive: Women, Ecology and Development. Vandana Shiva. London, Zed Books, 1989. *Hypatia, 6*(1), 206-214.

Salleh, A. (2017). *Ecofeminism as politics: Nature, Marx and the postmodern.* Zed Books Ltd..

Rana, N., Sati, S. P., Sundriyal, Y. P., Doval, M. M., & Juyal, N. (2007). Socio-economic and environmental implications of the hydroelectric projects in Uttarakhand Himalaya, India. *Journal of Mountain Science, 4*(4), 344-353.

Sarangi, S. (2002). Crimes of Bhopal and the global campaign for justice. *Social Justice, 29*(3 (89), 47-52.

Sen, S. (2020). Gender, Environment and Sustainability: The Journey from 'Silent Spring'to 'Staying Alive'. *Int J Adv Life Sci Res, 3*(2), 11-22.

Sereny, G. (Nov. 14, 1982). Life With Gandhi. The New York Times Magazine. Page 70.

Shankar, P (2021). Women and feminist groups demand gender equality and inclusion of diverse voices in COP 26. Mongabay Series: Environment and Her. Retrieved on December 12th, 2021 from https://india.mongabay.com/2021/11/women-and-feminist-groups-demand-gender-equality-and-inclusion-of-diverse-voices-at-cop26/

Sharma, S. (2021). Interweaving Environment, Ecology and Feminism: Ecofeminism as The Means of Environment Conservation. *ENVIRONMENTAL SUSTAINABILITY IN THE 21ST CENTURY: EMERGING ISSUES AND THE WAY FORWARD,* 244.

Shiva, V., & Mies, M. (2014). *Ecofeminism.* Zed Books Ltd.

Shiva, V. (2004). The future of food: countering globalisation and recolonisation of Indian agriculture. *Futures, 36*(6-7), 715-732.

Shiva, V. (2008). Globalization from below: Ecofeminist alternatives to corporate globalization. *Globalization and environmental challenges: Reconceptualizing security in the 21st century,* 15-20.

Shiva, V. (2016). *Water wars: Privatization, pollution, and profit.* North Atlantic Books.

Shu-lan, Z. H. A. N. G. (2001). Women, Environment and Development: Vandana Shiva's Ecofeminism and Its Critique.

Suresh, L. (2021). Understanding the Relationship Between Sustainability and Ecofeminism in an Indian Context. *Journal of Developing Societies, 37*(1), 116-135.

Sur, A. (2018). Feminists and Science: Critiques and Changing Perspectives in India. *Catalyst: Feminism, Theory, Technoscience, 4*(2).

Swain, A. (1997). Democratic consolidation? Environmental movements in India. *Asian Survey, 37*(9), 818-832.

The Economic Times (2006). Pesticide Cocktails in Coke and Pepsi brands. Retrieved from https://economictimes.indiatimes.com/industry/cons-products/food/pesticide-cocktail-in-coke-pepsi-brands/articleshow/1844556.cms?from=mdr

Wallis, V. (2008). On Marxism, Socialism, and Ecofeminism: Continuing the Dialogue. *Capitalism Nature Socialism, 19*(1), 107-111.

Warren, K. (2000). *Ecofeminist philosophy: A western perspective on what it is and why it matters*. Rowman & Littlefield.

Tøllefsen, I. B. (2011). Ecofeminism, religion and nature in an Indian and global perspective. *Alternative Spirituality and Religion Review, 2*(1), 89-95.

Vandana, S., & María, M. (1993). Ecofeminism. Bloomsbury Publishing: London, UK.

Véron, R. (2006). Remaking urban environments: the political ecology of air pollution in Delhi. *Environment and Planning A, 38*(11), 2093-2109.

Warren, K. J., Warren, K., & Erkal, N. (Eds.). (1997). *Ecofeminism: Women, culture, nature*. Indiana University Press.

Zakarriya, J. (2020). Identity, Land and Revolt in Egyptian Earth: An Ecofeminist Reading. *ISLE: Interdisciplinary Studies in Literature and Environment.*

Zavestoski, S. (2009). The struggle for justice in Bhopal: A new/old breed of transnational social movement. *Global Social Policy, 9*(3), 383-407.

ENDNOTES

1 Gowri Parameswaran is Professor and Chair of Educational Studies and Leadership at the State University of New York at New Paltz. She obtained her master's and Ph.D. in Cognitive/Educational Psychology from Rutgers University. She grew up in India and moved to the USA as an adult; since her move, she has gone back regularly to her country of origin where she has conducted cross-cultural research. Her explorations center on gender, socioeconomic status and culture and their impact on children and adult cognition both in the USA and in India. She is the co-editor of an introductory text for Women's Studies – Women: Images and Reality published by McGraw- Hill. She has also published books and articles on diversity and inclusion in education. In recent years she has written theoretical articles critiquing the historical assumptions around developmental psychology and how to teach about topics such as the privileging of the Global North over the Global South. She is currently working on exploring the exploitative consequences of the history of research on parenting in psychology in the age of structural adjustment and reduced government services for families in poverty. She can be reached at paramesg@newpaltz.edu

CHAPTER 5

Productivity to Precarity on Instagram: Digital Feminism in India during the Covid-19 Pandemic

Anhiti Patnaik[1]

ABSTRACT

This paper examines how digital feminism deconstructed neo-liberal ideals of technological productivity in India during the Covid-19 pandemic. By creating a productivity scale, I delineate new social disparities and risk factors brought on by the unprecedented shift to a work-from-home digital economy. Through theories of biopower, I argue that technology is not neutral, apolitical, or unequivocally in favour of equal access and human rights. The creation of a new social group termed the 'technoprecariat' during lockdown is discussed using a 'cripqueer' approach to digital feminism. I extend Judith Butler's early work on gender performativity to the neo-liberal ideal of gender productivity, where the onus of appearing perpetually 'productive' in lockdown was mainly on women. By analyzing how women debunked productivity on social media platforms like Twitter and Instagram, I examine queer influencers whose profiles demonstrated the cost of social non-conformism. I reveal how three feminist activists Priyanka Paul, Durga Gawde, and Roshni Kumar subverted gender productivity during lockdown through their distinct aesthetic and political standpoints.

Technoprecarity in the Pandemic

As a potential third wave of the coronavirus looms in India, it is worth examining how neo-liberal ideals of digital labour interacted with feminist activism on social media. With the spectre of mass death during the pandemic, the Indian State announced complete lockdown periodically between March 2020 – July 2021. This meant the closure of most major commercial, corporate, and government offices. The rapid transition to a work-from-home economy assumed the ubiquity of technological access and digital literacy that a large section of the Indian population does not possess, nor is likely to acquire in the immediate future. The average Indian worker lacks adequate internet bandwidth, fluency in English and technical communication, or the visual and mental ability to engage in uninterrupted productive labour online. In a recent interview, Gayatri Chakravarty Spivak claimed that "digital idealism" is nothing but a form of "digital colonialism" due to which the imposition of a complete lockdown by the State to prevent the spread of a virus ironically creates "humanitarian crises" (Spivak, 2020).

The first disaster that India witnessed in the summer of 2020 was not the spread of a viral plague but an exodus of daily wage labourers. With a sudden and unprecedented lockdown, migrant labour had to walk kilometres without food or water to return to hometowns and villages. This was a national crisis to be expected since it concerned a part of the population already living below the poverty line. The overnight shift into a digital economy during the coronavirus pandemic in India exacerbated existing forms of socio-economic precarity. However, we also witnessed an increase in deaths-by-suicide among high-school and university students and rising rates of health and reproductive disorders among middle-class working women. Since they had to work without childcare assistance or domestic help, the burden of managing both work and home fell completely on their shoulders (Afridi, Roy, & Dhillon, 2021). Studies showed that lockdowns also increased stress on LGBTQIA persons resulting in sexual detransition and PTSD-like symptoms (Policy brief: The impact of COVID-19 on women; and COVID-19 and ending violence against women and girls). The year ended with the farmers protests at the National Capital Region against the farm bills that openly supported the privatization of agricultural markets and grain distribution in a new digitally motivated economy.

Coercive lockdowns brought forth a perceptible expansion of the economic and gender precariat in India by shoring up a kind of toxic nationalism that permitted – on an almost Darwinian scale – the survival of only the *least* precarious. Those who had never faced shortage of food or water, incessant power cuts, patchy WIFI signals, job uncertainty, domestic abuse, online trolling, governmentality, or even the lack of something as essential as oxygen and pulse oximeters, were thrust into the condition of what may be termed "technoprecarity". According to recent research conducted by the Precarity Lab at Michigan, "technoprecarity" is a term associated with new risk factors and social inequality indices generated due to the proliferation of digital economies during the Covid-19 pandemic, "Technoprecarity is the premature exposure to death and debility that working with or being subjected to digital technologies accelerates. It is the unevenly distributed yet pervasive condition that the gig economy, toxic metals, denied welfare, and biometric surveillance systems perpetuate. We use the term technoprecarity to mark a contemporary expression of long-extant forms of violence under racial capitalism" (2020). A correlative to this would be the term 'technoproductivity' that connotes a minority of individuals working in the Global North and privileged parts of Indian society whose lives were least impacted by the pandemic. In both cases, however, the neo-liberal subject became a product of surveillance and "hyper-objectification" in his/her/their private and public life due to a shift to virtual realities.

Ironically, the more citizens stayed at home in lockdown, the more they were expected to *show* compliance with the neo-liberal ideal of technoproductivity on social media apps, government websites, and employer-generated digital platforms. As the researchers at the Precarity Lab note, "the digital is a medium of hyper-objectification. It is a fantasy of hyper-efficient and fulfilling capitalism. The digital automates and abstracts governance. It is also a commodity, a product of both hyper-visibilized and invisibilized labor. The digital is a set of technologies that mediates, intensifies, abstracts, reproduces, and generalizes existing forms of domination"

(2020). In an article on the impact of lockdowns on the Chinese digital labour market, Wu Yilong denies "the neutrality of technology and argue(s) that technology often serves as a political tactic to maximize and optimize social mobility, social productivity, and the security of the population" (2020). Therefore, "technology is essentially a type of biopower" in extension of Michel Foucault's work on modern liberal and neo-liberal cultures that govern people's political beliefs by controlling their health, basic resources, and fundamental rights. Foucault's extensive work on biopower reflects on the failure of the state to protect its citizens from the exacerbated effects of class and social inequality. Yilong gives the example of the Chinese government's replacement of the NAT standard with the CT standard in the second phase of lockdown so that worker 'productivity' was not compromised. The Indian State similarly monitored the circulation of medical data on Covid-19 and updated its vaccine policies in 2021 and policed popular discourses on social media pertaining to vaccine dissemination and the oxygen crisis in order to maintain its biopolitical control over the population.

In this paper, the extent to which biopower normalized a work-from-home economy during the pandemic is measured by constructing a *technoproductivity scale* using qualitative metrics. The scale reveals how known risk factors and systemic inequalities grew to include new forms of technoprecarity. Being technoproductive manifested in the willingness to conform to a neo-liberal work ethic in India, which is undoubtedly patriarchal, classist, casteist, and heterosexist. Those who were unable to participate in the digital economy entered a widening spectrum of technoprecarity. Clearly, the pandemic most affected social groups and bodies that have historically been relegated to various "zones of depletion" in India, however, this is not to say that the pandemic did not also affect "digital producers in enrichment zones" (Precarity Lab, 2020). With the expansion of the category of the 'technoprecariat' through more and more social groups being marginalized, disenfranchised, or "treated as disposable by algorithms that increasingly condition life chances" (2020), technology became a double-edged sword wielded both by those in power as well as marginalized groups. Social media platforms such as Instagram, Twitter, and Facebook have been the bastion of neo-liberal values like individualism, self-promotion, and social conformism. But in lockdown there were many trending hashtags in India that challenged the neo-liberal work ethic and promoted a sense of global altruism. Tweets and Facebook photographs began to move away from neo-liberal ideals such as fashion, food, disposable consumerism, world travel, and social conformity through marriage, career growth, and childbirth. Instead, there were status updates that performed technoprecarity in several ways.

In the summer of 2021, there were urgent requests on Instagram for instance to share information about oxygen cylinders, verified Covid resources, and available beds in hospitals. These status updates were monitored and regulated carefully by the State's IT cell as they constituted a living digital archive of precarious testimonies. Even personal statements about experiencing the death of a loved one, feeling disconnecting from friends and family, screen fatigue, job precarity, and disillusionment with State policies faced rigorous digital censorship (Scarr, Chowdhury, Sharma, & Dutta, 2021). Digital platforms brought forth into the public discourse lived narratives of horror, suffering, and loss, frequently implicating the State or various ideological state apparatuses like religion, media, and family. Influencers on the gender and disability spectrum shared posts on mental health awareness and advocated for fair trade, equal wages, the human rights of farmers and migrant labourers. They organized crowdfunded oxygen delivery campaigns and made pleas for a gender-neutral division of domestic chores that made them increasingly relatable to followers. Their posts highlighted the vulnerability of living on the margins of state welfare and social validation. More and more citizens who live above the poverty line empathized with issues pertaining to marginalized groups of India like women experiencing emotional burnout and domestic violence, the protesting farmers, or persecuted caste and religious minorities, migrant labour, or the differently abled. In the following sections, I study how three feminist activists Priyanka Paul, Durga Gawde, and Roshni Kumar subverted gender productivity during lockdown through their distinct aesthetic and political standpoints on Instagram.

Measuring Technoproductivity in an Intersectional Framework

It must be noted that in the initial stages of lockdown there was a euphoria around the ideal of technoproductivity. A Google search for "How to stay productive during quarantine" yielded over 1,00,00,000 results in the fall of 2020. There was a slew of 'listicles' or lists of things to do in lockdown ostensibly with the goal of being 'happy'. If happiness remained just out of reach but attainable through ceaseless productivity, one could avoid a nation-wide panic or existential crisis in lockdown. The biopolitical twist to traditional practices of self-care during this health crisis was that 'productive' work could induce a feeling of capacitation, a sense of purpose, and self-worth. Consequently, there was a "hyper-objectification" of traditionally female-dominated activities involving home maintenance and cleaning, nutrition and wellness, and arts and crafts on social media. If one received multiple 'likes' or shares for creating a new recipe or uploading a tutorial on how to wash dishes, then one exhibited technoproductivity.

The article "Mood of India During Covid-19 – An Interactive Web Portal Based on Emotion Analysis of Twitter Data" claims that on 1 May 2020, when the first nation-wide lockdown had been extended by two weeks, the largest part of 25440 tweets posted by Indians relating to Covid displayed a "happy" emotion (Venigalla, Vagavolu, & Chimalakonda, 2020). It categorized the emotions of the nation on Twitter into six basic groups "anger, disgust, fear, happiness, sadness, surprise" and "neutral" or non-emotive. The method employed was a sentiment analysis using data extraction of about 10,000 tweets pertaining to Covid per day, processing it by removing nouns and prepositions, ranking keywords that connoted these emotions, and finally subjecting the data to an emotion-based classification. Since the article was published, there have been two waves of the coronavirus and a severe health-care crisis resulting in thousands of undocumented mortalities. Even if the mood of the nation could be indexed in such a manner, there is no account for traumatized silences that are impossible to translate into social media vernacular. Grief, mourning, and loss after all, do not comply with the neo-liberal ideal of individual success, stoicism, and endless productivity in the face of death.

This raises questions of accessibility that prevent data mining outside the digitally fluent demographic in the country. Categorizing tweets in such a quantified manner does not consider what exactly affected the people who expressed sadness. It does not account for those lacking the ability to express themselves on social media and thus ignores the forces of biopower that dictate technological accessibility. What about the 'mood' of the migrant labourer walking home for hours without food or water? It reduces the "mood of the nation" to a smattering of uncensored, filtered, and conformist social media updates. Instead, an intersectional socio-cultural model that measures one's ability to be deemed technoproductive may yield a more accurate and long-term picture of technoprecarity. In Pierre Bourdieu's words, we need to analyze "the peculiarity of cultural capital, which we should call informational capital to give the notion its full generality, and which itself exists in three forms, embodied, objectified, or institutionalized" (Bourdieu, 1992). The productivity scale developed and illustrated below (Fig. 1) shows that to perform the neo-liberal ideal of technoproductivity in lockdown, an individual needed to possess at least three types of socio-economic capital. The scale is designed using qualitative analysis and in theoretical response to the case studies explored in detail in the subsequent section.

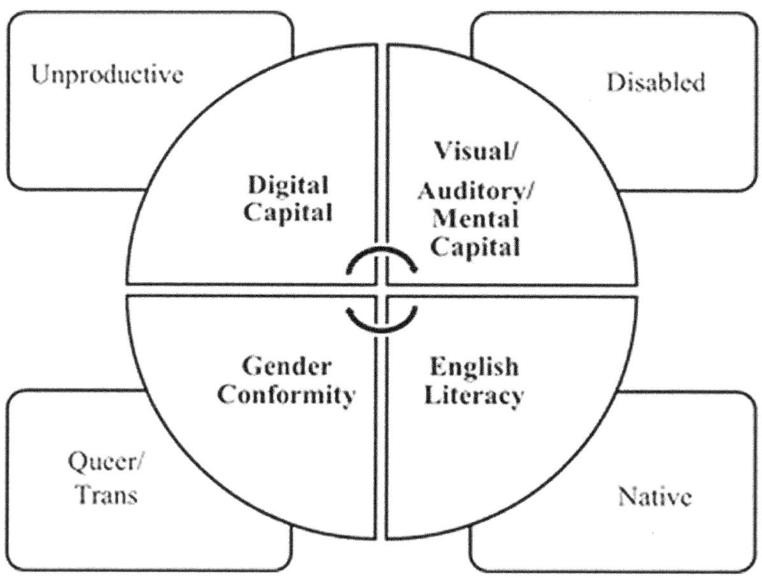

Figure 1: Productivity Scale during Lockdown in India 2020-21

The work-from-home economy first and foremost required digital capital to operate. Without a working personal computer or set of accessories like personal charger, headphones, microphones, storage devices or subscriptions to back up data, it was impossible to be employed or enrolled in school. Without even touching upon the medical technology requisite in a pandemic like the pulse oximeter, digital thermometer, and medical apps, it is quite clear that anyone lacking a smartphone or personal computer was rendered technoprecarious because of a new inability (or rather, *disability*) to work. Since they could not access digital capital in the workplace, many Indians fell below a new technoproductivity line (akin to the poverty line). This explains the 'happiness' of those who continued to express themselves on Twitter everyday versus the digital 'silence' of students and working professionals who dropped out, lost their jobs, or died-by-suicide. The fact that most individuals in any given society are always already on a spectrum of precarity is well known but the pandemic enabled us to bear collective witness to its myriad manifestations. The mass death of health care workers, refuse collectors, bus drivers, street cleaners, underprivileged students, and protesting farmers made a mockery of the neo-liberal ideal of technoproductivity. Their death is metonymic of a biopower that, like a pathogen, attacks us silently but surely.

Corresponding to the possession of digital capital was fluency in English and ownership of anglophonic capital. Although most digital platforms can operate in different languages, much official correspondence in India takes place in the language of the global hegemon. Fluency in English is considered evidence of socio-cultural capital in middle-class India and via its colonial roots enables a neo-colonial and neo-Protestant work ethic in urban centres. Studies show that even dating apps like Tinder, Grindr, and Bumble measure fluency in English to create compatible matches or filter out users who comment in Hindi, Hinglish, and other vernaculars (Birnholtz, Fitzpatrick, & Handel, 2014). Then there is the case of accessibility and how individuals on the disability spectrum in India responded to the work-from-home economy. Zoom meetings updated to include automatic closed captions, Twitter and Instagram posts began to appear with trigger warnings and image descriptions, laptops and smartphones developed more sophisticated speech-text and text-speech technology. But there was no corresponding professional or academic training provided to accommodate individuals with dissociative personality or bipolar disorder, manic depression, attention-deficit disorder, or those on the autism spectrum. Once digital platforms became the exclusive way to perform productivity, it precluded alternative modes of labour and learning, creativity, skill development, and socialization that are crucial for persons with disability. To cite the Precarity Lab, "We need new vocabularies for attending to the generalized production of precarity under contemporary racial capitalism. This is not the language in which the digital dream is advertised. In the promotional brochure for digital interconnectedness, these networked lives are pictured as always hyper-productive, virtuous, connective, and efficient. But it is clear to us that both these dreams and these networks themselves are broken" (2020).

When it came to gender conformity, it is interesting to observe that the very same State that prescribed complete lockdown to prevent the spread of the coronavirus would relax restrictions for weddings and ceremonies pertaining to childbirth. Various lists and tutorials being shared on home care and maintenance, health and wellness, arts and crafts, food and culture were dominated by female users and audiences. For example, "Lockdown List Ideas" (Fig. 2) uploaded by a female user "i wish i could wink" on Pinterest lists tasks that conform to idealized femininity.

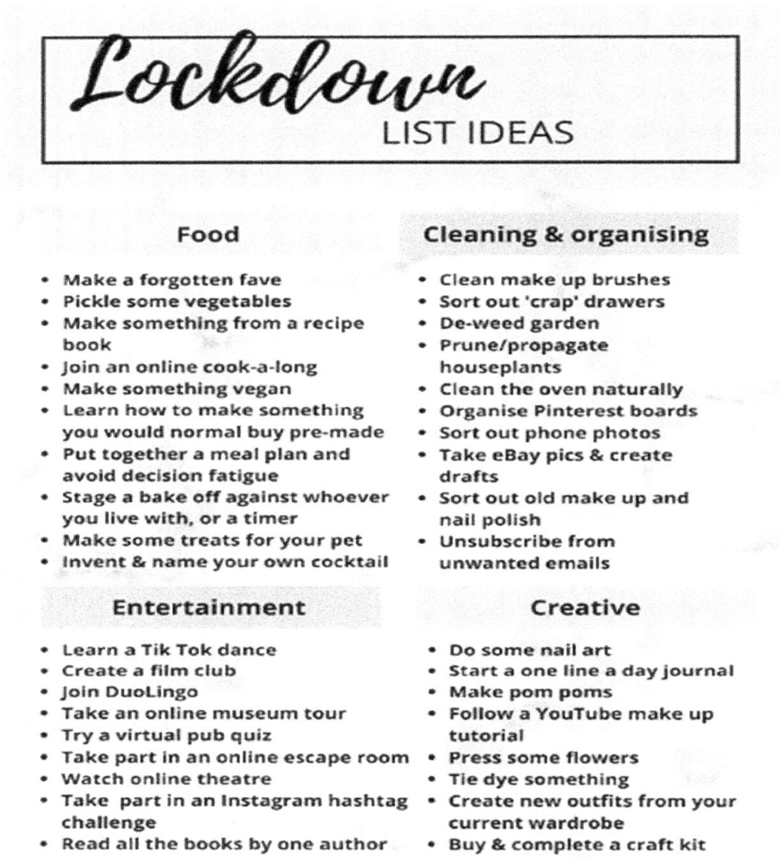

Figure 2: "Lockdown List Ideas," (April 5, 2020) I Wish I could Wink, http://www.iwishicouldwink.com/2020/04/my-lockdown-list-template-to-create.html#.YPbD2OgzY2w.

he pastel pink and marbled background of the listicle targets a female audience. But even within such blatantly gendered marketing lies the assumption that the tasks prescribed may be performed by women 'universally.' Tasks such as "de-weed garden", "learn a TikTok dance", "clean the oven naturally", "stage a bake-off against whoever you live with" require specific motor skills which would make the tasks impossible for a person with disability. Tasks such as "try a virtual pub quiz", "take part in an online escape room", "invent and name your own cocktail", and "read all the books by one author" become shareable only if one is fluent in English. And no doubt, such fluency is determined by economic, gendered, and systemic inequalities in the nation rather than an individual failure to be technoproductive.

Further, the neo-liberal ideal of the domestic goddess on social media did not translate for queer and trans communities, who suffer high rates of domestic abuse, unemployment, and homelessness (28 July 2020). For these individuals, the home is not necessarily a safe space to practice and perform aesthetic individualism on social media. The fact that queer and BIPOC users were trolled viciously for performing the very same activities glamourized in the above listicle, makes the heterosexism of the ideal of technoproductivity a glaring reality. Take for example, the ordinary task "create new outfits from your current wardrobe" and apply it to the transphobic reactions that the queer activist Alok V. Menon received on their Facebook and Instagram page for sharing fashion advice and photographs. Menon countered the trolls by posting a photograph where their body is cloaked by word clouds of hate speech (Fig. 3).

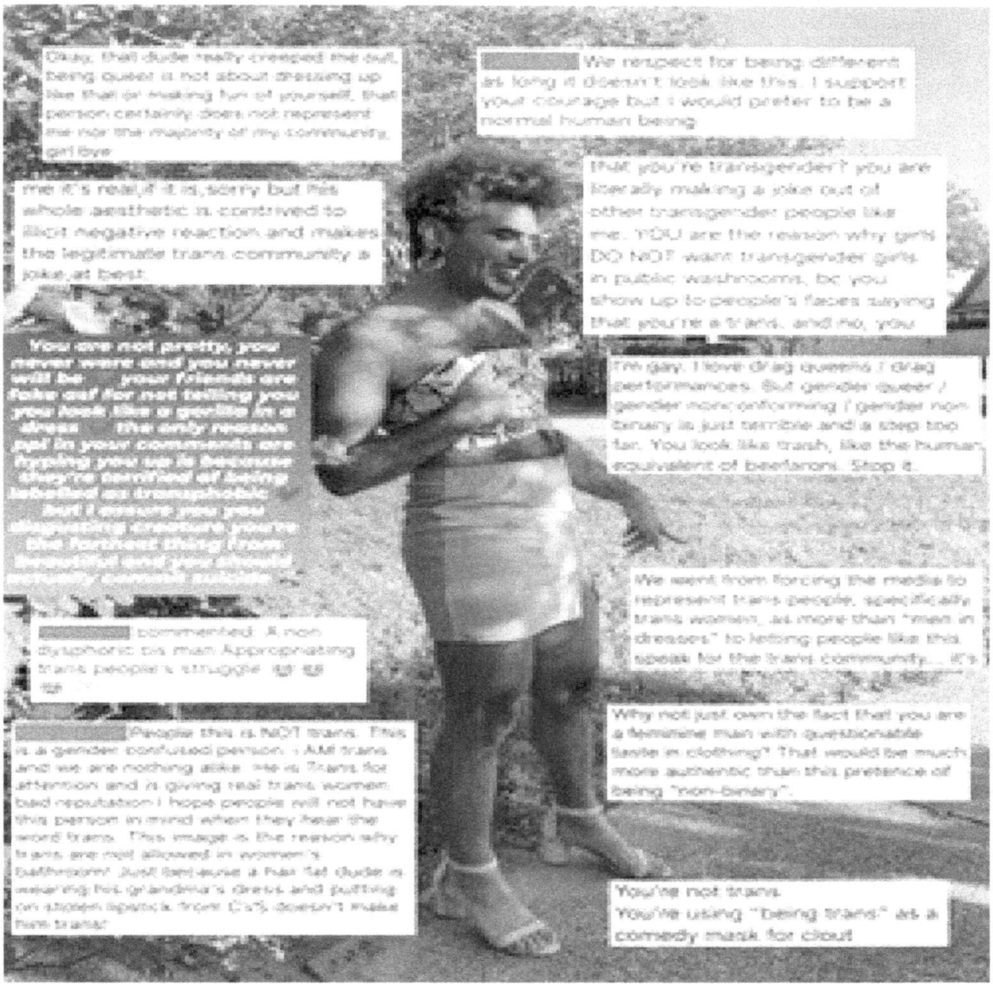

Figure 3: "Today on #NonBinaryPeoplesDay I wanted to be vulnerable" (July 15, 2021), Alok V Menon, Facebook, https://www.facebook.com/AlokVMenon/posts/today-on-nonbinarypeoplesday-i-wanted-to-be-vulnerable-with-you-all-my-entire-li/354221922740955/

They shared a long message holding these vitriolic comments accountable for promoting transphobia and cancelling their gender identity on a public platform:

> Today on #NonBinaryPeoplesDay I wanted to be vulnerable with you all. My entire life I've been harassed by the cis/hetero world. But if I'm being honest there's no pain quite like experiencing vitriol from your own. These are a few of the countless messages I receive all the time from other queer and trans people. I know that this is about internalized homophobia/transphobia, but that doesn't make it any less devastating and painful. These really hurt. There is an ongoing project of scapegoating gender non-conforming people instead of targeting the gender binary system. [...] Non-binary people aren't the problem. The gender binary is the problem. This was not about what we look like, this is about what they feel like. Queer/trans people should be able to look like whatever we want without being discriminated against. We shouldn't have to adhere to gender binary norms to be real, let alone safe. Our acceptance shouldn't have to be conditional on disappearing our difference. An earnest plea: Please challenge transphobia, even when it comes from trans people. Protect gender non-conforming people. Interrupt the cycle of violence. Create a more kind and just world.
>
> *(Menon, 2021)*

Clearly, Menon's attempt at technoproductivity did not comply with, what Judith Butler calls the "culturally intelligible" category of the ideal feminine. It would be erroneous for us to assume that digital economies are level-playing fields of productivity. In a bizarre reincarnation of colonial laws like the Criminal Tribes Act of 1871, the transgender community in India was marginalized as "corona transmitters". Their livelihood was destroyed because the rule of quarantine coincided with the contagion-model of policing non-normative sexualities in India. In her interview of a sex-worker Prerana, Banshikha Ghosh discovers that the identity of *kothi* women was literally erased during lockdown, because they had to shift to occupations that did not permit them to cross-dress (Ghosh, 2021). Butler's concept of "cultural intelligibility" raises some important theoretical questions regarding the agency of the individual living in lockdown, "If gender is constructed through relations of power and, specifically, normative constraints that not only produce but also regulate various bodily beings, how might agency be derived from this notion of gender as the effect of productive constraint?" (Butler, 1993).

A live talk given recently on Instagram by the journalist Gayatri Shah drew attention to the epidemic of "productivity anxiety" (Ferrao Walker, 2020) that came with the coronavirus pandemic. She discusses how her decision to hold an Instalive session stemmed from a desire to compete with the overflow of digital voices and rapid content generation. It was one thing for ordinary women to upload recipes or dance videos for social validation, but for female entrepreneurs it mandated an overnight adapting to massive social media engagement. Since lockdown spiked the global consumption of digital content, female entrepreneurs, independent researchers, journalists, activists and environmental workers were thrown into the deep end of a space where voices circulated with alleged freedom and plurality. All these women had to perform what Hemangini Gupta identifies as an "emergent form of entrepreneurial activism" to coercively declare their relevance as "desiring subjects of neo-liberal feminism in India" (Gupta, 2016). One must understand that even within feminist voices in India, there is a strong impulse towards neo-liberal ideals of individualism and personal heroism. The notion of the collective is rather stunted in these versions of digital feminism. And yet, there were some feminist activists on Instagram who invented new aesthetic and political standpoints to challenge neo-liberal and patriarchal ideals. The following case studies explore how lacking two important sources of cultural capital on the technoproductivity scale - gender conformism and mental ability – rendered certain influencers precarious on Instagram. Even though they possessed digital capital and reasonable fluency in English, their work was delegitimized and trolled. This violent erasure required them to evolve new dissident models of social media interaction that deconstructed the ideal of technoproductivity and created an archive of precarious bodies and subjectivities in the pandemic.

Case Studies of Digital Feminism on Instagram

Subverting the Ideal of Technoproductivity: Durga Gawde

Durga 'Shakti' Gawde is a Bangalore-based trans activist popular on Instagram as "India's 1st Drag King". Their posts advocate gender fluid fashion and photography and work to destabilize online models of misogyny. The subversive way that Gawde produces a non-compliant gender identity through layers of gender parody and performance is interesting. For one, their appropriation of the religious moniker "Shakti" subverts the myth of the *devi* or goddess in a Hindu-majority India. The label "drag king" is reminiscent of the Butlerian model of "drag" as a weaponized performance of gender non-compliance. But by opting for "drag king" rather than the more American "drag queen", Durga further challenged Western homo-normativity from the perspective of a BIPOC influencer. In a recent interview, they clarify that their aesthetic and political stance is a performance that parodies Western gender norms and fashion:

> Everyday, I am putting something on, taking something off. I go out with a beard, I go out with a really deep V-neck top – whatever I feel like. It doesn't matter as long as it's how I want and how I feel and choose at that moment. But when I'm performing, it is all of my life experiences that come together, and I perform that emotion. That's what drag gives to me.
>
> *(Mehra, 2020)*

When the first nation-wide lockdown was announced in March 2020, Gawde posted a self-portrait (Fig. 4) in their bedroom, which stood out for its anti-drag aesthetic. The caption declared "IT TOOK A PANDEMIC FOR THE MALE GAZE TO STOP INTERFERING WITH THE PEACE OF MY MIND". As a visualization of this statement, their face is turned away from the camera and folded legs convey a drawing of boundaries. Where the post celebrates a feeling of safety from the male gaze, it also communicates an anxiety of how to perform trans identity in isolation. Gawde confesses that "it is difficult to allow my femininity to come through" and signals towards the anxiety of trans-people to 'be' trans at home. Compared with the conventional posts by trans-persons on Instagram that promote personal acts of heroism and stoicism in a global crisis, Gawde reveals how gender dysphoria produces mental health concerns that may impact technoproductivity.

On May 20, 2020, Gawde organized a virtual fundraiser to raise menstrual health awareness and promote eco-friendly disposal practices among rural women in India called "Period Party 2: Periods in Pandemics" (Fig. 5). In terms of their location on the technoproductivity scale, their use of digital capital as an influencer and fluency in English is not a privilege being exploited here for social validation but used to forge social change. It promotes a campaign that reaches out precisely to those who lack digital capital in India. While there are countless such online campaigns, what is striking about the event poster is Gawde's promotional photograph. They are dressed in a black formal shirt with a red tie, hair brushed back in a butch aesthetic, with black lipstick. The post questions the controversial binary within Western feminism of those who are born women and termed "menstruators" versus those who become women and are termed "transsexual". Notably therefore, feminist influencers like Durga Gawde demonstrate through their dissident social media presence that gender precarity is not an individual failure to perform productivity in a pandemic. Gender precarity is a politically induced state of vulnerability engineered by the neo-liberal state and its impossible ideal of technoproductivity (Butler, 2009). Few escape the condition entirely but technoprecarity impacts marginalized communities more due to the multiple jeopardies they already suffer at the hands of class, caste, race, gender, and ableist hierarchies in contemporary India. This reality is precisely what feminist trans-influencers in India like Durga Gawde make apparent with their digital content.

Crip-queer Critiques of Femininity: Roshni Kumar

Roshni Kumar is a Mumbai-based photojournalist, artist, and activist who supports sexual diversity, body positivity, and animal rights through her sustained practice of veganism and queer-BIPOC friendly content on Instagram. Through her Instagram handle @rosh93, a large part of her transgressive identity on social media depends on her being a cancer survivor. Through intimate shots of her naked body, shorn head, and campy make-up and filters, her body challenges idealized femininity in middle-class India. Rather than conform to the image of the long-suffering de-sexualized female cancer survivor – whose 'beauty' resides only in a kind of toxic positivity or stoic technoproductivity – Kumar's self-portraits reveal that the disabled and diseased female body is a precarious but desiring body.

In the early days of lockdown, Kumar described how similar the experience of living in lockdown was to being confined to a hospital bed during chemotherapy:

> Isolation;
>
> What a wonderful paradox of feelings it's given me. From freedom to love to loneliness to independence to happiness. I was just thinking the last few days have been unnecessarily anxious and hard and wonder what may happen for the rest and there I stumbled on my Facebook memories - reminding me on this [sic] day in 2008 I'd kept cute little status of happiness because I was finally done with the hospital and my chemos and my treatments and I was going back into the real world. I stayed in a hospital for a good 6 months and hardly went home and called the hospital my home. I was in complete isolation from the world other than my family. I had to look at ceilings and the same window with the same view for all those days. I couldn't walk or eat real food, I missed so many things and I didn't do so many things but guess what? It didn't matter after. I survived and I came out stronger. (Kumar, April 25, 2020)

Such confessional posts subvert a neo-liberal culture of individual success-stories and personal heroism. Through the explicit connection Kumar forges between her personal experience of suffering from cancer in isolation to the suffering of millions experiencing debilitating symptoms of the coronavirus, anxiety, and loneliness in lockdown, she exposes the biopolitical agendas of the neo-liberal state. Margrit Shildrick claims that precarity is a kind of "embodiment" or "ontological state" that defines being marginalized or 'debilitated' in neo-liberal society. In response to the umbrella term "precarity," Shildrick uses the term "bioprecarity" to connote specific "material and ontological effects" (Shildrick, 2020) of biopower. Shildrick notes that the spread of the coronavirus has medicalized bodies so much so that erstwhile bodily norms – even those relating to the gender binary – have been disrupted. To continue to perform technoproductivity therefore requires a kind of impossible hyper-productivity where any semblance of humanness is wiped out.

Through a lengthy confession framed in the narratological device of the personal diary, Kumar performs gender non conformism rather than technoproductivity (Fig. 6). The self-portrait displays her seated with head resting on her arm in a symbolic gesture of exhaustion. We see evidence of the 'hands' that cleaned and maintained the home rather than a glossy image of her clean bedroom as a finished or fetishized image. The space fades into background as if it were one of the many homes where Indian maids and domestic assistants work every day. Almost exactly a year later, Kumar's Instagram posts chronicle her visual journey of mental disability. In the above photograph (Fig. 7), she erases her face and pinches her stomach to create an 'emoji' of sadness with her flesh. This is far more accurate picture of the 'mood of the nation' rather than a sentiment analysis of Twitter status updates. Kumar poses the imperfections of the female body to parody the selfies uploaded by health and fitness professionals during the pandemic. Kumar also denigrates the spirit of mindless competition on social media that generates "productivity anxiety". She not only critiques neo-liberal ableism in statements such as, "we all cannot function at the same capacity, and no one can function at a 100% everyday - all day" but also subverts the 'slow death' of all precarious bodies in the pandemic by draping her breasts with a white 'hospital' sheet that foreshadows the funeral shroud.

Whether it is her flamboyant mimicry of Lady Gaga and Katy Perry's wigs, or the prosthetics used by cancer survivors, Kumar's Instagram feminism is a good example of what a "crip-queer" resistance to the productivity ideal. Working through Robert Mcruer's concept of the "cripqueer" (2018), Shildrick states, "In feminist thought in particular, precarity mobilizes both a critical perspective on neoliberalism and a surprisingly transformative prospective. Against any simple expectation of negativity, the notion of precarious bodies can paradoxically signal the potential of communality and the strength of relationality" (2020). McRuer's "cripqueer" approach connects Disability Studies and Critical Race Theory to imagine a new kind of "relational" futurity where all forms of currently devalued and precarious embodiment signal a revitalization of global cultures in more sustainable and equitable directions. Shildrick invokes the term "crip" from McRuer to define a non-compliant stance against neo-liberal norms of technoproductivity. She argues that crip activism – such as Roshni Kumar's celebration of the cancer survivor's body, the domestic help's body, and queer and trans bodies on social media – may not resolve the real human losses brought on by lockdown. Nevertheless, they weaponize precarity and create new ways of resisting neo-liberal ideals that appear illegible, disorienting, or downright offensive to the digital norm.

Dalit Feminist Aesthetics: Priyanka Paul

Priyanka Paul is a Mumbai-based artist and queer BIPOC activist whose Instagram account @artwhoring was reported and trolled repeatedly during lockdown due to which it was temporarily closed. Signifying her failure to perform technoproductivity on social media, Paul's posts were vilified by casteist, ultra-nationalist, and heterosexist trolls for their gender non-conformist content and anti-caste activism. Her case stands out for the sheer volume of hate speech she received for not complying with the norms of technoproductivity; the closure of her account symbolizing a kind of digital 'suicide'. She regularly campaigns for Dalit and queer rights on social media and appeared in community-level projects. Prominently, she participated with Alok V. Menon and Fatimah Asghar in the international virtual event "Poets for Power: A Reading Featuring Queer South Asian Poets" on May 16, 2020. Composing from the vantage point of the gender and caste subaltern in urban India, Paul's art critiques the ideal of technoproductivity that rely on invisible layers of privilege. In the image given below for instance (Fig. 8), she lulls the viewer with a background of pink, passive, and ideal femininity. Then she launches her deeply scathing attack on pervasive discourses of Brahminical patriarchy that dominate trolling and social media violence in India. The figure on the right is a parody of Brahminical ideology symbolized by the three-heads of the Hindu godhead. Quite literally, the figure wears "caste" as a badge on its chest

Paul designs the figure's jacket with Pop Art images of Brahmins with well-built bare chests representing their toxic masculinity and muscular nationalism. In the tabular caste hierarchy written besides this figure, the "shudra" appears near the feet and the word is partially cut-off to refer to the "men from down under". This instance of gender and caste dissidence functions as a kind of narrative performance emerging from the experience of what Bhushan Sharma calls the "outsider within". Sharma employs standpoint theory, which claims that the unofficial perspectives of oppressed and marginalized individuals – such as Instagram posts – can provide a more objective account of social reality, and therefore, may be seen to challenge mainstream feminism. He highlights the importance of narrative representation in forging intersectionality, "As reality can only be known if it is represented, Dalit women penned their life narratives – social epiphanies – that then drove women impregnated with Dalit and feminist consciousness to trail the ethics of Black women writers" (Sharma, 2021). While much of Paul's artwork was lauded for gender non-compliance and anti-caste activism prior to the pandemic, it is important to remember that during lockdown her number of followers increased exponentially, many of whom were trolls invested in delegitimizing her unique brand of digital feminism.

For instance, a few months prior to closing her account, one of Paul's posts showcasing her new hair colour became viral as a Hindutva troll called @katuaslayer photoshopped and reposted her photograph with the caption "Why are we missing the signs of autism in girls?" (Fig 9). As may be seen from the image, Paul had to report the account and requested her followers not to share the image. Even as Paul tackled these trolls deftly by re-posting their hate speech so that her followers may block them, she was continuously attacked and ended up having to 'kill' her account. To transform her feminist activism into the precarity of a trolled and silenced subject on social media, the Hindutva troll employed a pejorative ableist vocabulary to invalidate her identity. Her harassment clearly demonstrates how intersections between the native woman, queer woman, Dalit woman, and disabled woman merge into a brilliantly precise image of gender precarity in neo-liberal India. The scale reveals how technoproductivity is both repression and repressive; it traps the precarious individual in a Sisyphean cycle of "hyper-objectified" labour that must comply with the norm. When users perceive their labour as being 'good,' likeable, or relatable on Facebook or Instagram, they erroneously believe they can pave the way to salvation in a global healthcare crisis. What of those who get mercilessly trolled and their digital labour invalidated, simply because it did not comply with the patriarchal and neo-liberal norms of technoproductivity?

It is clear that the very same ideological apparatuses in India that normalized technoproductivity and measured the 'happiness' of a nation reeling under a pandemic criminalized these examples of gender non-conforming feminist influencers. Who was lauded for being technoproductive on social media versus who were trolled for political and feminist dissidence indicates a discursive battle for what constitutes as normative labour in contemporary Indian capitalism. It is important to remember that capitalism sustains itself by invisibilizing labour and normalizing socio-economic exploitation. It prevents us from asking questions such as:

> How is disablement produced through global supply chains? Who is sacrificed? Digital economies contribute to the uncompensated breakdown of the mind and body. The precarious laborers of the digital sit at screens and filter violent or sexually graphic content, mine digital gold, operate tech support, mine literal cobalt/rare metals, assemble chips and screens, enter data, recycle or dispose of digital waste products, clean buildings in Silicon Valley, drive app-based rideshare cars, transcribe walls of text, write code, edit code, write fanfiction, produce videos, tweet, load computer chips on container ships, buy and sell stock. Some of these jobs are physically demanding, from mining to sitting hunched over at a desk. Others are psychically demanding, even traumatizing. The risks of labor, its likeliness to result in disability, sickness, trauma, stress, death, are organized by race, gender, and other categories that come pre-loaded with precarity.
>
> *(Precarity Lab, 2020)*

Going forward, the productivity scale designed in this paper may be used to measure how emergent feminist politics on social media platforms in India challenged the ideal of technoproductivity. The need of the hour is to redefine parameters by which we analyze the efficacy and impact of Indian digital feminism. We need to study the dissident strategies employed by young artists and activists that deconstruct neo-liberal ideals on social media. It is worth interrogating how such new non-conformist corporealities, aesthetics, and representations usher a more inclusive and intersectional future in Indian feminism.

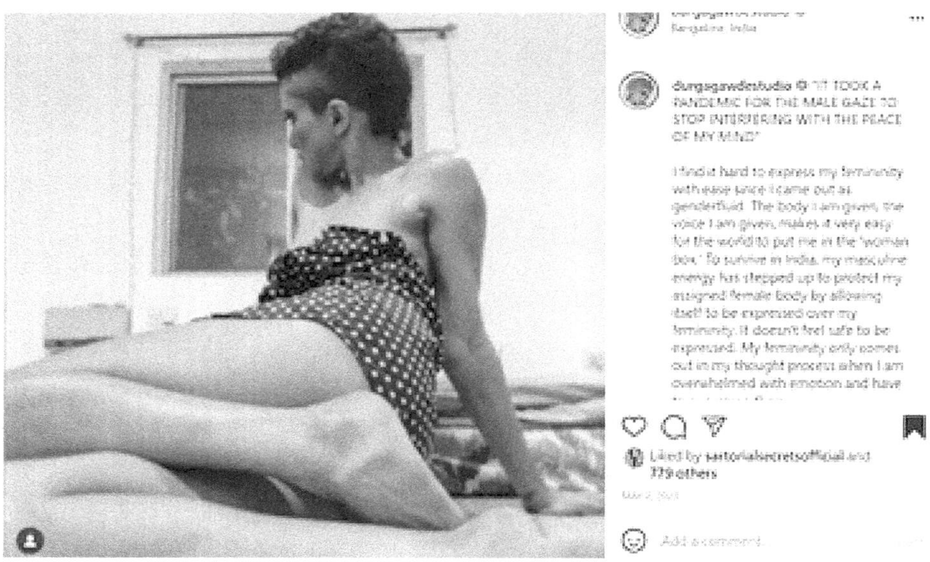

Figure 4: "IT TOOK A PANDEMIC"
(May 2, 2020), Durga Gawde,
Instagram https://www.instagram.com/p/B_sVd2MJMkx/

Figure 5 - "Period Party", (May 20, 2020), Durga Gawde, Instagram https://www.instagram.com/p/CAw-xZTJJd5/

Figure 6 - "Lockdown Diaries", (April 25, 2020), Roshni Kumar, Instagram https://www.instagram.com/p/B_Z0nVdFWh0/

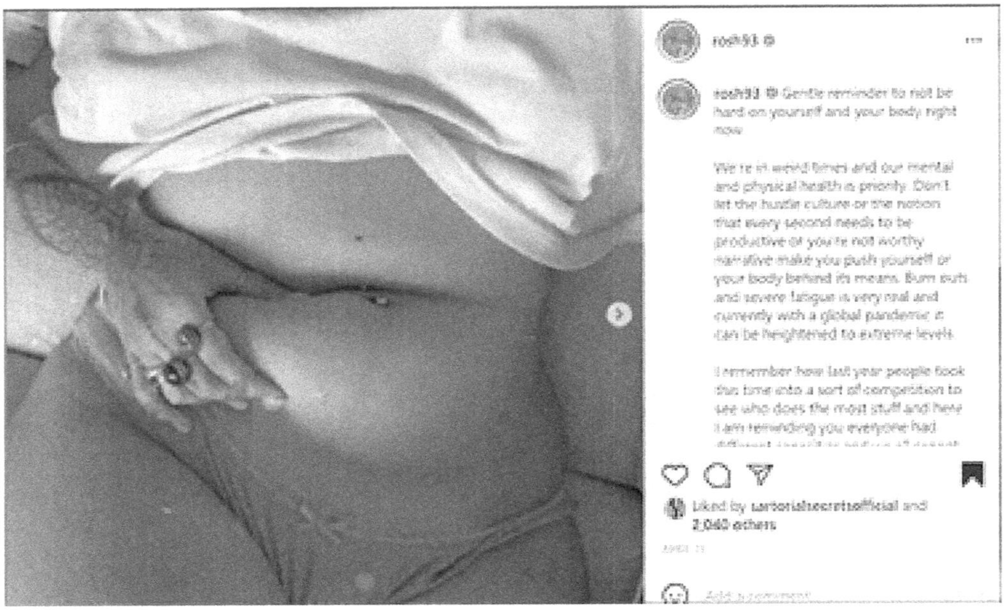

Figure 7: "Gentle Reminder", Roshni Kumar, April 15, 2021, Instagram, https://www.instagram.com/p/CNr0Og_l9_Z/

Figure 8. "I wrote from The Margins", Priyanka Paul, May 31, 2020, Instagram, https://www.instagram.com/p/CA26qvGDDJP/

Figure 9: "If you see any memes", Priyanka Paul, Stories, Instagram https://www.instagram.com/p/CAsgDmHjlo4/

REFERENCES

Afridi, F., Roy, S., & Dhillon, A. (2021). The gendered crisis: livelihoods and mental well-being in India during COVID-19. *United Nations University World Institute for Development Economics Research*. Retrieved from https://www.isid.ac.in/~fafridi/wp-content/uploads/2021/04/wp2021-65-Afridi-et-al..pdf (2020, July 8). *Violence and discrimination based on sexual orientation and gender identity during the coronavirus disease (COVID-19) pandemic*. UN General Assembly. Retrieved from https://undocs.org/A/75/258

Birnholtz, J., Fitzpatrick, C., & Handel, M. (2014). Identity, identification and identifiability: The language of self-presentation on a location-based mobile dating app. *Proceedings of the 16th international conference on human-computer interaction with mobile devices & services*, 3-12.

Bourdieu, P. (1992). *An Invitation to Reflexive Sociology*. Chicago University Press.

Butler, J. (1993). Preface. In *Bodies that Matter* (p. x). Routledge.

Butler, J. (2009). Performativity, Precarity, and Sexual Politics. *AIBR, 4*(3), i-ii.

Ferrao Walker, Gretchen. (May 12, 2020) People Are Using 'Pandemic Productivity' as a Distraction from Grief, Vulnerability. *The Swaddle.* https://theswaddle.com/people-are-using-pandemic-productivity-as-a-distraction-from-grief-vulnerability/

Ghosh, B. (2021). The Lockdown of Koti Intimacies. *Zurich Open Repository and Archives,* 29-33.

Gupta, H. (2016). Taking Action: The Desiring Subjects of Neoliberal Feminism in India. *Journal of International Women's Studies, 17*(1), 152-168. (n.d.). *Policy brief: The impact of COVID-19 on women; and COVID-19 and ending violence against women and girls.* UN Women Headquarters. EVAW COVID-19 Beirfs.

Mcruer, Robert. (2018). *Crip Times: Disability, Globalization, and Resistance.* New York University Press.

Mehra, Sanchi. (2020). In Conversation with Durga Gawde: An Artist, Activist, and Drag King. *Feminism in India.* https://feminisminindia.com/2020/10/19/durga-gawde-an-artist-activist-and-drag-king/

Precarity Lab (2020). *Technoprecarious.* Goldsmiths Press.

Scarr, S., Chowdhury, J., Sharma, M., & Dutta, P. K. (2021, May 7). How India's public, COVID-19 patients, and hospitals inundated Twitter with desperate pleas for help. *ReutersGraphics.* Retrieved from https://graphics.reuters.com/HEALTH-CORONAVIRUS/INDIA-TWITTER/oakpekqlrpr/

Sharma, B. (2021). Narratives of Dalit Women and 'the Outsider Within': Toward a Literary Practice of Dalit Feminist Standpoint. *Journal of International Women's Studies,* 22(4), 25-40. Available at: https://vc.bridgew.edu/jiws/vol22/iss4/3

Shildrick, M. (2020). *Bioprecarity in Neo-liberal Times: Ways of Rethinking Debility.* [Guest Lecture]. Birla Institute of Technology and Science- Pilani, Hyderabad.

Spivak, G. C. (2020, June 10). *Is Covid-19 a Global Equalizer?* (N. Mkrtchyan, Interviewer) Retrieved from https://www.youtube.com/watch?v=fTnUc95PQ4I

Venigalla, A. S., Vagavolu, D., & Chimalakonda, S. (2020). Mood of India During Covid-19 – An Interactive Web Portal Based on Emotion Analysis of Twitter Data. *Research in Intelligent Software & Human Analytics (RISHA) Lab,* 1-13.

Yilong, W. (2020). Witnessing the Pandemic with Foucault: Power, Politics, and Covid-19. *Canadian Social Science, 16*(8), 36-40.

ENDNOTES

1 Dr. Anhiti Patnaik is an Assistant Professor at the Department of Humanities and Social Sciences, Birla Institute of Technology and Science, Pilani. Her areas of interest include Victorian Literature, Cultural Criminology, Queer Theory, Postmodernism, and Critical Asian Studies. Anhiti completed her PhD in Cultural Studies at Trent University, Canada and is a Fellow of The School of Criticism and Theory, Cornell University and The Institute of World Literature, Harvard University. Her work has been published in *Neo-Victorian Studies, Journal of World Literature, Brontë Studies, Horror Fiction in the Global South* (Bloomsbury) and *Place Matters: Critical Topographies in Word and Image* (McGill-Queen's University Press).

CHAPTER 6

Networking Voices against Violence: Online Activism and Transnational Feminism in Local-Global Contexts

Sutanuka Banerjee[1], Lipika Kankaria[2]

ABSTRACT

Contemporary feminism manifests itself in the form of blogs, hashtags, e-magazines, and digitally planned protests through online communities that address the prevailing concerns of feminists in the digital age. This feminist approach to digital activism aims to reclaim the power of technology which is inherently hegemonic and masculinist by creating alternate spaces and modes of protest. Transnational feminism is increasingly being shaped by online discourses and the new digital space enables social movements in shaping feminist solidarity and complex netizen identities. This paper adopts discourse analysis of online contents that question the prevalent patriarchal system in South Asia and thus situate it in the changing socio-cultural context globally. Popular hashtag movements in various countries such as #YesAllWomen, #notallmen, #MeToo, #SheInspiresMe, #WomenMarch4Change, #WhyLoiter, #IWillGoOut, #AuratMarch #GirlsAtDhabas, #SafeCityIndia #PinjraTod as well as other online forums which raise the voices of women against various forms of violence will be analysed with a view to uncover their multi- layered impact. These multifaceted discourses on gender-based violence have reached a wider audience across the world through social media, and academic webinars during the Covid-19 pandemic have also largely contributed to the debate. The resonance of these dialogues has transcended the local to the global level; a close study of the transnational character of these digital messages in social media aims to examine the strict demarcation between the public and the private, thus challenging the concept of gendered spaces. This paper employs a multidisciplinary approach to methodologically analyse the online resources and nature of activism in India and investigate its global relevance. Additionally, the paper will also explore how the online campaigns are establishing networks notwithstanding time and place, by interrogating and understanding the relationship between online activism and its significance in conceptualizing transnational feminism.

Introduction

With increasing use of internet tools, digital technology has emerged as a key instrument in creating a space for feminist activism. This space has been variously utilized by specific communities and groups for advocating several activities such as organising protests, creating dialogues, and expressing dissent. The internet has added a new dimension to new-age feminist activism, which acknowledges the diversity and underlying differences in women's movements. This is increasingly being articulated in women's forums that can be termed as transnational in the sense that it caters to the debates on gender equity and advocacy in both local and global contexts (Dingo, 2012; Hesford, 2010; Hesford & Schell, 2008; Queen, 2008). This approach has added newer perspectives to feminist movements around the world. Transnational feminism focuses on "the diverse experiences of women who live within, between, and at the margins or boundaries of nation-states around the globe" (Zerbe Enns et al., 2020). A critical analysis of this theory can lead to the unravelling of new insights in the history of women's movements and the politics of solidarity.

Morgan's (1984) *Sisterhood is Global* focussed on women's lived experiences of patriarchy and the potential for building collaboration amongst women around the globe. This perspective underlined the commonalities between women rather than their innate differences, and how the commonalities formed the foundation for building a connected global women's movement. Mohanty (1988, 1992, 2003) critiqued the "Universal sisterhood" for its promotion of an essentialist, homogenous view of women as a cross-culturally singular category with similar interests, likings, perspectives, goals, and experiences. "Third World" feminists in both the global north and the global south started questioning the Western conceptualizations of feminism and examined differences among women in respect of race, class, sexuality, nationality, and located these differences in complex systems of identity and knowledge production. These critiques have prompted the scope of research from intersectional perspective which focuses on how the multiplicity of women's identities (based on race, gender, nationality, class and sexuality) and their specific interests shape feminist discourse (Basu, 1995; Grewal and Kaplan 1994; Kaplan, et al. 1999; Mendoza, 2002; Narayan, 1997). The increasing body of research on the diversity of women's movements and the presence of diverse feminisms in contrast to a single global women's movement concentrated on building coalitions linked by issues rather than drawing on parallels of uniformity. Transnational feminism as highlighted before, questions hegemonic feminist imaginings based on the models of global sisterhood underlying the meaningful differences between women both locally and globally and how it shaped and reshaped feminist politics (Nadkarni, 2017).

To critically investigate the nuances around the worldwide campaigns and coalitions for women's active resistance, the concept of "global village" (introduced by Marshall McLuhan in 1964) can be useful in this context. By global village, McLuhan (1964) implied that the world was increasingly becoming a smaller place as technology has connected everyone across barriers and this idea can also be applied in the analysis of online activism. This has been brought about by the internet which can be viewed as "international" or transnational as it connects geo-political spaces and aids in the exchange of communication beyond and between countries and the citizens (Kramarae, 2014). This paper will theorize the effect of online activism which aims to connect and mobilize people through different strategies and examine the relevance of the movements in virtual spaces which have reverberations in real world. Additionally, the paper will also focus on the Indian hashtag activism while examining how the campaigns against violence and discrimination are establishing networks notwithstanding time and place. While employing discourse analysis, the paper adopts qualitative approach and explores local-global intersections to understand the ramifications of digital feminism in South Asia. It has taken into account secondary resources available on the internet (blogs, e-papers, articles, e-zines and so on) to scrutinize the multi-layered nuances of online feminist activism. Along with providing a global overview of recent feminist online campaigns, it focuses on the Indian feminist activist discourse and contextualizes as well as situates it in the contemporary scenario.

Digital Revolutions and Online Activism

Feminist activism across the world has undergone a paradigm shift as feminist movements nowadays are rather mediated and *networked* instead of 1960s-era feminism which unfolded through activities of formal institutions (Clark-Parsons, 2018). Contemporary feminism manifests as blogs, hashtags, e-magazines, digitally planned protests, online communities and so on. Feminist solidarity and complex "netizen identities" (Chadha, 2017) are significant elements in understanding gender politics in online activism, spearheaded by the prevalence of media networks. Feminist social media feminism (Sebring, 2019) or cyberfeminism is variously understood as either a philosophy (Paterson, 1992) or a radical online pedagogy and digital rhetoric (Hocks, 2009; Torrens & Riley, 2009) that seeks to use internet and create online spaces with the aim to empower women.

Digital space as a location for transnational feminist intervention has witnessed a wave of feminist movements, which address various political issues— reproductive rights, verbal and non-verbal attacks, wage inequities, women's autonomy over bodies, and the effectiveness of such protests is considerably significant. The commonality of women's issues is a shared predicament, yet it cannot bring women together physically due to geographical and cultural barriers. When these debates are transported to the online platform, they have a broader connection where the local gets transposed to the global. For example, movements like #WhyIMarch which was a global campaign to unite voices for women's rights and other issues that started in the United States but with the help of internet spread to a number of countries. Further, in India #IWillGoOut proved to be a significant campaign for women to claim their agency and question patriarchal norms which have been discussed at length later in the paper.

Contemporary transnational feminist dialogues fundamentally include online feminist exchanges and mediations, writings, art and other productions. According to Kahn and Kellner (2004), a part of the Internet subculture comprises of personal and political blogging which also includes activism on social media platforms, such as Facebook, by connecting the real and virtual worlds. There were sporadic instances of women's digital activism in India from a long time but the Nirbhaya case is a landmark incident in the sense that the brutal gangrape in 2012 in Delhi sparked outrage and the internet seemed to play a crucial role in connecting voices across nations (Losh, 2014). Jyoti Singh Pandey, who was given the pseudonym of 'Nirbhaya,' was a young student who was gangraped in a moving bus and later thrown off the bus in a pitiable condition with an iron rod inserted into her vagina. Immediately after the incident social media users resorted to online platform to express their concern as they were shocked by the brutality of the crime. It received international attention and gave rise to public furore as it generated discussions about violence against women and their limited access to safe spaces. Social media acted as a platform to exchange information which amplified the response of people across the nation as they planned events to protest and demand justice by catalysing social change. Hashtags were used by social media users to draw attention to this incident and highlighted the question of women's safety in public spaces which eventually forced the government to amend laws for concrete action, and stringent punishments were introduced. In this light, it is crucial to situate gender-based violence in the broader context of transnational feminist activism that is being initiated through digital media.

Technology is instrumental in alleviating structural and physical barriers by uniting women for a cause but the economic structure of the society poses a major hindrance to the transnational networking of women due to digital divide. Studies have shown that economic inequality results in a huge gap leading to inaccessibility to internet (OECD, 2001). Although there is a presence of diverse voices online, it is important to question whether the digital space facilitates equal participation within the available limited resources. Usage of technology is based on internet penetration in remote areas and access to devices as well as literacy of women which restrict their involvement. The marginalized and the poorer section of women are the ones who are most likely to not have access to internet and therefore excluded from the purview of online activism. According to Mohan (2018), only 30 percent of the online users are women and further this percentage drops to 12 percent in rural areas. This class-based and region-based divide insinuate that those who have the resources and access to digital media can only vocalize their protest. The digital divide that echoes a separation between the information "haves" and "have-nots" has consequently led to a gender gap which becomes a growing concern especially if the power of technology is directly linked to voicing and exerting their agency.

New Media, Gender Question and Feminist Practices

Despite the limitations, internet has contributed to the democratization of feminist movements in the recent years by encouraging diversity and providing accessibility to the feminist struggle. The digital platform has forums and groups dedicated to particular issues which are enabling women to seek support, share and protest, thus, it has emerged as a site that redefines traditional notions of self, identity, and transnational feminism. New Media has become a significant propeller of transnational feminist activism. To define the term, it refers to any form of media ranging from blogs to podcasts that are delivered digitally. This implies that any internet- based communication disseminated through websites, emails, streaming platforms, online forums and so on can be considered new media (Siapera, 2017).

Digital feminism taking place in the online realm has gained popularity in the twenty-first century. In this connection, it can be highlighted that Fourth-wave feminism focusses on the use of internet tools, inclusivity and intersectional politics and takes into consideration the interlocking systems of power and how it disadvantages marginalised groups (Jain, 2020). It is increasingly contributing to scholarly discussions that involve a wide range of issues focusing on the connections between women's situated lives and changing dynamics of local-global interactions. Moreover, social media plays a pivotal role that allows people to engage in virtual communities that cannot be allocated strict geo-political locales.

The internet was initially conceptualized as a gender-neutral space as anonymity could be maintained while vocalizing any issue. However, it is no longer a neutral space as it is increasingly giving vent to opinions and expressions by people who are asserting their online identities (Cockburn, 1985; Wajcman, 1991). Citizens become netizens, who are able to voice concerns and initiate communicative action across an alternate medium. The existence of the virtual world has transformed the notions of the public and private domains by opening the window to a larger audience. In digital space, the idea of hashtag was initially conceptualized in 2007 on Twitter (Gannes, 2010) in order to facilitate the finding of information but it has grown in its scope that enables the users to specify context, emotion and meaning in their tweets while referring to a particular cause. The trend of hashtags has spread to other social media platforms as a means to draw attention to the trending topics, issues or news as well as to locate others who share the same views (Chen et al., 2018). The posts on any platform is targeted towards an imagined audience who are expected to perceive and participate in the discussions propelled by the hashtags (Marwick & Boyd, 2011). With the use of new media as a location of imagined communities, mediated social spaces create a sense of "virtual cosmopolitanism" (McEwan & Sobré-Denton, 2011). The notion of virtual cosmopolitanism as the space for mobilizing digital media (such as Twitter, Facebook, online support groups) is located at the intersection of social context and technological opportunity (Gillan et al., 2008). Feminists have judiciously made use of this relatively new aspect of hashtag as a means of attracting women to a cause (Eagle, 2015; Loza, 2016) wherein they can create a domain in the public space to come together virtually. However, Dean (2009) postulates that online activism maybe passive but the intimacy on the web space intensifies the emotions and feelings of solidarity.

A new term, *clicktivism*, is now being used when activists are resorting to online medium to galvanize protests and promote awareness. This highlights the potential that digital technology could play in the future of feminist activism by lending voice to protests against violence. To counter sexual harassment, Twitter and Facebook users are turning to the micro-blogging site by posting real life accounts of crimes and even organizing "slut–walks" and marches, mainly in metro cities. Social media also acts as a source of dissemination of information regarding marches or rallies. According to Carstensen (2014), social media has been able to "provide spaces for users to empower each other, to establish events and protests and mobilize for political action." Hashtag feminism has offered a powerful medium for voicing support for various feminist concerns and by doing so it has redefined "the ways we view the active components of feminism in our present society" (Dixon, 2014). However, there exists another point of view which emphasizes that online feminism may seem to be liberating through participation in a small way which is likely to prevent feminists from engaging in more involved ways of activism (Lee & Heish, 2013). This line of argument has given rise to the concept of slactivism which refers to the limited and low-risk participation in any initiative wherein individuals "confine their outrage to the computer screen" (Bastos et al., 2015). There are other terms such as "hactivism" which have become a part of critical media research and literary parlance as the reactionary nature of hactivism makes it an important tool in the landscape of online protests.

Global Visibility of Women's Issues and Online Activism in the South Asian Context

The varied forms of online activism have drawn global attention to women's issues through a number of ways made possible by technological advancements. To analyse the nuances of feminist movements and transnational connections within digital space, the interface between activism, gender, and technology needs to be critically examined. Hashtag activism as a field has emerged rather recently in order to "raise awareness for social issues on social media" (Xiong et al, 2019). Participation in such movements by sharing personal accounts and traumatizing stories is the assertion of the self where the personal becomes political and women assemble for a cause under the aegis of a hashtag. Various hashtag campaigns such as #MeToo, #EverydaySexism, #UrgentAction4Women, #ThisIsNotConsent, #EndFGM (Female Genital Mutilation) (Kangere et. al, 2017) and so on have sparked Fourth wave feminist discourses around the globe, incorporating a range of practices that are enabled by Web 2.0 digital technologies (Munro, 2013). Similar campaigns like #OrangeTheWorld, #GenerationEquality are conceptualized to express solidarity against discrimination and violence and promote gender parity. This feeling of comradeship generated by the hashtag activism has connected women and they are more likely to partake in significant efforts offline (Lee & Heish, 2013).

#MeToo became a massive scale movement where women from various sections of the society came out with their experiences of sexual abuse and molestation. Although the movement was initiated by Tarana Burke in the year 2006 "to stand with women of colour who have gone through sexual abuse and harassment" (Dixit, 2021), the worldwide resurgence of #MeToo across social media in 2017 was attributed to Hollywood personality Alyssa Milano. It commenced as a response to Hollywood's culture of sexual harassment but gradually grabbed global attention about the enormity of the problem for women across countries. This campaign has been successful in encouraging Indian women to uncover issues of violence, harassment and rape considering the intersection of power and politics. #MeToo movement in India garnered considerable attention largely due to the involvement of Bollywood celebrities and well-known personalities. A Google Trends visualization of hotspots for #MeToo search shows that there is a concentration of golden dots across India that reflects the interest of the readers and participants in a particular zone (Shrivastava et al., 2018). However, this predominantly digital movement indirectly excluded a large section of women from the ambit of the movement as the intersectional identities within and outside traditional feminisms excluded other marginally gendered bodies (Nanditha, 2021) and it has largely failed to discuss the lived experiences of sexual abuse of transwomen, Dalit women, LGBTQ and other marginalized communities. Even though there is some visibility of non- normative identities in online discourses like #loveforall and #pridemarch but it has failed to highlight the multi-layered forms of abuse and harassment confronted by these groups and communities.

The feminist activities on the online platform in India have been marked by the politics of inclusion and exclusion as the movement has been largely restricted to the elites, not proliferating amongst the working class and rural populations. Irrespective of that, #MeToo emerged as a movement which initiated conversations and opened doors to exchanges and debates concerning the ways to tackle the issues of sexual harassment and violence. A close analysis of the discourse of the tweets shows that they mostly reflect personal opinions of the celebrities and non-celebrities alike, although the celebrities receive far more visibility on such platforms. In her study, Nanditha (2021) found that these tweets generated recurrent words like "defamation", "harassment", "cases" and "allegations", indicating that many of these public accusations do not always follow the legal proceedings or generate debates surrounding the controversial issues of power and gender in public space. This has also led to counter arguments as the voicing of such opinions produced differing discourses with trending hashtags such as #fake, #fakecases, #mentoo and so on that gives vent to negative sentiments and hostility towards the movement. Online activism related to sexual harassment triggered a host of accompanying hashtags. #LoSHA, a similar name and shame campaign, was initiated by Raya Sarkar, a Law graduate from India now residing in the US, who published a list of professors as sexual predators (John, 2021; Pain, 2020). The list crowd-sourced names and cases of sexual harassment of students by their professors and it generated huge controversy and polarised feminists across the country (Chadha, 2017).

The biggest campaign in India in 2012 was in response to the brutal gangrape and murder of Jyoti Singh Pandey in the national capital and it drove urban populace to take recourse to social media to give to their anger and anguish. It was the digital activism that convinced people to go for street demonstrations impelled by online protests. Text messages, WhatsApp, Facebook and Twitter hashtags such as #Nirbhaya, #StopThisShame were used in a large scale to demonstrate collective rage against the persistent problem of sexual abuse and assault (Kurian, 2019). In 2014, Twitter saw a new wave of posts under #YesAllWomen, a campaign aiming to draw attention to the pervasiveness of sexism, chauvinism and violence directed towards women (Barker-Plummer & Barker-Plummer, 2017). This global hashtag became popular in India after the mass molestations that took place in Bangalore at New Year's Eve celebrations (De Bono, 2017) which encouraged Indian women to share their stories of sexual harassment. Indian feminists reclaimed that hashtag in response to #notallmen and asked users to post personal accounts of harassment and violence in Twitter, underscoring the reality that "yes, all women" have been subjected to sexual violence. #YesAllWomen created a transnational digital connection with reference to the Twitter campaign which documented women's experiences of everyday discrimination and sexism that generated widespread public outcry as disseminating awareness is the first step towards any social change. #KaunsiBadiBaatHai in 2019 in which UN Women partnered with TikTok, also highlighted the issue of gender-based violence (*FE Online*, 2019; Hu, 2019).

One of the most significant events that marked a new phase in Indian women's digital movement and online activism was the Pink Chaddi Campaign, which was initiated in February 2009 by a Facebook collective called "Consortium of Pub-Going, Loose and Forward Women" to demonstrate against the attacks in Mangalore by Hindu activists (Chattopadhyay, 2012). This was sparked by videos of young women being beaten up by men on the pretext that such activities were against the Hindu traditions and tainted the representation of ideal Hindu women. In response to this, the Facebook group called for a nationwide campaign to send pink underwear on Valentine's Day to the perpetrators as a mark of protest. The choice of pink underwear was symbolic of feminist freedom and sexualized consumerism. It aimed to question the appropriation of women's behaviour by patriarchal society through the act of showcasing intimate feminine underwear to bring the private to the public. The campaign got over-whelming response and it grabbed attention across the world as it was the first of its kind movement. Over the years, many such movements spearheaded by lawyers, students and organizations have taken over the digital space to fight against a monolithic idea of culture and all forms of violence.

In India, the reach of social media has played a pivotal role in uniting like-minded women for raising their voice and asserting their individuality. Around 2015, there was a spurt in hashtags relating to women's health, especially regarding taboo topics. A college student, Nikita Azad, started #HappytoBleed on Facebook to draw attention to the non-inclusion of women pilgrims aged 10 to 50 in Sabarimala temple, a very prominent Hindu shrine in India due to the belief that menstruating women might taint the holiness of the shrine (Varghese, 2015). It was aimed to empower women to take a stand against the social stigma surrounding menstruation and reclaim their autonomy over the bodies.

A large-scale movement over social media networks trended with #WhyIMarch in 2017 in a united response to the rising rhetoric of far-right populism (White, 2017). This globally synchronised protest also triggered discussions about gender equality and women's rights. The complex societal restrictions placed on women in the public arena led to initiatives like #WhyLoiter in India, which was aimed at encouraging women to reclaim streets and establish agency and independence (Phadke et al., 2011). By establishing their reasons for loitering, women propagated travel for leisure in an otherwise masculine space. The movement aimed at blurring the boundary between inner and outer spheres for women as they demanded equal right to public spaces, which is still mostly treated as a masculine privilege. The cyberspace, thus, was used to challenge prejudices and stereotypes and condemn street harassment as a pervasive form of oppression which hampers women's public presence and participation. #WhyLoiter in India and its counterpart #GirlsAtDhabas in Pakistan have been the pioneering movements that proliferated to the grassroots levels. #GirlsAtDhabas is a multi-city feminist initiative in Pakistan clinching the issues of safety and 'respectability' (Ansari, 2018). #Auratmarch in Pakistan on International Women's Day stressed on the similar motto of harassment free public space for women and came to the limelight receiving widespread attention. Further, the issue of safety was highlighted in a country-wide march across India with the hashtag #Iwillgoout which sought to demand women's right to equitable access to public spaces, galvanized by the reports of mass molestation on the New Year's Eve and series of sexual assaults in Bangalore in the year 2017. In 2019, in India the hashtag #WomenMarch4Change aimed at giving women and other marginalized communities a collective voice. Thus, the diversity of expressions that populates digital media makes it a fertile area for intersectional feminism which is evident through the posts and subsequent mobilizations. In keeping with the idea of reclaiming their bodies and spaces, hashtags such as, #SafeCityIndia, #BoardtheBus (Eagle, 2015, D'Silva, 2015) were introduced, which mostly focused on generating conversations about women's safety and their rights to mobility and safe public space. Furthermore, in this regard, #PinjraTod has received considerable attention as it was started by women college students who lived in hostels in Delhi and soon it spread to cities like Mumbai, Chennai and Thiruvananthapuram (Roy, 2016). It was aimed to unify women in claiming greater freedom for themselves and defy regressive and sexist rules, imposition of curfews and other restrictions in the garb of their safety. They also marched together to end moral policing and symbolically reclaim the night. There are other campaigns like #INeverAskForIt and #MeetToSleep which made an impact and caught headlines.

To propagate a space devoid of stigma, on International Women's Day (March 8), Twitter commenced #SheInspiresMe, the goal of which was to fashion a culture wherein women supported women, and empower female voices. UN Women Goodwill Ambassador Emma Watson, in the year 2014, welcomed men to support the movement for gender equality by participating in the HeForShe campaign. Since the campaign was launched, both men and women across the world used #HeForShe to profess commitment towards United Nations' goal for ending gender inequality by the year 2030. To encourage men and boys as supporters and agents of change in this effort to attain equality, HeForShe campaign was also launched in India. The impact of the national and local contexts is undeniable for the formulation of strategies for furthering women's rights and gender justice. MARD (Men Against Rape and Discrimination), launched in 2013 by Bollywood film director and actor Farhan Akhtar persuaded common public to consider men as allies in the struggle against gender inequality and raised awareness about gender based violence.

The space that internet has provided offers a platform for organized protests, not just in terms of hashtags but songs and offline performances as well. For example, "*Un Violador en tu camino*" ("The Rapist is You"), first performed in the port city of Valparaiso on November 20, 2019, was aimed at shifting the blame away from women who experience sexual violence (Abramovich, 2019). This protest song soon turned out to be the global anthem which became viral worldwide with the videos of flashmob performances, and it was replicated hundreds of times around the world in the space of a few weeks and translated in several languages in many countries including India, Bangladesh, Lebanon and so on (Hinsliff, 2020). This also highlights the transnational character of protest movements that intersects with multi-layered issues that netizens experience in the emerging social media platforms.

In the present situation, during Covid 19 pandemic, street protests became impossible and social movements had to reconsider their strategies and develop "online-only" formats (Haßler et al., 2021). There are reports about an increase in domestic violence in quarantine which is further reinstated by the rising statistics (Gupta & Stahl, 2020; Graham-Harrison et al., 2020; Grierson, 2020). Helen Lewis (2020), an author and journalist, has called the pandemic "a disaster for feminism" as during the lockdown domestic violence cases have increased 20% globally (Ford, 2020) and resulted in a parallel pandemic (Puhr, 2020). It has attracted global attention and a considerable number of women reported incidents of violence which resulted in discussions about coping mechanisms (WHO, 2020). Freie Universität Berlin organized a couple of webinars and interesting roundtable series such as *Transnational feminist dialogues in times of corona crisis* involving women activists and academics from various places across the world. Women from different parts of the globe participated in it and these types of online conferences, discussions and lectures thereby created a virtual space to share, exchange and discuss multi-layered aspects of discrimination and privilege. In India, various institutions organised webinars involving experts who helped in commencing a series of critical dialogues about crucial issues. For instance, Dr. Vibhuti Patel, a feminist social scientist delivered lectures on gender equity and how Covid-19 affected women's livelihood in the informal sector (Patel, 2020). Other scholars also shared their concerns and deliberated on this issue to combat the challenges posed by Covid-19 and Prof. Fawzia Afzal-Khan is notable among them (IWWAGE, 2020; Afzal-Khan, 2020).

Apart from the academic webinars in recent times, various non-governmental organizations have long been engaged in making contributions in creating awareness about gender- based discrimination and violence by utilizing digital media. For example, Breakthrough, started in Delhi in 2000, mentions on its website that it is working towards making "violence and discrimination against women and girls unacceptable" by using various strategies ranging from media and arts to music videos and animations. Other collectives, such as the Blank Noise Project, have used the online platform for feminist activism and intervention against street harassment in India and lack of access to public space. This project covered a wide array of activities such as blogging, workshops and strategizing to render public spaces as safe for millions of women who need to travel on a daily basis. Being an online effort, it advocated the use of new ICTs creatively to ascertain and resist sexual harassment, and at the same time recognizing that harassment is sometimes also perpetuated by technology. In this connection, mention may be made of another prominent organization, Digital Rights Foundation, a research-based advocacy NGO, run by the Pakistani Lawyer and Internet activist Nighat Dad, has contributed to women's rights in digital spaces by using ICTs to support human rights, freedom of expression, democratic processes and digital governance.

Apart from these, varied activist efforts have also culminated in feminist e-zines and web pages which give voice to women's issues. These emerging forums have changed the ways in which activism is being staged and individual opinions are brought to the forefront.Countercurrents.org started in 2001 is one of the first examples of cyber activism in India. From intersectional point of view it features articles from different sections of academic circle and activist network. In order to contribute to the ongoing conversation regarding global gender issues and add to transnational feminist discourses, many dedicated blogs and websites such as *Feminism in India* and *Women's Web* have become popular medium of expression. The authors are from various walks of life, including academics, journalists, independent researchers and NGO workers. These platforms aim to amplify the collective voices to develop feminist consciousness as it encompasses personal narratives by women, providing a means for resistance and liberation, outside the system of hierarchies.

Online Misogyny and Safety Concerns

Although digital feminism has revolutionized the ways of protest in many sense, the United Nations' Broadband Commission for Digital Development released a statement on "cyber VAWG," (Violence against Women and Girls) and commented that online harassment is a "problem of pandemic proportion" (Jane, 2017). Online bullying, trolling and harassment pervade the digital space and women are victimized on various accounts. It often blurs the contours between 'real' and 'virtual', with the after effects of online harassments peeping into women's offline lives. In many instances, the activists in online media have faced threats of violence, and even rape and death. Often as victims of online bullying, women resort to and reclaim the power of social media by registering their protests with the screenshots of the conversation. On the other hand, digital misogyny in the form of hate speech, physical threats and obscene language have a deep impact on women, that results in self-censoring, assuming an anonymous identity or a pseudonym, or withdrawing from online domains altogether (Day, 2013). This could prove to be very triggering and distressing to an extent that they are often forced to contemplate about taking down their blogs, Twitter handles and social media profiles. Many were forced to retract from online platforms and refrain from engaging in any online feminist debate. The global campaign "Take Back the Tech", begun in 2006, has been highlighting the question of violence against women perpetuated in the digital space. The campaign demands to take control of technology in the online and offline modes to advocate for ending violence against women.

Although online misogyny may be a new phenomenon, it resonates with patriarchal attempts to limit women's public presence and stifle their voices, viewing them as inferior (Jain, 2020). The prevailing regulations have proven inadequate to cover the entire gamut of gendered violence. In order to render online spaces as a fruitful space for feminist activism, implications of such acts of violence need to be addressed. For this purpose, the cyberfeminists seek to use digital media judiciously to create online spaces that are safe and liberating (Rowe, 2008). They have tried to harness the potential of internet by taking the feminist thinking forward and creating new opportunities by offering several tips. The initiatives, awareness and other learning activities are promoted by individuals and organizations to support women's equality and preventing the prevalence of gender stereotypes in the cyberspace (Breakthrough, 2015). Over the decades, women have developed various feminist ways of utilizing the social media to share stories, arrange meets, form coalitions and networks and so on. However, there is a need for more advanced forms of technology for creation of democratic spaces where activism and solidarity across countries can be promoted.

Conclusion

The potential of online spaces for global feminist networking offers an opportunity to be connected and be a part of the revolution, irrespective of geographical boundaries. It is a potent medium of heralding changes in the way feminist activism is propagated. While analysing the new media as building alternative spaces for opposition and resistance, the focus has been on how it de-territorializes location and permits alliances and intervention that cuts across identity and geo- political demarcations. The local-global nature of these feminist movements encourage transnational exchanges while keeping in view the local contexts as intersectionality is a major factor of critical analysis. The adaptation and localization of the global feminist engagements in India has influenced and shaped ongoing activism online. Multiple modes of expression in the form of hashtags, blogs, tweets and sites have lent women a voice irrespective of the underlying socio-economic and cultural differences. Despite the limitations, the active online space serves for creating a conducive environment for feminist movement in the digital platform. There is also a blurring of traditional binaries as women and men are forming networks and calling for action against sexual violence by turning "hashtag" protests into movements on social media.

The online space, thus, provides a medium that can accommodate diverse modes of protest, ranging from performances to posting on social media and creating webpages that initiate discourses and conversations about various women's issues. It has helped in building a transnational network that augment activism from various social groups and seek justice against the patriarchal prejudices of the society. On the other hand, the digital divide becomes a significant factor which marginalizes women in terms of class, caste, sexuality and they are often held back from asserting their rights and voices. It is essential that feminist activism in online spaces becomes more diverse, inclusive, decentralised, and democratic. Although a digital divide exists as these movements are mostly restricted to the urban section of the society, this space may be used as a potential site for raising the issues of the marginalized groups who are unable to access the internet. An intersectional and transnational approach to digital activism would lead to further inquiry into socio-political frameworks aimed for collective emancipation.

REFERENCES

Abramovich, P. (2019). *Chile anthem against sexual violence goes viral.* International business times. https://www.ibtimes.com/chile-anthem-against-sexual-violence-goes-viral-2880088

Afzal-Khan, F. (2020). Selection 1 - Resources - Love and Solidarity in the Time of Corona: Desi (South Asian) Feministas Envisioning Change Through Staying Engaged. *Journal of International Women's Studies*, 21(4), 6-8. https://vc.bridgew.edu/jiws/vol21/iss4/11

Ansari, N. (2018). Girls at Dhabas: challenging issues of safety, or 'respectability' in urban Pakistan? OpenDemocracy. https://www.opendemocracy.net/en/5050/girls-at-dhabas- safety-respectability-urban-pakistan/

Barker-Plummer, B., & Barker-Plummer, D. (2017). Twitter as a feminist resource:# YesAllWomen, digital platforms, and discursive social change. In J. Earl & D. A. Rohlinger (Eds.), *Social Movements and Media.* (pp. 91-118). Emerald Publishing Limited: Bingley.

Bastos, M. T., Mercea, D., & Charpentier, A. (2015). Tents, tweets, and events: The interplay between ongoing protests and social media. *Journal of Communication, 65*(2), 320-350.

Basu, A. (Ed.), (1995) *The Challenge of Local Feminisms: Women's Movements in Global Perspective.* Boulder: Westview.

Breakthrough. (2015). 16 Ways You Can Make Online Spaces Safer for Women. https://inbreakthrough.org/16-ways-you-can-make-online-spaces-safer-for-women/

Carstensen, T. (2014). Gender and social media: sexism, empowerment, or the irrelevance of gender?. In C. Carter, L. Steiner & L. McLaughlin (Eds.), *The Routledge companion to media & gender* (pp. 501-510). New York: Routledge.

Chadha, G. (2017). Towards complex feminist solidarities after the List-Statement. *Economic and Political Weekly,* 52(50). https://www.epw.in/engage/article/towards-complex-feminist- solidarities-list-statement

Chattopadhyay, S. (2012). Who's afraid of the pink chaddi?. In T. Carilli & J. Campbell (Eds.), *Challenging images of women in the media: Reinventing women's lives,* (pp. 77-86). Lanham: Lexington Books.

Chen, G. M., Pain, P., & Barner, B. (2018). "Hashtag Feminism": Activism or Slacktivism?. In D. Harp, J. Loke, I. Bachmann (Eds.), *Feminist approaches to media theory and research* (pp. 197-218). London: Palgrave Macmillan, Cham.

Clark-Parsons, R. (2018). *Doing It Ourselves: The Networked Practices of Feminist Media Activism* [Doctoral dissertation, University of Pennsylvania]. ProQuest Dissertations Publishing.

Cockburn, C. (1985). *Machinery of dominance: Women, men and technical know-how.* London: Pluto.

D'Silva, E. (2015). Guest Post: Tweet to @SafecityIndia to make your city safer. *blog.Twitter.com.* https://blog.twitter.com/2015/guest- post-tweet-to-safecityindia-to-make-your-city-safer-in

Day, E. (2013, December 8). *Caroline Criado-Perez: 'I Don't Know If I Had a Kind of Breakdown'.* The Guardian. https://www.theguardian.com/society/2013/dec/08/caroline- criado-perez-jane-austen-review-2013

De Bono, A. (2017). *#YesAllWomen resurfaces in India in the wake of mass molestation.* https://www.smh.com.au/lifestyle/yesallwomen-resurfaces-in-india-in-the-wake-of-mass- molestation-20170105-gtm76i.html

Dean, J. (2009). *Democracy and other neoliberal fantasies: Communicative capitalism and left politics.* Durham: Duke University Press.

Dingo, R. (2012). *Networking arguments: Rhetoric, transnational feminism, and public policy writing.* Pittsburgh: University of Pittsburgh Press.

Dixit, S. (2021). I refused to say #MeToo: Negotiating between individual agency and 'Imagined' platform constraints. *Journal of Creative Communications, 17*(1), 35-48. DOI: 10.1177/0973258620980550

Dixon, K. (2014). Feminist online identity: Analyzing the presence of hashtag feminism. *Journal of Arts and Humanities, 3*(7), 34-40. https://doi.org/10.18533/journal.v3i7.509

Eagle, R. B. (2015). Loitering, lingering, hashtagging: Women reclaiming public space via #BoardtheBus,# StopStreetHarassment, and the# EverydaySexism Project. *Feminist Media Studies, 15*(2), 350-353.

FE Online. (2019). *UN Women partners with TikTok to raise awareness against domestic abuse with #KaunsiBadiBaatHai campaign.* Financial Express Online. https://www.financialexpress.com/brandwagon/un-women-partners-with-tiktok-to-raise-awareness-against-domestic-abuse-with- kaunsibadibaathai-campaign/1775652/

Ford, L. (2020, April 28). 'Calamitous': domestic violence set to soar by 20% during global lockdown. The Guardian. https://www.theguardian.com/global- development/2020/apr/28/calamitous-domestic-violence-set-to-soar-by-20-during-global- lockdown-coronavirus

Gannes, L. (2010). The Short and Illustrious History of Twitter# Hashtags. *Gigaom Blog.* https://gigaom.com/2010/04/30/the -short-and-illustrious-history- of-twitter-hashtags/.

Gillan, K., Pickerill, J. and Webster, F. (2008). *Anti-War Activism: New Media and Protest in the Information Age.* Basingstoke: Palgrave Macmillan.

Graham-Harrison, E., Giuffrida, A., Smith, H., & Ford, L. (2020). *Lockdowns around the world bring rise in domestic violence.* The Guardian. https://www.theguardian.com/society/2020/mar/28/lockdowns-world-rise-domestic-violence

Grewal, I., and Kaplan, C. (Eds.). (1994). *Scattered Hegemonies: Postmodernity and Transnational Feminist Practices.* Minneapolis: University of Minnesota Press.

Grierson, J. (2020, April 15). *Domestic abuse killings 'more than double' amid Covid-19 lockdown.* The guardian. https://www.theguardian.com/society/2020/apr/15/domestic-abuse-killings- more-than-double-amid-covid-19-lockdown

Gupta A., & Stahl A. (2020) *For abused women, a pandemic lockdown holds dangers of its own.* New York Times. https://www.nytimes.com/2020/03/24/us/coronavirus-lockdown- domestic-violence.html

Haßler, J., Wurst, A. K., Jungblut, M., & Schlosser, K. (2021). Influence of the pandemic lockdown on Fridays for Future's hashtag activism. *New Media & Society.* 1-23. https://doi.org/10.1177/14614448211026575

Hesford, W. S. (2010). Cosmopolitanism and the geopolitics of feminist rhetoric. In E. E. Schell &

K. J. Rawson (Eds.), *Rhetorica in motion: Feminist rhetorical methods and methodologies,* (53-70). Pittsburgh: University of Pittsburgh Press.

Hesford, W. S., & Schell, E. E. (2008). Introduction: Configurations of transnationality: Locating feminist rhetorics. *College English, 70*(5), 461-470.

Hinsliff, G. (2020). *'The rapist is you!': Why a Chilean protest chant is being sung around the world.* The guardian. https://www.theguardian.com/society/2020/feb/03/the-rapist-is-you- chilean-protest-song-chanted-around-the-world-un-iolador-en-tu-camino

Hocks, M. (2009). Cyberfeminism intersects writing research: Studies in digital rhetoric. In K. Blair,

R. Gajjala, & C. Tulley (Eds.), *Webbing cyberfeminist practice: Communities, pedagogies, and social action,* (pp. 235-253). Cresskill, NJ: Hampton Press.

Hu, M. (2019). *TikTok teams up with UN Women to raise awareness about violence against women in India.* South China Morning Post. https://www.scmp.com/tech/apps- social/article/3040170/tiktok-teams-un-women-raise-awareness-about-violence-against- women?module=perpetual_scroll&pgtype=article&campaign=3040170

IWWAGE. (2020). Covid and women's livelihoods in India. https://iwwage.org/multimedia- webinar-covid-19-and-womens-livelihoods-in-india/

Jain, S. (2020). The Rising Fourth Wave: Feminist Activism on Digital Platforms in India. *ORF Issue Brief, 384,* 1-16.

Jane, E. (2017). Gendered cyberhate: a new digital divide?. In R. Massimo & G. W. Muschert (Eds.),

Theorizing digital divides (pp. 186-198). London: Routledge.

John, M. E. (2021). Feminism, sexual violence, and the times of# MeToo in India. In L. Fernandes (Ed.), *Routledge handbook of gender in South Asia* (pp. 335-350). London: Routledge.

Kahn, R., & Kellner, D. (2004). New media and internet activism: from the 'Battle of Seattle' to blogging. *New media & society,* 6(1), 87-95.

Kangere, M., Kemitare, J., & Michau, L. (2017). Hashtag activism: Popularizing feminist analysis of violence against women in the Horn, East and Southern Africa. *Feminist Media Studies, 17*(5), 899-902.

Kaplan C., Alarcon, N., and Moallem, M. (Eds.), (1999). *Between Woman and Nation: Nationalisms, Transnational Feminisms, and the State.* Durham: Duke University Press.

Kramarae, C. (2014). Web Science and Gender: The Languages of Technoscience Connections. In

J. Weber (Ed.), *Interdisziplinierung?: ZumWissenstransferzwischen den Geistes-, Sozial- und Technowissenschaften* (pp. 167-188). Bielefeld: transcript Verlag. https://doi.org/10.14361/transcript.9783839415665.167

Kurian, A. (2019). #StopThisShame, #GirlsAtDhaba, #WhyLoiter and more: women's fight against sexual harassment didn't start with #MeToo. *The conversation.* https://theconversation.com/stopthisshame-girlsat-dhaba-whyloiter-and-more- womens-fight-against-sexual-harassment-didnt-start-with-metoo-105711

Lee, Y. H., & Hsieh, G. (2013). Does slacktivism hurt activism? The effects of moral balancing and consistency in online activism. In *Proceedings of the SIGCHI conference on human factors in computing systems* (pp. 811-820), April 27 to May 2, Paris, France.

Lewis, H. (2020, March, 19). *The Coronavirus Is a Disaster for Feminism: Pandemics affect men and women differently.* The Atlantic. https://www.theatlantic.com/international/archive/2020/03/feminism-womens-rights- coronavirus-covid19/608302/

Losh, E. (2014). Hashtag Feminism and Twitter Activism in India. *Social Epistemology Review and Reply Collective* 3(12), 10-22.

Loza, S. (2016). Hashtag feminism, #SolidarityIsForWhiteWomen, and other #FemFuture. *Journal of Gender, News Media, and Technology* 5, 1–31. https:// doi.org/10.7264/N337770V.

Marwick, A. E., & Boyd, D. (2011). I tweet honestly, I tweet passionately: Twitter users, context collapse, and the imagined audience. *New media & society, 13*(1), 114-133.

McEwan, B., & Sobré-Denton, M. S. (2011). Virtual third cultures: Social media, cultural capital, and the creation of cultural spaces. In *Intercultural New Media Forum: Journal of International and Intercultural Communication, 4*, 252-258.

McLuhan, H. M. (1994, Originally published in 1964). *Understanding media: The extensions of man*. Cambridge, MA: MIT Press.

Mendoza, B. (2002). Transnational Feminisms in Question. *Feminist Theory, 3*(3), 295–314. Mohan, S. (2018). *12 million women across 110,000 Indian villages are becoming tech savvy,*

thanks to Internet Saathi. Yourstory. https://yourstory.com/2018/01/internet-saathi-impact- report/amp

Mohanty, C. T. (1988). Under Western eyes: Feminist scholarship and colonial discourses. *Feminist review, 30*(1), 61-88.

Mohanty, C. T. (1992). Feminist Encounters: Locating the Politics of Experience. In L. McDowell & J. Sharpe (Eds.), *Space, Gender, Knowledge: Feminist Readings* (pp. 94-110). London: Routledge.

Mohanty, C. T. (2003). Feminism without borders: Decolonizing theory, practicing solidarity.

Durham, NC: Duke University Press.

Morgan, R. (1984). Sisterhood is Global: the International Women's Anthology. NY: Doublday.

Munro, E. (2013). Feminism: a fourth wave? *Political Insight, 4*(2), 22–25.

Nadkarni, A. (2017). Transnational feminism. *Oxford bibliographies in literary and critical theory. New York, NY: Oxford University Press.* Retrieved from https://www. oxfordbibliographies.com/view/document/ obo-9780190221911 /obo-9780190221911-0006. xml.

Nanditha, N. (2021). Exclusion in #MeToo India: rethinking inclusivity and intersectionality in Indian digital feminist movements. *Feminist Media Studies*, 1-22.

Narayan, U. (1997) *Dislocating Cultures: Identities, Traditions, and Third World Feminism*. New York: Routledge.

OECD. (2001). *Bridging the digital Divide: Issues and policies in the OECD countries*. Paris: OECD.

Pain, P. (2020). "It took me quite a long time to develop a voice": Examining feminist digital activism in the Indian #MeToo movement. *New Media & Society, 23*(11), 3139-3155.

Patel, V. (2020). *Women, Labour and the Informal Sector*. https://www.youtube.com/watch?v=xXMeQwuMPTY

Paterson, N. (1992). Cyberfeminism. Electronic document at http://www.vacuum woman.com/CyberFeminism/ cf.txt

Phadke, S., Khan, S., & Ranade, S. (2011). *Why loiter?: Women and risk on Mumbai streets*. New Delhi: Penguin Books India.

Puhr, T. (2020, April 21). *Coronavirus is driving a domestic violence pandemic*. Devex. https://www.de- vex.com/news/opinion-coronavirus-is-driving-a-domestic-violence- pandemic-97028

Queen, M. (2008). Transnational feminist rhetorics in a digital world. *College English, 70*(5), 471- 489.

Rowe, C. J. (2008). Cyberfeminism in action: Claiming women's space in cyberspace. In S. Grey & M. Sawer (Eds.), *Women's movements* (pp. 148-160). London: Routledge.

Roy, S. (2016). Breaking the cage. *Dissent, 63*(4), 74-83.

Sebring, J. H. (2019). Hashtag feminism: Examining contemporary feminist concerns and social justice activism in a social media age. *Crossings*, (3), 49-62.

Shrivastava, B., Altstedter, A., & Chaudhary, A. (2018, October 23). *#MeToo's Twitter Gatekeepers Power a People's Campaign in India*. Bloomberg. Retrieved from https://www.bloomberg.com/news/articles/2018-10-22/-

metoo-s-twitter- gatekeepers- power-a-people-s-campaign-in-india

Siapera, E. (2017). *Understanding new media*. London: Sage Publications.

Torrens, K., & Riley, J. (2009). Women's studies 101: Online feminism in action. In K. Blair, R. Gajjala, & C. Tulley (Eds.), *Webbing Cyberfeminist Practice: Communities, pedagogies, and social action*, (pp. 207-34). Cresskill, NJ: Hampton Press.

Varghese, A.V. (2015). *Kerala Devaswom Chief Wants Machine to Scan Women for Purity at Sabarimala*. International Business Times, November 16. http:// www.ibtimes.co.in/kerala- devaswom-chief-wants-machine-scan-women- purity-sabarimala-654925.

Wajcman, J. (1991). *Feminism confronts technology*. Pennsylvania: Penn State University Press. White, C. (2017). *#WhyIMarch: People around the world explain why they attended The Women's*

March. BBC. https://www.bbc.co.uk/bbcthree/article/e7ab2d81-1c91-455a-a8a6- 3a8f9d861d7b

WHO. (2020). *Coronavirus disease (COVID-19): Violence against Women*. https://www.who.int/emergencies/diseases/novel-coronavirus-2019/question-and-answers- hub/q-a-detail/violence-against-women-during-covid-19?gclid=EAIaIQobChMI- P_Ct5z36QIVx00YCh1sEAV8EAAYAiAAEgI-C_D_BwE Accessed on 10 June 2020.

Xiong, Y., Cho, M., & Boatwright, B. (2019). Hashtag activism and message frames among social movement organizations: Semantic network analysis and thematic analysis of Twitter during the# MeToo movement. *Public Relations Review*, *45*(1), 10-23.

Zerbe Enns, C., Díaz, L. C., & Bryant-Davis, T. (2021). Transnational feminist theory and practice: An introduction. *Women & Therapy*, *44*(1-2), 11-26.

Websites/webpages mentioned https://inbreakthrough.org/ https://www.blanknoise.org/home https://www.heforshe.org/en

https://www.mvbz.fu-berlin.de/en/ueber-uns/dokumentation-eigener-veranstaltungen/20200623- 0714-transnational-feminist-dialogues-in-times-of-corona-crisis/index.html https://www.womensweb.in/http://www.therealmard.org/, https://twitter.com/mardofficial?lang=en

ENDNOTES

[1] Dr. Sutanuka Banerjee is an Assistant Professor in the Department of Humanities and Social Sciences, National Institute of Technology Durgapur in India. She obtained her PhD from the Department of Culture and Global Studies, Aalborg University, Denmark. Her research areas focus on Popular Culture, Gender Studies and Literature. She has presented several papers in international conferences in India and abroad and contributed book chapters in edited volumes by national and international publishers. She has also published papers in reputed journals.

[2] Lipika Kankaria is presently pursuing PhD in the Department of Humanities and Social Sciences, National Institute of Technology Durgapur, India. She has obtained her Bachelors' and Masters' degrees in English Literature from Calcutta University. Her research interests include Gender Studies and Colonial and Postcolonial Literature. She has presented several papers in international conferences in India and abroad as well as contributed book chapters in edited volumes.

CHAPTER 7

Reflections on Queer Literary Representations in Contemporary Indian Writing in English

Aakanksha Singh[1]

ABSTRACT

This reflection piece explores the importance of thinking beyond labels and categories for queer desires and queer expressions of love. Knowability and visibility of these desires through labels and categories has the potential and indeed does create awareness. This visibility, however, can inadvertently also create borders and perpetuate rigidity about queer desires, confining them to certain norms and limitations. The piece then reflects on mass media's role in creating these borders, particularly through the coverage of Pride Parades in India. Then by examining contemporary texts such as Amruta Patil's Kari (2008), Himanjali Sankar's Talking of Muskaan (2015) and Parvati Sharma's short story, "The Quilt," (2010) the piece argues how nuanced literary representations in contemporary Indian writing can allow readers to look beyond those labels and imagine myriad possibilities, leading to what Spivak calls, "sustained uncoercive rearrangement of desires". However, the article then concludes that existence of a body of literary work mustn't lead to complacency but to broadening of horizons and forging avenues for formation of queer literary writing in India through diverse forms: one example of this is bringing intersectional queer political themes within the ambit of literature as well.

Introduction

Queer visibility has been a significant aspect of asserting the right to merely exist in India, which becomes more so true for queer women. When the then Chief Minister of Maharashtra, Manohar Joshi stated that Deepa Mehta's film, *Fire* (1996), was "alien to our culture," it erased a reality of queer desire among Indian women (Jain and Raval n.pag.). Media's focus on these queer desires has been sporadic, often sensational or what Ashwini Sukthankar calls, "like scattered fireworks" that emphasise on events such as suicides or marriages of queer women (xv). While Sukthankar talked about media reportage in the 1990s' the trend has continued well into the 21st century where reports, albeit in a slightly optimistic manner instead of using a startling or surprising tone, continue to highlight expressions of these desires solely through heteronormative events such as marriage. These occasional news reports do bring in an iota of comprehension around queer desires, yet because of the patchy nature of the reports, they simultaneously also continue to 'other' these desires and frame their perception through distinct normative structures and connotations. In this reflection piece, I would therefore take a moment to think about how media reports coloured my own awareness about what queer desires mean and placed it into narrow confines. Using that as a jumping-off point, I argue then that literary representation of Indian women's queer desires in contemporary Indian writing can allow for what Gayatri Spivak terms as "sustained uncoercive rearrangement of desires" ("A Conversation" 615). What I put forward is that nuanced literary representations lead to such a rearrangement enabling individuals to look beyond and push against the borders of categories and connotations of queerness and the expression of desires. The literary representations can reorient the way individuals think of queerness to being borderless which makes room for exploring different queer subjectivities.

Invisibility Through Visibility

Putting the spotlight and creating awareness about queer individuals in India happened not only through erratic focus by media outlets but also through binary gender divides. Queer activism in India gained ground in 1990s' and is "inseparable from the history of neoliberalism, nongovernmental organizations (ngos), the politics and anti-politics of development, and the agendas of a modernizing state and a transnational public health apparatus" (Dave 10 - 11). Indian queer activism directed the media's attention particularly toward gay men and the issues associated with the spread of HIV/AIDS (Misra 22).

While it was transnational queer activism that concentrated on gay men's rights and violations, it was most possibly the vehement attack on the film, *Fire,* mainly by Hindu Right forces in 1990s' that led to an outpouring of outrage by queer women activists and members of different queer women's organisations, compelling them to show up and make themselves known. Hence, the placard proclaiming the two allegedly incongruous identities, "Indian and Lesbian" at the candlelight vigil in 1998 at Delhi's Regal cinema against the crackdown of the film, *Fire,* has become iconic (Dave 138). The conflation of two hitherto incompatible identities on this placard directly challenged not only the assumptions around what constitutes 'Indian' culture but also the alleged non-existence of queer women in India.

This new focus and visibility brought in repeated accusations from politicians and activists alike that queerness is a Western influence on Indian culture. The global and translational origins of this activism do not help in tackling these accusations. Moreover, the influence of global discourse on queer rights and activism is seen in the proliferation of Pride Parades in India. The first one was held in 1999 in Kolkata what was then named as Calcutta. This event was more like a walk than a Pride Parade, with participation of 15 men (Periwal n.pag.). After this event, Pride Parades have taken place in major metropolitan cities in India and since 2010 onward have been organised in smaller towns as well.

Pride Parades and Me

Pride Parades are a pivotal point for queer individuals and allies to exhibit their presence and continuing fight for their rights. The Parades do form a salient space for challenging the heteronormative structures of desire and love by expressing a plurality of desires. Needless to say, they bring in visibility and recognition, which is crucial in a nation that continues to arrange its socio-economic systems around heteronormativity. However, this positive visibility "curdles into representation" when media coverage, (both tv news channel and newspaper reports) though vital, diminishes the plurality of expressions within the Pride Parade to specific stereotypes about queer subjectivities: it is colourful, loud and flamboyant (Brighenti 333). Until I read books featuring queer characters, that was what I thought about queerness too. It seemed like an artifice, a performance, just a spectacle. Pride Parades perhaps need that quality of being a spectacle because "the spectacle is an *affirmation* of appearances" (Debord 9; emphasis in original). For much too long, queer individuals in India perpetually encountered only shame, ostracisation or denial and putting up a space such as the parade would offer an opportunity to celebrate themselves, their appearances and revel in the visibility never bestowed on them. The Pride Parade, indeed, do magnificently create a space where queerness could be voiced and proclaimed, yet the media coverage to a large extent reduced that space to nothing but a spectacle that only articulated and, in a way, emphasised upon selected appearances alone. The selected images propounded notions about how queer individuals looked like externally, perhaps unintentionally seeking to postulate certain us versus them narratives. The concentration on exteriority in these images solidifies that narrative that there are differences not just innate ones but also external ones: that somehow queer individuals will look, behave and function differently from those who are not queer. Why must these lines, these borders be drawn at all?

The media's endorsement of selective images often led to "a visible *negation* of life - a negation that has taken on *a visible form*" (Debord 9; emphasis in original). In my case, the visible form of negation came because I refused to participate in the Pride Parades as they had come to symbolise merely a one-sided representation that I could not inhabit. In retrospect, I think I felt that negation of life because when watching the coverage of the Parades on TV channels, I never felt connected to it, never understood the depth of the jubilation. My negation then took on the visible form of disconnectedness. Guy Debord adds that a negation leads to a further hierarchising of particular appearances and ways of being such that the spectacle becomes "a court where no one is allowed to speak" (12 – 13). Hence, though the Pride Parades in various Indian cities and towns were a uniquely 21st- century celebration, when reduced to a spectacle, they did not feel freeing to me by any measure. Questions running in my head remained unanswered and in the hierarchy of appearances in the Parade spectacle, it did not seem the questions would find a voice to speak or articulate themselves. Did queerness, its desires and subjectivities always mean out there and loud, or imply a more colourful attitude? What would it mean for it to be introverted and queer? In hindsight, I believe I felt what Suparna Bhaskaran refers to as "Curdled Otherness", because I was constantly trying to fit into versions of what others thought queerness is and should be (15). Supurna Bhaskaran uses this term to refer to people of colour in the US anthropology field and how for them, it is solely their race that marks their work and that it is the only category in which they are made to feel paradoxically caught between and having to justify their work through that constantly. In the scenario outlined about Pride Parades though, it wasn't colour or race that caused me to feel excluded and negated from those representations but on an analogous level, those media representations and their focus on certain symbols and moments of the Pride Parade, led me to feel constricted by those symbols, categories such that I felt that I could never belong. The negation was compounded because I perpetually failed to "recognize the potential limitations of using insider versus outsider in any pure organic sense" (Bhaskaran 15-16). It has only been a very gradual enlightenment (ironic, isn't it?) that has finally allowed me to understand how both differences and sameness will always exist simultaneously and it is important to grasp the potential and limitations of both these realities.

Here, I would like to mention briefly, that I do not have the same wariness for Pride Parades as I did earlier. I think I have learnt how and why they are essential, particularly in fomenting ties and communal spaces. Moreover, Pride Parades and other forms of activism have enabled greater acceptance of queer identities in India, legally, socially and often on individual and familial levels. Initially though, Pride Parades used to seem alien and something I could never connect to, simply because I didn't see myself as this flamboyant out-there person who could flaunt anything, let alone sexuality. I didn't possess a show-off kind of personality in general, and I wouldn't know how to do that in a Pride Parade. Images of the Parades streamed on news channels and appeared in the newspapers. These images focused on the joyousness of the occasion and its participants and of course the vibrancy of it, because there existed an association of the Parade with the rainbow and hence the colours were possibly emphasised. All this just only achieved in creating a disconnect because those were the only signs concentrated upon which is why such curdled representations had evacuated Pride Parades of any plurality of desires, expressions. I could not see myself fit neatly into that colourful and joyous crowd because I was still learning and understanding the various subtleties of my own self.

Going Beyond the Law

This is also where Spivak's conception of humanities as being about "sustained uncoercive rearrangement of desires" holds true ("A Conversation" 615). What she asserts by this is that quick solutions require sustainable and ceaseless work alongside, and the rearrangement she supports is one of understanding the importance of this work. Not just desiring an easy, stopgap solution but shifting that desire to acknowledge that a long road is ahead, even after the stopgap solution is implemented. One can think about laws through Spivak's paradigm that though changing laws is necessary, it shouldn't be the only recourse to change. In 2009, the Supreme Court of India decriminalised homosexuality by reading down the archaic Section 377. This verdict was appealed by private individuals and groups which eventually led to the regressive recriminalising of homosexuality by the Supreme Court in 2013. Five years later, the Supreme Court in a landmark judgement read down Section 377 (Dixit 1022). A reading down means that the entire Section 377 has not been struck down, but the part that criminalised consensual sexual acts has been declared as unconstitutional as it is "violative of Articles 21, 14 and 15 of the Constitution." (India Supreme Court 3). The provisions of Section 377 that criminalise non-consensual sex between adults, intercourse with minors and bestiality continue to remain applicable (India Supreme Court 46). These legal pronouncements undoubtedly led to moments of celebration and an eager expectation about changes that could now be ushered in among the population about desires different from heteronormative ones. Pride Parades are just one example of those moments of celebration.

However, the changes that laws bring do not happen overnight and sometimes, as seen in the 2013 verdict, laws can stand "ready to revert any moment" (Spivak "Can There be a Feminist World?" n.pag.). Hence, at this point, I must mention that I wholeheartedly agree with Spivak that it is fields within the humanities that can do the requisite slow, steady work of bringing about that reorientation in the mindsets and attitudes of the public. The desire for change shouldn't just simply be that the law is enforced fairly, but the rearrangement should be one where more long-term work is envisioned, one which involves imagining "the borderlessness that attends to borders" (Spivak "A Borderless World?" 47). In the case of Section 377 and queerness, the long-term work should therefore continue to labour toward imagining and giving life to a borderlessness of non-heteronormative desires rather than resorting to confining those desires solely inside certain categories and letters. Though the categories, like the legal verdicts, are beneficial in their own rights, they can and do, especially abetted by media representations, proliferate stereotypes, connotations and empty symbolisms too. They can generate borders and boundaries of paradoxically both belonging and non-belonging (the latter was the case with me!), by including individuals who can keep up certain appearances and excluding those who don't or cannot. The terms and media representations of queerness manufacture a forced kind of otherness, that also paradoxically is what upholds heterosexuality as an ideal, as a natural occurrence: "the signification of heterosexuality is made possible not simply by motivated analogy but through motivated opposition as well". (Baset 94). The exteriority that viewers and readers gaze at through media representations can thus become pregnant with reductive meaning/s and present a clear exposition of how queerness must be different from the natural, the so-called heteronormative. This is another reason for that disconnect that I felt from Pride Parades because of the reductive representations: I was made to feel othered when I felt that I just want to be; that I just am. I am no 'other' but was coerced to believe exactly that.

Should terms and representations be absolutely abolished then? When James Baldwin mentions in an interview to Richard Goldstein about his fantasy where, "No one will have to call themselves gay" and of course his idealist notion is in relation to United States of America, he does not automatically imply that it is easy to escape the limitations of language (73). Still, what continues to remain important is both accepting language's limitations and its function of tying you to a specific language just so that the one section of the population can validate their own existence, but also accepting that these limitations do not always entail enacting stereotypical iterations of queerness and its desires. Thus, though the Pride Parades form a focal point, and though the 2018 Supreme Court verdict was exceptionally historical, my own imagination and insights that queerness can go beyond designated borders occurred only when I read books that featured queer characters, who explored their desires and difference quietly and slowly and not necessarily always in outward, external manners. Those fictional characters, rather than the selected images broadcasted on the media, seemed more realistic and closer to how I felt and explored my own difference/s.

Chughtai's Urdu short story "Lihaaf" or the translated version in English titled, "The Quilt", introduced me for the first time to how desires different from a heterosexual one can exist. While it was when I read Shyam Selvadurai's *Funny Boy* and a translation, *Cobalt Blue* by Sachin Kundalkar, translated from Marathi to English by Jerry Pinto, that a series of epiphanies erupted within my mind about how it's alright to not burst onto a scene of visibility immediately, how desires can take their course in their own time and yes, how your feelings and sexuality are fluid. Chughtai's "The Quilt" is the only one in the aforementioned texts that depicts or rather brusquely hints at two women's sexual escapades beneath the quilt, but the story is set in a completely different milieu. These three texts formed the beginnings of my exploration into a world away from the limelight of mainstream media's conceptions of queerness.

Literary Representations that Embraced a Borderlessness

It was a random bookshop browsing stint that led me toward Amruta Patil's *Kari* (2008). I felt a heady mix of excitement because firstly, I randomly came across the book; secondly it was a graphic novel that was produced by a local writer and artist; and lastly, when I began reading it, I found out that the story was of a queer relationship between two characters, Ruth and Kari. It was a thrilling feeling to know that this was not just an indigenous graphic novel by a woman but also that the story was about a queer relationship. It was contemporary and chronicled the multiple realities of Kari who lived in Mumbai. The dominant colour tones that Patil uses in the graphic novel are grey, black and red. The former colours were ostensibly used by her to portray the grimness and pollution that perpetually engulfs Mumbai which she aptly renamed as 'Smog City'. They are far from the rainbow-coloured joyousness of the Pride Parades. Once again, I would like to add a caveat here that I am not some dour academic who wants queer individuals to live out their lives in some colourless smog city alone. Undoubtedly, there are moments of colour, of fantasy and joyousness in all queer lives and Patil also captures this in her graphic novel through the bursts of colour especially when the eponymous character thinks of her partner, Ruth. Moreover, the narrative showcases the character inhabiting spaces other than that of protest or demonstration. Kari works in an advertising agency and her close colleagues are aware of her relationship with Ruth. The same is true of Kari's flatmates. Patil also shows a glimpse of a younger Kari watching the singer, k.d lang's 1997 Grammy performance and marvelling at the genderlessness of the performer. Patil presents a quiet reflective moment for the younger Kari who felt mute "with no way to explain myself to myself or to anyone else" (Patil 80). Yet despite Kari's avowed inability to explain herself, watching the performer evoked strong feelings within her. Patil, thus, creates a character in this graphic novel whose queer subjectivity is formed through personal and individual moments and in spaces that do not necessitate acceptance only though a visible coming-out moment or participation in other forms of visibility. Kari participates in and allows her queerness to be visible through her own means and her own agency.

Therefore, representation matters, not curdled representations but vibrant and varied ones because a multiplicity in representation allows for subjectivities, including queer ones to form through a plethora of means and not through a set-in-stone means alone. Kari's different ways of showcasing her queerness helped me to understand how inhabiting a category need not mean you must box yourself inside a checklist set up by outside forces. While categories are important for administrative and legal processes, there should be occasions and moments for unboxing oneself too. Literature can aid in this unboxing, particularly though diverse representations. Variation in representation gives the reader looking at those representations a chance to belong differently, to understand at their own pace and to know how to navigate their own desires and emotions. Literature may not be the panacea to problems faced by queer individuals in India and may not always bring in social justice movements to fruition. But it still possesses the potential and power to steer and initiate silent, quieter moments of resistance.

For example, in Himanjali Sankar's 2013 Young Adult (YA) novel, *Talking of Muskaan*, Sankar depicts two female characters, Muskaan and Aaliya. The former is sure of her queerness while the latter is just beginning to understand the myriad shades of how her desires and attractions operate. Sankar portrays Aliya, through negotiations and reflections, coming to a tenuous clarity of her attractions being based on the person, rather than the sex. With this, Sankar then can throw light on the fluidity of sexual attraction and that queerness need not necessarily always be an innate feature. In an interview, Sankar, notes that she received feedback from a teenager that the book helped them understand their "own sexual orientation" (Banerjee 170).

Furthermore, Sankar has deftly utilised the setting of the 2013 Supreme Court decision to emphasise on how broader legal discourses impact the way young adults view relationships and categories of sexualities. For example, in the text, when Aliya's family discusses the Supreme Court's decision, Aliya's earlier clarity about accepting her varied attractions coagulates to vitriolic hate toward queerness. This hate is manifested when, over a phone call, she viciously brands Muskaan, her best friend, as a criminal too: "You know that you're a criminal? That you should really be in jail? You do know that right?" (Sankar 138). This climactic moment negates Aliya's earlier clarity about her own desires and the reader is bemused about whether Aliya would also label herself as a criminal in the light of the Supreme Court judgement.

The transformation of Aaliya's thoughts and actions from clarity to ironic cruelty toward Muskaan unpeels the burgeoning influence of homophobia. This one moment, one slip toward hate by Aaliya leads to damaging consequences for Muskaan. Furthermore, throughout the narrative, Sankar shows that Muskaan was horridly bullied by her school and classmates as rumours about her queer desires spread among them. Muskaan's bullying is another example of the vicious and vice like grip heteronormativity has within urban Indian societies. It is so prominent, that despite Aaliya accepting her fluidity earlier, she still reconciles to training herself to be heteronormative, "I could let the boy attractions grow [...]. It would make life that much easier if I could just do that" (100). Her declaration immediately follows the clarity she had which is why I termed her clear comprehension of her desires as momentary and tenuous. The momentariness abets her easy transformation toward hate for Muskaan, in spite of her avowal of her queerness. Sankar's tackling of the sensitive issue of how young adults navigate relationships and their queer attractions is commendable. The representations in her novel not only allow the readers to discern the nuances of and the problems of heteronormativity but also hold up a mirror to social mores and legislations that make heterosexuality normative in India.

Chughtai in her short story "The Quilt" had slipped into the narrative the existence of different forms of desire (although much debated whether what is portrayed is healthy sexual desire or a desire stemming from depraved self-loathing). Parvati Sharma's retelling of the story (also titled "The Quilt") highlights an acceptance of queer love among women. While Chughtai only insinuated at the potential of the two women characters underneath the quilt to be engaged in sexual activity, Sharma portrays precisely that in all its glory: two women making love to each other underneath the quilt and conversing and debating about Chughtai's original short story itself. This trajectory from the 1940s to 2010, exhibits the vast changes that conceptions and representations around queerness has gone through. Chughtai was charged for obscenity by the British Indian government in 1944 for merely hinting at a homosexual love (Sukthankar xiv). Sharma wasn't. Not that this should make us all complacent and blindly believe that yes being queer is now accepted, particularly with the regressive turn in Indian politics that are premised on divide and rule policies and on hate. But my intent in highlighting this retelling by Sharma, is to emphasise on how her positive representation is itself quite invigorating since it focuses on the sexual aspect of queer women's relationship; an aspect that is often missing because of the predominant use of the metaphors of friendships that are deemed more acceptable when comprehending queer women's relationships.

These are just three examples of how literary representations of queer women characters in contemporary Indian writing can enable diverse imaginations of queer desires' expressions and of living queerly. José Esteban Munoz notes, "Queer cultural production is both an acknowledgment of the lack that is endemic to any heteronormative rendering of the world and a building, a 'world making,' in the face of that lack" (118). Denial of queer existence was a norm so deeply entrenched that it emboldened political representatives (as in the case of the film, *Fire*) to make blanket statements about its non-existence, about its nothingness within India. Aided by transnational economic and cultural flows, Pride Parades emerged to proffer one form of world building. However, it is literary representations that have gone beyond the worlds constructed by those spaces, stretched the borders further, jettisoned stereotypes into the sea, so that newer ways of thinking about queerness and queer desires can arise and continue the process of reorienting and pushing perceptions about what queer lives can be.

Ashwini Sukthankar in the "Introduction" of the edited collection, *Facing the Mirror: Lesbian Writing from India*, exhorts the readers and queer women to refrain from thinking about silence and invisibility as a safe haven that allows for queer desires to blithely exist without any questions asked. She notes: "Silence is a zone we inhabit on sufferance. Easily invaded, easily demolished, it leaves us at the mercy of people who can simply choose whether or not to know and care" (xv). Yet Sukthankar's call for more visibility and claiming of public spaces is balanced on careful considerations of what those prior silences can also offer and have built over the course of time. Consequently, she furthermore emphasises on "how to negotiate an alternative" rather than only resolutely decide to "relinquish the safety of silence" (xviii). What the fiction texts discussed earlier also do, is throw light on formations of queer subjectivities, precisely at those gaps where visibility and coming out is not a solution at all or not within the framework of being, of existing; or where a flamboyance performative stance alone does not always validate one's existence. The authors' portraiture of the characters in those texts accomplishes a combination of both reclaiming public spaces but doing so also through alternatives that the characters negotiate at their own time and pace rather than by imbibing categories that can tend to fossilise into the universal and hence become exclusionary.

Literary representation must avoid falling foul of this tendency to crystallise categories into set definitions. Instead, it must continue playing with the amorphousness that is inherent within the terms and continue to "make up genealogies and worlds" (Munoz 121). It is actually easier to envision the indeterminacy of these terms as Akhil Katyal shows in his analysis where he lays bare that the definitions of what constitutes 'gay' or 'lesbian' writing are by their very nature amorphous. One instance where he demonstrates this is when he mentions about Hoshang Merchant giving a call for this anthology on gay writing (which ultimately was published as *Yaarana: Gay Writing from India*), Merchant was clear on who could qualify as a gay writer: someone who is out as gay (Katyal 239). Yet over the course of editing the submissions, Katyal notes that the term 'gay' "itself metamorphosed into a more flippant version in Hoshang's head – gay-shay [...]" (Katyal 252). There was a blurring of that earlier seemingly crystal-clear understanding of what can be termed as a 'gay writer'. Both Sukthankar and Merchant acknowledge the slipperiness of the terms in their respective anthologies and this acknowledgement is a good point at which literary representations can help to understand the different inflections of queer subjectivities within India rather than only perceive them through a lens of a media and Pride Parade spectacle.

The Way Forward

So, what can representation do from here on? Has it achieved all that there is to achieve? Literary representations have assuredly taken the lead in bursting out of curdled media representations about queer individuals in general and queer women in particular. But perhaps now is the time to take a cue from the intersectionality of queer politics in India. A few queer activist organisations such as PRISM in New Delhi in the 2000s adopted an intersectional ethos to understand and parse the different axes of power such as caste, region, religion, language and sexuality that converge in India (Sharma and Nath 87). By adopting such an approach, queer politics in India intended to mitigate the presumption that sexuality issues are problems only organisations dealing with sexuality, and not other rights-based organisations, have to tackle. An intersectional approach permitted for a dismantling of an 'us versus them' paradigm that had earlier alienated queer activists from other movements in the 1990s in India.

However, this adoption of an intersectional ethos by queer activists has been criticised by Ashley Tellis for being "only at the level of words" and that nothing substantial has been done in this regard through solidarity for different movements and problems affecting several sections of Indian queer individuals together (Tellis 150). Tellis's criticism is valid because queer activism has often been confined to upper- and middle-class English-speaking people residing in metropolitan Indian cities. Though an intersectional approach is important, an invoking of a queer Indian community is not free from its own issues. "To invoke community is immediately to raise questions of belonging and of power" (Joseph xxiii). This is exactly what Tellis calls into question: to confront the power dynamics in these parades, groupings and queer communities that can be skewed toward a particular demographic alone. Communities can bring in that much needed and much coveted visibility, but they then allow for the proverbial double-edged sword to raise its ugly head as any form of community, any form of visibility does create certain curated exclusions and inclusions. For example, Naisargi Dave, remarks on how organisations such as Sakhi and Stree Sangam in 1990s and 2000s India forged the path to create communities for queer women. Yet the moment communities came into fruition, so did a plethora of divisions. In this case, it was based on how politically active the women were. This division, Dave termed as "the politically competent and the politically incompetent" (46). These two terms themselves speak of how women could be in either of these categories depending on different axes of privilege and power they had access to including time and mobility.

The fact that communities and visibility can give birth to such strange paradoxes does not in itself form a sound reason to thoroughly dismiss or devalue communities. But then, is there a solution at all then? Solutions are coming in slowly and surely. In terms of intersectionality of queer movements in India, some progressive strides are becoming slowly prominent with Pride Parades. Pride Parades are being held in smaller towns too and queer groups are using Pride Parades in recent years as a site to voice their dissent about pertinent issues such as protesting against the Citizenship (Amendment) Act (2019) and the Transgender Persons (Protection of Rights) Bill 2019 (Pathak n.pag.; Desai n.pag). Although, the Transgender Persons (Protection of Rights) Bill 2019 had a progressive provision of self-determination, the Bill mired this "right to self-perceived gender identity" in bureaucratic red tape as the Bill stipulated that an identity certificate must be obtained from the District Magistrate (India Lok Sabha 3). Thus, even though the bill was touted as bringing in much-needed change, protestors and activists called for more nuanced changes to the bill. Pride Parades offered a platform, in such cases, for dissenting voices.

Like nascent Indian queer activism of the 1990s and early 2000s, literary representations of queer women so far have also largely been limited to English writing, urban settings and middle- or upper-class characters. Along with a focus on amorphousness of queer subjectivities in literary representations, one direction that authors in India must take is to embrace intersectionality in their writing too. Authors from different backgrounds must write stories that speak of diverging identity intersections, how characters function and understand their differing realities through them. This is a need both in English and non-English speaking contexts or in contexts that inhabit more than one language. An intersectional approach in literary writing would have profound implications for undoing assumptions that queerness in India is a Western import alone and this may very well pave the way for establishing numerous more modes of queer subjectivities that aren't invariably rooted in visibility, globalisation and transnational hegemonies.

REFERENCES

Baldwin, James. "'Go The Way Your Blood Beats': An Interview with James Baldwin". Interview conducted by Richard Goldstein. *James Baldwin: The Last Interview and Other Conversations*, United States, Melville House Publishing, 2014, pp. 57-74.

Banerjee, Suchismita. "Engendering Identities: Gay and Lesbian Characters in Contemporary Indian English Young Adult Fiction". *Asian Children's Literature and Film in a Global Age*, edited by Bernard Wilson and Sharmani Patricia Gabriel, Palgrave Macmillan, 2020, pp. 157-175. https://doi.org/10.1007/978-981-15-2631-2.

Baset, Al, Zaid. "Section 377 and the Myth of Heterosexuality". *Jindal Global Law Review*, vol. 4, no. 1, Aug. 2012, pp. 89-109, completejusticepodcast.s3.ap-south-1.amazonaws.com/Zaid+Al+Baset+-+Section+377+and+the+Myth+of+Heterosexuality+.pdf. Accessed 25 Mar. 2021. PDF download.

Bhaskaran, Suparna. "The Evidence of Arrogant Experience: Boomerang Anthropology and Curdled Otherness". *Made in India: Decolonizations, Queer Sexualities, Trans/National Projects*, Palgrave Macmillan, 2004. pp. 15-35.

Brighenti, Andrea. "Visibility: A Category for the Social Sciences". *Current Sociology*, vol. 55, no. 3, May 2007, pp. 323–342, *Sage Journals*, https://doi.org/10.1177/0011392107076079. Accessed 26 Apr. 2021. PDF download.

Chughtai, Ismat. "The Quilt". *The Quilt: Stories*. Translated by M. Asaduddin, Penguin Books India, 2011.

Dave, Naisargi N. *Queer Activism in India: A Story in the Anthropology of Ethics*. Duke University Press, 2012. *JSTOR*, https://doi.org/10.1215/9780822395683. Accessed 12 Feb. 2021. PDF download.

Debord, Guy. *Society of the Spectacle*. Translated by Ken Knabb. London, Rebel Press, 2006.

Desai, Rajvi. "Anti-NRC-CAA Protest Is Changing What Pride Looks Like". *The Swaddle*, 04 Feb. 2020, www.theswaddle.com/pride-anti-nrc-caa-protests/. Accessed 16 Feb. 2022.

Dixit, Pratik. "Navtej Singh Johar v Union of India: Decriminalising India's Sodomy Law". *The International Journal of Human Rights*, vol. 24, no. 8, Routledge, 2020, pp. 1011–1030, https://doi.org/10.1080/13642987.2019.1690465.

India, Lok Sabha. The Transgender Persons (Protection of Rights) Bill, 2019. *loksabhaph.nic.in*, http://164.100.47.4/BillsTexts/LSBillTexts/PassedLoksabha/169-C_2019_LS_Eng.pdf, passed 05 Aug. 2019. Accessed 10 Jun. 2022. PDF download.

India, Supreme Court. *Navtej Singh Johar v. Union of India & Ors*. 06 Sept. 2018. Supreme Court of India Judgements, https://main.sci.gov.in/supremecourt/2016/14961/14961_2016_Judgement_06-Sep-2018.pdf. Accessed 24 Sep. 2021. PDF Download.

Jain, Madhu, and Sheela Raval. "Deepa Mehta's Film Fire Creates a Furore". *India Today*, 21 Dec. 1998, www.indiatoday.in/magazine/society-the-arts/films/story/19981221-controversial-film-fire-is-sent-back-to-censor-board-matter-taken-to-court-827561-1998-12-21. Accessed 24 Sep. 2021.

Joseph, Miranda. *Against the Romance of Community*. University of Minnesota Press, 2002. *ProQuest Ebook Central*. Accessed 17 Dec. 2021. PDF download.

Katyal, Akhil. *The Doubleness of Sexuality: Idioms of Same Sex Desire in India*. New Delhi, New Texts Publications, 2016.

Misra, Geetanjali. "Decriminalising Homosexuality in India". *Reproductive Health Matters*, vol. 17, no. 34, Nov. 2009, pp. 20-28. *Taylor and Francis Online*, https://doi.org/10.1016/S0968-8080(09)34478-X. Accessed 20 Dec. 2021. PDF download.

Munoz, Esteban José. *Cruising Utopia: The Then and There of Queer Futurity*. 10th Anniversary Ed., New York University Press, 2019.

Pathak, Sushmita. "India Just Passed a Trans Rights Bill. Why Are Trans Activists Protesting It?" *NPR*, 04 Dec. 2019, www.npr.org/sections/goatsandsoda/2019/12/04/784398783/india-just-passed-a-trans-rights-bill-why-are-trans-activists-protesting-it. Accessed 16 Feb. 2022.

Patil, Amruta. *Kari*. New Delhi, HarperCollins Publishers India, 2008.

Periwal, Priyanka. "The Friendship Walk: India's First Pride March In 1999". *Homegrown*, 29 Jun. 2021, www.homegrown.co.in/article/805527/the-friendship-walk-india-s-first-pride-march-in-1999. Accessed 26 Feb. 2021.

Sankar, Himanjali. *Talking of Muskaan*. Chennai, Duckbill Books, 2014.

Sharma, Jaya, and Dipika Nath. "Through the Prism of Intersectionality: Same Sex Sexualities in India". *Sexuality, Gender and Rights: Exploring Theory and Practice in South and Southeast Asia*, edited by Geetanjali Misra and Radhika Chandiramani, Sage Publications, 2005, pp. 82-98.

Sharma, Parvati. "The Quilt". *Dead Camel and Other Stories of Love*. E-book ed., Zubaan, 2010. EPUB.

Spivak, Gayatri Chakravorty. "A Borderless World?". *Conflicting Humanities*, edited by Rosi Braidotti, and Paul Gilroy, Bloomsbury Academic, 2016, pp. 47-60.

--. "A Conversation with Gayatri Chakravorty Spivak: Politics and the Imagination". Interview conducted by Jenny Sharpe. *Signs: Journal of Women in Culture and Society*, vol. 28, no. 2, The University of Chicago Press, 2003, pp. 609-624, *JSTOR*, https://doi.org/10.1086/342588.

--. "Can There be a Feminist World?" *Public Books*, May 2015, www.publicbooks.org/can-there-be-a-feminist-world/.

Sukthankar, Ashwini. "Introduction". *Facing the Mirror: Lesbian Writing from India*. Penguin Books India, 1999.

Tellis, Ashley. "Disrupting the Dinner Table: Re-thinking the 'Queer Movement' in Contemporary India". *Jindal Global Law Review*, vol 4, no. 1, 2012, pp. 142-156. completejusticepodcast.s3.ap-south-1.amazonaws.com/Ashley+Tellis+-+Disrupting+the+Dinner+Table+-+Re-thinking+the+Queer+Movement+in+Contemporary+India.pdf. Accessed 13 Apr. 2021. PDF download.

ENDNOTES

1 Aakanksha Singh is a second-year PhD student at University of York, UK. Her research focuses on love between queer women characters in contemporary Indian fiction written by women. She can be contacted through her email address: aakanksha.singh@york.ac.uk

CHAPTER 8

Visiting the House of Bad's Mother: Queering Saadat Hasan Manto's "Thanda Gosht"

Namita Goswami[1]

ABSTRACT

This essay reads Saadat Hasan Manto's short story, "Thanda Gosht" (1950), depicting women's experience of sectarian brutality during the 1947 partition of India and Pakistan, to delineate the postcolonial significance Gayatri Spivak's concept of originary queerness. Manto's synecdoche ("cold meat") for an unnamed and raped female corpse, her Sikh abductor and violator, *as well as* for the story's readers, (re)figures reproductive heteronormativity as a process of unknowing that emplaces a gendered taxonomy, even when its victims are silent. Rather than reinforce sexual difference as a *finished* itinerary, however, Kulwant Kaur's repeatedly piercing question—*who* she *is*—queers "Thanda Gosht" by taking us to a "she" who we cannot imagine but *seem* to know. *This* tarrying with originary queerness "*in its place*" (Spivak, "Gender" 817, emphases added) dockets an unpredictable futurity made especially resonant by the chill that asseverates from Ishar's Singh's use of a peculiar affective idiom to describe his encounter with the unnamed and raped corpse, whose originary queerness inverts a teleological trajectory to manifest (the fight for) Nation as (visiting) "burre ki ma ka ghar" (बुरे की माँ के घर; the house of Bad's mother). *This* place, far from patriarchal honor and protection, makes a "zaalim" (ज़ालमि; bloodthirsty) of ("us") all, such that we cannot say what happened.

Introduction

> When the subaltern speaks, the world of knowing is moved.
>
> *(Josie Arnold, "The Un-named" 19)*

> Women's story is not the substance of great narratives. But women are curious, they have a knack for asking the outsider's uncanny questions, even though they are not encouraged to take credit for what follows.
>
> *(Gayatri Spivak, Outside 72)*

I. Subalternity → → Heterogeneity → → Originary Queerness

For Gayatri Spivak, the concept of originary queerness is one she cannot yet theorize. Such an inveterate dearth of aptitude seemingly reverses the course of critical inquiry. Although concepts are those concentrations of understanding that convey and uphold lived experience, originary queerness nonetheless divulges a palpable maladroitness. In a spot paradoxically mapped by an *incapacity* to refurbish a backstory, lives the heterogeneity that stays undecipherable, albeit while located in an assiduously interpellated lifeworld. Because lived experience cathects reproductive heteronormativity as a naturalized cultural logic (father, daughter, mother, son, etc.), originary queerness, in missing a commensurate "what happened," affects a curious freedom: "one cannot imagine what one seems to know" (Spivak, "Gender" 826). This essay reads Saadat Hasan Manto's short story, "Thanda Gosht" (1950), which depicts the sectarian brutality visited upon women during the partition of India and Pakistan in 1947, to delineate the postcolonial significance of originary queerness. I suggest that Manto's synecdoche ("cold meat"), for an unnamed and raped female corpse, her Sikh abductor and violator, *as well as* for the story's readers, (re)figures reproductive heteronormativity as a process of unknowing that emplaces a gendered taxonomy, even when its victims are silent.[2] In lieu of reinforcing sexual difference as a *finished* itinerary for the story's speaking parts, Kulwant's repeatedly piercing question—*who* she *is*—to Ishar Singh (much like the "kirpan" [करिपान; sword] she appends to kill her lover) queers "Thanda Gosht" by taking us full circle outside a suburban hotel room, where we encounter a "she" who we cannot imagine but *seem* to know. *This* tarrying with originary queerness "*in its place*" (817, emphases added) dockets an unpredictable futurity made especially resonant by the chill that asseverates from the story's "beginning"/"before" to its equally ignominious "end"/"after"[3]

In the following, I provide a few examples to show that Spivak's concept of the subaltern is conventionally grasped as a generalized negativity without a standpoint.[4] Due to the subaltern's irretrievable heterogeneity, our inevitably palimpsestic attempts at retrofitting a moot ventriloquism are only made possible by (once again) assuming a role in her gendering.[5] As such, if we understand this irretrievable heterogeneity as originary queerness, then, as Spivak contends, "what had seemed the historical predicament of the colonial subaltern can be made to become the allegory of the predicament of *all* thought, *all* deliberative consciousness" (Spivak, *Other* 204).

Secondly, I contest the reduction of subalternity to a deconstructive reading practice that offers inconclusiveness as a panacea, an ideological compensation for the overdetermined episteme of Europe and Its Others. Precisely because originary queerness cannot be circumscribed as merely an oppositional diagnostic and/or corrective stance, we may posit a heuristic metonymy: if proper postcoloniality is not native informancy but an excavation of foreclosure, then "writ[ing] the theoretically impossible ... self that is no more than an effect of a structural resistance to irreducible heterogeneity" (Spivak, *Other* 16) may yield an affective idiom that belies (a) *relationship* at ground level. In other words, originary queerness—what is diverse, dissonant, multiplicitous, manifold—stakes a claim to the constructive frame by conveying and upholding a non-antagonistic understanding of difference and, hence, enables "a modest shift from negation and interdiction to imagination" (Varadharajan, "Figure and Ground" 742).

Third, I suggest that the hermeneutic homology established here between subalternity, heterogeneity, and originary queerness calls forth a dexterity to mind a gap. Whereas cathecting the sanctioned descriptions allocated via reproductive heteronormativity turns an unnamed and raped female corpse into Kulwant's "sautan" (सौतन; the other woman), a "chudel" (चुड़ैल; demon-vamp), a "haramzadi" (हरामज़ादी; despicable, unholy, female bastard of a prostitute), a "bhadvi" (भड़वी; lady-pimp), "teri ma" (तेरी माँ; a beholden, emasculated Ishar's mother), or "meva" (मेवा; fruit), then Ishar's affective idiom as a not-yet-storied emergent—he calls the unnamed and raped female corpse "insaan kudiya" (इंसान कुड़यिा; human-girl) before he, too, turns into, and turns "us" into, "thanda gosht" (ठंडा गोश्‌त; cold meat)—can perhaps "*cross* identity" (Spivak, "Gender" 824) to secure some room to breathe. Specifically, the dearth of "what happened"—that is, the originary queerness of the "she" that is (now) "thanda gosht" (ठंडा गोश्‌त; cold meat), living beyond the *scene* of "life"—empowers the very "zinda lahu" (ज़निदा लहू; alive-blood), "ang" (अंग; organs), and "boti boti" (बोटी-बोटी; fleshy bones) that bespeak an effortful "storying of the vanishing present" (820). Such a proleptic act of attrition, however, as absurdly predicated on deficiency and lack, can *only* manifest for "an impossible readership" (824), for when we (or once we) get to originary queerness *in its place*, rather than to (different) places already mapped, it will (always) have been.

In the fourth section, I suggest that Manto's "Thanda Gosht" figures *how* originary queerness differs from meticulous information retrieval expressly by dint of the dismal fate of the unnamed and raped corpse. As an aperture for the irretrievable heterogeneity (that lives) apart from the story's "beginning" and "end" and, hence, *in* an illocutionary "before" and "after" (to be) perennially possessively memorialized as Ishar and *his* victim, "thanda gosht" (ठंडा गोश्‌त; cold meat) inverts a clandestine hotel room (in which we are also trapped) to stage an ubiquitous originary queerness that does not *queer* places. In fact, *places* queer it. Drained of apposite manhood by necrophilia even prior to dying by his own "kirpan" (करिपान; sword), a prosthetic left in Kulwant's hands at the "end," Ishar's *lived* failure as his "baap ka tukham" (बाप का तुखम; created from his father's sperm) ruptures the identity-based matrix of reproductive heteronormativity. The affective idiom of "Thanda Gosht's" vernacular (originally written in Urdu, I read a Hindi translation) drains reproductive heteronormativity of its symbolic force to convey and uphold those snippets of undifferentiated experience ("what happened?") by which we are borne across as a "person among persons" (Spivak, "Touched" 102). And so, (our) "zinda lahu" (ज़निदा लहू; alive-blood) becomes less congruent with the nationalist parlance that writes us into place, and more conducive to a postcolonial narrativization that looks (out) for originary queerness *in its place*.

II. Ghosts and Spirits

In her examination of subalternity, Priyamvada Gopal maintains that Spivak endeavors to nudge the unwitting anti-humanists of the Subaltern Studies group towards a more formalized association with deconstruction When critiquing Spivak's essay, "Subaltern Studies: Deconstructing Historiography," which introduces the volume *Selected Subaltern Studies* (1988), she enjoins that Spivak brings "quite different constituencies and philosophical resonances ... into such close proximity that they can be folded into each other" ("Reading" 147). Gopal's circumspection about conflating positivism, metaphysics, essentialism, and humanism may be merited, but the criticism itself recognizes that Spivak's project goes beyond its *merely* socio-political dimension. This implicit concession is further evident in Gopal's eschewal of "crises of self-representation and self-knowledge [as] the stuff of generalizable proclamation" (149) and her tongue-in-cheek query whether the subaltern would be "subaltern (enough)" if she "told us of things other than ghosts and spirits" (158).

According to Gopal, Spivak's deconstructive emphasis promulgates a "false choice" (Gopal, "Reading" 149) between text (discursive) and essence (identity) at the expense of appreciable histories that discomfit easily digestible binaries. Instead, we must espouse "the far more difficult ... work of examining the complicated engagement of selves, societies, bodies, histories, events, memories, interests, and desires that goes into the making of both consciousness and action" (148). By asserting that in principle "almost anything" (149) may be regarded as a "displacing gesture" (149), she observes of Spivak's analysis of Bhubaneswari's *sati*/suicide,

What is remarkable ... is the complete elision of [her] life and agency *as a nationalist revolutionary* with an anguished relationship to the assassination mission she was asked—and found herself unable—to carry out ... [T]he young woman's consciousness and interests are reduced ... to a ... *singular* discourse of female sexuality. (150)

Gopal correctly states that Spivak mentions the cause of Bhubaneswari's deliberated act—her inability to commit a political assassination—almost parenthetically. If considered alongside the scene of her death "in her father's modest apartment" (Spivak, *Critique* 306), however, the seeming diminution of Bhubaneswari's public role, insofar as Spivak's reading exceeds the socio-political as an ablative case, suggests that she rebuts the terms of making history.

Indeed, quite a few years later, we become aware of her familial relationship with Bhubaneswari, as Spivak reveals that Bhubaneswari is "my foremother" ("Response" 235); she is her grandmother's sister. In fact, Spivak situates Bhubaneswari *in* a women's genealogy: "I inserted the singular suicide of my foremother into that gap between the reasonableness of theory and the urgency of the revolutionary moment ... She made me read situations where no response happens" (235). When speaking of these family women in "If Only" (2006)—that is, her mother, great grandmother, paternal grandmother, and her mother's aunts—Spivak affirms, "These are the women who bred me. I am nobody's mother" ("If Only") Invoking her mother's demise, Spivak mourns the loss of a very particular ("that") archive, of women *in* life, at the margins of reproductive heteronormativity: "That is my relationship with these women. I am their repetition, with a difference" ("If Only").

A statement (negatively) docketing futurity via a women's genealogy is abruptly followed by a matter-of-fact denouement: "I am nobody's mother." Such a stipulated conclusion, pronounced after a stirring evocation of "the women who bred me," underscores Spivak's concern with the pathos of her exquisite grief.[6] In *this* figuration of a historical archive, when Spivak bluntly breaks the continuity of motherhood, being nobody's mother (like Bhubaneswari) extols the repetition, with a difference, that is a singular life. It is this originary queerness that is double crossed by an insidious historical logic that cinches culture into place. Following the trace of this foreclosure, therefore, summons a *forfeited* history of family women who are nobody's mother, an apocryphal genealogy written with whatever life can be squeezed (out) from our cultural saturation—Bhubaneswari's menstrual blood, Ishar's necrophilia and exsanguination—to expropriate reproductive heteronormativity. *This* genealogy of family women engenders *that* archive that can frame the headings decreed by either public nationalism or private domesticity as *machineries* that "ruse over" (Spivak, *Other* 15) what is diverse, dissonant, multiplicitous, manifold—that is, originarily queer—to impel seamless commensurability.

Consequently, Gopal's suspicions of deconstruction may be well-founded but, as Spivak emphasizes, to "read no more than allegories of unreadability ... [is to] ignore the heterogeneity of the 'material'" (*Other* 29), which is ceaselessly *excised* from the frame of the encounter for the normalization of silence. In other words, excavating the foreclosure of originary queerness, through which we are situated *in* the field of inquiry, is not a phantasmagoric palliative but the very *possibility* for mobilizing difference. Since subalternity is engendered by a "deliberately fragmentary record produced elsewhere" (287), *for* resistance to be conceived (at all), we must chart the artifices that effectuate antithetical dramatis personae (to be) cathected for a specific kind of story to be told, *as if* these functions were the sum total of all possible deliberations.[7] Spivak thereby proffers subalternity as the "absolute limit of the place where history is narrativized into logic" (207) because originary queerness countermands how appended *logical predicates*—Bhubaneswari's alleged unrequited love, Ishar's "kirpan" (करिपान; sword)—supplant "specific historical conditions" (Gopal, "Reading" 149) for a *purposed* transcription that consolidates our utterly contingent lifeworlds. Accordingly, if institutionally validated forms of subjectivity and agency further perpetuate our instrumentalization, then disclosing their historical provenance, rather than ennobling symbolic vagaries and abstruse neologisms such as radical alterity, perforce demands looking (out) for originary queerness *in its place* for a cosmogonic peek at how a world is (un)made.

III. The Subaltern (is) Dead

Victor Li, when scrutinizing the Subaltern Studies collective, similarly objects to the subaltern's representation as a "utopian ideal" ("Necroidealism" 276): if the subaltern marks a categorical threshold for culturally hegemonic knowledge production, then the most true-to-life example of subalternity is the dead subaltern. The collective, moreover, for Li, spiritualizes this dead subaltern as a portal to "a utopian ... mode of life" (276). As Li avers, "precisely this 'absence' ... results in the paradoxical condition in which utopia and death are linked ... [T]he subaltern's death or disappearance enables [her] to fulfill the ideal role of the ... inappropriable other" (277). Counter to such "cryptonomy" (280), Li figures the subaltern as the keeper of secrets and protector of singularities. (He does not, however, elaborate on *how* the subaltern fulfills this responsibility.) [8]

By casting the subaltern as incontrovertibly unrepresentable, moreover, Spivak marshals a a "sacrificial logic" (Li, "Necroidealism" 280) that accedes to an emblematic scapegoat for the "reassurance of a political ideal" (280), which, in turn, occludes extant subaltern struggles: first, the ambivalence and range of subaltern resistance is measured by "an empirically emptied alterity" (280); second, subaltern insurgency is not necessarily native informancy or ventriloquism but may mark aspirational efforts for mainstream insertion[9]; third, instead of tragic heroism, subaltern dissent perhaps establishes a transitional space between abjection and inclusion. By synonymizing the aesthetic with the aporetic, therefore, Spivak's necroidealism (Li's titular neologism) ignores the subaltern's "dense and throbbing lifeworld" (284) to epitomize a tautology: the subaltern (*is*) dead; the dead (*is*) subaltern

But, in Li's rendition of this rather dismal *fort/da*—it is the very nature of the subaltern (to be) dead to be continuously summoned, the subaltern is first equated with the dead, and then equated with utopia; utopia, in turn, is equated with the aesthetic, which is equated with the political; and, finally, Li posits this metonymic chain—the dead subaltern is a utopic ideal whose aesthetic figuration constitutes political protest—as how Spivak understands the work of historiography. As a result, Li appears to render (the question of) subalternity moot: if the subaltern *must* die to be worthwhile, then real life referents are superfluous. Why would Spivak refer to Bhubaneswari Bhaduri's *sati*/suicide, or any other confounding situation, at all? This gratuitousness would relinquish the very "dense and throbbing lifeworlds" (Li, "Necroidealism" 284) that Li appropriately insists we must strive to recuperate. In other words, permissible accounts of subaltern death impede an encounter with originary queerness—(to be) deciphered in *how* the subaltern dies, today, on *this* side of being, and not by way of her ineluctably anonymized, virtually prismatic presence.[10]

The prominence Rajeswari Sunder Rajan also gives to death in subaltern resistance avoids such disproportional metaphysical footholds by focusing on the quandary that subalternity poses to knowledge production. Death ought to include the subaltern in our common humanity, but subalternity as a structural exigency prescribes attentiveness to "the *meaning* of ... a particular death [as it] traverses the boundary between the living and the dead" (Sunder Rajan, "Death" 117, emphasis added). Against anointing a consummate paragon of exploitation, Spivak instead probes the "affective and ethical responses" (119) that Bhubaneswari's *sati*/suicide instigates. In abjuring the quest for a backdated authentic voice or motive will, subalternity figures the failure of a speech-act rather than its absence altogether. In fact, Spivak unequivocally chooses an "imperfect" (121) example of subalternity: Bhubaneswari is a middle-class Bengali girl; she is a participant in the nationalist struggle for independence; and she not only writes a letter, but waits for the onset of menstruation, before she hangs herself.

Sunder Rajan thereby underscores that "while the nonidentity of Bhubaneswari as subaltern might remain ... at the level of the individual or historical anecdote, there is no mystification ... at the structural level . . . Bhubaneswari's subalternity is produced" (Sunder Rajan, "Death" 123). She concludes, "There is no necessary syllogism here: x, y, and z die; they are all (produced as) subaltern; therefore subalterns (must) die" (130). Attending to a particular death's meaning, we inescapably probe the "specific historical conditions" (Gopal, "Reading" 149), to return to Gopal's prerogative, that mount a governing logic whereby difference is inherently oppositional. At that moment, whence (recalling Li) a "dense and throbbing lifeworld" (Li, "Necroidealism" 284) disappears into a taxonomical placeholder *meant* to understand the living, originary queerness may evince an affective idiom that belies (a) *relationship* at ground level to subvert the foreclosure that miraculates *place* and thereby procure a glimpse, as mentioned earlier, of a "person among persons" (Spivak, "Touched" 102).

Asha Varadharajan, similarly, to Sunder Rajan, attempts to "illuminate not only the singularity, but also [the subaltern's] remarkable prescience, continuing relevance, and abiding significance" ("Figure and Ground" 731). In using various rhetorical figures such as aporia, catachresis, metalepsis, etc., Spivak does not retroactively ferret out a perspicacious subjectivity that abuts an enforced silence (733) because subalternity "limns a predicament rather than names an identity" (734). Varadharajan's own prioritization of class consciousness and subaltern insurgency coheres with Spivak's more productive approach to bring colonial knowledge production to crisis, for the relentless shuttle between object- and subject-status as launched by the imperialist ("she was forced to die") and nationalist ("she wanted to die") sentences reinforces the widow's good wifehood. Pursuant to Varadharajan's insistence on the "vitality and dynamism [of] a figure ... thought only in terms of ... limits" (734), therefore, I suggest that subalternity's—that is, the subaltern's irretrievable heterogeneity's—heuristic homology with originary queerness may avoid the pitfalls of adequate representation allegedly gained via the epistemic strategy of particularization, whereby essentially historical categories of identity (race, class, gender, etc.) dispense a purportedly more tortuously acquired adequate representation.

If "[w]e are a part of the records we keep" (Spivak, "Explanation" 22), then Manto's ironic and melancholic transpositions of originary queerness—"insaan" (इंसान; human), "insaan -kudiya" (

इंसान कुड़ियाँ; human-girls), "zinda lahu" (ज़िनदा लहू; alive blood), "ang" (अंग; organs), "boti boti" (बोटी-बोटी; fleshy bones), and "thanda gosht" (ठंडा गोश्त; cold meat)—figure a vital and dynamic entity trapped in the vicissitudes of a system's logic, for nationalist history *should* merely recapitulate male honor, valor, and enlightenment; they are, after all, their "baap ka tukham" (बाप का तुखम; created from father's sperm). Instead, on *that* fateful night, we *all* visit "bure ki ma ka ghar" (बुरे की माँ के घर; the house of Bad's mother)—that is, (another) Mother India. *Here* are: hotel rooms, not marital bedrooms; lovers, not spouses; looters, abductors, and rapists, not patriots; promiscuity, not chastity; intrigue and abeyance, not principled war; a spurned woman, not devoted wife; necrophilia, not conquest and acquisition; jealous female murderers, not sacrificed women; emasculation, not virility; banal evil, not righteous good; sexual arousal, not patriotic fervor; and, a card game, not history. *These* are the ingredients of a not-yet-storied emergent that, as stated above, can "*cross* identity" (Spivak, "Gender" 824) to docket an unpredictable futurity, for by the time we get to this hotel room, at the margins of reproductive heteronormativity, rather than to Mother India already mapped, it will (always) have been. This is how Mother India becomes less congruent with the nationalist con-text that writes us into place, and more conducive to a postcolonial narrativization that looks (out) for the inhabitants of "burre ki ma ka ghar" (बुरे की माँ के घर; the house of Bad's mother) *in its place*.

V. Originary Queerness

Because originary queerness is "a position without identity" (Spivak, "They" 2), it cannot be adduced by feminist varieties of neoliberalism (nationalism, democracy, rights, etc.). Neither is this non-position derived from "straight," nor does it signify feminine excess; indeed, as per Spivak, sexual difference qua humanism "nestles" *in* originary queerness (2). Inasmuch as originary queerness is disclosed by forms of cultural evidence appreciable only via a non-antagonistic understanding of difference, its difference from reproductive heteronormativity is "continuous" (3).[12] Furthermore, this irretrievable heterogeneity is neither reasonable nor unreasonable but (lives as) the heuristic yet perennially anachronistic "before" and "after," "beginning" and "end," of the standpoint, whose cartographic specificity incarnates the bounds of the known. Whereas the determinants of knowledge production rely upon a generalized form of gender coding, as animated by institutionally validated forms of subjectivity and agency, the effort to look (out) for the heterogeneous avouches (a) relationship at ground level and, hence, (a) responsibility *in* originary queerness.

Susceptibility to the irretrievably heterogeneous *in its place*, therefore, in contravention of rationalized lived experience, is an imaginative endeavor to be borne across sanctioned registers, which promulgate Woman as a semiotic resource *par excellence*, the tangible undifferentiatedness of "the diversity of daily life" (Spivak, "Gender" 816) forming a wishful disclaimer to the "peopled impersonality of an inherited record" (816). In order to enervate a heedlessly didactic yet dramatized logical sequence—sex, gender, marriage, reproduction—as Spivak notes, "the question of gender … *must be felt*" (816, emphases added). Altering all (else) that follows, originary queerness *in its place* conveys and upholds an inability to capture the fundaments in which (as it happens) we *actually* live. For this recounting, futurity is geo-graphed by our deficiency and lack, which thereby "stance the negotiation in directions of greater virtuality" (818); in other words, we forego the claim to identity for "the bottom layers" (819), where (all) failures are honorable.[13] *Here*, a negotiation's polymorphic consanguinity does not warrant discretional yet globalized lifestyle options: "sautan" (सौतन; the other woman), a "chudel" (चुड़ैल; demon-vamp), a "haramzadi" (हरामज़ादी ; despicable, unholy, female bastard of a prostitute), a "bhadvi" (भड़वी; lady-pimp), "teri ma" (तेरी माँ ; a beholden, emasculated Ishar's mother), or "meva" (मेवा; fruit), which endorse the frame of a cultural logic; alternatively, we recognize, *in* (our) originary queerness, that "a decision … makes us rather than we it" (818).

Spivak thereby calls "queer" ("Gender" 818) *this* irretrievable heterogeneity *in its place*—that is, those rudiments wherein we can bear witness to an essentially historical double bind because *here* difference is not intrinsically functional. Contrary to an overdetermined historical billing made possible under the auspices of reproductive heteronormativity, irrespective of what will (always) have happened at ground level, stancing identity *in* originary queerness, in the direction of *greater* virtuality, releases the "unmaking of the negotiation … a virtualization of the virtuality of the queer" (824). Thus, identity may be indispensable to have (a) predictable place, but this identity is (to be) unpredictably stanced as virtual. By projecting the "queer" as virtual, however, identity's virtuality, disavowed by a foreclosure of (a) relationship at ground level, secures its ill-begotten mandate. What ensues is an irresolvable "nonpassage" (826) between virtual and nonvirtual, or predictable and unpredictable, as (autochthonous) identity and (virtual) "queer" are not antonymic but aporetic. As a result, the unpredictability of moments of *crossing* identity serves as an "imperfect analogy" (824) for *how* "something that engages as sexual difference plays, marking time, defining and activating space" (Spivak, "Touched" 101). In these imaginary homelands, "one never stops (not) translating" (Spivak, "Translating" 39) originary queerness because irretrievable heterogeneity *in its place* requires articulation to get anywhere (at all).

Like Ishar Singh's primevally bloodied "kirpan" (करिपान)—bloodied not just by his victims or even by his own murder, but by millennia-old palimpsestic piercings of flesh—Spivak's double negative "stake[s] a claim to be *une forme tachée*" ("Touched" 103) to putatively finished itineraries. In granting a crucial role to the indefiniteness of our most intimate but eventually unsayable materialities (hence the onus on the "zinda lahu" [ज़निदा लहू; alive blood] of affective idiom), which registers history as turning (our) originary queerness into "thanda gosht" (ठंडा गोश्त; cold meat), Spivak asks us to imagine the cuts required for (an) "us" to be written. Recalling "that from which sexual difference differs" (101)—that is, the heuristic yet perennially anachronistic "beginning" and "end," "before" and "after," of our intoned parts—puts "the question of Being in drag" (Spivak,

"Touched" 102): as such, we may *be* men and women (irretrievable heterogeneity in drag), but the *dearth* of a backstory is how we are borne across identity, whose originary queerness will (always) have been.

While an "interminable conversation" (Spivak, "Gender" 98) ensnares this queer everydayness into an abyssal regime of "sexual sameness [as] sexual difference" (102), I suggest that the world about the hotel room, as refracted by the unnamed and raped female corpse's "thanda gosht" (ठंडा गोश्त; cold meat), which is also (like us) not, in fact, *there*, but left in some bushes, turns Mother India into a joke on "us." When the question of gender is felt in *this* chimerical place, we may recognize that the critical force of subalternity emerges precisely from "being the ... limit of the epistemic project of [information] retrieval" (Chowdhury, "Post-deconstructive" 165).In the context of post-independence failures of decolonization, therefore, originary queerness, as "shared *in* the rhythm of working together" (Spivak, "Gender" 821n21), may "dheere dheere" (धीरे-धीरे; slowly-slowly) (the repetition is an "Indian" affective idiom) lead to "ek baat" (एक बात; one telling, or one thing to tell) about "insaan kudiya" (इंसान कुड़ियाँ; human-girls) as indeed strange things.

IV. The Scene

To recall Li's neologism "necroidealism," it seems that the subaltern in "Thanda Gosht" (ठंडा गोश्त) is (a) subaltern in every possible way: *she* is dead; *she* does not speak; she is (not) *there*; she has no name, no family, no religion; she *is* "thanda gosht" (ठंडा गोश्त; cold meat), left to rot in some bushes. If colonialism and nationalism both buttress good wifehood as Hindu women's aggregate ontology, then partition narratives posit their rape-ability as an intransigent *is*. In *this* hotel room, where the entire story takes place, rape is like a lover cheating or tasting fruit, a happenstance, an entitlement, or cause of murderous jealousy due to a "chudel's" (चुड़ेल; vampish and demon-like) seduction. Consequently, a full-blooded Punjabi woman is also her father's daughter *when* she exacts revenge, because her lover fell prey to another woman's charm—a patriarchal glossing of violence that dovetails with historical scripts of defended rectitude and concomitantly conferred status.

The confines of the hotel room, which segregates a visible interior world from an unseen exterior one, contain only two characters—Ishar Singh and Kulwant Kaur—who are Sikh Punjabi lovers. We immediately come upon Kulwant as she waits for Ishar. When he arrives, she uses her "tej tej nazron" (तेज़-तेज़ नज़रों; quick-sharp-expressive eyes) to look at him "ghoorkar" (घूरकर; a hard and hostile stare). She moves forward to lock the door. It is twelve o'clock at night (resonant of the midnight hour of India's independence, which Jawaharlal Nehru will have just described as India awakening while the world sleeps) and a "rahasyapur" (रहस्यपूरण; mystery-imbued) silence saturates the "chaya(s)"(छाया; shadows) of the locked enclosure. (The use of a high Hindi word to describe the silence adds an epochal tension to a run of the mill situation of a woman waiting for a man.) Not only is the tumult of the exterior held at bay by the locked door, but even the hotel room is not fully perceptible—the shadows outside are also present inside.

Kulwant returns to sitting cross-legged on the bed with an air of miffed expectation and entitled hurt. And *here*, Manto begins the steady process of undressing Ishar Singh, albeit in private quarters. At first, Kulwant leaves Ishar alone as he unravels the tangled threads of his disparate thoughts. Still holding his "kirpan" (करिपान; sword), he stands in a corner.[14] That Ishar does not stride into and thereby command this space, as well as his continued silence, further shroud the already darkness-filled room. Ishar seems hesitant, as though ashamed of having committed a misdeed, even when Kulwant shifts positions and starts to swing her legs.

Manto describes Kulwant as "bhari bhari" (भरे-भरे; full-full). (Punjabi Sikh women per stereotype are "fair" and "healthy." "Healthy" is a euphemism often used for not "slim.") The pregnant pause during which this vernacular is used will later birth Ishar's exsanguinated corpse, itself an inversion of Kulwant's affectively embossed fullness. In lieu of Ishar's manly presence, Manto directs our imaginative gaze to Kulwant's muscles, which ripple as they are "gosht se bhare hue" (गोश्त से भरे हुए; filled with meat). Using the Urdu word "gosht" instead of the Hindi word "maans" (मॉस) renders Kulwant less weighty or obese and more a meaty bone to be chomped on. Her breasts raised very high on her chest, and her "tej tej nazre" (तेज़-तेज़ नज़रों; quick-sharp-eyes), alert for predators, augment her animalesque irruption in suspended time. Having waited for a while, her upper lip shows signs of her "gubar" (गुबार; pent up feelings), as though this swollen lip announces her swollen emotions. When gussied up, Manto confirms that she is a "dharlledar" (धड़ल्लेदार; impressive, larger-than-life) woman. (The use of "daar" [दार] after the adjective renders this formidableness synecdochic.) Unlike Kulwant's andean aspect, Ishar's diminution proceeds apace, despite his manly features and muscular body, but this incremental shrinkage does not obviate Ishar as "yogyatar" (योग्यतार; capable and deserving) of Kulwant. (The use of "daar" [दार] after the adjective renders this deservingness synecdochic.) Still quiet in the corner, Ishar's kirpan-bearing hand starts to shake whilst his tightly bound turban disassembles.

At this point, the two have not exchanged a single word, the expectant lull also imbued in Kulwant and Ishar's physicality and full-bloodedness. That this quiet hotel room is a sanctuary is refuted by their awkward bodies: Kulwant's grows more impatient, Ishar's steadily decomposes. Kulwant suddenly leaps up but, regardless of her by now vituperative "tej tej nazren" (तेज़-तेज़ नज़रों; quick-sharp-expressive eyes), can only sputter his name. Ishar's eyes refuse to meet Kulwant's gaze; he turns his face away and looks at the floor. (Punjabi Sikh men per stereotype are "aggressive" and "virile." "Virile" is the euphemism for well-endowed manly men whose sperm produces well-endowed manly sons.) Upon spewing his name once more, Kulwant immediately suppresses her tone, seeming to concede how far she can goad him. Her query about his whereabouts, however, uncovers his disappearance for several days. And here, Manto also commences to let Ishar run dry.

Moistening his cracked lips with his tongue, a dryness that will eventually reach its physical *and* logical conclusion, Ishar tells Kulwant that he cannot provide his whereabouts. Ishar's unknowingness not only marks his seeming trauma but also gestures to (another) Mother India wherein independence is impetuous pillage. Kulwant is angry, accusatory, and disquieted with his "ma ya jawab" (माँ-या जवाब; non-answer). (माँ means "mother"; Ishar's non-committal response is like a naughty child's upon getting caught.) To distract from his obfuscation, Ishar throws his "kirpan" (करिपान; sword) to the side and lies down. His girth still fills the bed, but he has been sick for some time. Seeing her lover in such straits further fills an already "bhari bhari" (भरे-भरे; full-full) Kulwant with "sahenbhuti" (साहानुभूती; forbearance and sympathy). (Throughout, Kulwant's and Ishar's coarse eroticism is counterbalanced by high Hindi words such that her "normal" reactions become noble, magnanimous, or supernal, whilst the extremity of Ishar's transgressions precipitates mawkish self-pity. As such, the cleavage between anatomy and senses peculiarly sheaths their final acts with vindication and comeuppance at once.) For now, Kulwant strokes his forehead whereas he stares at the ceiling. His chronic reticence, gradual feminization, contracting posture, and desiccated lips (the obverse of the "gubar" [गुबार; pent up feelings] of Kulwant's upper lip), suggest something truly horrific. He is still only able to say Kulwant's name in a voice filled with "pida" (पीड़ा; pain and sorrow), another high Hindi word that sublates Ishar's opportunistic savagery as the generic kernel of "life."

Despite the "gubar" [गुबार; pent up feelings] of Kulwant's upper lip, or perhaps because of it, Kulwant begins to playfully bite him. *Now* begins their foreplay, which seems misplaced given Ishar's demeanor. (Perhaps Kulwant tries to distract him.) Manto portrays Kulwant as relentless in her pursuit of sexual satisfaction and Ishar as a man up to the task. At this moment, however, Ishar removes his turban and gazes beseechingly into Kulwant's eyes. He does spank her "gosht bhare kulhe" (गोश्त-भरे कूल्हे; meat-filled hips), another descriptor synonymizing sex, violence, and gorging of animal flesh. After he snaps his head back to express incredulity at women's crazy minds (he may be amused at Kulwant's inappropriate unseriousness, but later revelations suggest this utterance displaces responsibility for *his* deliberated actions onto the unnamed and raped female corpse), his hair comes undone. In a further role-reversal, Kulwant, the sexual aggressor, runs her fingers through his long tresses. She again lovingly asks him where he went for all these days. He again deflects by saying he was at "bure ki ma ke ghar" (बुरे की माँ के घर; Bad's mother's house). (This domestic idiom personifies "bad[ness]" by giving it a mother and a natal home.) Manto's gendered morphology induces dread, for this familiar proverb is at once insult and warning. It tells the reader that what Ishar witnessed was seriously awful (not just "regular" awful) because he visited the *origin* of badness, a sacrosanct site of being and belonging transfigured into hell, as though where he was before this "visit," remarkably, were a prelapsarian dwelling, even as the affective idiom used reinforces the primeval and autochthonic nature of *that* place, where all badness is birthed and bred.

He swears to god that Kulwant is a "jaandaar" woman (जानदार; full of life) when he starts rubbing her ample chest. Knowing that she has him where she wants him, she gracefully shakes his off hand. We learn that they are in a suburban hotel room because Kulwant tells him to swear on her head before enquiring whether he went into the city's commercial districts, where the looting is taking place. Due to the cocoon-like quality of the hotel room, which is also the site of an illicit dalliance, the mayhem outside seems far removed. Ishar impulsively fastens his bun in one swoop, as though trying to put himself back together. He responds negatively. Kulwant now appears womanish in her constant nagging. Convinced that he won't share his looted bounty, she refuses to believe him. Ishar curses anyone who lies to her: "voh apne baap ka tukham na ho" (वह अपने बाप का तुखम न हो; not created from his father's sperm). (Mothers give birth to "bad," but fathers' sperm-filled scrotums breed "honesty.")

Although momentarily reassured by this fealty, she blurts out that she still does not understand what happened. He was totally fine that night when he lay next to her, after dressing her in pilfered ornaments, receiving her caresses. Suddenly, he got dressed and left. Either because of her persistence or his triggered memory, Ishar's face falls. Kulwant notes he is turning yellow. At this juncture, she indeed knows that "daal mein kuch kaala hai" (दाल में कुछ काला है; there is something black in the lentils). Again, the affective idiom is domestic: an almost daily staple, lentils symbolize antediluvian motherly care, an unvarnished maternalism that turns rotten by something black (an inauspicious and sinister color). Kulwant is rightly suspicious. He tries to lie with his lifeless voice. She presses on her upper lip as her suspicions grow stronger. Forcefully enunciating every word, she taunts his manliness (we also learn he has been missing for eight days). Ishar sits up straight as if assaulted. To reassure her that he is the same man, he embraces her forcefully with his "shishali" (शशिाली; formidable and mighty) arms; she must suffocate from his squeezing so that the heat leaves her bones. Kulwant may not interfere, but she sticks to her complaints. He repeats, he went to "Bad's mother's house" (बुरे की माँ के घर; bure ki ma ke ghar). But, then again, there is "kuch nahin" (कुछ नहीं; really nothing) to tell (her).

V. House (or Hotel Room) of Cards

By now, we've been *in* suspense for half the story, that is, the hotel room pumps this affective enervation in all directions—outwards, inside, towards us. The story *nestles* in suspense, a peculiar lover's foreplay that throbs with the potential to change everything. Indeed, Ishar's constant deflection suggests that we must witness what's not (actually) *there*. This (black, inauspicious) something, on the other side of a locked door, exaggerates (like the "gubar" [गुबार] of Kulwant's upper lip) Kulwant's incredibly banal repartee; she is womanfully (भरी भरी [filled] like her) melodramatic—Ishar must set her on fire if he lies—yet also coquettishly curious. This potential combustion enhances the room's already corpulence-induced erotic charge, which Ishar "manages" by encircling Kulwant's neck with his hands and his lips crushing hers. Readers may anticipate this fluidity between sex and violence because Punjabi Sikhs are *expected* to be full-throttled: in their language, music, clothes, jewelry, dance, food, and it follows, in their lovemaking. As Ishar's "kirpan" (करिपान; sword) attests, they are a warrior people. Further catering to stereotype, Manto's characters now use equally corny analogies for obstreperous copulation.[16]

The moment's intensity breaks when Ishar's facial hair gets into Kulwant's nostrils, and she sneezes. Both laugh. Looking at her lustfully, Ishar invites her to play cards. Despite the beads of sweat above her upper lip, Kulwant rolls her eyes, professing "dafaan ho" (दफान हो; let the burial happen). (Sex and death, like phallus and "kirpan," are predictably interchangeable.) He bites her hips; she suffers, pushes him away, halts him. Kulwant melts when his teeth catch her top lip. Taking off his kurta, Ishar announces the "turp chaal" (तुर्प चाल; card game). Like skinning a slaughtered goat, Ishar removes her *salwar kameez* over her head. Strenuously kissing her arm, he stares at her naked body, swearing she is a very "karaari aurat" (करारी औरत; spicy-hot woman). Kulwant's upper lip trembles in arousal.

Seeing the red mark on her arm, she (foreshadowing her own consummation of this sexual interlude) calls him "zaalim" (ज़ालमि; bloodthirsty). Ishar smiles through his black moustache (which mirrors Kulwant's cupid's bow, itself a proxy for her vagina). Pursuant to his pronouncement that "julm" (जुल्म; oppression) should occur today, he inflicts them: he bites her earlobes, presses her "ubhre" (उभरे; heaving) chest, licks her hips with loud smacks, fills her cheek-filled face with kisses, sucks her all over, and wets her body with saliva. Notwithstanding Kulwant reaching a boiling point like a pot over "aanch" (आँच; high fire-heat), Ishar cannot get an erection. Whatever techniques he remembers, he tries as though a losing "pahlvaan" (पहलवान; athlete). Stretched like an instrument with chords at the highest pitch, Kulwant is irritated: it is time for this muscled and sinewed man to "putta faink" (पत्ता फेंक; throw his card, make a play).

Upon hearing her, the entire deck of cards slips from Ishar's hand. Breathing heavily, he lies "pahlu" (पहलू; next, military flank) to Kulwant. She warms him up, for a layer of cold sweat covers his forehead. With her tense "ang" (अंग; organs) sorely disappointed, she leaps out of bed, "jaldi jaldi" (जल्दी-जल्दी quickly-quickly) covers herself with a sheet, flares her nostrils, and demands in a scattered voice *who* squelched him dry, *who* the "haramzadi" (हरामज़ादी; despicable, unholy, female bastard of a prostitute) *is*, *who* the "chudel" (चुडे़ल; vampish-demon) and card-thief *is*. A panting Ishar reassures her in a "nidhal" (नढ़िाल; resigned and unenergetic) voice, but she boils with rage.

Placing her hands on her hips, Kulwant informs him with "drirta" (दृढ़ता; sternly-strongly) (her hardness a procuration of his erection) that she will find out, even after bitterly making him swear his fidelity, as she is Sardar Nihal Singh's daughter. He lies and she will suck his "boti-boti" (बोटी-बोटी; fleshy bones) until desiccated (a role reversal given their foreplay). As soon as he shakes his head sorrowfully, she loses her mind. She springs for the "kirpan" (करिपान; sword), removes its casing—as if peeling a banana (his undressing her was akin to skinning a goat), and a bloody fountain gushes from Ishar's throat. Not yet satisfied, she scratches his hair like a jungle-wild cat, swearing at her "sautan" (सौतन; rival) with "moti moti" (मोटी-मोटी; fat-fat) curses. Ishar beseeches in a dolorously soft voice, and she backs off. As the blood flies into his moustache, we near the end of Ishar *and* of the story, but we *still* do not know what happened.

Although reproachful of her impetuousity, he thanks her. What happened, he says, happened for the better. Her jealousy awakening anew, Kulwant asks *who* "teri ma" (तेरी माॅ; your mother) *is*. (He is an emasculated, beholden mama's boy.) After tasting his blood, a ripple or current runs through Ishar's body. His "dhundhlali" (धुँधलाली; murky) eyes get a slight "chamak" (चमक; shine-light) when confessing that he, a bastard, killed six people with that "kirpan" (करिपान; sword). She needs to stop swearing at that "bhadvi" (भड़वी; lady-pimp), but Kulwant is obsessed, yelling that she's asking him *who* she *is*. Spreading his hand on his neck, he smiles when he sees his "zinda lahu" (ज़निदा लहू; alive blood). With a stifled voice and slit neck, he calls humans strange things. Kulwant interjects he focus on matters to hand.

Ishar's broadening smile also broadens his moustache (a synecdochic expression of *another* [im]possible masculinity, somewhere else). A fresh layer of cold sweat covers his forehead. His pierced neck means that he can only tell her "saari baat" (सारी बात; whole telling, whole thing to tell) very "dheere dheere" (धीरे-धीरे; slowly-slowly), even as he cannot *actually* tell her what happened. Not only humans, but "insaan kudiya" (इंसान कुड़ियाँ; human-girls) are also really strange things. Looting in town like everyone else, he gave her all the filched jewelry, ornaments, and money. But he did not tell her "ek baat" (एक बात; one thing, one telling, one thing to tell). Howbeit he grimaces in torment, Kulwant declines to pay him any mind. Pitiless, she commands him to spill (the spilling of blood makes him spill the "truth"). In his rejoinder, Ishar blows the spurting blood upwards onto his moustache so that it flies in front of him.

The house he attacked contained seven people. He killed six, but the seventh was a very beautiful girl. Kulwant listens quietly. Planning to kill her, he then (referring to himself in third person) determined to taste this new "meva" (मेवा; fruit) since he enjoys Kulwant daily. Propping her on his shoulders, he went to the bushes alongside the railroad tracks. At this juncture in his "ek baat" (एक बात; one thing, one telling, one thing to tell), his tongue is arid. Kulwant swallows her spit, urging him to resume. With immense exertion, Ishar confesses he did "patta faink" (पत्ता फेंक; throw the card, make his play). Kulwant shakes him when his voice drowns out. Opening his eyes, he sees Kulwant's every "boti boti" (बोटी- बोटी; morsel of meat) palpitating. The girl was dead, a "laash" (लाश; cadaver), completely "thanda gosht" (ठंडा गोश्त; cold meat). Acquiescing to his request for her hand, she realizes that Ishar's is colder than ice.

VI. Human-girls (इंसान कड़ियाँ) in One Telling (एक बात)

When charged and tried for obscenity, Manto argued that Ishar represents hope even for evildoers—that is, a recuperable or redeemable humanity.[17] Obviously, if necrophilia is what causes self-awareness, then our standards are incredibly low. Kulwant and Ishar's clichéd repartee and sexual foreplay is coupled with the equally clichéd continuity between sex, food, animality, and violence. Somewhere along the line, Kulwant is compared to a cat. Alongside military imagery, sex and rape are likened to a public card game played by men in teashops, parks, town squares, etc. Domestic imagery includes slaughtering and skinning goats, boiling water, spices, meat, bones, and peeling a banana as well as motifs such as daughtership, motherhood, and patronymy. Though part of a sexual dalliance in excess of traditional mores, Kulwant calls the victim her "sautan" (सौतन).

Phallogocentric irony (Kulwant penetrates Ishar; blood bursts from the neck, not semen from the phallus; Kulwant's back is erect, not Ishar's penis; Ishar's unravelling hair and clothing) as well as pedestrian swear words— "chudel" (चुड़ैल; demon-vamp), "haramzadi" (हरामज़ादी; despicable, unholy, female bastard of a prostitute), "bhadvi" (भड़वी; lady-pimp), demonize the victim to hold *her* responsible for Ishar's predation and Kulwant's jealousy. Both women are cast as vampire-like beings imbibing Ishar's life force: if the abducted woman shrivels Ishar's "kirpan" (करिपान; sword) and blocks his "chaal" (चाल; move), Kulwant's possessiveness wizens his "boti boti" (बोटी-बोटी; morsel of meat) by exsanguinating him of "zinda lahu" (ज़निदा लहू; alive blood).

The originary queerness of the unnamed and raped female corpse, her "thanda gosht" (ठंडा गोश्त; cold meat) a synecdoche for the incapacity to generate her backstory, despite her dismally overdetermined gendered fate, becomes appreciable by an affective idiom: "insaan kudiya" (इंसान कुड़ियाँ; human-girls) whose "zinda lahu" (ज़निदा लहू; alive-blood) forms (lives as) the "before" and "after," "beginning" and "end," of the "ek baat" (एक बात; one thing to tell) overheard in the hotel room: *that* is *all* we know. As such, Kulwant's incessant, uncanny questions— *who* squelched him dry, *who* the "haramzadi" (हरामज़ादी despicable, unholy, female bastard of a prostitute) *is*, *who* the "chudel" vampish-demon (चुडे़ल) and card-thief *is*, evince that, heedless of our habitual systems of hatreds—she becomes "chudel" (चुड़ैल; demon-vamp), a "haramzadi" (हरामज़ादी; despicable, unholy, female bastard of a prostitute), "bhadvi" (भड़वी; lady-pimp), or "meva" (मेवा; fruit), "zinda lahu" (ज़निदा लहू; alive-blood) moves inexorably into chaos, which experience *in its place* exsanguinates Ishar.

Ishar expects the ubiquitous, but something else happens, which he tries to revoke by using "insaan kudiya" (इंसान कुड़यिा; human-girl), the word "kudiya" (कुड़यिा; girl) reiterating his infantilization of women. *She* who is also "kuch nahin" (*कुछ नहीं;* really nothing) to tell, left in bushes by railroad tracks (an imperial mapping of India as [a] place), *crosses* identity with a "bhari bhari" (*भरी भरी;* full full) undifferentiatedness, even when not (in fact) there. Here, behind a locked door (Kulwant's first act when Ishar returns), therefore, which sunders *all* signs of life on one side but not the other—words used to describe Kulwant: "karaari" (करारी; spicy-hot), "aanch" (आँच; high fire-heat), "moti moti" (मोटी-मोटी; fat fat), "jaldi jaldi" (जल्दी-जल्दी; quickly quickly), "ubhri" (उभरी; heaving)—"the question of gender ... *must be felt*" (Spivak, "Gender" 816, emphases added).

As we remain ensconced in these quarters, the hotel room forms (for "us") the aperture for a consummate unknowingness trapped in the vicissitudes of lovers' logic. Exceeding the trappings of domestic, communal squabble and public, patriotic fervor, the unnamed and raped female corpse's very impersonality captures the fundaments in which (as it happens) the partition actually *takes* place. And so, condemned as we are to witness Ishar tortuously die and overhear Kulwant's unanswerable question, (our) futurity must now be geo-graphed by our deficiency and lack. Since Ishar's affective idiom momentarily breaches a foreclosure of *relationship*, we may stance the patronymic in the direction of *greater* virtuality. Because irretrievable heterogeneity *in its place* foils the predictability of rationalized itineraries of reproductive heteronormativity, we can never have "ek baat" (एक बात; tell one thing, have one thing to tell) about what happened. In other words, *her* originary queerness, despite her *being* cold brute matter (in drag), upends the entire card game.

The unnamed and raped female corpse thereby recalls for ("us") "that from which sexual difference differs" (Spivak, "They" 101) because her *dearth* of a backstory generates an ethical crisis that sexual difference cannot ruse over for continuity and homogeneity. This backstory, whose originary queerness will (always) have been, must be ceaselessly *excised* from the frame of the encounter for "thanda gosht" (ठंडा गोश्त; cold meat) (human only in outline) to dispense with the very intransigent inconstancy (in this, Kulwant and the corpse are foils) that brings Ishar into (a) disavowed *relationship*: he is (dis)figured because he feels *responsible*. Thus, irrespective of a readily arrayed interminable conversation— hot/cold, suburb/city, fire/ice, kirpan/flesh, haven/peril, home/hotel, life/death, lover/wife, animal/human, vital/desiccated, ignorance/knowledge, animal/human, reality/game, and so on—we cannot bequeath "saari baat" (सारी बात; whole telling, tell whole thing, whole thing to tell) about this entropic encounter with a "strange thing" (now) called "insaan kudiya" (इंसान कुड़िया; human-girl).

Because (our) "before" and "after," "beginning" and "end," mark (an) unknowing, we may only "dheere dheere" (धीरे-धीरे; slowly-slowly) exsanguinate identity to perhaps become "jaandar" (जानदार; full of life) enough to have "ek baat" (एक बात; tell one thing, have one thing to tell). Who she *is* metamorphoses a vestibulary space into a gland pumping dread into a "shishali" (शशिाली; formidable and mighty) nation's "boti boti" (बोटी- बोटी; fleshy bones). Her originary queerness, therefore, inverts a teleological trajectory to manifest (the fight for) Nation as (visiting) "bure ki ma ka ghar" (बुरे की माँ के घर; the house of Bad's mother). Here, in this place, far from honor and protection, like Kulwant we notice that "daal mein kuch kaala hai" (दाल में कुछ काला है; there is something black in the lentils): that "teri ma" (तेरी माँ; your mother) might, indeed, make a "zaalim" (ज़ालमि; bloodthirsty) of ("us") all. Just the same, no one knows what happens next.

REFERENCE

Chowdhury, Aniruddha. *Post-deconstructive Subjectivity and History: Phenomenology, Critical Theory, and Postcolonial Thought*, Brill, 2014.

de Kock, Leon. "Interview with Gayatri Chakravorty Spivak: New Nation Writers Conference in South Africa," *Ariel: A Review of International English Literature*, Vol. 23, No. 3, 1992, pp. 29-47.

Priyamvada Gopal, "Reading Subaltern History," *The Cambridge Companion to Postcolonial Literary Studies*, edited by Neil Lazarus, Cambridge University Press, 2004, pp. 139-161.

Li, Victor. "Necroidealism, or the Subaltern's Sacrificial Death," *Interventions* vol. 11, no. 3, 2009, pp. 275-292.

Pandit, Prakash. Toba Tek Singh Aur Anya Kahiniya (टोबा टेक सघि और अन्य कहानयिा), Rajpal, 2013.

Spivak, Gayatri. "Translating in a World of Languages," *Profession*, 2010, pp. 35–43.

—. "In Response: Looking Back, Looking Forward," *Can the Subaltern Speak?: Reflections on the History of an Idea*, edited by Rosalind C. Morris, Columbia University Press, 2010, pp. 227–236.

—. "They, the People," *METAFISH: Biopolitics, Trans-Nationalism, Apocalypse,* Community, 2009, pp. 1–5. <https://metafish.wordpress.com/2009/08/16/gayatri-spivaks-presentation-they-the-people/>.

—. "If Only," Writing a Feminist's Life: The Legacy of Carolyn G. Heilbrun (Guest Issue), edited by Nancy K. Miller and Victoria Rosner, *S & F Online*, Vol. 4, No. 2 Spring 2006, http://sfonline.barnard.edu/heilbrun/spivak_01.htm.

—. *A Critique of Postcolonial Reason: Toward a History of the Vanishing Present*, Harvard University Press, 1999.

—. "Gender and International Studies," *Millennium*, Vol. 27, No. 4, 1998, pp. 809–831. Print.

—. "Explanation and Culture: Marginalia," *The Spivak Reader*, edited by Donna Landry, Routledge, 1995.

—. *Outside in the Teaching Machine*, Routledge, 1993.

—. "Interview With Gayatri Chakravorty Spivak," *Ariel: A Review of International English Literature*, vol. 23, no. 3, 1992, pp. 29-47.

—. "Can the Subaltern Speak?," *Marxism and the Interpretation of Culture,* edited by Cary Nelson and Lawrence Grossberg, University of Illinois Press, 1988, pp. 271-313.

—. *In Other Worlds: Essays in Cultural Politics*, Routledge, 1988.

Sunder Rajan, Rajeswari. "Death and the Subaltern," *Can the Subaltern Speak?: Reflections on the History of an Idea*, edited by Rosalind C. Morris, Columbia University Press, 2010, pp. 117–138.

Varadharajan, Asha. "'... half-sick of shadows': Figure and Ground in Gayatri Chakravorty Spivak's Imagination of the Subaltern," *Cultural Studies* 30, Vol. 5, 2016, pp. 730-753.

ENDNOTES

1 Namita Goswami is Professor of Philosophy at Indiana State University. She works in continental philosophy as well as postcolonial, critical race, feminist, and queer theory. She has published in a wide range of journals such as *Hypatia, SIGNS, Angelaki, Journal of Speculative Philosophy, Contemporary*

Aesthetics, and *Critical Philosophy of Race* and in edited volumes such as *Rethinking Facticity* (edited by Eric Nelson and François Raffoul), *Asian and Feminist Philosophies in Dialogue: Liberating Traditions* (edited by Ashby Butnor and Jen McWeeny), *Phenomenology, Embodiment, and Race* (edited by Emily Lee) and *Constructing the Nation: A Race and Nationalism Reader* (edited by Mariana Ortega and Linda Martin Alcoff). She is the author of *Subjects that Matter: Philosophy, Feminism, and Postcolonial Theory* (SUNY Press, 2019) and co-editor of *Why Race and Gender Still Matter: An Intersectional Approach* (Cambridge University Press: Pickering & Chatto, 2014). She is currently completing a book on Gayatri Spivak.

2 In a previous reading of "Thanda Gosht," I emphasized that the abducted corpse crosses the sexual differential that emplaces women in overdetermined narratives of honor and sacrifice because of Ishar's necrophilia. It is Kulwant's culminating action, however, that pivots our understanding of women as passive victims toward forms of complicity with which partition history has yet to grapple. Ishar's affective idiom, in that context, suggested an ironically secular grappling with nationalism as a consummate *opportunity* for sexual violence. See "Crossing the Sexual Differential Into Utopia: The Subaltern is (Better Off) Dead," *theory@buffalo*, Vol. 19, Winter 2016, pp. 129-152.

3 When I first examined originary queerness in Salman Rushdie's *Shame*, I focused on how Rushdie's marvelous and voluminous amount of storytelling precluded the novel's female characters from reductive interpretations. Highlighting the novel's raucous funniness, its dialogue meant to be read out loud, I suggested that what we *hear* is an originary queerness that turns everydayness into a melodramatic Bollywood scene. See "Raddi, Phisaddi, and Bekar: Locating Spivak's Originary Queerness in Salman Rushdie's *Shame*," *Angelaki: Journal of the Theoretical Humanities*, Vol. 26, No. 5, 2021, pp. 38-56.

4 See, for example: Sangeeta Ray, "Reading Singularity, Reading Difference: An Ethics of the Impossible," *Gayatri Chakravorty Spivak: In Other Words*, Wiley Blackwell, 2009, pp. 67–106; J. Maggio, "'Can the Subaltern Be Heard?': Political Theory, Translation, Representation, and Gayatri Chakravorty Spivak," *Alternatives*: Global, *Local, Political*, Vol. 32, No. 4, Oct.-Dec. 2007, pp. 419-443; Jane Krishnadas, "The Sexual Subaltern in Conversations 'Somewhere in Between': Law and the Old Politics of Colonialism," *Feminist Legal Studies*, Vol. 14, 2006, pp. 53–77; Celia Lury, "From Diversity to Heterogeneity: A Feminist Analysis of the Making of Kinds," Economy and Society, Vol. 31, No. 4, Nov. 2002, pp. 588-605; Forest Pyle, "'By a Certain Subreption': Gayatri Spivak and the 'Lever' of the Aesthetic," *Interventions*, No. 4, 2002, pp. 186-190; Benita Perry, "Problems in Current Theories of Colonial Discourse," *Oxford Literary Review*, Vol. 9, No. 1, pp. 27-58.

5 See Spivak's discission of this appropriation in the "History" section of *A Critique of Postcolonial Reason* (pp. 198-311). I discuss how this appropriation often takes the guise of a retroactive search for the subaltern's "free will" in "De-Liberating Traditions: The Female Bodies of *Sati* and Slavery," *Asian and Feminist Philosophies in Dialogue*: *Liberating Traditions*, edited by Ashby Butnor and Jen McWeeny, Columbia University Press, 2014. Pp. 247-270.

6 A clear articulation of what Spivak learned from deconstruction is "Touched by Deconstruction," *Grey Room* 20, Summer 2005, pp. 95-104.

7 Upon learning of Bhubaneswari's death through family rumors, Spivak asked a female relative for more details, but this philosopher and Sanskritist critiqued Spivak's interest in the "hapless" (*Critique* 308) Bhubaneswari, not her accomplished sisters or liberated descendants. Waiting for menstruation could be construed as a remonstrance of this physiological destiny, her brother-in-law's taunts that at the age of seventeen she is "not-yet-a-wife" (307) could be precipitous, as could her failed mourning for her dead father, not to mention the letter (found ten years after her *sati*/suicide in 1926) confesses her inability to commit a politi-

cal assassination (307). Spivak laments these prodigiously legible scripts, which contrast her with allegedly more empowered women of post-independence India (311).

8 Spivak states, "[I]f ... our ontological commitments are dependent on various forms of coding, we can presuppose a variety of general catachrestic names as grounding" (*Other* 16).

9 Li introduces "cryptonomy" but does not develop it further. For an excellent analysis of subaltern secrets see Sandhya Shetty and Elizabeth Bellamy, "Postcolonialism's Archive Fever," *Diacritics*, Vol. 30, No. 1, 2000, pp. 25-48.

10 Here, Li ignores, for example, Spivak's statement, "You don't give the subaltern a voice. You work ... against subalternity" (de Kock, "Interview" 46).

11 I allude here to Theodor Adorno's critique of metaphysics that perpetuate dehumanization and functionalism when they conflate the absolute abstraction of experience with transcendence of cultural determinism. See *Metaphysics: Concepts and Problems*, Stanford University Press, 2000.

12 Spivak contends, "[S]ubjectship ... is different from ... originary queerness ... [O]ratures ... can make visible that self-elaboration as such is not necessarily a historical question in the sense in which we understand history. And the originary queerness ... supposed upon such terrain is no secret origin ... Self-elaboration ... temporize[s] a life as a person among persons ... I don't mean 'individual' ... [O]ratures [...] [are not] in locatable archives [, which] does not make them 'without history'" ("Touched" 102).

13 I am drawing here on Spivak's characterization of Rushdie's *Shame* as an "honorable failure" (*Outside* 223) insofar as the intangible undifferentiatedness of our everydayness that constitutes "the bottom layers" (Spivak, "Gender" 819) cannot not (in *Shame*'s case, spectacularly) fail to cathect identity.

14 Aniruddha Chowdhury contests Benita Perry's assertion that Spivak's subaltern is thoroughly mediated. Not only does Spivak's career-long ethico-political project move her to the heterogeneous subaltern margins of authorizing discourse, but she also characterizes the gendered subaltern "as the space of sheer heterogeneity" ("Post-deconstructive" 164, 154). Given post-independence failures of decolonization in the global South, strategically deploying subaltern heterogeneity "can make visible the phantasmatic nature of a merely hegemonic nationalism" (Spivak, *Other* 79)

15 Sikh practice centralizes what are known as the 5 k's: *kesh* (hair), *kach* (undergarment), *kirpan* (sword), *kanga* (a wooden comb), and *kada* (a steel bangle).

16 For specific discussions about sexuality, see Ayesha Jalal, *The Pity of Partition: Manto's Life, Times and Work Across the India-Pakistan Divide*, Princeton University Press, 2013; Naveiñ Reet, "Capturing Obscenity: The Trials and Tribulations of Saadat Hasan Manto," *Nordic Journal of Law & Social Research* (NNJLSR), No. 5, 2014, pp. 15-40; Saadat Hasan Manto, "Afsana Nigar Aur Jinsi Masail (The Short Story Writer and Sexual Matters)," *Manto Nama*, Sang-e-Meel, 1995; Saadat Hasan Manto, "Panchwan Muqadimah (The Fifth Trial), *Manto Kahaniyan*, Sang-e-Meel, 1995; Aziz Ahmad, Manto Ka Muqaddama: Obscenity Trial-1," *All Things Pakistan: Pakistan, Pakistani, Pakistaniat*, 29 September, 2009, pakistaniat.com/2009/09/29/saadat-manto-trial/.

17 Manto seems to be referring to a card game popular in Iran, India, and Pakistan.

18 See Sarah Waheed, "Anatomy of an Obscenity Trial," *Himal South Asian: A Review Magazine of Politics and Culture*, 1 July, 2013, himalmag.com/anatomy-obscenity- trial/. It is possible that they are married and seeking refuge in a hotel room. It is also unclear whether they are single or married to other people and having an affair.

CHAPTER 9

Dissenting Bodies, Disruptive Pandemic: Farmers' Protest and Women's Participation in Mass Mobilisation in India

Paromita Chakrabarti[1]

ABSTRACT

While authoritarian states promoting neoliberal forms of governance have taken advantage of COVID-19 to weaken the foundations of civil society, there has also been a significant rise in contemporary struggles for a more democratic society during and around the pandemic. From December 2019 to November 2021, India has seen a significant number of protests. The timeline of collective resistance against the state and its divisive, violent and neoliberal agenda represents a critical juncture in Indian politics. This paper focuses on the farmers' protests that started from last November and recently ended in a stunning, hard-earned victory. In a sector that is overwhelmingly male-dominated and deeply patriarchal, women farmers have come out on the streets protesting the controversial Farm Laws hastily passed by the Indian government in September 2019 that threatened to corporatize farming and increase exploitation and marginalisation of small farmers. What is most interesting about the farmers' protests is large-scale participation of women across caste, class, occupational, and religious divide which has changed the composition and dynamics of collective resistance and demonstrate how organised and collective resistance can become symbols of solidarity and intersectional dissent. The paper will examine the role of gender and female agency in protests by female occupying bodies in physical spaces particularly when under the pretext of COVID -19 crisis management the state has severely pushed back against citizens right to dissent and fight for justice. The farmer's protest has brought to the fore women's role in mass mobilisations. Women's participation in the protest has tremendous significance for women's movement for justice, equality and rights and can pose a real challenge to the return of the 'Strong State'.

Introduction

History has witnessed instances of individual protests injustice and brutality such as the famed image of the young man standing in front of the army tank in Tiananmen square, China.[2] The world has also seen spectacular mass movements of resistance and rebellion such as the French Revolution, the Russian Revolution, global struggles for independence from colonial rule in parts of Asia, the Caribbean, Africa; anti-war protests, anti-slavery abolition movements, the Civil Rights Movement in the US, the anti-Apartheid movement in South Africa, the Arab Spring, among others; that have changed the course of nations and transformed societies. Protests have been a defining feature of our world and modern history is replete with evidence of popular uprising, political and civil rights movements, mass rebellion, demonstrations, picketing, rioting etc., that have challenged existing power structures and, on many occasions, have also successfully overturned them.

We are currently living in times of protest. Protests against, protests by, protests for, protests within are not simply hashtags. There are virtual protests and protests by occupying bodies in physical spaces. We have seen protests such as the #MeToo movement, Black Lives Matter movement, Occupy Wall Street, the Arab Spring in North Africa, the *gilet jaunes* in France, the Youth Strike for Climate, #NiUnaMas and anti-femicide movements of Latin America, the Right to Abortion in Argentina, Poland and Ireland that have rocked the world; while closer home in India, we have witnessed massive resistance and ceaseless protests in Kashmir, the anti-rape and anti CAA (Citizenship Amendment Act) protest and the farmers' protests in India. These protests have demonstrated how organised and collective resistance can become symbols of solidarity and intersectional dissent. They are stunning examples of mass participation on a very large scale which has revitalized collective resistance in our present times. Protests have the ability to energize a restive populace by bringing them together in harmony, shot with the force of solidarity that comes through collective political action. Protests also can become sites of discordance and tension as they bring divergent bodies and discrete views together in a common struggle for equality and justice. A viable protest that has any chance of being successful has to be constantly open to negotiation and interrogation of its own position and an acknowledgement of the diverse character and divergent positionalities of the protesting publics.[3] Large scale mobilisation of people in the current moment in history is extremely interesting for feminist scholars as well as for those studying social movements. Examining women's mass mobilisation can offer insight into questions of identity, sexual relations and power structure and how women negotiate them through their participation in these mass movements.

Today protesting bodies on the streets are made highly conspicuous through media and other streaming devices. These images are shared widely through social networking feeds and often become the most visible moment in the history of collective struggle, 'overshadowing other temporalities, sites and modes of protest' (Cohen, Forbis and Misri, 2018: 15). Visibility is seen as agency and the deploying of protesting bodies in public sphere is construed as defiance. Streets on which demonstrations take place are thus marked as sites of resistance and has an immediate performative appeal. However, there is a whole repertoire of tactics that often comprise less visible acts of organized resistance and expands beyond the public sphere to include sonic, visual and digital practices along with the textual.[4] Visible protests in the public sphere often exclude or obscure those acts of individual or collective resistance that fall outside of them due to the threat of retaliatory state violence, immediate danger to life and liberty, disability, job precarity, child care, citizenship status etc. There is an urgent need to engage with forms of protest that exists beyond the boundaries of the visible, break free from an ableist framework and expand the discourse on organised resistance and collective struggle (Cohen, Forbis and Misri, 2018: 15).

Acts of organised resistance can be thus mapped on a huge scale which spans multiple registers and repertoire of strategies and tactics to fight oppression and exploitation. They address the pressing material and social concerns of our times and help build solidarity and partnerships across divides. Both individual and group struggle for an equal and just world has led to many a liberation movement and strengthened the contest against neo-imperialism, racial, gender and religious discrimination, and state violence. This paper looks at the organised struggle against steady corporatisation of the economy and neoliberal offensives by the state particularly through the mass mobilisation of women and the broader impact of women's participation in collective struggle in general on questions of gender and in particular the effect it has on gender roles, gender relations and gender equality in India.

Indian protest scene and farmers agitation

From December 2019 to November 2021, Indian streets have exploded in demonstrations, agitations, blockades, and conflict.[5] Streets have become the most visible sites of occupation by the protesting bodies and one of the many violent sites of state repression. With the pandemic raging, the heavy-handed way in which the state responded to collective protest reveals the precarious nature of Indian democracy. The central government curbed civil liberties, shut down the internet at protest sites, clamped down on news in the media, arrested political opponents/students/dissidents/protestors all in the name of restoring order and managing COVID-19 crisis along with the usual excuse of weeding out the 'anti-nationals' who apparently pose a threat to India's security and unity. Despite severe repression, the protests have continued unabated, particularly the ongoing farmers' protests which have the potential to seriously challenge deregulated capitalism and state oppression. The government brought in COVID -19 control regulations and tried to forcibly clear out the sites of protests, ban gathering of people and implemented a slew of measures that restricted access to public spaces making it very difficult to organise any kind of mass protests. In spite of COVID-19 regulations being in place and series of enforced lockdowns, the Indian protestors found a way to mass mobilise and storm the capital with demonstrations.

Since November 2020, Indian farmers have been staging one of the biggest protests that the country has seen. The farmers have been fighting against the implementation of three farm bills that the government tabled at the Parliament and rushed it through based on strength of numbers, and it passed in the form of the controversial Farm Laws in September 2020. The three controversial Farm Laws hurriedly passed without proper debate in the parliament were: Farmers' Produce Trade and Commerce (Promotion and Facilitation) Act, 2020; Farmers (Empowerment and Protection) Agreement on Price Assurance and Farm Services Act, 2020 and Essential Commodities (Amendment) Act, 2020. According to the government, the new Farm Laws signal a new era which will give more freedom to the farmer, more autonomy as s/he will no longer have to depend on a middleman for selling and can send produce across state borders as well as to large agro-businesses and grocery chains. The Modi government made loud proclamations that deregulation will open up agriculture to market competition thus boosting farmer income; open Indian agriculture to foreign markets; attract private investment; modernise the sector; improve infrastructure and all transactions would go digital. Foregrounding how this elimination of a public regulatory system will make farming more profitable, the government has opened up agriculture for big players from the corporate world. The government very carefully framed the argument for deregulation in the rhetoric of rights discourse saying that farmers will now be able to widen their networks, move freely across artificial, restrictive borders and create alliances transcending them.[6] Since the current BJP ruling party is a technocratic-populist one, the entire attempt was to justify the new laws as progressive and welfare-oriented through the adoption of a language which privileged technocratic interventions for problem solving and free-market logic that pretends to offer choice.[7] De-regulation will usher in a new era in farmers rights and bring with it greater opportunities. However, farmers fear that inequality and exploitation will exacerbate in a sector that has been reeling under massive poverty and has been divided by caste, gender and class differences.

The agricultural sector has never been a level playing field and neoliberal interventions will render it even more inequitable. With 85 percent of marginal farmers who have no access or minimum access to markets or transportation facilities, profit making through liberalisation and de-regulation will be in favour of big corporations who are already beginning to make their presence felt in the field. Farmers fear that de-regulation and entry of giant corporations will drive down prices, increase exploitation and marginalisation of small farmers and create havoc particularly during times of uncertainty such as over-supply as well as crop failure. Thousands of farmers especially from the states of Punjab, Haryana and western Uttar Pradesh started long marches to Delhi, the seat of power and have been camping at three Delhi border points: Tikri, Singhu and Ghazipur since 26th November 2020, demanding an immediate repeal of the three controversial laws. They also demanded a legal guarantee on Minimum Support Prices (MSP) for their crops.

From November 2020 to January 2021, 11 rounds of talks had been held between the government and the farmers' union. Under the coordination of 'Samyukt Kisan Morcha' and 'All India Kisan Sangharsh Coordination Committee', at least 22 farmers' union participated in the protests. The farmers' union received direct and indirect support also from other trade unions prominent among them is the All-India Motor Transport Congress (AIMTC). In the last round of talks that ended in January, the government offered to suspend the Farm Laws for one to 1.5 years. The farmers' union decried the proposal stating firmly that they will accept nothing short of complete repeal of these pro-corporate Farm Laws. The matter then moved to the Supreme Court which had passed a stay order on the laws and ordered to set up a four-member committee to resolve the impasse over them between the Centre and farmers' unions protesting at the Delhi borders. Unflinching in the face of police action, rampant arrests and threat of escalating violence, the farmers' union persisted in continuing their protests and finally won a stunning victory on 19th November 2021 when the Modi Government announced the repeal of all three Farm Laws. The farmers' unions welcomed the announcement but decided to continue their stir until the minimum support prices (MSP) is guaranteed by the government.

Farmers' Protests and Women in Mass Mobilisation

The farmers' protests are very interesting because of several reasons. They are one of the biggest that we have seen in recent times; they have been supported by trade unions from various sectors including service and manufacturing; the protests and blockades have spread to different states with simultaneous sit-ins and marches organized across state borders; several state governments tacitly extended their support to the protests (in keeping with their dissent against the bills before the Farm Laws were hastily passed); they received wide media coverage both national and international; they have seen overwhelming support from civil society and large-scale participation of women across the caste, class, occupational, and religious divide.

It has brought the women of the Anti-CAA movement and the women farmers together on the same platform; strengthening each other's fight and offering solidarity. The farmers' protests have brought to the fore women's role in mass mobilisations. Women's participation in the protests has tremendous significance for women's movement for justice, equality and rights. The clarion call for women to join in large numbers to mark March 8th at the protest sites is cause for celebration as it has been one of the largest gathering of women protesting against privatisation, corporatisation and neoliberalism in the world.

In January 2021, the Chief Justice of India (CJI) asked lawyers to persuade women, children and the elderly to leave protest sites and go home as it could be very difficult for them to brace the biting cold winter, especially when they are involved in sit-ins and hunger strikes and there may be considerable danger to their person if they continue to participate in such acts of resistance. The court also indirectly suggested that women's participation in the protests was as care givers, providing cooking and cleaning services; insinuating thousands of women farmers who were stung by the reductive attitude that treated them as frail and weak, did not see them as equal partners in the struggle and failed to recognise them as farmers in their own right. The CJI's remarks drew large scale ire across the protest lines as it was seen as not just as an attempt to exclude women from the protests, but also as a warning of violence to come against the protesters.

Unanimously rejecting the CJI's appeal with a resounding 'No' these women farmers continued their protests at the blockade sites along with male farmers asserting their identity as farmers and upholding their right to be seen as equal stakeholders. Bhowmick's report for *Time* mentions how women have risen up in fierce resistance. She quotes women farmers extensively from her interviews: "We either die and go back, or win and go back," said a woman protester. "Something snapped within us when we heard the government tell the women to go back home," says Jasbir Kaur, a 74-year-old farmer from Rampur in western Uttar Pradesh. Bhowmick finds out that Kaur has been bravely camping at the Ghazipur protest site for over three months, only returning home once. "Why should we go back? This is not just the men's protest. We toil in the fields alongside the men. Who are we—if not farmers?" (Bhowmick, 2021). The protest sites became an alternative space for women as they converted it to a place to resume their daily activities such as cooking, cleaning etc. Photo journalist Pundir's interviews with several women farmer protesters show how they have been not only defiant of the CJI's appeal but also developed a deeper sense of solidarity and community through their experience of being part of a collective struggle. When Pundir asked the women when would they go back home, one protester replied: "this is my home now, with a bigger family" (Pundir, 2021).

The protest has drawn women of all ages and diverse backgrounds from across India. From Septuagenarian Gurmer Kaur from Uttar Pradesh to 41-year-old widowed mother of two Amandeep Kaur from Punjab with her children, from 18-year-old farmers Sahumati Padha, and Hiraath Jhade who came from the central state of Chhattisgarh to Bindu Ammini Dalit rights and women's rights activist from the southernmost state of Kerala, this protest has witnessed pan-Indian support and solidarity. The protestors through their overwhelming and active participation have successfully challenged the traditionally accepted gender roles of simply being caregivers and housewives who help the family in farming. They have also been able to resist gender discrimination through an assertion of identity as farmers and protesters in the public space.

Changing mindsets in states where sexual violence, femicide, and gender discrimination are rampant has been a persistent challenge for activists. For her report, Bhowmick interviews Sudesh Goyat, the firebrand gender rights activist from Harayana. Goyat tells her: "We have been working to bring about gender equality in these parts for so long—but the process has been slow." Goyat declares how during the first few days of protests in Tikri, she was the only woman from Haryana there. But after the court suggested women leave, Goyat says proudly how women "started to pour in. They came with their families. They came with other women. They came alone. It's no less than a miracle." (Bhowmick, 2021).

The sites have also become important venues for discussion and debate on gender equality. The men and women have had to occupy spaces in close proximity and a deeper understanding of gender imbalance is beginning to emerge among both men and women who have had to share spaces for several months. Taking advantage of this rare situation, activists held frequent discussions on women's work and their contribution to the rural economy. Regular announcements from the stage about treating women as equals echoed around the protest sites throughout the day. Bhowmick's other interviewees, such as the young and passionate Harsharan Kaur who left a job in Dubai to volunteer at the protest site draw courage from and display her faith in the mass mobilisation: "I like this India" she tells Bhowmick. (Bhowmick, 2021).

Gender rights activists have been working with women and men at these sites and have been able to normalise conversations around taboo topics such as menstruation. At the Ghazipur site, Bhowmick interviews the 29-year-old Ravneet Kaur, a law student from Bangalore, who has set up a mobile sanitary napkin store where the products are displayed openly. Kaur tells Bhowmick: "The men got used to it soon enough." "Now these conversations are normal around here. Men don't flinch when they say sanitary napkins anymore" (Bhowmick, 2021). Sudesh Goyat, the gender rights activist has been at the Tikri protest site since the very beginning, helping mobilize women and organize for January 18 to be recognized as Women Farmers Day. She tells Bhowmick: "Women work equally in the fields with the men. It's only right they should be here to protest. The awareness among women about their own power has never been higher than now" (Bhowmick, 2021).

Whether such sentiments will spread beyond the protests is unclear, but for now, female farmers are being seen, heard and acknowledged—offering a new vision of what gender equality might look like for the country. In an interview with Sukh Deep Singh, a young farmer from Punjab, Bhowmick quotes him: "We have looked upon them as mothers, sisters, wives," he says, "but now we see them in a different light" (Bhowmick, 2021). Singh's awareness signals an interesting shift in gender relations and reveals how participation in mass struggle can dislodge deep seated gender stereotypes. The large presence of women in public spaces, holding their own, also has a significant impact on how they are viewed by their male counterparts. From being seen simply as mothers and wives to becoming comrades in a battle is a really important shift that can have very decisive transformation on gender relations in particular. What is most important is women have begun to see themselves differently. There is a rising consciousness among women protestors who now understand their oppression and exploitation and know that they have to stand up and fight. This self-awareness has led to agency and made these women vocal and brave. In Tikri, Sudesh Kandela, a 55-year-old farmer from Haryana, whom Bhowmick interviews tells her while she watches a play being staged by a local theatre group, enraptured by the spectacle: "I didn't know what I was capable of beyond the expectations of me as a woman, a wife and mother." She confesses to Bhowmick that she has never been to a protest or taken her veil off outside her home. "But I am here now," she says, clenching her fists, "and I cannot be oppressed. I cannot be intimidated. I cannot be bought" (Bhowmick, 2021).

Taking Centre stage: Women's radical activism through mass protests

On March 8th, India witnessed a new Women's Day. Wearing bright yellow scarves representing the colour of mustard fields, the women took centre stage at key protest sites, chanting slogans, holding small marches, and making speeches against the laws. Holding flags of farm unions, the women gather around women leaders from the farming community and around those activists who had joined the swell of protests from all over the country. These women leaders made fiery speeches against Modi government's complete lack of concern towards women farmers and its apathetic attitude towards women in general. Some protestors went on a day-long hunger strike demanding an immediate repeal of the Farm Laws. The women protestors were joined by thousands of women from all walks of life and those who have been sitting at Shaheen Bagh in protest of the draconian CAA since November 2019. There were speeches, plays, songs, dance, poetry readings that highlighted women's contribution to farming among others. The stage was managed by women, the speakers were all women and the issues tackled were about farming in general and women farmers in particular and the contribution of women farmers in this movement. While the focus was primarily on women farmers and their concerns, there were many discussions and speeches made around women's role in the economy, their contribution to society, exploitation of and violence against women, and the importance of collective struggle for gender justice and equality.

What is extremely significant about these protests is the emergence of a new crop of feminist activists who co-organised and co-ordinated the protests that brought both men and women together. These new women activists demonstrated a high level of political consciousness by recognising the common struggles of both factory/industrial workers and farmers. Nodeep Kaur who has been organising male and female industrial workers to demand better working conditions and assumed a leadership role in this organisation lead a rally of thousands of industrial workers – men and women – in support of the farmers' movement.

The case of Disha Ravi is a very interesting one. On 13th February 2021, twenty-two-year-old old environmental and gender activist Ravi was arrested by the Delhi Police on the allegation of providing an online toolkit to defame India, allegedly taking and offering support to pro- Khalistani separatist group (which wants to create a separate country in Punjab) under the garb of farmer's protest. There was a global outcry and widespread protests in India against her arrest. The way she was arrested once again confirmed the heavy-handed way in which the current government tried to muffle dissent and scare young activists by jailing them under sedition laws on the flimsiest pretext of spreading disaffection and ill will against the government (*Al Jazeera*, 2021). Ravi was later released for lack of evidence by the Delhi High Court which pronounced the toolkit at the centre of controversy as an innocuous one with no evidence of any call for violence. In her support to the farmers' cause, Ravi said: "My grandparents, who are farmers, indirectly birthed my climate activism." She explained in detail why climate activism and the farmers' protest against the three Farm Laws resonated with her. Ravi said in her statement after her release:

> "Climate Justice isn't just for the rich and the white. It is a fight alongside those who are displaced; whose rivers have been poisoned; whose lands were stolen; who watch their houses get washed away every other season; and those who fight tirelessly for what are basic hu-

man rights. We fight alongside those actively silenced by the masses and portrayed as 'voiceless', because it is easier for savarnas[8] to call them voiceless. We take the easy way out and fund saviourism rather than amplify the voices on ground" (Dutta Roy, 2021).

Ravi's activism and support to the farmers' protests is a case in point where women have come out in the open to argue against the government's neo-liberal offensives and successfully make links with the larger social, environmental and political struggles that define our century and those of caste, gender and class that divide Indian society.

The massive participation of women in the protests has garnered worldwide attention. The protests have attracted the attention of activists, politicians and celebrities around the world, such as singer Rihanna, climate activist Greta Thunberg, legal activist Meena Harris (the niece of US Vice President Kamala Harris), the Hollywood film actress Susan Sarandon, UN human rights chief Michelle Bachelet and the UK Green Party member of parliament Caroline Lucas. They have all extended support to the farmers' protests against the three Farm Laws brought in by the BJP government.

Women, food and farm labour: The optics of protest

The prominent presence of women in what was perhaps the world's largest ongoing protest movement till early December 2021, and certainly one of the biggest domestic challenge facing Prime Minister Narendra Modi's government, has put a spotlight on the important role women play in agriculture in India. It also marks a milestone in women's struggle for equality, and their leadership in resistance movements. Most of the protesting farmers have come from the three north Indian states of Haryana, Uttar Pradesh and Punjab, states that have the worst male to female sex ratio, highest record of violent crimes against women, rampant practice of dowry in marriage, and lowest property and land ownership among women in the country. The large presence of protesting women from these states is thus extremely significant and quite remarkable (Nabourema, 2021).

Women farmers comprise an invisible workforce in India's vast agricultural sector. Most spend long hours of hard farm labour but own no land. Women who are protesting the Farm Laws worry that these laws will not only threaten their livelihoods but may drive their male relatives to desperate measures such as suicide and abandonment. Mitra and Shroff argue that farmers' suicides have acquired epidemic proportions in India spiralling out of control. The loss of competitiveness with the opening up of India's agricultural economy in the mid-1990's by several states was a major reason for farmers suicides. Most farmers' suicides are brought on by their inability to repay loans taken from private moneylenders and banks (Mitra and Shroff, 2007:73).[9] Statistics on farmers' suicides reveal the extent of catastrophe and indicate that it is mostly men who take their lives leaving the women and children in abject poverty. Widows of farmers and agricultural labourers have had to bear the excruciating burden of childcare and work to provide for food, education and shelter for the family. It is no wonder that women are fiercely contesting the laws that they believe will exacerbate poverty, exploitation and financial hardship.

The farmers' protests have also rekindled women's demands for land reforms. According to an Oxfam India report, more than 85 per cent of rural women in India are engaged in agriculture, yet less than 13 percent of women owned land. Nearly 75 percent of rural women in India who work full-time are farmers, and the numbers are expected to rise as more men migrate to cities for jobs (Oxfam India, 2018). According to the India Human Development Survey conducted by National Council of Applied Economic Research (NCAER), 83 percent of agricultural land is inherited by male members of the family and less than 2 percent by females. The lack of formal ownership makes it very difficult for women farmers to access bank loans, government assistance, subsidies, support of the agricultural cooperatives etc. Furthermore, women, especially those whose spouses have committed suicide, are unable to gain the right to the land they farm due to gender-biased inheritance laws particularly in the north Indian states of Punjab, Uttar Pradesh, Haryana among others . Inheritance provisions are governed by multiple laws and in the case of women farmers assertion of land rights through marriage or birth is further complicated with different states implementing land laws that clearly reflect gender bias through covert or overt favouring of the male of the family. This reality, coupled with the inability of female farmers to access subsidies, insurance, loans and aid programmes, has driven women to join the protests in large numbers and demand wider reforms (Nabourema, 2021). The odds are particularly stacked against single women farmers as they juggle home and work, land and law; if the new laws are passed the market for agricultural produce is bound to become more distant and hence more competitive and exploitative.

Women are keenly aware that their presence at the protest sites offers some level of protection to the men from police brutality and tough action by security forces; they are also conscious of their contribution to the cause of resistance as they maintain a steady supply of rations and daily necessities at the camp sites. Many women farmers participated in the protest by rotation as female family and community members took turns to look after children and tend to the farms back home. This has strengthened affective networks and consolidated the fight against state sponsored capitalist takeover of their lands and labour. Women protesters are now a formidable group forging alliances with the wider struggles of the working-class movement. Pundir notes that the predominantly non-violent nature of the protests has also encouraged large scale participation of women and the elderly in the protests and the visible presence of women farmers at the camp sites have inspired other oppressed groups in society and particularly minority women and students, both urban and rural; to come out openly in support of the protestors and combine forces to fight the government's anti-people, anti-farmer measures (Pundir, 2021).

The role of gender and female agency in protests by female bodies occupying physical spaces particularly when, under the pretext of the COVID -19 crisis management, the state has severely curtailed citizens' right to dissent and the fight for justice must be seriously considered. The collective struggle against the encroachment of corporate capital has weakened gender, caste and communal divisions. Although there are divisions between small and medium farmers the encroachment of corporate capitalism represents a danger to both and on this basis, women have taken a prominent role in organising resistance even among those communities that are traditional, and male dominated. The farmers' protests has brought to the fore women's role in mass mobilisations and has tremendous significance for the women's movement for justice, equality and rights. Their participation represents a crucial dimension in resisting the return of the 'Strong State'. The farmers' protests need to make links with larger urban struggles and the workers movement in order to move beyond its current impasse. The struggle of the working class needs to be unified under a leadership that can bring diverse trade unions together to bargain for collective rights and push back against the behemoth of corporate capitalism that has weakened many labour organisations. Currently the impasse is trade unions organising separately and not joining forces to secure greater rights for its workers to fight against austerity measures. Until all trade unions of the country come together on one plank and demand an end to rampant privatization, corporate take-over of public institutions, induced precarity and push for the return of a welfare state, the farmers' victory may be a short lived one.

Conclusion

The protests have highlighted both the role women play in farming and revealed their skills of organising and mobilising. The presence of women in the protests also challenges the stereotype of Indian women as being passive victims of social injustices and violence. Women have seized the opportunity presented by the protests to demand not just the repeal of the controversial Farm Laws, but also to end discrimination and inequality (Nabourema, 2021). It is yet to be seen to what extent women's mass mobilisation transforms the existing structures of gender relations and succeeds in addressing current social and economic inequalities.

However, there is no doubt that these massive protests have shaken the very foundations of the country and brought ordinary people from all walks of life to lend support to the cause of the farmers. It is this collaborative aspect of the mobilisation that seems to be one of the most interesting dimensions of the struggle. Women farmers' participation in the protests have given rise to new coalitions of activists and inspired spirited critique on women's empowerment, women's roles in agriculture, women and land rights, gender relations and patriarchy, among others. The interactions that have taken place between women at the protest sites cut across class, caste, religion and geographical divides, revealing the importance of doing intersectional feminism and reviving the possibility of social egalitarianism.

The farmers' protests to a large extent have been able to successfully contest the onslaught of privatization and the associated dismantling of the public sector and decline of social welfare measures particularly in the field of agriculture. These protests have been able to expose the consequences of privatization and neoliberal market reforms such as inequities of distribution and consequent threats to livelihood. Fiercely resisting the state's insistence on a restructured partnership as a strategy for survival in neoliberal times by submitting to the demands of the private marketplace, the farmers have shown immense resilience through their yearlong sit-ins. Demanding social provisioning and guaranteed welfare protection from a state that has clearly embraced free market neoliberalism, the farmers' protests encapsulate the challenge that defines our current moment of crisis. Should we organize and fight for a more protectionist state that provides us social services and is not undermined by transnational corporations that circumvent state regulations and structures? Or should we celebrate the weakening of the state in favour of globalization, NGOization, free flow of resources and transnationalization of public welfare? The debate between a statist and non-statist mode of political economy as a favoured form of political space lies at the heart of the farmers' protests. All the actors involved in the protests are highly critical of the state-in-retreat. The farmers' protests as a social movement demands a certain kind of role from the state, it envisions the state as a provider of welfare provisions with responsibility towards its citizens that can be fulfilled through uncompromising public institutions that are accountable.

What is interesting is that the current famers' protests not only demand a protectionist state that fights off privatization but as a social movement seeks to democratize it. This aspect of the protests is extremely crucial as we witness a slow demise of the welfarist state while also noticing the frightening rise of a police state that relies on force, surveillance and other methods of control to regulate and subjugate. The farmers' protest thus occurs at a critical moment in time when the state is poised to withdraw from public welfare and yet strengthen its disciplinary apparatus to impose its will on the citizens. It offers us a nuanced perspective on contestations, oppositional discourses, intersectionality, self-organisation at local levels, the power and reach of mass mobilisation and the various dimensions of governmentality. It shows us the importance of organising based on class and yet considers gender, caste, religious differences that if ignored can fracture the movement and lead to its defeat. The biggest strength of the farmers' protests lies in their egalitarian, democratic and participatory character. They offer us an insight into what larger struggles against neoliberal capitalism can achieve by organizing based on changing class relations, by diminishing the agrarian/non-agrarian divide, and by considering multiple axes of oppression based on social relations such as gender, sexuality, caste, race, ethnicity, religion, tribe etc.

After a year of sit-ins, road blockades, marches, demonstrations, rallies, the farmers have won. The government's repeal of the controversial Farm Laws has turned one of the most important organised struggles of our times into a success story. The farmers have resisted and triumphed for now. What remains to be seen is whether this particular social movement can sustain itself and yet merge into larger struggles for social justice, economic empowerment, gender equality, political freedom and communal harmony in India. One takes hope from the fact that the movement and mass mobilisation of both men and women seem to be going from strength to strength and there are no signs of anyone involved giving up.

REFERENCES

Aljazeera. (2021, February 15). 'Disha Ravi: Arrest of young Indian activist triggers outrage.' https://www.aljazeera.com/news/2021/2/15/indian-climate-activists-arrest-causes-outrage

Bhowmick, Nilanjana. (2021, March 4). "'I Cannot Be Intimidated. I Cannot Be Bought." The Women Leading India's Farmers' Protest.' *Time*. https://time.com/5942125/women-india-farmers-protests/

Cohen, E., Forbis, M., & Misri, D. (2018). Introduction: Protest. *WSQ: Women's Studies Quarterly, 46*(3 & 4), 14–28. Retrieved July 27, 2021, from https://www.jstor.org/stable/26511329

Dutta Roy, Divyanshu. (2021, March 13). 'Pronounced Guilty By Seekers Of TRPs": Activist Disha Ravi Hits Back.' *NDTV*. https://www.ndtv.com/india-news/activist-disha-ravi-releases-statement-pronounced-guilty-by-seekers-of-trps-2390128

D'Souza, Radha. (2018). *What's Wrong with Rights?: Social Movements, Law and Liberal Imaginations*. London: Pluto Press.

Friedman, J. (2020). *Power Without Knowledge: A Critique of Technocracy*. Oxford University Press.

Friedman, J. (2019). 'Populists as Technocrats.' *Critical Review*, 31(3-4), 315-376.

Moffitt, B., & Tormey, S. (2014). 'Rethinking Populism: Politics, Mediatisation and Political Style.' *Political Studies*, 62(2), 381–397.

Mitra, Sidhartha and Sangeetha Shroff. (2007). 'Farmers' Suicide in Maharashtra,' *Economic and Political Weekly*, 42(49), 73-77.

Nabourema, Farida. (2021, March 3). 'In India Women Propel World's Largest Movement.' *US Institute of Peace* (USIP). https://www.usip.org/publications/2021/03/india-women-propel-worlds-largest-protest-movement

Ostiguy, P. (2017). Populism: A Socio-Cultural Approach. In C. R. Kaltwasser, P. Taggart, P. O. Espejo, & P. Ostiguy (Eds.), *The Oxford Handbook of Populism*. Vol. 1, 73– 100, Oxford: Oxford University Press.

Oxfam India. (2018, November 15). "Move over 'Sons of the soil: Why you need to know the female farmers that are revolutionizing agriculture in India." Gender Justice, *Oxfam India: A movement to end discrimination*. https://www.oxfamindia.org/women-empowerment-india-farmers

Pundir, Pallavi. (2021, March 9). 'In Photos: The Women on the Front Line of India's Farmers' Protest.' *https://www.aljazeera.com/news/2021/2/15/indian-climate-activists-arrest-causes-outrage*Schwartzberg, Melissa (Ed). (2020). 'Protest and Dissent.' *Nomos LXII: Yearbook of the American Society for Political and Legal Philosophy*. New York: New York University Press.

ENDNOTES

1 Dr. Paromita Chakrabarti is Professor and Head of the Department of English and Director, Global Research Initiatives (GRI) at H.R. College of Commerce and Economics, University of Mumbai where she has been teaching since 2001. Her research areas include migration, diaspora, postcolonial studies, gender and nation. She has been a 2010-11 Fulbright-Nehru Doctoral Research Fellow at the Department of English, Indiana University, Bloomington. Dr. Chakrabarti has published several articles in international journals and is the assistant editor of the peer reviewed journal *Writing Today: International Journal of Studies in English*. She has been a joint editor for the peer reviewed journal *Baltic Worlds* from Södertörn University, Stockholm and has been a resource person at University Grants Commission (UGC) sponsored refresher courses and short-term courses for faculty across colleges and universities in India. She annually teaches a Master's level semi-

nar class on Feminist Critical Theory at the University of Sheffield, UK, and has been an invited speaker for seminar lecture at several universities and colleges both in India and abroad. In her spare time Paromita enjoys trekking and travelling. E-mail contact: drparomitachakrabarti@hrcollege.edu

2 This iconic image of an unidentified man who stood in front of a column of tanks leaving Tiananmen Square in Beijing, June 5, 1989, blocking their path, after the violent crackdown of the Chinese govt against protests is seen today as a symbol of fearless resistance against censorship and state authority. He is known as "Tank Man".

3 For more on this see Melissa Schwartzberg edited 'Protest and Dissent' in *Nomos* LXII and Cohen et al.

4 Photography, paintings, graphic art, literature, theatre, dance, cinema, songs and speeches on radio (sonic protests), memoirs, oral history, testimonies, community storytelling, food, clothing, digital culture and subcultures, can operate as sites of protest and struggle for transformation outside of the very visible demonstrations of collective resistance that take place on the street.

5 One of the most significant protests that drew in thousands across the country was the Anti-CAA demonstrations that reached a crescendo in December 2019-January 2020. Protesters demonstrated against the implementation of the controversial and discriminatory Citizenship Amendment Act (CAA) of 2019 that makes provisions for Indian citizenship to persecuted religious minorities from neighbouring Afghanistan, Bangladesh and Pakistan. This provision is for only Hindus, Sikhs, Buddhists, Parsis, Jains and/or Christians. The CAA specifically excludes Muslims. The Act has come under severe criticism as it clearly makes religious identity as a criterion for Indian citizenship.

6 Radha D'Souza (2018) provides a detailed critique of the way governments and businesses use the rights discourse to justify neoliberal policies and globalisation. She also exposes the ways in which governments court big businesses and suggests corporate capitalism as a means to improving people's lives.

7 See Friedman's work on how governments use technocracy as an approach to governance. In this system technical expertise is prized over democratic representation. Also see Ostiguy and Moffitt's work on performative-relational approach towards populism. The politics of both technocracy and populism are viewed as hostile to representative democracy and pluralistic politics.

8 Upper caste people are the savarnas.

9 The maximum number of suicides reported are from those states of Karnataka, Maharashtra and Andhra Pradesh. It is interesting to note that these are the states that have adopted the economic reforms of 1990's in totality and aggressively promoted market-oriented model of agriculture while withdrawing state support and welfare measures for farmers. In promoting market-oriented production systems, these states have also pushed for the cultivation of cash crops for profit (predominantly cotton) even when the land and the supporting ecological system may have been unsuitable for such cultivation.

CHAPTER 10

Women's Agency and Pastoral Livelihoods in India: A Review

Aayushi Malhotra[1], **Sailaja Nandigama**[2],
Kumar Sankar Bhattacharya[3]

ABSTRACT

The role of women in promoting and sustaining pastoral livelihoods remains an under-researched area across the world. Often, studies discuss pastoralism as a male-oriented enterprise, thus overshadowing or ignoring the part played by women in such livelihood practices. In India, where pastoralism itself is essentially a neglected area of research, such discussions remain even sparse. Pastoral communities depending on migratory livestock rearing practices for their livelihoods exhibit gender-based differences in their everyday life in terms of division of labour, mobility patterns, and rights over resources. Women play different roles and responsibilities at the household and community levels that remain intertwined with their pastoral livelihoods. Drawing from the available literature, we aim to synthesize the situated agency of these pastoral women in their everyday lives and their collective activism in the face of mainstream models of development. We engage in a thorough analysis from a gender perspective in this paper to discuss specific cases of Indian women and their influence on pastoral livelihoods and interests. We aim to reframe and undo the invisibility women in pastoralism have faced thus far by re-telling their stories from a gendered perspective.

Introduction

Pastoralism involves migratory livestock rearing practices that vary according to socio-ecological landscapes resulting in a wide range of diversity. FAO (2021) defines pastoralism as an animal husbandry practice that follows a specific grazing itinerary across spatio-temporal scales. It includes rearing different types of livestock in variable ecological conditions extending from dry, arid rangelands to the mountainous alpine grasslands, while following appropriate mobility patterns. An estimated 500 million people across the globe derive livelihoods from this practice (Manzano et al., 2021). While in India, a considerable population of around 13 million depends on the traditional pastoral activities to earn a living (Kishore & Köhler-Rollefson, 2020). Despite such an expanse both in terms of nature and praxis, pastoralism is limited to discussions within academic circles with a major proclivity for ecological governance and resource management-related aspects. The remaining socio-cultural predicaments within pastoral livelihoods are not adequately examined yet, despite being frequently acknowledged. Gender within the pastoral communities and households is one such underexplored aspect.

Gender, just like the other intersectional attributes of society, plays a vital role in structuring pastoral livelihoods. Within the gigantic livestock economy of India, women comprise a majority of the available workforce, especially at the rural and household level enterprises (Ramdas & Ghotge, 2006). Nonetheless, most of the available scholarship either overlooks the gendered underpinnings or overtly discusses pastoral issues from a male vantage point, leaving out concerns and challenges of women. Very few scholarly studies (Bhasin, 1991, 2011; Eneyew & Mengistu, 2013; Flintan, 2008, 2011; Fratkin & Smith, 1995; Hannah, 2007; Kipuri & Ridgewell, 2008; Köhler-Rollefson, 2018; Ramdas & Ghotge, 2007; Rangnekar, 1994; Venkatasubramanian & Ramnarain, 2018; Verma & Khadka, 2016) have dealt with the gendered differences across the pastoral contexts essentially influencing the division of labour and resources, workload, ownership rights and access to resources, along with the decisions regarding mobility and marketing. These studies, even if numerally limited, indicate the relevance of gender as a crucial analytical lens to understand how pastoral livelihoods are organised. A gendered focus is essential for the pastoral livelihoods to be mainstreamed, as is acknowledged by the international bodies like the Food and Agricultural Organization (FAO). A recent compilation on variability in pastoralism by FAO (2021) highlights the lack of disaggregated data and research on pastoral women, who despite their integral roles in pastoral livelihoods stay in the back benches of socio-economic development. According to this report, such an information deficit and skewed focus is likely to result in misplaced priorities regarding the gender dynamics, thus hampering the overall socio-economic development within the pastoral contexts. Women in pastoralism acquire different roles considering the type of pastoral activities[4] prevalent within their household and the communities (Verma & Khadka, 2016). In India, around 46 specialized community groups have traditional pastoral affiliations, rear a variety of livestock[5] and follow different mobility patterns[6] suiting their geographical positioning (Kishore & Köhler-Rollefson, 2020). These basic criteria play a major role in defining the contributions of women towards livestock, land and households, and also, govern their resource ownership, control and access rights (Jaweed & Khan, 2015). For instance, among the agro-pastoral community of *Gaddis* located in the hilly terrains of Northern India, women do not migrate along with the herds, only men perform all the animal husbandry related activities on the move. However, in the case of semi-nomadic *Raika* pastoralists of Rajasthan who rear camels, or the buffalo rearing *Van-Gujjars* of Uttarakhand, the whole family migrates as a unit. Such variations--in types of livestock reared, patterns of migration followed, along with intersectional and socio-cultural factors that are exclusive to pastoral livelihoods--have far reaching impacts on the role played by the pastoral women and their ability to exercise agency.

Despite the diversity of pastoral contexts, women in-general play a significant role in sustenance and maintenance of pastoral livelihoods (Flintan, 2008; Verma et al., 2016). Apart from being the caretakers of the livestock and the family, they often play the roles of a herder, trader, knowledge-bearer, healer, as well as a political activist (Ramdas & Ghotge, 2007; Rangnekar, 1994) when needed. Requirements of mobility, arranging the resources for self and livestock and trading activities put these pastoral women at the forefront where they negotiate and bargain on an everyday basis (Köhler-Rollefson, 2018). Although, pastoral women in India are constrained by predominant patriarchal norms that often put them in positions of subjugation--to assume them as powerless victims would be misleading. Therefore, there is a need to challenge such assumptions and recognise their central roles in functioning and sustenance of pastoral livelihoods in tune with their situated agency.

A majority of the existing studies on pastoral contexts take the gender aspect into peripheral consideration, arriving at conclusions that point towards women to be subservient and doubly marginalized or situated at the margins of the margin (Bhasin, 2011; Eneyew & Mengistu, 2013; Kipuri & Ridgewell, 2008; Verma & Khadka, 2016). These simplified inferences are often borrowed without contextual assessment and critical engagement to claim that pastoralism, in addition to the mainstream gender-based discrimination, adds onto the existing vulnerability of women (Bhasin, 2011). They consequently label pastoral women as oppressed and voiceless, which further leads to the inception of skewed development interventions that often do more harm than good (Köhler-Rollefson, 2018). We do not intend to entirely discard the assertion that pastoral women are vulnerable to various hardships; however, rendering them deprived of voice and agency in the context of their livelihoods is highly problematic as well as deceptive. Therefore, in this paper we aim to question these generalized inferences and their policy based implications by discussing the role of women in influencing pastoral livelihoods within the Indian context. To this end, in our assessment of selected literature, we bring to light the exercise of 'situated agency' by pastoral women as it has a significant bearing on the survival of pastoral practices and futures.

Situated agency as a concept has been applied across disciplines in several ways as it provides ample space for multiple localized interpretations (Gammage et al., 2016; Nandigama, 2020). However, to clarify from the outset, in this paper we borrow from the work of Naila Kabeer (1999), where she conceptualizes agency to be more than the decision-making ability-- that extends to bargaining, negotiation, deception, manipulation, subversion, and resistance--both in individual as well as collective capacity. Such processes are situation-specific where the aspects of agency including voice or actions could manifest in various ways. In this paper we review the cases of Indian pastoral women, using this conceptual framing to challenge the reductionist idea that assumes them to be doubly disadvantaged and marginalized. Through an in-depth analysis of literature, we conclude that Indian pastoral women navigate patriarchal norms with their situated agency and are not necessarily marginalized, in the way marginalization in pastoral contexts is generally percieved. With their integral roles and positions, pastoral women influence pastoral livelihoods in multiple ways. Essentially, we argue that there is a need to look beyond the conventional lens of resource ownership, control or access to understand pastoral women's everyday agency in influencing their traditional occupation.

In this paper, we address the inconsistency in literature where pastoral women are often labelled as marginalized and voiceless because of their patriarchal subjugation, but are also recognised as active agents influencing the direction of change within pastoral livelihoods. Thus, to untangle what role women play in pastoral systems, we ask the following key questions: What kind of implicit or explicit actions do women take? How do those actions affect pastoral livelihoods? And finally, what do these roles and actions say about their situated agency? To answer the same, we look at women's everyday decisions, actions and choices that otherwise get neglected under the assertion of their weaker socio-economic positions. Although the narrow literature available in this direction limits our capacity for generalization, we recognise that whatever finite information is available remains noteworthy to initiate this much needed discussion. This further lays a foundation for future research in pastoral studies probing comparable contexts with a renewed focus on gender dynamics, pastoral women and their situated agency.

Women in Pastoral contexts

Pastoral livelihoods that revolve around migratory animal husbandry remain dependent on women in more than one way. Apart from their direct contributions within pastoral systems that include rearing the livestock, milking, taking care of calfs and the sick animals, feeding and arranging fodder, women also are responsible for other tasks including subsistence agriculture, household chores and subsidiary economic activities like weaving, cheese-making and producing other by-products (Rangnekar, 1994; Rota & Sperandini, 2010; Verma & Khadka, 2016). However, they continue to remain invisible without due acknowledgement both in research and practice as their roles in pastoralism are rarely recognised (Rangnekar, 1994). Lack of gender disaggregated data from pastoral households limits the scope for understanding actual gender relations in pastoral communities. This often leads to sweeping generalizations of pastoral women as voiceless and vulnerable within the dominant discourses on gender inequality and paternalistic prejudices (Köhler-Rollefson, 2018; Rota & Sperandini, 2010). Inadequate narratives and superficial representations of pastoral women as victims of patriarchy, deprived of resource ownerships and access with excessive unpaid workloads stay in circulation without any contextual examination and critical analysis. Gradually, such arguments also become the basis for their socio-economic development and policy interventions to introduce various measures for women's empowerment. Such policy narratives seem to operate at various levels without fully engaging with the consideration of pastoral women's already existing agency (Flintan, 2008; Köhler-Rollefson, 2018; Rota & Sperandini, 2010), and could very easily go against their interests as is shown below in the case of pastoralists from the Deccan region and Rajasthan among the others.

Indian pastoral women and their situated agency

Out of the existing accounts that outline the struggles and contributions of pastoral women in maintaining and supporting pastoralism, we identified some cases that shed light on their situated agency. Although, these studies engage with the issues of women's resource rights, impacts of climate change on women's labour and their possession of local ecological knowledge (Bhasin, 2011; Köhler-Rollefson, 2018; Ramdas & Ghotge, 2007; Venkatasubramanian & Ramnarain, 2018), we utilize them to critically interpret the role of women in pastoralism and to provide a base for conceptualizing the exercise of their situated agency.

Beginning from the North of the country, among the *Gaddi* agro-pastoralists of Western Himalayan region, women play an important role in the dual enterprise comprising migratory herding and agricultural activities as documented by Bhasin (2011, 2013) and Mehra (1992). These pastoralists rear herds of sheep and goats following a seasonal vertical movement across the plain and hilly terrains in search of pasturage. In this community, men carry out traditional migratory pastoral practices while women stay in the settled villages where they look after the larger cattle that need to be stall-fed. As men stay on the move year-round, women take charge of most of the household chores and decisions. They also are significantly responsible for agricultural activities that supplement household nutrition as well as their earnings. Agro-pastoral pursuits within this community continue because of this gendered division of labour at the household level. With their sedentary status, *Gaddi* women assert a stronghold over the household economic decisions and indirectly contribute in sustaining the migratory pastoralism by mutually sharing the workload with their male counterparts. Such a combination of factors including the absence of men because of their constant migration, economic contribution of women through participation in cultivation activities and rearing of animals can be considered as some of the underlying reasons for the alleviated social status and autonomy of the *Gaddi* women (Mehra, 1992).

Similarly, in the case of the *Raika* pastoralists of Rajasthan, women actively participate in nomadic pastoral shepherding where they watch over both the livestock and finances along with their men. In common parlance, very often they are expected by the *Raika* community to act dociley in face of the stringent patriarchal norms that govern their education and marriage, and are lauded for their veiled outward appearance, and their silent behaviour around men. However, Köhler-Rollefson's (2018) account on *Raika* women explains how they wield the power behind the scenes. According to her, *Raika* women perform exceptionally well in managing the money matters and are at times addressed as the 'family finance ministers' by their male counterparts (Hannah, 2007; Köhler-Rollefson, 2018). While the *Raika* men are out grazing their livestock, women handle the interactions with traders and agriculturalists to finalize animal and manure related transactions, which facilitates their economic independence. Their role and position in pastoral practices, which involves caring for the new-born calfs, handling family income and managing the camps during migration are also highly valued within the community and remains crucial for keeping the pastoral economy of the *Raikas* intact. Despite the stringent patriarchal norms prevalent in Rajasthan, *Raika* women are able to uphold strong social as well economic positions by the virtue of their participation in pastoralism. However, in recent times women of the community expressed a declining interest in pursuing a migratory lifestyle with the emergence of numerous challenges including dwindling resources, state imposed restriction on grazing, children's education and their own aspirations for a modern sedentary lifestyle. Acting on their will, they are shunning the marriage alliances with the pastoral men, leaving deeper impacts on the generational renewal of *Raika* pastoral practices. Considering their centrality and strategic role, Köhler-Rollefson (2018) identified the *Raika* women as the lynchpin when it comes to the continuance of traditional practices of migratory sheep husbandry.

The case study of *Dailibai Raika,* (Hannah, 2007), the owner of a small herd and a traditional animal healer, provides a vantage point to our understanding of the situated contexts in which women's agency get articulated during the pastoral lifestyles. *Dailibai* is known for representing her community across several important governmental and non-governmental platforms to voice concerns regarding declining access to the grazing lands that affect the pastoral pursuits. She steers across powerful patriarchal settings to raise the livelihood related problems pastoral women and men face at multiple public forums despite the aversion of a few powerful community members. By doing so, she challenges the general perceptions regarding the pastoral women being inarticulate and voiceless. This bias against politically active women has been observed among many other pastoral contexts across the world (Eneyew & Mengistu, 2013; Kipuri & Ridgewell, 2008). According to *Dailibai,* 'if *Raikas* are not able to safeguard their pastoralism, not only many valuable livestock breeds, but also a large pool of knowledge would be lost. People would also have to settle for low paid city jobs that hold no honour'(Hannah, 2007). More voices like hers are needed to protect the pastoral interests and also raise the issues of pastoral women to draw required support.

Another significant illustration of pastoral women's agency is documented by Ramdas & Ghotge (2007) where they discuss the collective resistance of pastoral women against the state. *Kurma, Kurba* and *Dhangar* pastoral communities of the Deccan region in India, who depend on livestock rearing for the majority of their earnings, have been constantly subjected to the state's development measures that claim to promote gender equality and promote women's empowerment. Restrictions imposed on these shepherding communities by the forest department amidst the already shrinking common grazing resources, and introduction of foreign breeds of livestock that can be stall-fed, led to a collective mobilization of women against such sedentarization policies of the state. Pastoral mobility and resource dependence on the commons have always been the points of contention since colonial times in India (Chakravarty-Kaul, 1997; Ramdas & Ghotge, 2007). Following this outlook, when the pastoralists in the region were dissuaded from entering the forests and using the common state-owned grazing resources on which they have traditionally depended, women-led groups resisted such changes. For these pastoralists for whom the small livestock including goats and sheep remain integral assets, losing access to common grazing grounds and shifting towards larger cattle rearing, meant a weakening of their socio-economic status and deprivation from the traditions of independent decision making (Ramdas & Ghotge, 2007). They also perceived the introduction of non native breeds of livestock as a looming threat to the indigenous genetic resources held within the native breeds that they rear. Therefore, as an act of resistance the women of these communities collectively rejected the foreign livestock breeds that promoted stall feeding and also countered the state measures that prevented their mobility and resource access through deliberate everyday actions. Ramdas & Ghotge (2007) call these, acts of non-cooperation where pastoral women acted against state impositions through actions like taking their livestock to forest plantation areas for grazing, or intentionally using the wrong lopping[7] methods to collect fodder. These everyday forms of resistance used by women pastoralists in their situated contexts, boldly asserted their agency and the choice of livelihood as well as their access and user rights over common resources they protected for generations.

One more example echoing a similar sentiment surfaces from the Barmer district of Rajasthan, where women acros caste and class groups came forward to protect their breed of cattle from getting diluted. These women organised themselves into an informal network referred to as *Janki Mahila Mandal* to protect the indigenous '*Tharparkar*' bull breed native to their region (Flintan, 2008). This pure breed was under continual threat by the ongoing crossbreeding initiatives and dwindling fodder availability in the region. Taking charge collectively by defying the stringent caste hierarchies and class driven social structure, women of this region established a local help group that facilitated livestock rearing practices and established a credit system to help members in times of need. According to Flintan (2008), this case reflects how women-led initiatives not only strengthen pastoral pursuits but are also equally important to eliminate the social evils rooted in caste, class and gender based discrimination.

Furthermore, the *MERA declaration* that took place in 2010 at Gujarat in India brought together women pastoralists from 32 countries and is another example of women's agency and activism to safeguard their pastoral livelihoods. In this unique international gathering, women pastoralists participated and collaborated to propose a shared agenda regarding their common demands and form alliances to develop a global support network. Their declaration boldly affirmed that "It is by remaining pastoralists that we can be of great service to the entire human community" (*Mera Declaration of the Global Gathering of Women Pastoralists,* 2010). This participatory women-led movement demanded recognition for pastoral livelihoods, especially for the women of these communities who contribute immensely to the functioning of pastoral systems. They demanded the due recognition for their livelihoods as well as their specific roles that are usually unacknowledged by the development agencies including the governments, as a lack of such recognition adversely impacts their rights over resources and land. According to this declaration, rights to mobility, safety, representation, education, and capacity building remain the most important concerns of pastoral women. They believe that pastoral populations have been denied their fundamental rights, which jeopardises their livelihoods and significantly increases their vulnerability. The main objective of this united statement was to generate a political document that could serve as the basis for action for international development agencies to secure the pastoral futures. Apart from the above, this gathering reflected on the potential of pastoral women's collective agency towards protecting their unique way of life. This, till date remains one of the historic landmark events that instigated an important discussion on commons, land rights and women in pastoralism across the world.

Similarly, the case of *Maldhari* pastoralists of Gujarat who are commonly subjected to land grabs and declining grazing lands saw mobilization of women against unjust laws, extractive capitalist interventions. The state's ignorance towards this pastoral community's interests is pointed by the *Maldhari* women when they argue that there is an urgent need for the pastoralist women to come to the forefront and articulate their demands (Duncan & Agarwal, 2017). According to these women, their participation in such activist movements increased due to the failure of their male counterparts in securing their pastoral futures. "Lots of land was available 15 years ago. Now it is not possible because of industry and land pollution. Land, grazing land, is not available. Before, men took care of women. Now there are no animals, no money and you see more violence. Men do not take care of women"(Duncan & Agarwal, 2017, p. 68), explained one of the *Maldhari* women when asked about the effects of declining pastoralism. In their opinion, collectivising and voicing the concerns on local and state levels would help the pastoral women in pushing their demands for securing the pastoral livelihoods and this also could help resolve the tensions between men and women that are stemming from the loss of livestock. According to them, 'to be a *Maldhari* is to own livestock' and thus, protecting their pastoral interests remains imperative to the survival of their community.

All these cases represent the uniqueness and diversity of pastoral contexts besides the specific motivations and constraints that drive the pastoral women's agency in individual as well as collective capacity. Their actions and choices by virtue of their position within pastoralism remain integral for safeguarding their pastoral interests as well as securing their gendered opportunities.

Conclusions

In this paper, we reviewed the literature offering specific cases of Indian pastoral women to locate their situated agency in the context of their livelihood activities. Women in pastoralism are often portrayed as highly vulnerable and oppressed under the combined burden of their livelihoods and gender. However, in contradiction, our assessment of the literature using the lens of situated agency proves otherwise, and allows us to queer the existing representations available in the scholarly as well as the policy circles. The cases of Indian pastoral women discussed above provide enough evidence to support the claim that women in these communities are not simply passive or voiceless victims. Based on their situated contexts and within the limits of their roles and responsibilities, pastoral women found ways to exert their agency in everyday lives by the means of representing, bargaining, negotiating, subverting and resisting. As an outcome, their actions and choices influence the pastoral livelihoods in a myriad of ways that are contingent on various contextual factors.

The situated agency of pastoral women is manifested through diverse ways on an everyday basis. Strategic dependence of the entire community on women's roles within various pastoral practices, such as their crucial contributions to animal rearing and household economies, the emphasis placed on their choices of marriage alliances, and their migration, along with their collective actions to resist and demand external interventions, are but a few of these manifestations. In some pastoral communities, women hold independent ownership rights over a variety of livestock that remain their major assets (Ramdas & Ghotge, 2007). Besides, they also have extended control over the financial matters at the household level (Köhler-Rollefson, 2018). As far as the other resources including land are concerned, pastoralists in-general get marginalized amidst the shrinking commons and lack of access to formal land tenures. As stated in the *MERA* declaration, secure land tenure remains the foremost demand of all pastoralists across country contexts irrespective of their gender. However, additional recognition to women pastoralists in such areas certainly is a desirable step towards strengthening their socio-economic status.

In our review, we also corroborated on how the gender-based division of labour in pastoral households acts as a source of situated agency for the women. Absence of men during migratory periods often translates in increased responsibility and autonomy over household decisions for women. The complex gender dynamics that pastoral communities showcase while being located within the patriarchal settings are crucial for managing and sustaining the overall pastoral practices. It is almost as if pastoral women run an efficient parallel sub-system that works hand-in-glove with the mainstream patriarchal set-up, which often results in mixed outcomes for women. For instance, cases such as the *Raika* women, exemplify both negative and positive impacts that women's agency can generate for pastoral livelihoods. Where, on the one hand, women's active participation streamlines the functioning of nomadic pastoralism among the *Raikas*, on the other, women's declining desire to migrate in the face of increasing uncertainties generates undesirable outcomes (Köhler-Rollefson, 2018). Such negotiations within the existing paternalistic rubrics manifest either as acquisition of valuable economic roles or as expressions of dissent for marriage alliances with the pastoralists are some of the indirect ways in which *Raika* women assert their situated agency. Their choices implicitly influence the continuity and future of the community's pastoral way of life as well as their livelihoods.

Apart from the individual and household level influence, we also discussed the cases of collective agency and activism reflected through *MERA* declaration, protest demonstration by the women of pastoral communities from the Deccan region and the formation of *Janki Mahila Mandal* to safeguard an indigenous breed and organise a self-help group. These variety of examples from across the country become relevant in establishing that pastoral women's collectives harbour enormous potential to raise their needs and demands on the national and international fora. This form of collective agency bringing together a multitude of voices in a coherent manner is crucial for putting the needs of pastoralists on the table and to seek appropriate interventions to secure the future of pastoralism in India. The so-called patriarchal pastoral leadership across various regions of India, could learn a thing or two from their women and their confident assertions of situated agency for productive purposes.

In our analysis, we found diverse situations that interacted with women's agency leaving notable impacts on the functioning of pastoral systems on the whole. Therefore, to avoid premature judgements and extrapolations regarding the status of women in pastoralism, we propose that a careful scrutiny of contextual differences should be considered. In addition, a layered analysis of the actual forms of women's oppression attempted through the lens of situated agency, rather than using the assumed forms that are readily available in the literature, would contribute to a deeper understanding of the ways that women need support and how their societies can advance the status of their women.With limited research insights available on this matter so far, a potential for further empirical enquiry exists that could systematically explore the terrains of gender dynamics, women's agency, and transitions in pastoral livelihoods. This would help in filling the existing knowledge gap and would simultaneously inform the policies that could secure the current pastoral livelihoods as well as their futures.

REFERENCES

Bhasin, V. (1991). Status of Women in the Himalayas: A case of Gaddis. *Journal of Human Ecology, 2*(2), 107–116. https://doi.org/10.1080/09709274.1991.11907709

Bhasin, V. (2011). Status of Women in Transhumant Societies. *Journal of Sociology and Social Anthropology, 2*(1), 1–22. https://doi.org/10.1080/09766634.2011.11885543

Bhasin, V. (2013). Pastoralists of Himalayas. *Journal of Biodiversity, 4*(2), 83–113. https://doi.org/10.1080/09766901.2013.11884746

Chakravarty-Kaul, M. (1997). Transhumance- A Pastoral Response to Risk and Uncertainty in the Himalayas. *Nomadic Peoples, 1*(1), 133–150. JSTOR. https://www.jstor.org/stable/43123514

Duncan, J., & Agarwal, M. (2017). "There is Dignity only with Livestock": Land Grabbing and the Changing Practices of Pastoralist Women in Gujarat, India. In B. B. Bettina & S. Shortall (Eds.), *Gender and Rural Globalization: International Perspectives on Gender and Rural Development.* CABI. http://ndl.ethernet.edu.et/bitstream/123456789/47639/1/92.pdf#page=61

Eneyew, A., & Mengistu, S. (2013). Double Marginalized Livelihoods: Invisible Gender Inequality in Pastoral Societies. *Societies, 3*(1), 104–116. https://doi.org/10.3390/soc3010104

FAO. (2021). *Pastoralism- Making variability work.* FAO, Animal Production and Health Paper No. 185. https://doi.org/10.4060/cb5855en

Flintan, F. (2008). *Women's Empowerment in Pastoral Societies* (p. 144). IUCN-WISP. https://www.iucn.org/sites/dev/files/import/downloads/gender_format.pdf

Flintan, F. (2011). Changing Nature of Gender Roles in the Drylands of the Horn and East Africa: Implications for DRR Programming. *Regional Learning and Advocacy Programme for Vulnerable Dryland Communities,* 80.

Fratkin, E., & Smith, K. (1995). Women's Changing Economic Roles with Pastoral Sedentarization: Varying Strategies in Alternate Rendille Communities. *Human Ecology, 23*(4), 433–454. https://www.jstor.org/stable/4603176

Gammage, S., Kabeer, N., & van der Meulen Rodgers, Y. (2016). Voice and Agency: Where Are We Now? *Feminist Economics, 22*(1), 1–29. https://doi.org/10.1080/13545701.2015.1101308

Hannah, J. (Ed.). (2007). *Women Pastoralists: Preserving Traditional Knowledge Facing Modern Challenges.* Secretariat of the United Nations Convention to Combat Desertification, International Fund for Agricultural Development.

Jaweed, T. H., & Khan, N. (2015). Review of Status of Tribal Women in Tripura by Malbika Das Gupta. *Pastoralism, 5*(1), 5, s13570-015-0026–0029. https://doi.org/10.1186/s13570-015-0026-9

Kabeer, N. (1999). Resources, Agency, Achievements: Reflections on the Measurement of Women's Empowerment. *Development and Change, 30*(3), 435–464. https://doi.org/10.1111/1467-7660.00125

Kipuri, N., & Ridgewell, A. (2008). *A double bind: The exclusion of pastoralist woman in the East and Horn of Africa.* Minority Rights Group International.

Kishore, K., & Köhler-Rollefson, I. (2020). *Accounting for pastoralists in India.* League for Pastoral People and Endogenous Livestock Development, Ober-Ramstadt.

Köhler-Rollefson, I. (2018). Purdah, purse and patriarchy: The position of women in the Raika shepherd community in Rajasthan (India). *Journal of Arid Environments, 149,* 30–39. https://doi.org/10.1016/j.jaridenv.2017.09.010

Manzano, P., Burgas, D., Cadahía, L., Eronen, J. T., Fernández-Llamazares, Á., Bencherif, S., Holand, Ø., Seitsonen, O., Byambaa, B., Fortelius, M., Fernández-Giménez, M. E., Galvin, K. A., Cabeza, M., & Stenseth, N. Chr. (2021). Toward a holistic understanding of pastoralism. *One Earth, 4*(5), 651–665. https://doi.org/10.1016/j.oneear.2021.04.012

Mehra, P. (1992). Women, Worl & Position: A Study among the Gaddis of Palampur, H.P. *Indian Anthropologist, 22*(2), 41–55. JSTOR. https://www.jstor.org/stable/41919689

Mera Declaration of the Global Gathering of Women Pastoralists. (2010). https://www.wocan.org/sites/default/files/mera_declaration_of_the_global_gathering_of_women.pdf

Nandigama, S. (2020). Performance of success and failure in grassroots conservation and development interventions: Gender dynamics in participatory forest management in India. *Land Use Policy, 97,* 103445. https://doi.org/10.1016/j.landusepol.2018.05.061

Ramdas, S. R., & Ghotge, N. (2006, August). India's Livestock Economy. *The Forsaken Drylands.* Seminar. https://www.india-seminar.com/2006/564/564_s_r_ramdas_&_n_s_ghotge.htm

Ramdas, S. R., & Ghotge, N. S. (2007). Whose Rights? Women in Pastoralist and Shifting Cultivation Communities: A Continuing Struggle for Recognition and Rights to Livelihood Resources. In S. Krishna (Ed.), *Women's Livelihood Rights-Recasting Citizenship for Development* (pp. 41–61). SAGE Publications India.

Rangnekar, S. (1994). Women Pastoralists, Indigenous Knowledge and Livestock Production in Northern Gujarat. In *Rajasthan and Gujarat: A collection of papers* (pp. 15–16). Overseas Development Institute. http://agris.fao.org/agris-search/search.do?recordID=GB9504614

Rota, A., & Sperandini, S. (2010). *Gender and Livestock. Livestock Thematic Papers: Tools for Project Design.* IFAD. https://www.ifad.org/documents/38714170/39148759/Gender+and+livestock.pdf/67c6dca9-4a11-4f53-931e-2ccb46105a3c

Venkatasubramanian, K., & Ramnarain, S. (2018). Gender and Adaptation to Climate Change: Perspectives from a Pastoral Community in Gujarat, India. *Development and Change, 49*(6), 1580–1604. https://doi.org/10.1111/dech.12448

Verma, R., & Khadka, M. (Eds.). (2016). *Gender and pastoralism in the rangelands of the Hindu Kush Himalayas: Knowledge, culture, and livelihoods at the margins of the margins*. ICIMOD.

ENDNOTES

1 Aayushi Malhotra is a Ph.D. candidate at the Department of Humanities and Social Sciences, BITS PILANI, Pilani Campus, India. She is currently working on the socio-ecological transitions in the pastoral context in India.

2 Prof. Sailaja Nandigama is an Associate Professor in the Department of Humanities and Social Sciences, BITS PILANI, Pilani Campus, India. Her research interests include human and environmental systems, climate change, forest governance, gender, social justice, and policy issues.

3 Prof. Kumar Sankar Bhattacharya is an Associate Professor at the Department of Humanities and Social Sciences BITS PILANI, Pilani Campus, India. He works in the areas of Cultural Studies, Ecology, and Environment, Postcolonial Theory, and Trans-national and Global Literature.

4 Types of pastoral activities include- pure pastoralism, where only herding is practiced as the main economic activity or agro-pastoralism where migratory herding and subsistence agriculture are practiced in combination.

5 Pastoral communities across India rear different livestock based on their geographical and ecological conditions. It ranges from yaks, buffaloes, sheep, goats, and camels to ducks, horses and donkeys. Many times, traditional pastoral communities also have mythological reasonings for the type of livestock they rear.

6 Diversity of mobility patterns are followed by the pastoralists to secure the critical resources for their livestock. Pastoralists can be nomadic (without permanent settlements), semi-nomadic (have permanent settlements but migrate for most of the time in year) or can follow transhumant patterns (seasonally defined movements between fixed points).

7 Lopping means methods of cutting the branches of trees that used as fodder for the livestock.

CHAPTER 11

Subverting Patriarchal Interpretation of the Ramayan through a Feminist Lens: A Critical Study of Sita's Ramayana

Shruti Chakraborti[1]

ABSTRACT

"Re-vision – the act of looking back, of seeing with fresh eyes, of entering an old text from a new critical direction – is for us more than a chapter in cultural history: it is an act of survival", writes Adrienne Rich in her seminal essay, "When We Dead Awaken: Writing as Re-vision". Rich firmly advocates that women authors should create spaces for subversion of patriarchal values and ideals through their literary works. Revisionist mythmaking, from a feminist literary perspective, evolves through challenging a preceding text which predominantly manifests androcentric ideas. The present paper aims to examine a female reinterpretation of Ramayan, *Sita's Ramayana* by Samhita Arni, as a revisionist text. *Sita's Ramayana* is a graphic narrative in which Arni's retelling is complemented by *patachitra* or scroll painting by Moyna Chitrakar, a female *patachitra* artist from West Bengal, India. Sita's character is one of the major literary tools through which women writers often attempt to re-view the Ramayan and subvert the male-centric reading of the epic. This paper seeks to understand the elements of revisionism in *Sita's Ramayana* in the context of a sixteenth century retelling of Ramayan, *Chandrabati's Ramayan*, a verse narrative composed by Chandrabati, the first women poet of Bengal. *Chandrabati's Ramayan*, a fierce Sita tale, has been the primary influence on Arni in subverting the patriarchal, popular representation of Sita's character. This paper attempts to interpret how Arni has altered the patriarchal understanding of the epic by foregrounding the tale through Sita's viewpoint. It also aims to analyse how these female authors, Arni and Chandrabati have assigned Sita's character an agency to challenge the androcentric notions that dominate the interpretation of Ramayan. Further, the paper seeks to interpret how the folk-art form of *patachitra* contributes to the meaning-making of a contemporary subversive retelling of the grand epic.

Introduction

"Mythology in India is not just an academic or a historical subject, it is a vital and living topic of contemporary relevance. The complex social, political and religious attitudes of 'modern' India cannot be understood without an understanding of our myths and their impact on the collective faith of our people" (Gokhale XIV) writes Indian writer, Namita Gokhale, in the introductory note, entitled "Sita: A Personal Journey", of her book, *In Search of Sita: Revisiting Mythology*, which is co-edited by Malashri Lal, Retired Professor, University of Delhi. The Indian epic, Ramayan, not only constitutes a substantial part of Indian mythology but also influences the socio-cultural, religious, and political landscape of India to a large extent. Hence, creative minds through ages and across different cross-sections of Indian society have re-interpreted and re-created this epic narrative, in varied forms and through diverse media.

Female reception, internalisation, and interpretation of the Ramayan essentially differs from male perspectives. Female authors, readers, artists, performers, and audiences often choose to ignore the narrative factors that are prominent in an androcentric representation of the epic. Eminent Indian author and comparatist, Nabaneeta Dev Sen, outlines certain narrative approaches that appear in female retellings of Ramayan, in her essay, "Lady Sings the Blues: When Women Retell the Ramayana". In this essay, Dev Sen strongly suggests that these female songs or verses or narratives for that matter, are tales of Sita which are far removed from the mainstream narrative on Ram. She specifically refers to four narrative alternatives that get manifested when female authors retell the epic. According to her, primarily, a female author might follow the traditional narrative mode and attempt to write 'like' a male author, the second alternative – the epic might be re-told through a feminist lens; as the third alternative, she suggests that the re-presentation might reflect an ideological dimension, or, fourth, it might be the story of any woman narrated in the context of Sita's tale which is a common cultural practice amongst rural women across India.

> "Just as the Rama myth has been exploited by the patriarchal Brahminical system to construct an ideal Hindu male, Sita too has been built up as an ideal Hindu female to help serve the system. .... But there are always alternative ways of using a myth. If patriarchy has used the Sita myth to silence women, the village women have picked up the Sita myth to give themselves a voice"
>
> *(Dev Sen 19).*

The interpretation of the Ramayan by rural women becomes crucial in the context of the present paper. This paper seeks to examine, a contemporary Indian author, Samhita Arni's graphic retelling of the Ramayan, *Sita's Ramayana,* as a revisionist re-interpretation of the epic in the context of another female retelling, *Chandrabati's Ramayan* written in the 16th century by Chandrabati, a rural Bengali female poet who hailed from a village now located in Bangladesh. Chandrabati's text is an episodic re-presentation of Ramayan approached through the lens of female interpretation. Arni's narrative is largely modelled on Chandrabati's verse re-presentation of the epic. Hence, the perspective of reception, interpretation, and retelling of the epic by the rural women emerges with immense significance. Further, the paper also seeks to present an understanding of the graphic illustration that accompanies Arni's text, locating its socio-cultural connection. It is a particular folk art form called *patachitra* (Scroll Painting) which is widely created in different rural parts of the eastern Indian states, West Bengal and Odisha. Moyna Chirakar, a female *patua* (Scroll Painting artist) from West Bengal, India, creates the *pata* illustrations for *Sita's Ramayana.* The *pata* paintings of Moyna Chitrakar, in a terse and precise manner, narrate the story of Ramayan, especially, the parts of the epic which are closely associated with Sita. She presents to us the wide-eyed, soulful, thoughtful, suffering, enduring yet resilient Sita, the one who is central to Arni's narrative. Thus, this book demonstrates the combination of Arni's and Moyna's exploration of the Ramayan, placing the retelling in a distinctive female narrative tradition.

Background of the study

As already mentioned, the narrative of *Sita's Ramayana* has been modelled on *Chandrabati's Ramayan*. Hence, it becomes imperative to present a critical analysis of the model text which ensures a better understanding of the primary text. The present paper attempts to analyse the prominent narrative elements present in a 21st century graphic narrative, *Sita's Ramayana* that is revisionist in nature, and further seeks to understand how those elements got transmitted from a 16th century verse retelling of Ramayan written by a rural Bengali female poet. In this context, *Chandrabati's Ramayan* emerges as the key secondary textual resource which has been translated from Bangla to English by Nabaneeta Dev Sen. Two essays by Dev Sen on female retellings of Ramayana, entitled "Lady Sings the Blues: When Women retell the Ramayana", and "Rewriting the Ramayana: Chandrabati and Molla" are pivotal texts to understand the narrative traits inherent in the re-interpretation of Ramayan when perceived by female authors, and to locate the socio-cultural significance of Chandrabati's narrative respectively. Another text that offers an elaborate perception on Chandrabati's life and her works is *A Woman's Ramayana: Chandrabati's Epic,* a book jointly written by Mandakranta Bose and Sarika Priyadarshini Bose. This text has also been referred to as a secondary resource to understand the social factors that were at play during Chandrabati's time, along with insights into her personal experiences, which together contributed to Chandrabati's retelling of the Ramayan. The other book by Mandakranta Bose which is of key importance in the context of the paper is, *The Ramayana in Bengali Folk Paintings.* In this book, Bose presents extensive research on the *pata* images and their genealogy of West Bengal.

Feminist writer, Adrienne Rich a key figure in the domain of revisionist mythmaking, who has advocated in favour of the requirement of a revisionist literary dimension. In her essay, "When we Dead Awaken: Writing as Re-Vision" she clearly outlines the purpose and significance of a revisionist outlook:

> "Re-vision – the act of looking back, of seeing with fresh eyes, of entering an old text from a new critical direction – is for woman more than a chapter in cultural history: it is an act of survival. Until we understand the assumptions in which we are drenched we cannot know ourselves. And this drive to self-knowledge, for women, is more than a search for identity: it is part of our refusal of the self-destructiveness of male-dominated society"
>
> *(Rich 18).*

In this seminal essay, Rich challenges patriarchal social constructs and highlights the fact that old texts need to be reinterpreted, re-evaluated, and revised from a new critical perspective, which should essentially be a feminist perspective. She further suggests that this act of revision is not only directed in search for an identity but must be launched as a way to survive male-dominated society. The feminist thinkers and authors who promote the notion of revisionist myth-making, highlight the dire necessity of applying a feminist critical approach to evaluating theses myths. In patriarchal societies, myths are constructed according to the androcentric terms, and they perpetuate a phallocentric cultural system. Reality is often subdued and a perceived reality surfaces and dominates the cultural landscape of a specific society. The mythic images of women are often stereotypical in nature and these stereotypes contribute to imposing a gender identity on women in a given social structure. This imposition subsequently hinders the growth of a feminist outlook and a feminist resistance that would liberate women from the entrapment of a constructed reality. The revisionist writers challenge this tendency of subjugating the female voice in a narrative.

Indian author, Beena G. comments in her book, *Vision and Re-vision: Revisiting Mythology, Rethinking Women,* "Revisionist myth making counters hegemonic narratives and is commonly used as a strategy by writers with an objective of revaluing the experiences of the marginalized people" (G 13).

These core concepts of revisionism are pivotal to the development of the whole study as presented in this paper.

Chandrabati's Ramayan: The Text

Dev Sen, in her essay, "Lady Sings the Blues: When Women retell the Ramayana", refers to the revisionist approach commonly observed in the appropriation of Ramayan done by the rural women in India. She writes,

> "Rural women do not care for the court nor the critic. What they care for is something with which they can identify themselves. Therefore, Sita and her suffering becomes an inseparable part of their existence. They sing songs on Sita, not on Ram. They are not interested in Ram as an ideal man, nor as a valorous warrior or a just king. The interest of rural female folk tradition lies in episodes like, Sita's birth, her marriage, her love life with Ram, her abduction, her childbirth, and most importantly her abandonment, injustice and suffering, hence the Balakanda and Uttarakanda of Ramayan are favourites
>
> *(Dev Sen 18-19)."*

In the context of *Chandrabati's Ramayan,* Bose and Bose state,

"But Chandravati's work further distinguishes itself by going beyond the usual domestic or local ambit of folk narratives to venture upon the epic theme of the catastrophe that overtakes an entire people. Even though it side-lines battles, the typical subject of the epics, and turns away from Rama, the conventional hero of the Ramayana, to his wronged wife Sita and centralizes her agony, it no less urgently concerns itself with the public doom that falls upon Lanka, where she is incarcerated, and upon Ayodhya, of which she is the queen. Chandravati's poem is indeed about Sita, but it is no less about her world"

(Bose and Bose 1).

This statement, which appears in the "Introduction" of their book, *A Woman's Ramayana: Chandrabati's Bengali Epic,* summarizes the narrative component and significance of *Chandrabati's Ramayan* from the revisionist perspective. The theoretical idea of revisionist mythmaking emerged in the 20th century. Hence, Chandrabati did not follow the domain of 'revisionism'. Her retelling was a spontaneous reflection of her personal experience and realisation and inspired by the cultural and religious environment around her.

Chandrabati belonged to an impoverished Bengali Brahmin family in Maimansingha which is presently located in Bangladesh. Writing religious verses was already a practice in her family. Moreover, Krittivas, one of the key literary figures of medieval Bengal was a forerunner to Chandrabati. The 15th century *Krittivas Ramayan* is one of the significant mainstream Ramayan narratives in India. Following Kamban's *Iramavataram,* composed in the 12th century, this was the first major work after a span of three hundred years which has remained a dominant Ramayan narrative since then. However, in both, style and content, Chandrabati's Ramayan largely differs from Krittivas'. Perhaps the most significant difference lies in the reception of these two texts. *Krittivas' Ramayan* occupies a canonical position in the Ramayan discourse in India. However, Chandrabati's text was lost in the course of time, both, in India and Bangladesh. Dineshchandra Sen and K.C. Moulik, noted literary historians and Bengali scholars of the Bangla literary domain in 20th century, played a key role in reviving Chandrabati's text. The modern Bengali scholarship became aware of this text in the 20th century after it was documented by Dineshchandra Sen in his *Maimansingha Geetika* in 1916, and K.C. Moulik's *Purvavanga Geetika* in 1976 (Dev Sen 165). ßthis parenthetical phrase is awkward—introduce them before you first quote them not in a parenthetical phrase; also, is Dev Sen the same as D.C. Sen? If so, use one name consistently throughout, and again, only cite the last name in parenthesis. The key resource for Sen was a long poem, *Chandrabati* composed by a balladeer Nayanchand Ghosh. This poem was composed fifty years after Chandrabati's death. According to this poem, Chandrabati was in love with a young man from her village named Jayanand. Jayanand too was a Brahmin and both their families had agreed to their marriage. On the day of their wedding, Chandrabati came to know that Jayanand had fallen in love with a Muslim girl, converted to Islam, and married her. This left Chandrabati heartbroken, and she refused forever to marry. She was adamant in her decision and devoted herself to serving Lord Shiva in a temple in her village. After some time, Jayanand realized that he still had a deep-rooted love for Chandrabati. He returned to her and pled for forgiveness. Chandrabati locked herself in the Shiva temple. He wanted to see her for the last time before committing suicide; he knew that because of his religious conversion neither Chandrabati nor the Hindu community would accept him further. However, Chandrabati refused to even meet him. She was determined to decline the person who had betrayed her and her religion. Once his continuous pleading stopped Chandrabati came out of the temple only to discover Jayanand's floating dead body in the river adjacent to the temple.

Upon "seeing his dead body floating in the river, Chandravati stood bereft of sense" (Bose and Bose 7). This betrayal and the subsequent intense grief that Chandrabati suffered was reflected in the inherent melancholy of her writings. Her personal experience, correlated to her creative performance establishes a clear direction towards her empathy for an abandoned, dejected female figure like Sita. This is a potential reason behind her re-creation of the Valmiki Ramayan in which the focus shifts from the glory of Ram to the suffering and resilience of Sita. The suffering yet resolute character that Chandrabati herself was, found its expression through the characterization of Sita in *Chandrabati's Ramayan*.

However personal emotions might be at play, there was also a larger socio-cultural perspective which undeniably had a major role to play in the context of Chandrabati's retelling. The tremendously popular and dominant understanding of Valmiki's Ramayan often ignores the essence of Ram's character that Valmiki had portrayed in his epic creation. Valmiki's Ramayan demonstrates Ram as the ideal man, the best amongst mortals. But the subsequent mainstream readings and interpretations of the Ramayan have established Ram as an avatar of Vishnu, and he gradually transcended to a heavenly entity, perceived as the reincarnation of Vishnu himself. This transformation happened predominantly under the influence of the Bhakti movement which substantially changed the philosophical and theological landscape of India from the 7th century till the medieval period. Nevertheless, a different approach towards receiving this interpretation emerged in interpreting the Ramayan in the eastern part of India, after Krittivas. The epic was being scrutinised through a culturally critical lens and alternative narratives appeared.

Bose and Bose comment, "But later still one may see an altered consciousness, strongly responsive to gender concerns, which signals the beginning of a tradition of looking at the epic from below, from the viewpoint of the victim rather than that of the victor. The conventional practice of narrating the epic has thus been radically altered and sometimes altogether subverted" (Bose and Bose 4).

Both Nabaneeta Dev Sen and the duo, Bose and Bose focus on this tradition of alternative writing from the perspective of the rural women community across India. There were numerous retellings that were created during this period, however unfortunately, the large portion of it could not find a place in the canon of the Ramayan discourse. *Chandrabati's Ramayan* too falls into this category. She earned the reputation of being the first Bengali woman poet for two of her ballads, *Sundari Malua* and *Dasyu Kenaram*, however, not for her Ramayan. The 700 hundred-couplet verse that comprises her Ramayan is a fragment, which the Bengali male scholars and critics have conveniently pushed to the margins. Bengali scholar and literary historian, Sukumar Sen is of the opinion that Chandrabati's retelling lacked the potential to even be considered as a retelling in the first place. Another pivotal Bengali literary historian and author, Asitkumar Bandyopadhyay has recognised Chandrabati's authorship but has ascribed some episodes to her narrative which do not even exist in the original Chandrabati text. This exhibits a significant lack of reverence towards Chandrabti's work. Thus, the initial critical reception of *Chandrabati's Ramayan* did not do any justice to the work, rather, it was considered as a dismal failure, from the literary perspective.

Dev Sen, in her essay, "Lady sings the Blues: When Women retell the Ramayana", mentions that *Chandrabati's Ramayan* is the first female retelling of the Ramayana that had triggered her own interest in exploring the domain of female retellings of the Ramayan in 1989.

"For me it all started in 1989 with an accidental re-reading of the Chandrabati Ramayana. That is where I discovered that a women's Ramayana tells a different story. Since then, I have been fascinated by women's retellings of the Rama tale" (Dev Sen 18). In her essay, "Rewriting the Ramayana: Chandrbati and Molla", she explicitly expresses her disappointment in how Chandrabati survived in the memories of the common people in Bangladesh as a historic character, not for her Ramayan but for her personal life:

> "Although her Ramayana is no longer read or even known, Chandrabati herself is all remembered fairly well for her tragic love with Jayananda. Even after 400 years, the love story, as told by Nayanchand Ghose, holds our interest, like the story of Tristan and Isolde, or Laila and Majnu. Chandrabati, a historic character, has thus turned into a legend, and lives on in the ballads herself. But in these ballads, Chandrabati the poet and the writer of the Ramayana is hardly given any importance, it is simply the sad tale of a young woman, and her lost love"
>
> *(Dev Sen 168).*

Quintessentially like a revisionist author and critic, Dev Sen seems to be worried about the identity that patriarchal reception of Chandrabati has created. Male critics, and male bards and balladeers, be it in the 20th century or back in the 16th century have been more concerned with Chandrabati's personal life and less about her creative acumen.

Dev Sen comments that, issues related to gender roles and its manifestation, foregrounding of silenced voices, and the tensions between the established socio-cultural normativity regarding interpreting the Ramayan narrative and Chandrabati's feminist re-presentation of Ramayan led to the extinction of the text's existence in the public memory. Further, Dev Sen elaborately explains the reason why this text had not been accepted in the Ramayan canon. The narrative features and narrative elements of *Chandrabati's Ramayan* which are essentially transgressing and subversive in nature might be 'responsible' for the text being labelled as a dismal failure in the patriarchal cultural domain.

Chandrabati chose to write her Ramayan in Bangla and not in the revered language, Sanskrit. The prologue or *bhanita*, which Dev Sen presents in her translation, has been taken from *Sundari Molua*. It includes mention of her parents, goddess Manasa and also the small river Phuleshwari of their village. However, there is not even a customary mention of Ram. In fact, in the whole composition, Ram has never been glorified at any point. The composition is not about Ram's glory or his valour, it is about Sita's life. *Chandrabati's Ramayan* is one of Bengal's own versions of Ramayan which can be considered more as a narrative on Sita than on Ram. It narrates Sita's sufferings. Her experiences as an abducted woman by Ravan, her plight in Lanka, her rescue by Ram, her return to Ayodhya, Ram's betrayal to her and her subsequent exile, the humiliation she suffered, and her final submission to Mother Earth. It is explicit that Chandrabati aimed at re-creating the Ramayan in which Sita's plight worked as a framework based on which, Chandrabati aimed building a resistance towards the patriarchal domination of women in the sixteenth century, which still stands out with so much relevance. As Dev Sen keeps emphasising it throughout her essay, "Rewriting the Ramayana: Chandrabati and Molla", and also do Bose and Bose in their book, *A Woman's Ramayana: Chandravati's Bengali Epic*, that Chandrabati's text was a text written by a woman, written about a woman, and the target recipients were the uneducated, ever-suffering rural women of Bangladesh (erstwhile undivided Bengal) who identified their plight with Sita's suffering. The patriarchal presence, neither in the content which would involve Ram, nor as the audience was desired. Chandrabati, had a Brahminical orientation. She was trained in Sanskrit, she was also well versed with the style of ballad writing which is manifested in her other works; yet, she chose to retell her Ramayan in an unconventional form with unconventional contents from the point of view of epic writing.

The narrative is for the most part manifested in the *Baromaasi* form, the songs that women of many parts of rural India and Bangladesh sing to describe their everyday life, their plight and suffering. The word *Baro* in Bangla means twelve and *maas* means month. The word, "baromaasi" (also known as baromashya) refer to the songs that rural women sing, essentially to a female audience, recounting the experience of their female existence. This is a part of the folk cultural tradition in India and Bangladesh. Moreover, *Chandrabati's Ramayan* was composed to circulate as an oral narrative. It was to be sung as a ballad, predominantly by female singers to female listeners. According to the traditional Bardic tradition of singing ballads in Bangla, the crowd is addressed as "Suno sabhajana", which means "listen, members of the court" (Dev Sen 171); however, the refrain that Chandrabati uses in her verse is' "Suno sakhijana", which means, "listen my girlfriends" (Dev Sen 171). This is a massive subversion, from all angles, socially, culturally, and a deviation from the established literary tradition. Therefore, the great epic narrative tradition is absent in the composition.

Further, the epic war has been ignored in this text, as has Ram's heroic valour. The narrative technique is quite unique; the war is described through Sita's dreams. Chandrabati had an intriguingly fascinating narrative logic. According to her, since Sita was not present with Ram during the war, how would she know what exactly had happened. Hence, she had dreams of the war, and she narrated them. Chandrabati's primary concern was to depict Sita's sorrow. Her composition is a tale of love, longing, pain, and separation. Her deliberate rejection of the apparent glorious war from being included in her narrative was a reason potential enough to label her retelling as inferior and substandard according to the androcentric understanding of an epic poem like Ramayan. Dev Sen firmly believes that *Chadrabati's Ramayan* was deprived of an inclusion to the canon not because of its fragmented composition, but because of its subversive, non-traditional approach. Two voices operate in the text, one is Chandrabati's rebellious voice, and the other is Sita's soft and subdued yet irrepressible voice, and both together have displaced Valmiki's, or for that matter, any male narrator's voice. Dev Sen further comments,

> "In fact, Chandrabati's Ramayana was never even properly read for what it actually was: the story of Sita's journey from birth to death. Instead of praising Ram, Chandrabati often intrudes into the narrative to comment on Rama's foolishness, to advise and guide him and to accuse him of the devastation that awaits Ayodhya. It is clearly not a devotional text, but a secular one; the story is presented as a plain human drama and not as a divine mystery"
>
> *(Dev Sen 171).*

Chandrabati had the rebellious, analytical mind to de-mystify the divine elements and heroic epic grandeur from the Ram-tale and transformed it into a Sita-tale. Dev Sen suggests that this subversion of epic convention has led to the text being denied an inclusion in the domain of the mainstream, authoritative Ramayan narratives.

The scope of this paper does not remain limited to a comparative study of two texts, *Chandrabati's Ramayan* and *Sita's Ramayana*. Rather it aims at locating *Chandrabati's Ramayan* as a point of departure for many other female retellings of Ramayan in the subsequent time. The contemporaneity of Chandrabati's text is reflected in its immense potential to influence authors five centuries apart. Dev Sen reminisces her experience of visiting Chandrabati's village in Bangladesh.

To her utter disappointment she found that Chandrabati is remembered for her ballads and also for her and Jayanand's love story. But she is hardly associated with her Ramayan. The Ramayan songs are still popular among the rural women community, but they are not ascribed to her. The songs have survived; but the poet has been forgotten since she refused to follow the authoritative patriarchal understanding of Ramayan. That she chose to write solely on Sita, did not fit into the male dominated Ramayan discourse. However, it is undeniably true, that the rural female community indeed identifies themselves with Sita. They have internalised this epic heroine as one suffering human who is one of them. Towards the end of her essay, "Rewriting the Ramayana – Chandrabati and Molla", Dev Sen writes,

"Even to this day Sita provides a voice to our silent, suffering women. We are sisters in sorrow, be it in India or in Bangladesh" (Dev Sen 177). Arni's *Sita's Ramayana* is one such text in which the author has internalised the spirit of *Chandrabati's Ramayan.*

Sita's Ramayana: Textual Analysis

In *Sita's Ramayana,* Arni approaches the age-old epic from the same perspective that Chandrabati had done almost five hundred years ago. It is unfortunate that *Chandrabat's Ramayan* is considered a fragment, and thus it never received recognition amongst the mainstream narratives of Ramayan, but Arni certainly aims to offer some justice to it in her 21st century novel. However, it is a graphic narrative, thus, much colourful and appealing in nature. The text is written in the autobiographical mode that captures a part of Sita's account of the Ram-tale in flashback. The tale emerges with a revisionist dimension. The narrative opens with Sita in Dandakaranya after being abandoned by Ram. She is expecting her first child and the nature around her thoroughly sympathizes with her plight, as she recounts the whole series of events of her life post-marriage. This recollection essentially centres around Sita – the initial days of her happy married life, her decision to accompany Ram to the forest and the subsequent crisis that befell her after she was abducted by Ravan, her agony as a captive in Lanka, and the painful days she spent over there resisting Ravan's repeated insistence to marry him with the sole hope that Ram would definitely appear and rescue her. Ram indeed rescues her only to abandon her again. Sita's first-person narration ends with her being abandoned in Dandakaranya by Lakshman on being instructed by Ram. After that, the third person narration starts, which captures the events of her children's birth, her stay at the hermitage of Valmiki, Ram's encounter with Lav and Kush, and finally her voluntary acceptance of death. The primary revisionist feature that is demonstrated in the text is that the narrative initiates from the events that followed after Ram was exiled for fourteen years; after his arrival to the Chitrakut forest with Sita and Lakshman, Sita's recollection of the happenings of her life begins hereafter. The narrative emerges to be significantly revisionist in nature when, like Chandrabati, Arni too chooses to be episodic in selecting episodes from Ramayan that are significantly related to Sita. Like Chandrabati, she too overlooks the entire episode of Kaikeyi and Manthara's plotting against Ram to deceive him and deprive him of the throne of Ayodhya which he was rightfully supposed to ascend. Ram's apparent generosity and the act of being the ideal son in accepting to go to exile bearing the burden of his father's commitment is altogether removed from Arni's narrative, which otherwise occupies a key narrative space in the dominant Ramayan narratives. Arni, displays no preference in representing Ram either as an ideal man or as a gallant warrior. Rather, she interprets him as a lover-husband of Sita, who again wretchedly fails in emerging as the hero in his wife's life. Apparently, *Sita's Ramayana* might seem to be another comparatively shorter retelling of the Valmiki Ramayan. However, a close reading of the text is bound to reflect that it is quite different from the *adi kavya* (Valmiki is often referred to as the *adi kavi* which means the earliest poet and thus the Ramayan becomes the *adi kavya* or the earliest verse) and from other popular discourses of the Ramayan that have dominated the readers' mind across ages.

The revisionist approach manifests itself in not only assigning Sita the centrality but also ascribing her an agency to critique the acts of men in Ramayan which for ages have been celebrated as valorous and virtuous acts. Sita's interpretation of Lakshman's act of mutilating Surpanakha is subversive: Violence breeds violence, and unjust act only begets greater injustice" (Arni and Chitrakar 16). Sita explicitly states that Lakshman's deed was unfair, and she had to suffer the consequence of it later in her life. Here, one cannot miss feeling the presence of the subtle empathy that Sita feels towards Surpanakha. As a distinctive revisionist text, Arni creates space for other female characters of the epic who have remained unheard and unnoticed, or misperceived. She highlights the character of Trijatha, Vibhishan's daughter. Trijatha has been ascribed with magical powers and a soft heart. She became Sita's friend during her days of captivity in Lanka. Trijatha empathised with Sita, but not for one moment did she want to leave Lanka and take refuge under Ram. Whereas her father Vibhishan betrayed his brother, Ravan, and with the favour of Rama became the King of Lanka after Ravan's death. Trijatha's approach had an ideological perspective. She and Sita shared a bond of female companionship which did not percolate beyond their personal relation. She refuted the idea of accepting Ram as the superior and the victor. Trijatha stands out as the second important female character in the text. She has been placed almost like a parallel to the character of Sanjay in Mahabharat who was blessed with divine power to witness the War of Kurukshetra sitting at Dhritarashtra's court and narrate it to him. Trijatha does the same thing. She narrates to Sita the war that had taken place between Rama and Ravan which she witnessed in a dream. Arni incorporates a similar narrative logic as Chandrabati. In *Chandrabati's Ramayan,* Sita experienced the war in her dream, in Arni's narrative, she does it through Trijatha's dream. Both Chandrabati and Arni establish the narrative formula in which Sita is essentially dissociated from Ram's 'valour' as a warrior and the 'glory' of the war. She stands alone with her plight, resilient towards her suffering, critiquing Ram.

Sita, in this graphic retelling, appears to be highly verbal about making her position clear on the issues of deception and lack of personal integrity. As already mentioned, she had not approved of Lakshman's act towards Surpanakha. She maintains an ethically and ideologically stoic position, irrespective of the person, whether it is about Ram or Lakshman. She disapproves of Ram's killing of the Vanara king Valin. Further, Sita condemns the way Indrajit, Ravan's son was killed craftily. The invincible Ravan too was killed by deceit which Hanuman had designed and executed under Ram's instruction. Sita does not hesitate to sympathize with the denizens of Lanka after Ravan's defeat. Even after being freed by Ram, she chooses to take sides with the vanquished; she critiques the destruction that befell Lanka: "Lanka was destroyed, Ravan was dead. Kumbhakarna, Indrajit and thousands of other Rakhshasas had perished on the battlefield. But I could see their women crying. My friend Trijatha lamenting" (Arni and Chitrakar 119). On the same note, she articulates her thoughts about the destruction that a war causes. Since the text is a distinguishing female narrative, Sita comments on women's situation in a war: "War, in some ways, is merciful to men. It makes them heroes if they are the victors. If they are the vanquished – they do not live to see their homes taken, their wives widowed. But if you are a woman – you must live through defeat" (Arni and Chitrakar 120). According to her, victory or defeat is for me; women are the ever- vanquished lot.

The misery of women has been underlined through the characters of Tara and Mandodri as well. Sita laments the fact that her husband Ram was responsible for these women's woe that they suffered at the bereavement of losing their husbands. Another striking narrative element in the novel is that both Ram and Ravan appear as lovers. It seems as if the war took place between the two lovers of Sita. Ravan has been portrayed as Sita's lover, but also a demon who knew his ethical limits. There is no mention of him making physical advances to Sita.

Hanuman's contribution to the whole scheme of affairs has been more prominently highlighted in this Sita-tale, compared to the other popular narrations. Hanuman is dominantly portrayed as one who had submitted himself to Ram and Sita, and his presence in the epic is highly overshadowed by Ram. This is obvious, as the structure of Ramayan has been to project Ram as an ideal hero in every way. But in this narrative Hanuman stands out as an ally to Ram, who equally if not more, contributed to rescuing Sita. And Hanuman is seen to be sympathising with Sita more than Ram has done. Not only Hanuman, but the other non-human beings like, Jatayu, Gadur, and the trees, flowers, and birds of Dandakaranya all have been shown to have been thoroughly better ones than the human beings. Arni gives a prominent voice to the ecological elements in her text.

However, the most prominent revisionist perspective, in this text, is manifested through Sita's criticism of Ram and the overall re-interpretation of Ram's character. In this context, Arni again follows the narrative elements and arguments of *Chandrabati's Ramayan* which are essentially subversive in nature. Arni, like Chandrabati, deliberately chooses to overlook Ram's glory as an ideal man, an ideal son, an ideal husband. His commitment as a son, his uprightness as a hero, his valour as a warrior remains overlooked in *Sita's Ramayana*. Neither Chandrabati back in the 16th century, nor Arni in the 21st century felt it necessary to highlight Ram and his acts.

For them Sita and her perspective have been of more importance. Until Sita was freed from Lanka, she was unaware of Ram's mindset and intentions. After the war was over, Ram was busy crowning Vibhishan, the king of Lanka instead of hastening to meet Sita. When he was asked about this, he said that he fought the war because it was a matter of his honour, and he was no more interested in Sita, since she might have lost her chastity. Sita was left totally flabbergasted at this. Her reverence for Ram seemed to be a mere illusion that diluted immediately. Subsequently, Sita held Ram responsible for the loss of innocent lives in the war and the destruction that Lanka succumbed to. She decided to end her life in fire. But the fire god, Agni, refused to devour her, and Ram took her back to Ayodhya. Still, her happy life in Ayodhya was transient. She was again abandoned by Ram when she was an expecting mother. She gave birth to her children in Valmiki's hermitage in the forest and refused to let Ram have any knowledge about her sons. Finally, during the 'Ashwamedha yajna' (a Vedic ritual that involved horse sacrifice performed by a king to celebrate his supreme authority) when Ram discovers the identity of his sons and brings them back to Ayodhya along with Sita, she declined to live with Ram in Ayodhya. To avoid being subjected to further humiliation in life, Sita chose to accept death. A return to the lap of Mother Nature was more honourable to her than living her life with a man who had least concern, sympathy, love for his wife. She says, "I do not wish to be a queen. I have been doubted once, twice, and I do not care to be doubted again" (Arni and Chitrakar 145). This statement is full of resistance and dislike not only towards Ram but also towards the entire patriarchal system. In her final statement to Ram, after which she disappears, she says: "Let me go. Take care of our children. Having gained a father, they now lose a mother. You must be both to them" (Arni and Chitrakar 147).

Patua Graphics or Patachitra

In Bengali, "pat" means "picture" and "patua" or "chitrakar" means "painter". *Patachitra* or scroll painting is a popular folk-art form which is practised in the eastern part of India, mainly in the states of West Bengal and Odisha. This art form has an ancient tradition, whose roots stretch far back in time, yet it is very contemporary in nature, since the discourse of this art ranges from traditional myths to current news and socio-cultural issues. To briefly comment on the form and content of this kind of painting, it can be said that colourful, painted scrolls are unfolded to tell stories of different kinds. Each 'pata' narrates each episode of a long narrative. This art form combines the elements of art, storytelling, and performance. The painters are like troubadours, who go around from one place to another with their scrolls of paintings, primarily narrate the stories in the mode of singing. Another quintessential trait of this art form is that it is thoroughly connected to the indigenous folk tradition of its respective geographical locale, be it Bengal, or Odisha, or any other place. It is essentially an oral tradition that incorporates local culture, customs, religious beliefs, along with legends, myths and epics, in its broader perspective. In this book, *Sita's Ramayana*,

Moyna Chitrakar, a female *patua* graphic artist from West Bengal paints the narrative of Ramayana. She has ascribed to the characters bright colours and the traditional features of *patachitra*. Her artistry has made the book far more appealing, and quite close to our modern-day graphic novels. She does complete justice to Arni's text, as well as Chandrabati's take on the Ramayan. Sita becomes so living throughout the book, both in her moments of glee and her phases of plight.

The *patachitra* illustration in *Sita's Ramayana* has multiple significant factors associated with it. It is not merely a graphic art form that has been employed to render a visual effect on the written text. The socio-cultural background of the *pata* artists, their approach towards painting Ramayan in the rural areas of West Bengal, and the contents of the Ramayan paintings, all together have a distinct connection to the narrative content of Arni's retelling. Rather, a close look at *Chandrabati's Ramayan* also exhibits a deep connection. The *patua* graphics might be considered as metatextual in relation to both the retellings, although it has no physical presence in Chandrabati's narrative. Mandakranta Bose, in her seminal book, *The Ramayana in Bengali Folk Painting*, writes that the *pata* artists have an inherent "empathy with the disempowered of the world" (Bose 12). Hence, it can be assumed that *patachitra* representation of the Ramayan narrative would also be concerned with portraying the characters and episodes which involve silenced voices and subaltern epic characters. Like the two retellings that have been examined in this paper, and many other alternative re-interpretations, the *patua* Ramayan painting too is episodic in nature. The artists choose to foreground certain episodes while they ignore others. For instance, episodes involving Kaikeyi and Manthara are often ignored in *pata* paintings which immediately refers to the similar omission of these episodes in Chandrabati and Arni's texts. The *patuas* or the *patachitra* artists exercise an autonomy to select the subjects of their paintings, which in itself, is an act of subversion.

Pata paintings, as noted, is a folk-art form in India. Socially, they belong to the marginalised section, both in terms of their caste and economic status. They are illiterate and mostly belong to the significant segment of rural subalterns. Bose writes that these artists and their art have never been approved by the dominant Brahminical society in ancient times, and unfortunately that segregation still latently continues. However, the *pata* artists chose to voice their protest through their art and interestingly that tradition too continues.

According to Bose, "They decided the best way to broadcast their victory would be to paint it and then travel from village to village telling and showing others what happened" (Bose 11). The essential point to be noticed is that any departure from the authoritative versions of a dominant narrative agitates the governing sections of the society. Chandrabati's text was rejected for the same reason that it digressed from the dominant reading of Ramayan, similarly it has happened with the indigenous scroll painters of West Bengal. This is perhaps the primary factor that connects the three narratives, *Chandrabati's Ramayan, Sita's Ramayana,* and the *patachitra,* the indigenous form of folk art that constitutes the graphic elements in *Sita's Ramayana*. The overall socio-cultural picture of oppression and subsequent subversion pertaining to the Ramayan narrative connects deeply to the apt application of Moyna Chitrakar's *patua* paintings to demonstrate *Sita's Ramayana*. Chandrabati's subversive narrative is revived and manifested in Arni's retelling, complemented by Moyna's feminine consciousness as an indigenous subaltern artist. All this together, renders *Sita's Ramayana* the quality of a distinct female alternative narrative that re-interprets the Ramayan as a Sitayan (a tale that revolves around Sita).

Conclusion

According to Gokhale, "Sita was not only an immortal daughter of the Earth or an incarnation of Lakshmi. She was also intensely human, although her vulnerabilities are lost in the accretions of myth and reverence. But Indian myth is never static, it is constantly in the process of reinterpreting and revalidating itself, and the society that it defines" (Gokhale XVII).

The female revisionist interpretations of the Ramayan are essentially directed towards a search for this human Sita whose image has assimilated with the social, cultural, and emotional life of the common Indian women. They own Sita's tale and identify with it. Further, it is manifested in their stories and through other creative discourses. This paper has sought to examine three such Sita tales composed by three different female creators across a span of five hundred years. Chandrabati's retelling was way ahead of its time. Its contemporaneity emerges suitable as the foundation for Sita's Ramayana which again finds expression through an indigenous folk-art form. Chandrabati composed her verses of the Ramayan for oral circulation. This folk tradition percolates in the inclusion of the folk-art form of *patachitra* in Arni's narrative. The present paper traces this travel of Sita's tale, its female reception and interpretation across media which is a dynamic literary and creative process and affirmatively subversive in its own right.

REFERENCES

A.K.Ramanujan. "Where Mirrors are Windows: Towards an Anthology of Reflections." *History of Religions,* vol. 28, no. 3, 1989, pp. 187-216. www.jstor.org/stable/1062747. Accessed 31 July. 2020.

Arni, Samhita and Moyna Chitrakar. *Sita's Ramayana*. Tara Books Pvt. Ltd., 2018.

Bose, Mandakranta and Sarika Priyadarshini Bose. *A Woman's Ramayana: Chandrabati's Bengali Epic*. Oxon: Routledge, 2013.

Bose, Mandakranta. *The Ramayana in Bengali Folk Painting*. Niyogi Books, 2017.

Dev Sen, Nabaneeta. *Chandrabati's Ramayana*. Zubaan, 2020.

—. "Lady Sings the Blues: When Women Retell the Ramayana." *Manushi,* no. 108, pp. 18-25. ninapaley.com/Sitayana/Manushi_LadySingstheBlues. Accessed 15 September. 2020.

—. "Rewriting the Ramayana: Chandrabati and Molla." *India International Centre Quarterly,* vol. 24, no. 2/3, 1997, pp. 163-177. www.jstor.org/stable/23005443. Accessed 20 October. 2020.

G, Beena. *VISION and RE-VISION*. Notion Press, 2019.

Gokhale, Namita. *In Search of Sita*. Ed. Malashri Lal and Namita Gokhale. Penguin Books, 2018.

Luthra, Rashmi. "Clearing Sacred Ground: Women-Centered Interpretations of the Indian Epics." *Feminist Formations*, vol. 26, no. 2, 2014, pp. 135-161. www.jstor.com/stable/43860745. Accessed 15 August. 2020.

Ostriker, Alicia. "The Thieves of Language: Women Poets and Revisionist Mythmaking." *Signs Journal of Women in Culture and Society*, vol. 8, no. 1, 1982, pp. 68-90. www.jstor.org/stable/3173482. Accessed 26 November. 2020.

Rich, Adrienne. "When We Dead Awaken: Writing as Re-Vision." *College English*, vol. 34, no. 1, 1972, pp. 18-30. www.jstor.org/stable/37521. Accessed 15 August. 2020.

Acknowledgement

I thank my research supervisor, Prof. M.G. Prasuna (BITS Pilani, Hyderabad Campus) for her support and guidance. I thank S. Saritha Sasidharan (PhD scholar, BITS Pilani, Hyderabad Campus) for useful discussions and valuable input.

ENDNOTES

1 Shruti Chakraborti is a doctoral research scholar in the Department of Humanities and Social Sciences, BITS Pilani, Hyderabad Campus, Telangana, India. Her research focuses on Narratology, and contemporary Indian English mythic fiction. She obtained her postgraduation degree in English literature (M.A. English) from University of Calcutta and has completed PGCTE and PGDTE from The English and Foreign Languages University, Hyderabad. Shruti has a few publications in different anthologies and journals which include research papers on British Literature, Postcolonial Literature, and Indian English Literature. While her passion lies in reading, she also has a deep love for sketching, painting and doodling. Email: p20170105@hyderabad.bits-pilani.ac.in

CHAPTER 12

Performing Dalit Feminist Youth Activism in South India: Rap, Gaana, and Street Theater

Pramila Venkateswaran[1]

ABSTRACT

Young Dalit men and women are changing the narrative of casteist oppression in India. Youth activists perform protest songs in the genre of rap and *gaana*, using elements of slam poetry and rap from African American artists and blending them with local musical innovations. The performances have deliberate messaging, signaling particular caste and gender injustices, both current and historical. This paper will analyze Dalit youth performances of rap, *gaana*, and street theater (*koothu*) in South India, particularly in Tamil Nadu, to understand the poetics of protest against caste and gender oppression. It will look at the notion of space in these performances. Since social space has historically been restricted for marginalized groups such as Dalits, and even private space has never existed for Dalits, more so for women, the performance space—the screen, the theatre, or street—becomes a heterotopia, or a third space for voicing injustice through song. Taboos are tossed aside in this space; transgressive, private-public fused in-your-face musical phrasings appear on every audio and visual device through the globalization of the internet. Rap and *gaana* queer accepted caste and gender narratives. This paper will look at youth rappers, such as Arivu, the latest sensation, *gaana* performer, Isaivani's performances, as well as "The Casteless Collective" and inquire into the reasons for their appeal despite their iconoclasm. Affect is another area of inquiry in the analysis of Dalit performance, since caste and gender oppression meant invisibilizing Dalits and not seeing them as humans with emotions. Examining the value of affect within performances as well as its effect on audiences is important, since both coalesce to make historically restricted speech appealing and far-reaching in effecting change.

Introduction

Dalit youth anti-caste activists in India, particularly in Tamil Nadu, are vibrant in their powerful feminist messaging, as seen in their multimedia performances. One of their latest music video sensations is *Enjoy Enjaami*, with its powerful amalgam of rap, hip-hop, and indigenous rhythms celebrating the musician Arivu's grandmother, an indentured laborer in Sri Lanka under the British. The video captures the wealth of nature and Dalit women's labor, both of which have been oppressed by the institutions of caste, capitalism and gender. Dalit artists use pop music, marginalized musical forms and *koothu* (theater) to make their statement challenging the burden of caste and gender oppression, a burden that continues to exist even if untouchability is illegal in India. Dalit feminism addresses caste and gender oppression; therefore, Dalit musicians and artists are feminists raising awareness of Dalit oppression. Young Dalit activists today see the power of music and theater to change oppressive social conditions. For example, little did Indians imagine that a provocative song critiquing the denial of women's access to the Sabarimala temple, sung by Isaivani, as part of The Casteless Collective, a grassroots anti-caste collective, would contribute to the Supreme Court upholding the decision in September 2018 to allow women to enter the temple (Supreme Court Observer).

Dalit communities have always expressed themselves in song, drumming and dance. This oral, expressive culture is communal, seasonal, and celebrates rites of passage or community gatherings with song, percussion and dance. Description, wit, and humor characterize these aural and kinesthetic expressions. However, the separation of castes since Vedic times[1], which brought with it the systemic oppression of Dalits by upper castes, coincided with a divide between "high" classical arts populated by Brahmins and the "lower" folk arts of Dalit communities and other lower castes (Scheduled Castes and Other Backward Castes, as termed officially) (Chanda-Vaz, 2019, para. 13). Dalit arts remained on the fringes of society, both physically and psychologically, since "they have not yet been widely recognized as valuable forms of representative earthy literature" (Singh, 2018, p. 189).

Caste became a wedge issue during India's independence, as we see in the debates between Mohandas Gandhi and Dr. Bhimrao Ambedkar (the former known for fighting for India's freedom from British rule, and the latter who questioned national freedom that failed to get rid of the caste system that oppressed millions of Dalit men and women)[2]. The central government's failure to challenge the sacerdotal caste system further invisibilized Dalit arts, while making more visible the young republic's pride in the classical arts, thus privileging "knowledge production" (Ingole, 2020, p. 92). "Popular Dalit folk songs, dramas, and humor are yet to find a respectable place in mainstream Indian academia" (Ingole, 2020, p. 95). Historically, Dalit women singers, dancers, and musicians have kept their art within the private sphere of their community gatherings or their homes. But, during the Nationalist movement for Indian Independence, Dalit women, for example, who participated in the Dalit youth organizations "staged poems, plays and songs based on their experiences . . . which became the key ingredients for the Ambedkar Movement to assert its identity as one driven by rebellion and demand for justice" (Singh, 2019, p. 50).

Dalit songs and *therukoothu* (street theater), (*koothu* for short) barely migrated to upper caste communities; their transmission into urban cultural hubs is recent. Any reference to the songs and dances of the marginalized were introduced as auxiliary acts in concerts and were mainly seen as entertaining rather than having any intrinsic artistic or cultural value. For example, in a classical dance concert such as Bharatanatyam, the *korathi* (gypsy) dance was seen as purely for entertainment rather than as having artistic expertise. Similarly, the folk song which was introduced at the end of a classical (Carnatik) music repertoire was judged the same way. The prejudice against folk arts is slowly beginning to dissipate in younger generations.

In this paper, I argue that young Dalit lyricists, singer-activists, and theater directors create performance spaces that function as heterotopias,[3] which allow for oppressive norms to be reversed. Michel Foucault defines heterotopia as an open space, a "counter-site" to closed spaces in society. Heterotopias are "real sites," which "are simultaneously represented, contested, and invented... Places of this kind are outside of all places, even though it might be possible to indicate their location in reality" (Foucault, 1984, pp. 3-4). In this paper, I use heterotopias to refer to spaces where Dalit women and men create their political identity. For Dalit feminist artists, heterotopias become the spaces where they create their art and feminist expressions to end society's injustices toward Dalit people. Current rap, hip-hop, *gaana* and *koothu* artists break barriers for women and lower castes by occupying these heterotopian spaces, such as the stage, the studio, cyber networks and music videos to speak out their contested realities.

I also argue that the materialist and rationalist philosophies of Ambedkar and E.V Ramasamy Naicker (popularly known as Periyar) nourish the lyrics produced by Dalit music artists in India. It is important to note that Periyar's rational and materialist ideology is in opposition to Hindu Vedic spiritual idealism, and so it needs to be understood within the Dravidian culture and the context of Tamil Nadu. It has to be distinguished from European Enlightenment rationalist thinking. Dalit lyrics reflect Periyar's rationalism, which "invested in the surface materiality of things" (Gajarawala 2013), rather than the metaphysical world, in order to use human imagination and will to bring about change. Dalit feminism takes inspiration from Periyar's feminism, which addresses, through the use of logic and reason, the origins of women's enslavement and charts the ways to end it.

Today, young Dalit men and women have changed the narrative of casteist oppression in India. Youth activists perform protest songs in the genre of rap and *gaana*, using elements of slam poetry and rap from African American artists and blending them with local musical innovations and theatrical elements. Their deliberate messages in rap, hip-hop and *gaana*, are earthy, connecting to people's lived experiences, just as Periyar had expatiated[4]; they address caste and gender injustices, celebrate Dalit leaders, and lampoon current politics and society. Dalit singer-activists break with traditional expectations of their presence in theatrical spaces. They challenge caste restrictions by commandeering public spaces as their stage, such as the theater, the street, and the internet and make them heterotopian spaces where they mirror Dalit reality, challenge assumptions and invent artistic ways to assert their feminist and democratic ideals. Additionally, Dalit youth use musical technology as well as social media to garner the kind of psychological and emotional affect, in both depth and international reach, that previous iterations of protest attempted to capture.

In this paper, I analyze the visual and lyrical language of rap, *gaana*, and *koothu*, which intersect in Dalit youth performances. Such an analysis not only uncovers the poetic and artistic elements used by Dalit artists but also depicts how Dalit feminism is embodied by Dalit performers in heterotopian spaces, such that the audience is affected by the themes of Dalit women's oppression and Dalit feminist activism. I use intersectionality of gender and caste as a tool in my analysis of Dalit artistic productions.

In the last three decades, rap music performance has spread like wildfire in different Indian languages, particularly among Dalit youth. In Tamil Nadu, rap and *gaana* are popular among youth activists challenging caste oppression. Rap, which originated in Jamaica in the 1960s and spread to the black ghettos of New York in the 1980's (Baxter, 1988, p. 30), was a form of spoken word protest, accompanied by beatboxing, that spread among marginalized black youth in the US, and caught fire among youth globally. *Gaana,* a term used by Tamil Nadu youth activist-singers, began in the working-class neighborhoods of Chennai, Tamil Nadu. It is like rap but also uses Dalit song traditions. It is "edgy folk music characterised by a hard-driving rhythm and earthy lyrics" (Deeksha, 2018, para.11). As Isaivani explains, the *gaana* form uses rap, folk, and melody (Aadhan Tamil, 2019). Aspects of *koothu* can also be seen in the staging of rap and *gaana.*

Dalit Feminist Themes in Rap and Gaana

Both rap and *gaana* are provocative in their address of feminist themes that queer mainstream notions of feminism. I use the verb form "queer" to denote the unsettling of normative assumptions, and the discourses and practices based on these assumptions ("Queer"). Queering established assumptions helps us discover the blind spots in our theories and practices. In this paper, queering feminist practices in India reveals caste as deliberately invisibilized in discourses about women's empowerment. Contemporary feminists point out that Indian feminists mainly advocated for Brahminical, middle class, and other upper caste women. Dalit women's oppression did not enter feminist discourse until intersectionality was used as a tool of analysis in feminism (Arya and Rathore, 2020, p. 5). Caste has only recently entered the gender-class-sexuality nexus. Even today, the media reflects the lack of representation of caste; "only upper-caste women and their issues receive recognition by the media, by the leaders of mainstream movements as well as by 'mainstream' feminists, who simply assume they can speak for Dalit women" (Tharu, 2020, p. 184). Dalit rap, *gaana,* and *koothu* play vital roles in articulating caste, gender, and class in their lyrics and performance.

Koothu's avant garde elements can be seen in women cast as lead singers, the way the stage is populated, the use of lighting, sound effects, props, and visuals offering dramatic effects, such as anticipation, climax, wit and humor, and the musical conversations between singers and percussionists. This intersectionality of musical and theatrical forms is true to Dalit artists' "transgressive notions: a command over experiences of untouchability that only a person treated as untouchables can express" (Singh, 2019, p. 189).

Dalit songs and music videos on feminist themes intersecting caste and gender critique Brahminical taboos against the eating of beef, lack of Dalit women's access in temples, pollution taboos for both men and women that keep them out of essential social spaces, caste persecution, land rights, reservation, condemnation of manual scavenging, voting, murder of young couples who transgress caste rules, and gender politics. The lyrics make fun of vegetarians, the hypocrisy of priests and the upper castes. As one of the lyricists of The Casteless Collective, Arivarasu Kalainesan, says, Dalit music and theater "is not only about pain ... but also on their triumphs, their victories." (Deeksha, 2018, para. 22). He adds, "'In Tamil, there are no songs about many crucial matters, like a woman's preferences in life, liberalism, reservation or casteism. Our songs are about the unsung and the unnoticed people and issues. Yes, we and our songs are political'" (Mohandas, 2019, para.3).

Enjoy Enjaami is a feminist statement about caste and ecological violence. This music video offers a view of Dalit past that has been made invisible by institutions of caste, capitalism, and gender. The hero of *Enjoy Enjaami* is the lyricist Arivu's grandmother who suffered as an indentured laborer in Sri Lanka during British rule. She returns to Tamil Nadu, cut off from her family, and pieces a life together. The *oppari* mourns the losses suffered by the laborers as well as the losses suffered by nature, intersecting feminism, ecology, class, caste, and colonial subjugation. The repeated call "Cuckoo cuckoo" is haunting, as it echoes the pathos of trees lost to cities and the "civilizing" force of capitalism. Drumbeats of *parai,* a percussive form which originated in Dalit villages, capture the endurance of the oppressed laborers who survive through their faith in nature and their music. A forest of color decorated ancestral women, the figure of a younger woman presented as a queen, and alternately the crone seated on a throne, and the drummers, with Arivu entering with spoken word segments, create a powerful message of reclaiming Dalit identity.

Dalit feminist heterotopias

Dalit music performances are collective heterotopias, where both spectators and the performers have agency and embrace solidarity. The staging of Dalit feminist themes in music and *koothu* is a heterotopian space that represent Dalit suffering and activism, contest accepted norms, invent intersectional indigenous forms to question casteist and sexist customs, and teach anti-oppressive ideas. So, in the interstices of a casteist society, Dalit feminist youth activism in music creates heterotopias that are both symbolic and functional. The Casteless Collective formed by Pa. Ranjith can be seen as a heterotopia that presents music that critiques caste oppression. Their title, "Casteless," is telling, since the mission of this group is to eradicate caste. This collective, comprised of musicians from different castes, and including men and women, does live performances as well as makes music videos which are distributed via the internet.

In the heterotopian space of the stage, we see women singers breaking taboos of gender boundaries and upper caste restrictions of public space. Isaivani, one of the lead singers in The Casteless Collective, declares that she experiences equality on stage and feels the collective empowers her to be her authentic self. Having resonated with the message of the collective and her love for songs carrying anti-caste and feminist messages, she feels she has found her niche in *gaana* and rap (Aadhan Tamil, 2019). Isaivani's song on Ambedkar, an example of Dalit feminism, celebrates the leader's unrelenting work for the freedom of Dalits (Praba, 2019). As one of the architects of the Indian Constitution, Ambedkar asserted that Hindu religious literature, or *Shastras*, were directly responsible for upper caste Brahmins continuing to subjugate Dalits. Isaivani's lyrics, quoting Periyar and Ambedkar, praise Ambedkar's dress, his education, and his beliefs; the chorus is Ambedkar's and Periyar's slogan, *jatiya ozhikatam* (annihilate caste). In this music video, Isaivani dresses in a style similar to Ambedkar; she wears a pair of trousers, a white shirt, a black jacket and sneakers. Her long hair hangs loosely down her back. With no makeup, she represents the professional woman in urban space claiming her daily reality. The video opens with her walking into the center of the screen from down a driveway, showing her comfort in using public space. Walking down a driveway signifies one's ownership of oneself and one's destination. Her stance makes a statement about Dalits not having to fear being seen or approaching anyone or any building or space from the front, in contrast to the submissive gestures and body language of ex-untouchables a century ago. Her voice which rises from the belly carries the timbre of power, consistent with *gaana* tradition, as opposed to the high-pitched falsetto of Tamil film singing required for women. *Gaana* singers, particularly female, disrupt this expectation of femininity. Rhythm and melody, accompanied by a percussive dance beat popular in *koothu* and folk-dance offer energy to her voice and match the heavy subject matter of the lyrics.

Dalit feminist heterotopia breaks accepted notions among the elite that music that is not classical is second rate (Deeksha, 2018. para. 11). This is like the division in Tamil literature, between poetry and novel written in literary Tamil, or *cen* Tamil, considered high art and those written in spoken Tamil, considered kitsch. In fact, in common upper caste parlance, non-classical music, particularly that of marginalized communities, is called *dabankoothu*, a derogatory term denoting lack of class and lack of aesthetics of the *koothu* form and its performers. In domestic scenarios, when there is an argument or a fight, family members usually exclaim, *ena koothu*! referencing derogatorily to the musical forms of the slums as unappetizing as well as the slum dwellers being uncivilized. This societal division between classical and non-classical forms like rap, *therukoothu* and film music is slowly beginning to change as a result of feminist activists such as The Casteless Collective, Isaivani, Padma Mangai, among others. Today, talented artists in the film world and in heterotopian art spaces have diffused the borders between classical and non-classical. Music directors, Pa Ranjith and A.R. Rahman, have taken the music world by storm with their interesting musical innovations. *Enjoy Enjammi* is an example of such an innovation, combining *oppari*, or mourning song, which is the Dalit form of hip-hop, rap, indigenous rhythms, and spoken word, lifting this assemblage into art, thus dissolving the high/low binary, as well as disrupting casteist spaces by performing their feminism.

Transformation of the voice and the body of the performers is also seen in theatrical productions by anti-caste theater activists such as Padma Mangai (Singh, A, 2013) and Ashwini

Kasi (Pragati, 2021). Similar to Dalit music activists, Mangai and Kasi have brought art forms within Dalit and other "lower" caste communities onto the stage, making them the center of culture. In their mission to transform society, they have revived *therukoothu* to tell stories that relate to contemporary society and bring awareness of gender and caste oppressions (Pragati, 2021, para.13). They innovate traditional myths and use unconventional spaces, thus subverting age-old caste and gender divisions and separations. Women and marginalized groups are given agency in the democratizing spaces of *therukoothu,* and arts such as *tappattam* traditionally done in Dalit communities are revived in the curriculum of dramatic arts (Nathan, 2018).

Mangai calls the diverse musical and dance forms of Tamil Nadu as "living forms in Tamil Nadu" (Singh, A, 2013, p. 497), discarding casteism and sexism. "Also, if one sees through these forms, a new idiom can evolve. The forms are inherently flexible and have been changing and evolving with the times" (Singh, A, 2013, p. 497). "Mangai traverses boundaries constructed within theatre work, bridging an assortment of forms—*therukoothu, isai natakam,* and modern drama. . . .Much of her work is sourced from marginalized aesthetic forms (such as domestic all-female rituals and the colloquial, sociolinguistic practices of the disenfranchised) and is performed in marginal sociocultural spaces (such as the courtyards of housing projects)" (Singh, A, 2013, p. 493). She recasts classical female characters, such as Avvai and Manimekalai, as agentic, transcending restrictions.

Contrary to men acting women's roles in traditional productions, activist directors and producers break gender norms. Women now act in *therukoothu* and other plays; issues such as transgender oppression, caste killings, and women leaders make their way into the plays. Isaivani embodying Ambedkar, a Dalit woman playing a male leader's role, is the intersection of theater and *gaana* to create Dalit feminist heterotopia. Thus, women characters as well as women actors and musicians find voice on stage. The stage, which can be the street, a building, a TV studio or the internet, becomes the political space for the arts activists, whether they are producers, directors, or actors. We can call these spaces, which are sometimes spontaneous, heterotopias of dissent which galvanize awareness in society and bring about policies to protect vulnerable populations.

Dalit Women's Performance Spaces

The history of Dalit women has consisted of restrictions placed on them by the institutional structures of caste, gender and class, the latter two tightly bound by upper caste Brahmin rules which have spilled across castes. In Dalit women's singing and *koothu* performances, we see them queering social caste and gender expectations regarding occupying physical space of the stage or the screen, the street corner and home, as well as occupying mental and emotional space. True to the foundational feminist ideas of Periyar, enunciated in *Why Were Women Enslaved?* (2020), Dalit women's bodies occupying public space is a retort to upper caste restrictions. Since caste and gender proscriptions become internalized, we see Dalit women discarding psychological barriers to their freedom by claiming public space in their performance. They are not only performing their art but are also performing their transgressive act of crossing boundaries. Thus, through their "freeing acts," they traverse "mental and defined moral spaces" (Singh, R., 2019, p. 44).

Isaivani demonstrates her (and her community's) active queering of conventional caste narrative by performing her songs and her activism in her easy movements on stage, often occupying the entirety of the stage, walking to and fro covering its width, or breaking into *koothu* movements. Her voice has audacity or sauciness, a tone of defiance mixed with humor that draws her audience to her. She has a powerful earthy voice emanating from her belly, very unlike the shrill falsetto of the Tamil film voice culture. Her voice, her stride, her gestures, the lift of her head, all produce what she calls "thimir" or audacity (Aadhan Tamil, 2019). For example, in her song, *I'm sorry Ayyappa,* the lyrics delivered in her defiant tone, convey the content of the opening lyrics: "I am sorry Ayyappa/Naan ulla vantha ennappa/bhayam kaatti adakkivaykka/pazhaya kalam allappa [I am sorry Lord Ayyappa / What will happen if I enter your place, mister? / Old times are no more / Don't use fear to suppress us]. The end rhyme with its profane diminution of the god Ayyappa to a casual stranger (appa), followed by the wagging of a finger at the god and the rule makers to discard gender and caste rules and wake up to the times, rouse the audience into consciousness of caste oppression. *Bayam* and *Adakkuthal*—fear and oppression—used in the same line is a lightning rod to rouse the audience into applause. It is interesting that *adakkivaykka* which means "to oppress" has the same root as *adakkam* which means modest and is used as a moral code only for women, to keep them in their place. In one fell swoop, Isaivani discards the rule of *adakkam* and substitutes *thimir* as the code for her and for oppressed communities. She feels it is important to project audacity in order to lend power to the words of the songs, which are songs of protest against restrictions on women and Dalits. Isaivani creates a psychological space for the viewer of her videos to imagine a world where they are indeed free of the shackles of caste. The songs themselves are generated from the freedom of the lyricist in the framework of the page; on stage, the singer experiences the emancipation of the imagination by bringing the song alive to the audience, and the viewers participate in the power of the imagination which opens up mental and emotional avenues for them.

The psychological space that singers like Isaivani clear for performers and the audience simultaneously becomes a political space where performers and the audience experience agency. The stage becomes a heterotopia or alternate space where Dalit performers can "allow for social and cultural norms to be contested or reversed" (Andrews, 2021). Describing a *kummi* song, Roja Singh observes that the character in the song transforms "mud into gold," thus reversing "the idea of polluted fated to further pollute into an agent of purification (2019, p. 206). We can see Isaivani as the agent in the song alchemize the given social dross of women as untouchable into the gold of egalitarianism for all genders and castes to access public worship spaces. As Isaivani says, "When you speak your message through song, it will reach everyone. Music is an easy way to voice social issues" (BBC NewsTamil, 2021). Performers experience the power of self-expression and knowledge in this space, which shapes the socio-political context for both the performers and the audience.

Isaivani expresses her feminist agency in her performance as a Dalit woman, a trained singer, as well as her performance as an activist who desires change for Dalits and for Dalit women. As viewers, we are energized to participate in change making. The audience as well as the singers "feel and enter untouched and unknown spaces that are life-giving and identity-binding (Singh, 2018, p.211). As Isaivani opines, "A woman speaking out is criticized. A woman speaking out about casteism is criticized. I just keeping doing what I do. Change is the goal" (BBC Tamil).

Dalit musician-activists believe in making any space into their stage. As Arivu says, "If you need to convey a message, you don't need a stage or a mic. If you don't have a path, make it!" (Mohandas, 2019, para. 9). Sujata Gidla (2017) describes her uncle, K.G. Satyamuthy, or Satyam as he was called by his family and friends, a Maoist leader in Andhra Pradesh, who organized members of the lowest caste of manual scavengers, the *pakis*, to act in a local dance and music competition. When members of the troupe win the competition, Gidla describes how Satyam's appeal to the communist association to fund his troupe to perform in the villages was rejected. But Satyam persists in organizing the troupe to put on performances every evening, collecting a fistful of rice in return from each of the households in every village, which the performers would sell to fund their expenses, such as fuel and food. Satyam exposes the hypocrisy of the communist association and inspires his troupe to demonstrate their joined conviction about denouncing oppression of Dalit women and men. In organizing *pakis* to perform in plays that depicted abuse of Dalits by landlords and critiquing antiquated technology such as using men as beasts of burden to pull rickshaws, he created the space for them to find freedom of movement in public space and self-expression that music and *koothu* allow. Gidla shows the feminist expressions of Dalits like Satyam using poetry and theater to subvert caste, gender and class rules. It is this persistent pushback against the forces that restrict space that we see in Dalit youth's music and theater activism.

Just as contemporary Tamil poets create work that dissolves the high/low, caste and gender binaries, Dalit feminist youth activists use language and form in music that bring marginalized vernaculars into the center. As Arivu, the lyricist of *Enjoy Enjaami*, says, "The language one hears throughout the song is that of people who do not find representation in mainstream media" (Padmanabhan, 2021, para. 9). In one of her interviews, Isaivani gives examples of the idiom of slums, such as *jamma jamnakattu*, which she describes as jolly and without any specific meaning (Aadhan Tamil, 2019). Young people, regardless of caste or creed, enjoy the verbal gymnastics of these idioms, which are witty, musical and humorous, understood within their contexts. The use of the local vernacular is feminist since feminism is iconoclastic and, in this case, breaks the accepted binary of "high" culture and "literary" language, since they stratify society into powerful and powerless. For Dalit performers, bringing their speech into the heterotopian space of the stage is a border-crossing act.

Choice of language and idiom fuel the energy of rap, *gaana,* and *therukoothu.* Periyar's Self-Respect movement pushed for Tamil to gain ascendency as the language of the state of Tamil Nadu to counter the British Raj as well as the dominance of Hindi.[6] Periyar and his party, the Dravida Kazhagam, which later became the DMK (Dravida Munetra Kazhagam), saw Tamil as superior to English and Hindi and unifying all the states in the South. The fight to overthrow English and write in regional languages has been part of the postcolonial argument (Iyer and Zare, 2009, p. x). To this day, *bhasha* (regional language) writers claim their value, while Indian-English writers argue that theirs is a unique language, which historically has used the master's tools to answer back to empire (Iyer and Zare, 2009, p. xxii). At the same time, ironically, Dalits question non-Dalits' lack of access to English, whether in education, writing, publication, or work (Iliah, 2020, para 1). Dalits see English as their political choice, in order to challenge the restriction of Dalits in English medium schools. In postcolonial India, English became the currency for jobs. Dalits were denied education and they were denied literacy in Sanskrit and English, two hegemonic languages. Kancha Ilaiah argues for Dalitization, not Sanskritzation (upper caste oppressive domain), so every Dalit person learns English to counter language oppression and spread their message of revolution nationally and internationally (Ilaiah, 2020, para. 1), a radical position that influences Dalit feminism.

Dalit feminists tame hegemonic languages, be it *cen* Tamil or English, and use them to serve their aesthetic and political purposes. Rap and *gaana* videos produced by Dalit music activists show their use of spoken Tamil, folk Tamil, and the blending of idioms heard within *cheri* (slum) and rural communities, with English. They mix idioms and pun on words, with surprising results. For example, in *Enjoy Enjaami,* we hear the double entendre in the title, employing both Tamil and English meanings. *Enjaayi,* which means *mother,* sounds like the English lexicon *enjoy*. The denotation of the English word "enjoy" disrupts the narrative of the mother's pain enduring the oppression of laboring under imperialism. *Enjaami,* a Tamil phrase which means *my god* and sounds like a name to the non-Tamil speaker, moves the mother god (Arivu's grandmother) into the center of the musical narrative.

Another rap and *gaana* piece, "I'm sorry, Ayyappa," inspired by Periyar's speeches on women's rights,[5] addresses the god Ayyappa in the repeated chorus, but the song itself is not about the god, but about women's rights. Within this song, the apology in English sounds casual. This is deliberate because the serious matter of the song is about women challenging their lack of access to the Sabarimala temple, and a Dalit woman voicing this challenge. Isaivani can achieve this tonal contrast in her rendition, offering the token apology in a high note beginning the song and shifting to the powerful voice and lyrics celebrating herself and all women as Periyar's granddaughters and debunking rules that keep women down.

Isaivani interweaves idioms used in the slums along with Tamil-inflected English words, such as "taste-la," "sugar-u," "power-u" and "housefull-u," as in her *Beef song*. Different registers of Tamil and English give verve to the lyrics sung in fast tempo, with intricate rhythmic, tongue-twisting phrases alternating with lines sung or spoken in slower tempo. Sometimes, two musicians on stage have conversations, or repartees, mixing languages, which are swift and full of innuendo and humor. The singers' command of the pace of rap and *gaana* is exhilarating, outwitting the flashing disco lights and visuals on stage. We witness the transformation of Dalit feminist voices that meld the aesthetic and the political in vibrant heterotopian imagination.

Origin of Dalit Feminism in Oral Tradition

It is useful to reflect on the music and poems in Dalit women's tradition, such as the earliest songs called *Therigatha* composed by the Buddhist nuns in the 6th century, BC ("Therigatha," 1991). These were songs of protest about a woman's place in society and the expectations on women sung by Buddhist nuns asserting their need for liberation; they painted images of oppression in the domestic sphere and their longing for freedom from "mortar and pestle" (Tharu and Lalitha, 1991, p. 68). *Bhakti* songs of Chokamela, Kabir and women saints addressed a divine being, but were earthy in their imagery, which portrayed the material reality of people's suffering and decried caste oppression. *Bhakti* and Buddhism were counter narratives to mainstream Hinduism which was based on the *varna* (caste) system (Kumar, 2019, p. 43). These poets asserted the path to the divine lay through the heart. *Bhakti* poets were able to create *bhakti* or the feeling of devotion that changed conservative Hindus. *Bhakti* or devotional songs opened up a space for non-Brahmin Hindus to declare allegiance with a loving creator who did not see differences in gender or caste. In fact, naked saints who imitated the nakedness of god, (*digambara* or cloud clad) are still celebrated by Hindus, for they don't see division between people but perceive the highest unity between spirit and matter realized in the everyday. However, women across caste did not experience this metaphysical truth in their mundane lives. Their space was restricted by caste taboos.

Dalit feminists today, in poetry and music, continue the tradition of Buddhist and *bhakti* poets and musicians. We see in recent decades, feminist musicians delving more into the ancestral spaces of their people, both in exploring their land as well as in learning about the past by listening to the stories from their lineage. They interrogate their history of oppression and their cultural production in order to create music and theater that show creativity, imagination, and insight. Emboldened Dalit feminist voices, as in *Beef song*, *Enjoy Enjaami* and *I am sorry, Ayyappa*, refuse to be cowed down by hegemonic institutions and ideologies. We see in these music videos the performance of Dalit subjectivity. Where Dalits were invisibilized, the youth singer-activists command attention in both physical bearing and voice. As Arivu says, "It's a world of hypocrisy – a woman who, in popular songs, is depicted as a goddess, is killed for making a choice about her life. *Thaadikkaran pethi*, [also known as *I am sorry, Ayyapa*], is a song in a feminist viewpoint– of a woman's preferences about job, life partner and the dress she wears. It's a liberal anthem where the woman speaks her mind" (Mohandas, 2019, para. 7). The theatre, stage, or screen become heterotopian spaces where the once-invisible Dalit women and men move into the center.

While the atrocity on the Dalit body makes their oppression a spectacle where there is no accountability, the stage offers a transgressive space for the oppressed to voice their emotion and show their bodies in action, carried by the aesthetics of song. The theatrical / video production of *Enjoy Enjaami* carries feminist, ecological themes challenging labor oppression and destruction of nature. It begins with the frantic beat of *parai* (Dalit drum), accompanied by ululation and the visual image of a hand lifting a handful of soil from a trembling earth. The tone of the video informed by these images anticipates the music of people of the soil and nature. It is interesting to note the subversion of the musical forms in the video: *parai,* which is perceived by the upper caste as funereal, becomes a music of joy in the video; *oppari,* which is a lament, sung by women, is lifted from the cemetery and placed on the stage to represent the lament of Dalits and is fused with a hip-hop rhythm; ululation which is used to commemorate birth also becomes part of the fabric of this musical creation. The lyrics convey the displacement of Dalit ancestors, their land and forests. This feminist lament is expressed in the grave tones of singer Dhee: "Thottam Sezhithalum En Thonda Nanaiyalaye, / En Kadale Karaye Vaname Saname, / Nelame Kolame Edame Thadame [my garden is flourishing, yet my throat remains dry / Oh, my sea, bank, forest, people, / land, clan, place, and track]" (Lyricsraag, 2021).

In the video, the younger woman, dressed in full-sleeved shirt and pants and adorned in traditional jewelry and sitting on a throne in the forest, contrasting with the matriarch who is the laboring woman—the grandmother—attuned to nature, calls people to unite and take care of the earth and nourish the people of the soil. The lyrics tell of Dalit youth revisiting their origins when laborers toiled in the fields and forests, which belonged also to the birds and animals. They recall nature offering its energy for their survival. The ecological connection is lucid: "Pattan Poottan Katha Boomi, Atam Pottu Kattum Sami, / Ratinandha Suthi Vandha Seva Koovuchu / Adhu Pottu Vachcha Echamdhane Kada Marichu, / Namma Nada Marichu Indha Veeda Marichu [My ancestors guarded the land. The devotee that dances / As the earth rotates, the rooster's / excretions fertilized the forests, / transformed into our country, then into our home too]" (Lyricsraag, 2021). The singer, Arivu, asks in the voice of the grandmother "Ena kora, ena kora," [what more do you want, what more do you want], indicating the fullness of what Dalits had, and now have, in their spiritual and body memory. Thus *Enjoy Enjaami* has a positive message for all people to unite and become nurturers of the soil and the forests for our survival. "Enjoy" is the operative word in the chorus. The call of cuckoo, which is the chorus, signals sunrise, a metaphor for awakening. The cuckoo, a traditional metaphor for a fair-skinned woman, is deliberately used in the song to subvert casteist aspersions on Dalit women. The ululation and the *parai* (Dalit drum) that begin and end the song are harbingers of life, beauty and joy.

Dalit feminism and democracy in Dalit youth activists' rap, gaana, and koothu

The arts have always been a vehicle to awaken people, especially during times of crisis. Although protests against caste and gender oppression have been ongoing, times of crisis give rise to a flood of anti-caste, feminist, artistic and intellectual production. The struggle for Independence was one such moment which sparked major debates and produced a wealth of writings across the country. Increased violence against Dalits in recent years has seen a peak in anti-caste and feminist-themed music and artistic productions. As with earlier historical moments, currently, Dalit allies among upper caste musicians participate in spreading awareness of caste privilege and the socialization of aggression toward lower castes. For example, T.M. Krishna, a famous Carnatik musician, in his book, *Sebastian & Sons,* brings to light the invisibilisation of the talent and expertise of *mridangam* makers who belong to the Dalit caste. Krishna points out the hypocrisy of the Brahmin artists who regard the makers as impure while they *use* the *mridgangams* which are made out of cow, buffalo and goat skins. While they maintain their caste through vegetarianism and despotic benevolence, they display their hypocrisy by not admitting that they are in touch with animal skin and keep their instruments in their *puja* or prayer room, which is barred to the makers. Moreover, while the upper caste male artists are celebrated and awarded prestigious prizes, the makers (Dalit men and women) who are a constant presence in the artists' lives and possess considerable musical knowledge, are invisible. Although threatened with loss of music gigs, T.M. Krishna speaks out against caste injustice that the majority of upper castes would prefer to ignore (2020).

As Dalit scholars reiterate, casteism and gender injustice thwart democratic values. In the casteist economy of space, both the existence and the cultural production of Dalits are invisibilized. "Democracy not only opposes caste, but also provides a space to represent the experience of the excluded subjects" (Ingole, 2020, p. 98). Hugo Gorringe (2016), in his exploration of caste wars as wars to occupy or restrict space, believes that "continued contestation of spaces of exclusion and division is vital to Indian democracy" (p.173). Young activists from across the caste spectrum use the arts to cast out pernicious divisions which restrict spaces for the vulnerable. As Padma Mangai explains, theater by definition is a collective and is democratic (Singh, A, 2013, p. 493). Aswini Kasi, P. Rajagopal, and Padma Mangai are a few among many who innovate newer art forms from marginalized traditions as well as from other cultures (Nathan, 2018).

Unlike much of the music industry in Tamil Nadu which focuses on individual aspiration and fame, Dalit feminist activists see their performance as a collective mission to bring about change. This democratizing principle encompassing feminism, as influenced by Periyar, and Marxist ideology and socialism, informs their lyrics, their choice of language, performance techniques, choice of instruments, technology, and dress in order to augment messages of change. They flout gender and caste norms and reclaim their history, music and *koothu*, thus changing society's engagement with history and current politics.

In the efforts made by feminist anti-caste art activists to democratize spaces, it is important to distinguish between cultural appropriation and allyship. Unlike cultural appropriation, where a superior group speaks in the voice of the group from which it appropriates, activists in the arts bring men and women from across the caste spectrum to create egalitarian presentations that both the performers and the audience can relish. Thus, they transgress and transform conventional spaces to make them democratic. Mangai and T.M. Krishna are cultural allies who believe all artists and all arts need to have social and political spaces to thrive.

Music technology plays a role in contesting restriction of space for the marginalized. From the simplicity of using the phone as a recording and broadcasting device, to the complexity of recording songs and videos in a recording studio, music technology has galvanized the production and dissemination of rap and *gaana*. The internet has helped easy exchange and dissemination of the knowledge of both music and music technology. The current generation was born in the age of the internet and its rapid spread of information, thus displacing centuries-old restriction of knowledge to some. This shared epistemology is nowhere more visible than in the widely broadcasted competitions and award-winning shows, such as Behindwoods Gold Mic Awards. Behindwoods' directors unabashedly articulate their support of singers like Arivu and Isaivani on The Casteless Collective, as well as other emerging Dalit artists, thus demonstrating the centrality of anti-caste language, feminist themes, and their reception in urban centers of Tamil Nadu (Behindwoods TV, 2019).

Cyber space keeps information permanent, which makes any imposed restrictions on cultural productions moot. Young Dalit female and male rappers and *koothu* artists find their freedom in the space of technology, and their audiences are whichever corners of the globe airwaves reach. Arivu, who believes this "is an era of cultural renaissance" (Mohandas, 2019, para.7). is committed to fight for a caste-free system and discrimination-free world. He says, "Our songs discuss the ignored facts – the thousands of manual scavengers whose average lifespan is 40 years as they die every day in drainages; those landless farmers who are never there on the list of any government benefits and live in poverty; the IIT washrooms where wash basins are reserved for vegetarians; the common men who speak loud about oppression and discriminate their sisters at their homes..." (Mohandas, 2019, para. 7).

Affect as Resistance

What are the reasons for the appeal of Dalit activist songs, music videos and *koothu*? Is it purely their iconoclasm? Affect is another area of inquiry in the analysis of Dalit feminism, since caste and gender oppression meant invisibilizing Dalits and not seeing them as humans with emotions. Social restrictions when internalized transform into inner walls that keep people oppressed. Examining the value of affect within performances, as well as the effect of performances on audiences, are important, since both coalesce to make historically restricted speech appealing and far-reaching in effecting change.

Emotional affect was very much part of *bhakti* song tradition, which was counter cultural to Brahminic or Vedic Hinduism, both in the recitation and in the reception. The *bhakti* (devotion) *rasa* (taste or emotion) transcends gender (Kumar, 2019, p. 43). One can argue that the same people who may be moved to tears hearing a recitation may not be moved by the murder or rape of a Dalit woman. But the affect that young Dalit performer-activists seek to evoke is through emotional persuasion of social messaging, which is earthy and have no other-worldly themes.

The performance of rap, hip-hop, *gaana*, traditional folk song and *koothu* attest to the emotions felt by the singers, irrespective of their audience. For example, the spontaneous singing at work or in the fields, laments or leisure songs, which created an alternate space of freedom of movement, "were not necessarily sung in a group but were often built into a group session as women chose to join in. These spaces were not performance spaces because there was no specific audience for these songs. Even if all the women did not sing, everyone participated by joining in the chorus or keeping rhythm with their swaying bodies" (Singh, R., 2019, p.192). Self-expression using voice, tone, and body movements becomes a medium of connection with the audience. As Leslie Kan ("Spectacle," n.d.) describes, spectacles, such as music performances or even communal parades or festival gatherings, are cathartic for the performers and for the audience.

Dalit folk song, rap, *gaana* and *koothu* expand the psychological space for the marginalized, thus spurring the imagination to create art, as well as expand the topography of the movement of Dalit bodies. Psychologists examining concepts of space and time in the experience of listening to music point out that "our representation of space and time is alterable and malleable. Both entities are a product of conscious and unconscious processing, affected by perceptions, memories, moods and emotions, our interests and current goals, and our physiological condition" (Schafer, Fachner and Smukalla, 2013, para. 1). Rhythm enhances the musician's and the listener's perception of space; space can be altered "during intense experiences with music," such that "attention has turned inward and . . . the representation of the outer world has faded into the background (Schafer, Fachner, and Smukalla, 2013, para. 45). These neurobiological findings about space in music help us understand how Dalit music activists find expressions of rap, *gaana* and *koothu* as positive spatial experiences for the gendered body.

In the case of the spectacle of the stage or YouTube video, Dalit performers, such as The Casteless Collective, create the spectacle of change-making, perfecting the musical art form as well as the social messaging in the lyrics, while paying attention to the technologies of sound. They project a world where gender and caste restrictions can be overcome. This iconoclasm, through the catharsis produced by the emotions of watching and listening, creates the possibility in viewers to imagine themselves as part of change-making. Music performances by young Dalit activists open up the boundaries of activism in the arts, thus broadening political spaces of the marginalized and moving them into the center of feminist activism. They use their talent, imagination, and collaboration to innovate newer forms to appeal to the public. Their didacticism evident in their intersectional feminist messaging is both overt and covert. Their songs are subtle and militant, humorous and hard hitting, witty and argumentative. Their body movements using the beats of *koothu* accompanied by percussion and song are both transgressive and lively. Above all, Dalit performances are fun; the rappers and musicians know how to blend entertainment with their snappy social and feminist messages.

Today, we see young Dalits and non-Dalits in the diaspora perform Dalit musical forms at concerts. For example, musicians have elevated *parai* to its rightful place by teaching it and performing it widely. I saw a *parai* performance in 2019 in New York at the Ward Melville Heritage Organization, where Tamil men and women, as well as children, performed a complete repertoire to much acclaim. Performing once-marginalized art forms is a tongue-in-cheek response to classical *mridangam* and *tabla* players as recognized artists. Similarly, the rap-loving younger generation embraces Dalit performances with gusto, such that Dalit performances move from transgressive acts toward becoming mainstream, which is transformative indeed. In the words of a song by Arivu and Isaivani: "Eppadi, eppadi, eppadi, itha kekalaina eppadi / eppadi eppadi eppadi /itha mathamlaina eppadi" (How, how, how, / how can we not ask this? / How, how, how, / how can we not erase caste?] [translation mine]). For their goal is clear: "nama thambi, thangachi, ellorume sirikanam / nama thambi, thangachi, ellorume padikanam (our brothers and sisters, all need to smile / our brothers and sisters, all need to be educated) [translation mine].

Dalit performers' concerted effort to dismantle systemic oppression is clear in the moving and catchy rhythms of rap, *gaana*, and the myriad theatrical forms. Their message is to sing with courage and live fearlessly. Dalit activism in music and *koothu* in Tamil Nadu reveals feminism's intersectionality as a challenge to hegemonic systems. It casts the spotlight on Dalit feminist imagination as an aesthetics of liberation, with a history and vision for the future of Dalit people. It widens the possibilities of democracy both within literature, theater, and art forms and in the larger society. Tamil and English become modes of richly interwoven, textured communication with the other regions in India and internationally. Society reaps rich dividends from Dalit feminist heterotopias that value creativity and freedom across identity markers.

REFERENCES

Aadhan Tamil. (2019, May 16). *Isaivani Exclusive Interview* [Video]. YouTube. https://www.youtube.com/watch?v=Y2ELzJHebOI

Agier, M. (2011). *Managing the Undesirables: Refugee Camps and Humanitarian Government.* (D. Fernback, Trans). Polity. (Original work published 2008)

Andrews, G. (2021). YouTube Queer Communities as Heterotopias: Space, Identity and "Realness" in Queer South African Vlogs. *Journal of African Studies,* Vol 33. https://www.tandfonline.com/doi/abs/10.1080/13696815.2020.1792275

Arasiyal, Tamil. (2019, Jan 4). *I'm sorry Ayyappa Thaadikaaran Pethi song* [Video]. YouTube. https://www.youtube.com/watch?v=C3IasST65Z4

Arya, S. & Aakash, S.R. (Ed.). (2020). *Dalit Feminist Theory. A Reader*. Routledge.

Babu, V. (2020, Jan 22). E.V. Ramasamy: A controversial legacy and why he continues to shape Tamil Nadu politics. *Hindustan Times.* https://www.hindustantimes.com/india-news/ev-ramasamy-a-controversial-legacy-and-why-he-continues-to-shape-tamil-nadu-politics-analysis/story-NoQ1AGX9TJgEzuhhf1JvkL.html

Baxter, Lawford. (1988, June 15). Rap Music Began on Jamaica in the 1960s. *The New York Times.* https://timesmachine.nytimes.com/timesmachine/1988/06/15/659388.html?pageNumber=30

BBC News Tamil. (2021, March 14). *Gana Isaivani Interview* [Video]. YouTube. https://www.youtube.com/watch?v=ksCVhuY20WM

Behindwoods TV. (2019, Nov 27). *Casteless Collective Arivu Chumma Kizhi* [Video]. YouTube. https://www.youtube.com/watch?v=Y9Pawofy_ys

Chanda-Vaz, U. (2019, Jan 27). How a radical collaboration between a classical and a folk art form is redefining the boundaries and possibilities of performative tradition. *Scroll IN.* https://www.academia.edu/38266545/Karnatik_Kattaikuttu_The_art_of_erasing_boundaries

Deeksha, J. (2018, Oct 29). Viva la Vada Chennai: How youngsters here are using hip-hop, rap and gaana to rewrite music history. *The New Indian Express.* https://www.edexlive.com/people/2018/oct/29/viva-la-vada-chennai-how-youngsters-in-the-region-are-using-hip-hop-and-gaana-to-rewrite-music-hist-4281.html

Foucault, M. (1984, October). Of other spaces: Utopias and heterotopias. (J. Miskowiec), Trans.). *Architecture / Mouvement/ Continuité.* https://web.mit.edu (Original work published 1967, March)

Gajarawala, T. J. (2013). *Untouchable Fictions: Literary Realism and the Crisis of Caste.* Fordham UP

Gidla, S. (2017). *Ants Among Elephants.* Farrar, Strauss, and Giroux.

Gorringe, H. (2016). Out of the cheris: Dalits contesting and creating public space in Tamil Nadu. *Sage.* 19(2), 164-76. DOI: 10.1177/1206331215623216

Ilaiah, K. (2020, October 3). Why The Farmers Need English Education? *Indian English Day Diary.* www.kanchailaiah.com

Ingole, P. (2020). Intersecting Dalit and Cultural Studies: De-brahminizing the Discisplinary Space. *Caste: A Global Journal on Social Exclusion,* 1:2, 91-106.

Iyer, N. & Zare, B. (2009). Ed. *Other tongues: rethinking the language debates in India.* Rodopi.

Kan, L. (n.d.). Spectacle. University of Chicago: Theories of Media. http://csmt.uchicago.edu/glossary2004/spectacle.htm

Krishna, T.M. (2020). *Sebastian & Sons.* [eBook edition]. Context. https://www.amazon.com/Sebastian-Sons-History-Mrdangam-Makers-ebook/dp/B082W2BP75

Kumar, R. (2019). *Dalit Literature and Criticism.* Orient Blackswan.

Lyricsraag. (2021, June 18). *Enjoy Enjaami lyrics* [Video].YouTube https://lyricsraag.com/enjoy-enjaami-dhee-arivu/

Maajja. (2021, March 6). *Enjoy Enjaami* [Video]. YouTube. https://www.youtube.com/watch?v=eYq7WapuDLU

Mohandas, V. (2019, Jan 4). Voice of the Voiceless. *Deccan Chronicle,* www.deccanchronicle.com/lifestyle/viral-and-trending/040119/voice-of-the-voiceless-1.html.

Nathan, A. (2018, Sept., 12). Documentary Koothu puts the Spotlight on a Vibrant Theatre Tradition from Tamil Nadu. *Scroll In*. https://scroll.in/reel/893665/documentary-koothu-puts-the-spotlight-on-a-vibrant-theatre-tradition-from-tamil-nadu.

Padmanabhan, S. & Kanna, A. (2021, July 11). What Arivu's Enjoy Enjaami Tells us about the Cultural Resistance to Caste. *The Wire*. https://thewire.in/caste/what-arivus-enjoy-enjaami-tells-us-about-the-cultural-resistance-to-caste.

Periyar, T. (2020). *Why Were Women Enslaved?* Ebook edition.

Praba, G. (2019, July 26). *Annal Ambedkar Song gana Isaivani* [Video]. Youtube. https://www.youtube.com/watch?v=1QkKOhgcTwM

Pragati, K.B. (2021, Sept., 9). A Woman in a man's world. *The Hindu*. https://www.thehindu.com/entertainment/theatre/a-woman-in-a-mans-world/article36391563.ece

"Queer." Encyclopedia of Sex and Gender: Culture Society History.. Retrieved June 11, 2022 from Encyclopedia.com: https://www.encyclopedia.com/social-sciences/encyclopedias-almanacs-transcripts-and-maps/queer

Schäfer, T., Fachner, J., & Smukalla, M. (2013). Changes in the representation of space and time while listening to music. *Frontiers in psychology, 4*, 508. https://doi.org/10.3389/fpsyg.2013.00508

Singh, A. (2013). An Interview with Mangai. *Asian Theatre Journal, 30* (2), 486–505. https://doi-org.ncc.idm.oclc.org/10.1353/atj.2013.0044

Singh. R. (2019). *Spotted Goddesses: Dalit women's agency-narratives of caste and gender violence*. Zubaan.

Supreme Court Observer. (n.d). *Judgement in Plain English*. https://www.scobserver.in/reports/sabarimala-temple-entry-indian-young-lawyers-association-kerala-judgment-in-plain-english/

Vikatan TV (2015, April 15). *Eppadi, Eppadi*. [Video]. Youtube. https://www.youtube.com/watch?v=Znk6tYHF39c

Tharu, S. (2020). "The Dalit woman question." In A. Sunaina & A.S. Rathore (Eds.), *Dalit feminist theory: A reader* (pp. 182-187). Routledge.

"Therigatha." Tharu, S. & Lalitha, K. (Eds.). (1991). *Women writing in India: 600 BC to the present*. Vol.1. p. 68.

ENDNOTES

1 Pramila Venkateswaran, poet laureate of Suffolk County, Long Island (2013-15) and co-director of Matwaala: South Asian Diaspora Poetry Festival, is the author of *Thirtha* (Yuganta Press, 2002) *Behind Dark Waters* (Plain View Press, 2008), *Draw Me Inmost* (Stockport Flats, 2009), *Trace* (Finishing Line Press, 2011), *Thirteen Days to Let Go* (Aldrich Press, 2015), *Slow Ripening* (Local Gems, 2016), *The Singer of Alleppey* (Shanti Arts, 2018), and *We are Not a Museum* (Finishing Line Press, 2022). She has performed the poetry internationally, including at the Geraldine R. Dodge Poetry Festival and the Festival Internacional De Poesia De Granada. An award-winning poet, she teaches English and Women's Studies at Nassau Community College, New York. Author of numerous essays on poetics as well as creative non-fiction, she is also the 2011 Walt Whitman Birthplace Association Long Island Poet of the Year. She leads writing workshops for breast cancer patients in their healing journey. She is a founding member of Women Included, a transnational feminist association and the current President of NOW Suffolk, Long Island..

CHAPTER 13

Looking at the Nation through a Lover's Eye: N. Padmakumar's Film, A Billion Colour Story

Shreerekha Pillai Subramanian[1]

ABSTRACT

Cinematic response in India to social justice movements, even when aimed at rectifying communal violence and tensions, reifies entrenched orders separating Hindu from Muslim, citizen from the 'Other,' native from the diasporic. To the polyphony of films focused on interfaith love, a recent indie film adds a new 'look'. Narasimhamurthy Padmakumar's, *A Billion Colour Story* (2016) focalizes on a child's point of view in a black and white filmic narration to dismantle old hatreds and re-ignite love of culture and nation for the very diversity that has become pixelated, walled, entombed and reactionary. More like Nollywood in its reliance on a smaller budget, a do-it-yourself *chutzpah* and decolonial vision, the story revolves around a child, Hari Aziz, who becomes the instrumental force behind rendering his parents' dream true of making a film about their beloved nation, its teeming diversity, and its border-crossing love. The director, Padmakumar, addresses a host of current crises faced by those living in the shadow of Late Capital, culturally steeped patriarchies, and right-wing Hindu fundamentalism, while pointing to the billion colours that make up this teeming 'democracy' that might make its most significant issues clear in the binary of black and white. A close reading of this film reveals its decentering and decolonizing of hegemonic notions of nation, gender, class, and religion,-and of the hegemony of the Bollywood Gaze that dictates who will love whom, to what degree, at what costs, and to what end. What Narasimhamurthy Padmakumar provides in the diegesis, alongside the love story of a Muslim man and his Hindu wife, and the 'product' of their love, a child, is a film that encapsulates their 'looking' at the world. However, his looking leaves a lot to be desired on two registers: his looking does not see the active youth-led contestations taking place on the ground against the Hindu-led political hegemony and his looking refuses to call out the culprit, the excesses of violence performed by the nation-state and its Hindutva brigade against its minoritized 'Muslim' and othered subjects.

Introduction

A Billion Colour Story won the eighth Bagri Foundation prize (Rubin, 2017) for independent cinema from India in London. Dedicated by the director to the victims of recent lynchings by the Hindutva-centered national hegemony, the film sets up a modern moral tale against the backdrop of the film capital of Mumbai where the expat inter-religious couple, Imran Aziz (Gaurav Sharma) and his wife, Parvathy (Vasuki) move with their prepubescent son, the innocent young child narrator, Hari Aziz (Dhruva Padmakumar, son of the film's director). The film's diegetic order remains firmly grounded in the gaze of the lover, one who loves intensely, i.e., the couple, their son, and their way of looking at the nation they consider home.

To briefly summarize the film, the basic plotline charts how the child bears witness to the parents' wonder and idealism and speaks about their identities as Indophiles who love all the colours that make up the nation – the sweets, festivals, customs and people that make up the nation. While stumbling to find funding for their initial 'cute' love story, the two give up as they also struggle to find housing as an inter-religious couple finally landing on a small flat in a Muslim enclave where the wife continues to arouse anger from the conservative gatekeepers. As they lose the little bit of funding through their missteps, they move into an even smaller home, sell all their belongings and shelve the earlier film to make one about an inter-religious couple during the 1940s whose love undoes the historical march forward into partition and ultimately imagines India and Pakistan as one people. The character of the progressive elder, Anand Shashtri who endorses the vision of the father, is assassinated for his outspoken peace work in the face of retrograde Hindutva that remains the echo chamber of the film's diegesis. Heartbroken, as the father is called to give his testimony at the police station, the son interrupts his football game to leap onto his father's back, a match cut that shows his leap interrupting\a hidden marksman's gun set to kill the dad, instead finding its aim in the son's body. Even though the screen is black and white, we imagine red, going back to the colors that open the film's narrative identifying love, violence and hatred as red. Just as the dead child's narratorial voice guides us from the beyond, the child had rendered a video asking for funds for his father's project of love in order to render poetry back in his life, and monies had come pouring in. As the film closes on the parents setting to leave the country having given up on their ideals, the son rescues the father's dream by securing funds and faith from beyond the grave.

A couple of decades ago, Vinay Dharwadker published the essays of A. K. Ramanujan posthumously (1999) since one of the great tellers of tales, a translator, folklorist and poet himself, Ramanujan wrote a much studied and cited work on the many versions, tellings, and translations of the epic, *Ramayana.* In the layered translation-related wisdom Ramanujan imparts regarding an epic that is not a single text but a compendium, multiplicity proliferates and lives as separate but related organisms. Resonant with Edouard Glissant's rhizomatic complexity (1989) that is a profound truth of Antillean life and postcolonial transnational truism, Ramanujan's multitextuality is akin to the South Asian banyan, a variant of the ficus that casts down roots and continues to live on, the many trunks of story overlapping, shading over, and growing their own forests in their own times and places. Ramanujan writes, "In this sense, no text is original, yet no telling is a mere retelling-and the story has no closure, although it may be enclosed in a text. In India and in Southeast Asia, no one ever reads the *Rāmāyana* or the *Mahābhārata* for the first time. The stories are there, 'always already'" (p. 158). Diminutive and humble as a man, Ramanujan's untimely death in 1993 was demoralizing to all of us who continue to bask in the long shade he provided, a shade long and dark enough to shake up the Hindu supremacists who outlawed his essay at Delhi University a decade or so ago (Roy, 2011), considering it a threat to their vision of singularity that is pureed into Hindu authority and hegemony in the public sphere. Taking a small hint from Ramanujan's points about an epic text, the story of border-crossing love is 'always already' part and parcel of the fabric of South Asian discursive order that relishes the Laila-Majnoon (Hasson, 2018) and Heer-Ranjha love stories that end in dead lovers and living stories. In times marked by the rise and cementing of Hindu supremacist nationalism in India where such stories are buried alongside the great lovers who remain like ghosts, immortal and hovering just over the horizon like hope, the supremacists recast the mythopoetics and history of cross-cultural mingling and further cement religious divides that mark Muslim and minoritized bodies as other in the nation's body politic.[2]

The dog whistles to mobilize the pious to violent action, continued unrestricted in temples and pilgrimage sites, with a political order that tacitly, and more often, actively supports the anti-Muslim discourse permeating the public sphere.[3] The film, dedicated to the victims of lynching in recent years, grapples with responding to these rising tides of religious fundamentalism, as manifested in the conservative Hindu and Muslim neighborhood committees (to counter Land Jihad) that govern who is included, allowed, tolerated or ejected from the artificial urban communities of apartment complexes and such. However, what has marked Indian national history through its twentieth century anticolonial struggles and nation-building post-1947, as marked by the watershed moment of Gandhi's assassination by a member of the Hindu Right is the birth of Hindu fascism as inspired by its corollaries in Europe (Hameed 2020), is its long hibernation and flourishing in the late twentieth and twenty-first centuries as the reigning ideology and political power. In the wake of each of the major communal riots, a great number of the lives of the minoritized subjects, mainly Muslim, have been lost since Babri (1993) , Godhra (2002), Dadri (2006), Muzaffarnagar (2013), just to name a few recent tragedies that have functioned as pogroms against Muslim communities. The film charts the frustrated clamor for justice by those who have suddenly been disappeared from the nation's fabric, the voices of the dispossessed haunting the film, as in the character Parvathi's question in the film, "Did the Godhra victims get justice?" (25:21). Here the camera pans to the curious son who is telling us the story and piecing together the catalog of injustices that inspire his parents to counter with their fictional works to right the wrongs of the nation they love and call home. Expressed recently by Anjali Arondekar in the conference, "Dismantling Global Hindutva," (Sept. 10-12, 2021), it is a spirit of andolan/resistance that fuels the filmic order that desires to unsettle the violence and loss through a spirited engagement with alternative possibilities for rethinking our past and reimagining our futures in South Asia and its diasporas. As Nandini Sundar concludes in her remarks at the same conference, which she attended and presented despite the prolific amount of death threats received leading up to Sept. 10 and on, she speaks about how Hindutva has hijacked all discourse but still, we need to move forward into the "India of our dreams," the catch-all ambition of this film as well. This conference is evidence of long decades of work by South Asianist scholars, historians such as Romila Thapar, Irfan Habib,

Wendy Doniger, Sheldon Pollock, Jeffrey Kripal, Christopher Jaffrelot who have written about the complex, multi-religious and cultural milieu that construct Indian identity, an effort at combating what I observed in an earlier article, "a colonizing space of Hindu-nationalist hegemony" (Subramanian 2011). More recently, these tensions have boiled over in textbook controversies between diasporic groups who identity as Hindu believers battling for positive images of Indian, i.e., Hinduism in textbooks over the South Asia studies scholars in the US who are seen as colonizing (Redden 2016). On the ground in India, youth-led resistance has been at the forefront fighting against the demagoguery of the right-wing government and its majoritarian policies. In the same period that Padmakumar labors on his film and it is released in 2016, student protests against the oppressive tactics of BJP fomented across dozens of universities.[4]

Death, Dispossession, and the Dream Shot from the Child's Perspective

In resolving past the tired binaries, the film writes its way into transgressive border-crossing love of the kind that mark the history of commercial blockbuster Hindi cinema, from *Mughal-e-Azam* (1960) to *Bombay* (1995), *Jodha Akbar* (2008), *Veer Zaara* (2004), Padmavati (2017) and so many such films that highlight the love stories of couples whose love survives the entrenched hatred and norms rendering such transgressions next to impossible. Nilanjana Paul's analysis (2017) of the film, *Padmavati* addresses the layered registers at work in the censorship and discourse compelled by Hindutva political order, the ruling order since 2014 that has exacerbated the violence faced by vulnerable minority populations such as Muslims, migrants, and other vulnerable individuals identified as dissidents by the ruling party. Anderson observes, "Hindutva since 2014 appears to be more confident, proud, brazen, and belligerent than ever before" so that, he develops in his article, "Hindu nationalism now permeates into new spaces: institutional, territorial, conceptual, ideological."

In thinking against the binaries that condition South Asian cultural mores from male/female, Hindu/Muslim, rich/poor, native/diasporic, adult/child, licit/illicit, mainstream/arthouse, faithful/faithless, patriot/traitor, the director renders this film in black and white which makes the story vivid and dreamy at once, a memory tale rendered intense in the absence of the usual Bollywood technicolor and glitz. Its title addresses the body politic as a billion colours, the very subject of the film, and the inspiration that leads the protagonists to return to their home locale. Similar to 'black and white' that are global film successes like Marjane Satrapi's *Persepolis* (2007) and Alfonso Cuaron's *Roma* (2018), the film attempts to drive the story of colors home through the heightened sensuality and visuality of black and white. As the child narrator of Bapsi Sidhwa's novel, *Cracking India* (1988) brings us the guilt memoir of the author/child witness to the trauma of partition (Subramanian, 2013), this film centers the child's voice to bring home lessons on death, dispossession and the dream of an alternative nation not founded on Hindu supremacy but rather an inclusion, permission, transgression and blurring of differences as depicted, with room for doubt, questioning, and defiance.

Walter Benjamin writes, "Death is the sanction of everything the storyteller can tell. He has borrowed his authority from death. In other words, it is natural history to which his stories refer back" (p. 84). The power of the storyteller derives its authority from death, a direct relationship of looking into one's mortality that is the source and inspiration of the story, what makes the work timeless, unforgettable, and meaningful in its exact details to "warming his shivering life" (p. 88). The film, from the opening reflections on colors, diversity and the flag of the nation meditates on the impossibility of this child's being, prefiguring an ending that gives the story its breath, enlivening its point from the abyss of infinity. The film prefigures the child's death, or a dead child talking because each interaction portends the death of the child born of a union delegitimized by the prevailing order of Hindutva. When Hari Aziz meets his new friend, Sofia in the building they move into, she has a goat on a leash, a pet she names Julie to which her father's rejoinder is that Julie is only a temporary guest since she will be sacrificed as meat offering to Allah during Id celebrations. Sacrifices, as the event of Abraham's 'testing' in the biblical tradition of willingness to give up his son Isaac, Ishmael in the Qur'an, upon the command of the Lord, is key. In the Islamic theological tradition, Baqri-Id is a significant ritual, the day the goat is ritualistically offered to Allah as sign of one's submission to the one and only God.

For the father in this film, Imran Aziz whose religious conviction is displaced by love for a nation, his son is indeed sacrificed to bring his dream to living color. As the plot line shares the forced impoverishment on the parents who have to repeatedly uproot their home and homeschool their son as the school tuitions are beyond their pale, the child narrator wisely quips that there is no room for self-pity with nine civil wars raging across the globe. His is a voice of transnational empathy and cross-border wisdom, a voice that recollects his father's memory of living in a Bombay chawl in 1992 in the wake of Ayodhya-incited communal riots where his neighbors stayed up to guard the lives and safety of six Muslim families against the Hindu mobs. Against the onslaught of sectarian divisions that mark the violence of the everyday (Das, 2006), the child's memory sheds light on an alternate nation where Hindu majority protects, stands guard, and fights against the right-wing Hindutva ideology. In this imaginary, the 'right' conduct of a Hindu prevails over rights of the Hindu majority.

Akin to the street theater that works to help the masses 'see' the perniciousness of Hindutva, Ghosh notes, "Janam has responded to the demand from various mass organizations of the Left for a play to counter Hindutva politics" (p. 77). Deepa Reddy's (2018) post-script on the Charter put forth on Hindu Rights in 2018 urges for a closer reading of the apolitical and anti-political discursive orders built into Hindutva that helps in undoing the political stalemate between the Right and the Left in India. The film's denouement on the son's death followed by the capital pouring in to realize the father's dream can be figured as the transcendence of the nation over the limitations of its people. Religious fervor is replaced with faith in the nation, a corrective against the corrosive nationalist patriotism that deems Hindus as rightful citizens and all others, Muslims, Dalits, Christians, Queer and minoritized bodies as suspect especially after the passing of the Citizenship Amendment Act (Bhat, Ramachandran). Instead, faith in India's secular tradition summarizes the film's polemic, "India's poetry is still alive. A billion people can't be wrong." Unlike the clarity of the 'mob' that carts away Shanta, the central Ayah character who is symbolic of a prelapsarian pre-partition peace in Deepa Mehta's literary adaptation in her film, *Earth*, here the bullet that kills the child is left unmarked as originating from a Hindu Right or Muslim or other state/non-state actor. Beyond the film, or sadly, what it refuses to spell out is that in the current socio-political discursive order in India, it is militant Hindutva that takes down, through direct violence and other means, critics of its establishment (Deb 2019). The film raises sharp questions in the voice over of the sage child, a critical theological presence that resonates with the Upanishadic texts, a child of the ilk of Nachiketas who questions death itself and gains immortality, "Was my death communal?" since Hari Aziz's religion remains ambiguous. However, it is quite significant that in a film that meditates on the child's point of view, the diegetic order disappears the active grassroots work happening all over the nation by youth protesting the retrograde boundaries of class, gender, caste, religion, sexuality, and nationalism in which their lives remain confined.[5]

The medieval mystics of South Asian subcontinent, the Sufis and the Bhakts, were passionate in their quest for the divine. Desirous of a union with the supreme being, they often short-circuited existing forms of piety and hierarchy finding the powerful men of religion to be obstacles en route to God. For them, temples and mosques, rather than distinct emblems of religious establishments, were embodiments of God. Charged often for flouting the laws of religious practice, they sought the love promised within. Their message too radical even today, fifteenth century poet Kabir resonates here on whose death, it was not clear whether the people would bury or cremate him with a scuffle ensuing between his Muslim and Hindu devotees (Hess and Singh, 1983, p. 4). Upon lifting the shroud, they find a heap of flowers that they appropriately divide to complete their separate rituals of burial and cremation. In so doing, they end up missing the point of his teaching wherein he had castigated them for loving ritual over God, division over faith. Arguing over difference, they forget the essence of the divine, as Kabir emphasizes in his many *dohas*, "Hindus say, "Burn my body,"/ Turks say, "Follow my Pir."/ They fight religious wars./ The swan discerns, says Kabir" (p. 72). For Kabir, the amphibious bird belongs to all the worlds – water, land, air, and never claims any one as its own. Although the child's death cannot be marked as one or the other, the diegetic order of the film points to communalism as the pernicious ideology that kills the dream of a united radically inclusive nation. It is a body politic constituted by a billion who can, in fact, agree on the sentiment of loving 'poetry' that comes to stand for love of the other who is minoritized, marginalized, dispossessed and shot dead in mid-life thus despite the ambiguity of his religion, becoming as Walter Benjamin observes regarding the storyteller, "an incarnation of the devout"(p. 92). In dying, the child ascends to become the one who is the fount of wisdom and knowledge, the one who can tell the story with the veracity and authority of the sage, see past difference as Kabir asked, and become the 'one' voice of the nation.

The Costs of Dreaming/Limits of Padmakumar's Vision

The meta-diegetic aspect of the film is that Padmakumar's vision is also about filmmaking. In highlighting the struggles faced by the nascent couple, mainly the father who is the primary driver behind their film, the mother recedes to the background as the nurturer and primary caretaker of the child. The film addresses the great struggle behind the costly and capital-heavy collaboration necessary for filmmaking. For any film makers who are pushing the envelope, from feminist (Citron) to experimental, art house, or anti-realists, the capital investment is the hurdle that sends many a project to the back shelves never to be completed or shared with any audiences, big or small.

From the film's opening, the curious and observant voice of the child narrator apprises us of the struggles faced by his idealistic father who believes in the teeming diversity and splendor of India which he seeks to encapsulate in a 'cute' film that just never seems to find sure footing through producers. The costs of the father's dream downsize the son's life – from a return abroad to an apartment complex in Mumbai, to smaller and smaller dwellings, homeschooling, the curtailing of life's little treats to the impossibility of buying new football kicks and a ball to finally, the cessation of life itself. The challenges of funding their film project leads to whispered conversations to avoid worrying the son, but the keenly observant narrator fills in the gap from looking up what he does not know and coloring in the rest. The lack of funding leads to the change of plans, and to an even larger vision, a film project that re-imagines the origins of the modern nation-state and imagines itself undoing the violence of partition through love.

Upon the death of Anand Shastri, a figure who might remind the audiences of Anand Patwardhan, the filmmaker who has been documenting and resisting the censor boards for decades (MacFarlane), the father finally gives up. Then, as they pack to leave the country, the representative from the bank reaches them just in time, a deus ex machina figure who magically blesses them with serious money raised by the son's evocative video speech on behalf of his father's dream. With a sum of thirteen crores in hand, the child's voice sums up, "India's poetry is still alive. A billion people can't be wrong." The film's logic, in the neat summation that resonates with the archetype of the sacrifice of Isaac, rights the wrongs of right-wing fundamentalisms, religious extremism, petty bourgeoisie differences, traditional mores, and at its core, Hindutva, through the capitalist correction. The father is able to fund his dreams, and since it happens with public support, the film's discursive order suggests that the viral video's popularity has somehow negated or cured the toxic virality of Hindutva. The film's logic signals that the teeming diversity of India can come together and rout the rabid ideologies of Hindutva. Upon the film's conclusion, diversity, in a material sense, translates into capital.

Rather than the hollow symbol of diversity that often remains a functionary of capitalism, it is necessary to remember the present and past work of youth-led resistance. The lifelong focused work of historian, Irfan Habib, speaks of the ways of remembering a figure like Bhagat Singh who is celebrated for his anti-colonialist work, but not as much for trenchant critiques of "caste system, untouchability, and communalism" (xx), so remembering in the current climate of communalism can also be a form of misremembering. The resistance to Hindutva is coterminous in twentieth century with its birth and inception, as Habib's introduction to Bhagat Singh's lesser-studied writings cautions. The contemporary discursive order writes toward a homogeneity, a strain of the unity in a diversity thematic that sublimates difference and marginalizes the multiplicity of voices. Rather than constructing a true radical democracy that includes and makes the nation a safe home for all, as Bhagat Singh dreamt of in the early twentieth century, the film too participates in consensus across difference as made evident in the successful accumulation of capital.[6] The weird circuits of capital work contiguously; the same pockets that subsidize 'cute' videos that sentimentalize a film project can also support videos and faith-work on promoting Hindutva-centered work at home and in the diaspora, promoting ideological work under the western alibi of countering putative anti-India sentiments.[7]. The immense backlash faced by the organizers of the recent conference comes at the heels of decades-long dissent and renders apparent the surfeit of capital that flows in multi-directional ways cementing Hindutva and its project of turning the 'secular' nation into a 'Hindu Rashtra'.

Tanika Sarkar's keen analogy parallels how the spurious science of race difference forms the building blocks of Nazi ideology asserting here that similarly, the spurious hold on history aids the project of Hindutva.[8] Hindutva ideology remains firmly locked in place, and post-film release as the director receives four minutes of standing ovation at the London Indian Film Festival (LIFF) in Britain on November 3 (2016), the suffering of minoritized bodies alongside the ones protesting the violence continues unabated on the ground. Youth-led protests and its suppression took center stage from the start of Bharatiya Janata Party (BJP from here on) ascendancy to power, and it continues to reign supreme into an uncertain future. As Angana Chatterji reminds us in tracing the fracture of the democratic enterprise always already in its inception in 1947, "At the intersections of history, geographicity, and residual conflict, the dominance of Hindus, fraught relations to Othered-subjects, and a multi-party system shaped India's 'conflicted democracy'" (p. 401). The film here, despite its idealistic efforts, falls prey to neoliberal interpellations. In sentencing the child to death in its diegesis, it also effectively silences the possibility of love across religious lines to thrive.

Since the collusion of right-wing Hindu ideologies with the governing party in power in 2014, the oppression of minoritized bodies has been severe. So, has the resistance to it. Yet, Padmakumar's film fails to nod towards the real. Moumita Sen writes, "... since the election of Narendra Modi in 2014, and the coming to power of the BJP (as part of the National Democratic Alliance), the language and politics of blasphemy have featured prominently in national media debates. Lynching of Muslim men in the name of cow vigilantism and cattle protection (Venu 2017), talks of rebuilding the contentious Ram Mandir (Press Trust of India 2017) and the witch-hunting of intellectuals as 'anti-nationals' (Bhattacharjee 2017) have been standing topics in the national media from a year or so after the BJP came into power in 2014. The rights and freedoms of minority groups such as Muslims, oppressed castes, indigenous groups and women have been the most threatened by the ideology of Hindutva, or Hindu nationalism" (p. 149-150). Sen's summary of the rise of Hindutva, especially in the era of BJP governance, a position echoed by scholars across the disciplines (Thapar, Chatterjee, Prashad, Muralidharan, Jaffrelot, Truschke, Valiani, Balagopal) addresses the straight lines connecting capital and religious nationalism to Hindutva, a point that is elided in the neat feel-good conclusion of Padmakumar's project. It is not really about whether a billion people can be right or wrong; in the complex simulacra of neoliberal capitalism in which the media-consuming subjectivities are interpellated. It is possible to drop a dollar supporting the child's video homage for his father while also supporting in literal, figurative, orthodox and orthopraxic terms the ideology of Hindutva that prospers across the layered domains of contemporary geopolitical landscapes that constitute India. Romila Thapar's (2013) lifelong work on Indian antiquity presents a corpus of work that sheds light on historiography, source-checking, and methodology, scholarly practices that have been devalued in a public sphere dominated by Hindutva that has taken it upon itself to fantasize and mythologize a pure Hindu nation. Thapar points out that ironically the debunked colonial history is the very corpus of textual authority Hindutva cites to concoct its alternate past. In trying to play nice and remain palatable to a wide-viewing audience, the film fails to name the specter of Hindutva that is undoing the radical experiment of a nation meant to be an inclusive and safe home for all.

Destabilizing Prevalent Tropes in Dreaming Toward the New

Padmakumar's film utilizes the extreme close-up, a photographer's eye for the detail of objects, landscape, faces in order to bring the story home. In an attempt to destabilize existing tropes around nation, gender, class, religion, region, and even Bollywood, the film revels in the details that make the story of these three lives – the father, Imran, the mother, Parvathi, their son, Hari Aziz and the little community around them, an attempt to counter ideology through individuality. The struggle and its limitation are the premise that imagines an 'individual' way out of the ideological chokehold of Hindutva; the film refuses to name Hindutva as the toxin undoing the edifice of secular democracy as such, laying out the blame evenly on the rise of fundamentalist fervor from all ends, and fails to call out Hindutva as the culprit. Scholars such as Tanika Sarkar point to the pervasiveness of Hindutva in all projects, "a lethal mix of ethnic pride and ethnic hatred" (p. 169), then not naming it for the violence it perpetuates presents a serious gap in the 'feel good' conclusion of Padmakumar's diegetic order. In celebrating the billion colors of its title, translating the teeming diversity of its people into the 'tiranga' of its tri-color flag, the film signals toward a religio-nationalism that is holding its people at siege. During the most recent upsurge of youth protests in India, a young poet Armaan Yadav raps in his poem, "Saffron Ablaze," "My country's up in flames, and the flames look saffron./ Sentiments ablaze in the haze of violence/ No free speech, just days of silence."[9]

Hari Aziz explicates the meaning of colors in the opening montage with the camera zooming in on the bloom of a flower or tears on a face, a sequence that culminates in the long shot of an Indian flag fluttering on a landscape dotted by snowclad mountains, a generic trope that is often employed in the decades-long border skirmishes with Pakistan over Kashmir. Instead of the flag standing as symbol of a bellicose patriotism, the child narrator unpacks the colors anew – saffron for renunciation, white for truth, green for vegetation and the wheel for dharma. His classmates break it down in communal terms – saffron is for Hinduism, green for Islam and white for all other religions. In both interpretations, the nation emerges from either a Sufi/mystical or interfaith nexus. By decentering Hindutva, the children 'get' it wrong much to the chagrin of the irate teachers who expect a verbatim regurgitation of Hindu nationalism vis-à-vis textbook patriotism, but in doing so, the children hint at the deconstruction of Hindutva that needed to be more pronounced in the film all along.

The parents of Hari Aziz, always already transgressive as a Hindu-Muslim couple also broke ground in coming together across the North-South dynamics that continue to haunt the Indian ecosystem.[10] In bringing to light the petty grievances of either side, the child narrator claims an omniscience that rises above old frictions. The film fails to absorb how the neoliberal order in India absorbs and markets Muslim representations, such as clothing, language, culture, as it does with regional cultures all over India within the hegemonic neoimperialism of Bollywood. In its reigning simulacra, Bollywood manages to disappear histories of struggle with the same speed with which 'difference' appears on its screen, the regional variations signified via a tableau of exoticized bodies.

The parents remain outside the gender prescriptions of normative heteropatriarchy; at one point, the father does go out to work a 'regular' job for a television show but at this period, the mother stays home to home school and teach the son for whom they cannot afford school tuition fees. At another point when the father shelves his old film and begins a new project on partition, it is the mother who writes the new film script. The couple embodies an equality founded on mutual respect and collaboration in raising their child and nurturing their family sidelining old hierarchies that raise eyebrows all the same.[11] As the child of an inter-religious couple, the very thing outlawed by the Love Jihad ideologues, Hari's very existence is anathema. Hari shares with his father that his classmates call him '377', referencing the Indian penal code handed down from nineteenth century colonial annals that criminalizes homosexuality, pejoratively calling the boy 'gay' for his sensitivity, thoughtfulness and articulate speech, marking at once his alterity and the ideological right-wing policing that is part and parcel of everyday discourse. Paola Bacchetta, in charting the genealogies and iterations of homophobia in Hindutva, writes, "The self-identified queer

Muslim (or other Other) stands at the intersection of xenophobic queerphobia and queerphobic xenophobia" (p. 378). As a diasporic child returning to the homeland, and a child who stands as 'sign' of his parents' transgressions, Hari Aziz is othered and subject to what Bacchetta names as xenophobic queerphobia.

Padmakumar's directorial vision rejects the formulaic gestures of Bollywood; there are no song and dance numbers, no fantasized famous actors, but rather, the cast is an ensemble of lesser-known theater or arthouse actors, models, and the amateur youngster, the director's son as the central lever of the film's momentum. The film gives off the glow of an afternoon special, a homemade feel-good film that can be consumed but it tarries with the do-it-yourself *chutzpah* and small budget that exudes a decolonial aspiration, an unyoking from the behemoths of Hollywood and Bollywood to generate a kitsch all the more successful due to the unique qualities of its cast of characters and storyline. Where the film falls short is that in presenting a syuzhet packed with mystical wisdom interspersed in the film's chronology, the frenetic workings of Hindutva in the fabula remains unaddressed.

Utopias and Counterrevolutions: Representations and Misrepresentations

As the father figure in the film moves from a 'cute' love story to a love story for the nation, and revives the age-old dream of the anticolonial freedom fighters, some on opposite ends of British India, from the Khudai Khitmatgars (Khan Abdul Ghaffar Khan) of the North West frontiers (Banerjee) to Mohandas Karamchand Gandhi, Maulana Abul Kalam Azad, Zakir Husain, Mohammad Abdur Rahiman, Muhammad Ali Jinnah and other elders of the freedom movement who saw partition as a carving of a body politic that was violent, communal, and colonial. His vision is repeatedly lauded by his friends and well-wishers, and the elderly Indian progressive who sees in his work the eye of a Sufi, Imran Aziz revives the old Indian secular nostalgia for the nation pre-partition.

The seismic events of the moment bear witness to the India that is today a majoritarian state that suppresses dissent, punishes intellectuals, scholars, activists and journalists, and arrests students. The period of unrest marked by the BJP victory in 2014 leads into authoritarian tactics last seen during the Emergency, imposed by Prime Minister Indira Gandhi in 1975-76. Student union leaders, at prestigious institutions like Jawaharlal Nehru University, Jamia Millia Islamia in Delhi, Aligarh Muslim University in Uttar Pradesh and dozens of others rise up against the draconian 'Citizenship Amendment Act' (CAA), 'National Register of Citizens' (NRC), and 'National Population Register' (NPR) policies that target Muslims and other minoritized subjects.[12] Student protests that began coterminously with the reign of the new regime now proliferates as recorded evidence on social platforms. They "negotiate with the seemingly impenetrable state apparatus, heavily guarded by the might of capitalist businesses, the security state, and geopolitics"[13] through poetry, song, parody and comedy. Comedian Munawar Faruqui tells audiences about his childhood in Gujarat referencing the 2002 pogrom against Muslims, "I think I survived because the government is not good (a good pause here) in completing its targets."[14] Poet Varun Grover pens the poem, "Hum Kagaz Nahi Dikhayenge" (We Will Not Show Papers) against the dictum of NRC in which he reclaims the nation as a place of radical love. He recites in his opening stanza, "Tum zehar ki chai ubaaloge,/hum pyar ki shakkar gholke usko/gatt gatt gatt pee jayenge/hum kagaz nahi dikhayenge" ("You will boil poison tea/ We will stir in the sugar of love/We will glug it down/ We will not show papers" - translation mine).[15] In the great tradition of dissidence, the poet protester refuses to cooperate with unjust state edicts, and yet, stands ready to suffer the consequences. Here we are, in fact, looking at the nation through a lover's eye.

The film absents the activisms and visionary groundwork on border-crossing peace projects (Waikar) that exist across the urban, rural and South Asian subcontinent. Anjali Arondekar's close reading of the megacity of Bombay through a colorful cast of characters helps "unmoor us from settled understandings of how identifications and representations of difference and belonging operate within a city like Bombay" (p. 234). The work of on-the-ground activists is part of the knowledge production that should push into and be refracted as part of the film's syuzhet. Padmakumar's characters, and the father's zeal for such a love story for undoing the violence of partition ties into decades-long literary, artistic and filmic imaginaries and contemporary ongoing activist labors that need to somehow be catalogued. What Imran Aziz begins in this film is evident as already having begun and what he births is work that is already in progress all over the South Asian subcontinent. From the minimalist stories of brutal cruelty of the partition recorded by Saadat Hasan Manto in *Mottled Dawn,* to Amrita Pritam's poem that was recited by all in the decade after independence, "I call upon Varis Shah Today,"[16] writers such as Qurratulain Hyder, Khushwant Singh, Bapsi Sidhwa, Bhisham Sahni, Salman Rushdie, film makers such as Ritwik Ghatak and scholars such as Urvashi Butalia have kept alive a critical imaginary of the genocidal violence of 1947-48. In the most recent reincarnation of earlier activisms, the beloved poet Faiz Ahmad Faiz's poem resisting the dictatorship of Zia-ul-Haq in Pakistan, "Hum Dekhenge" (1981) resurfaced as the song of the times for the youth protesting against the oppression of religio-nationalist government of Modi. Faiz's verses speak of bearing witness and winning against injustice, which the students render into their march song that takes off on campuses all over India, "Inevitably we shall witness/ the day that has been promised/ that has been etched on the pages of eternity/we shall witness/ when mountains of tyranny/shall be blown away like cotton."[17]

The surface mien of the film is activist; the director wishes to transform hearts and minds through a narrative that arises out of a literary and cultural milieu of sentimentality. Rather than being reduced to tropes of maudlin afternoon soaps, the film could have claimed legitimacy since its imaginary arises out of a South Asian subcontinental interfaith milieu that prizes the performance, theatre and artistry of a sentimental ethos as well-represented in its literary and theatrical arts spanning several millennia. The moral caution here directly urges spectators to stop the faith-based bickering and boundary-making, allow individuals to choose partners across lines of faith and belief, and if they fail to do so, society bears the cost of losses of the worst kind. The key thematic of the film, a son's sacrifice that serendipitously becomes the conduit to realizing the father's dream, resonates with the founding episode in the life of Abraham which the Tanakh calls "The Sacrifice of Isaac" (Genesis 22:1-19). The Qur'an references it in several surahs, as orders that arrive to Ibrahim in a dream that he shares with his son, Ishmael. Argued eloquently with a close reading of the Islamic account as one that is not in concert with patriarchy and asserts the autonomy of the son to respond and devise his own response to God's command, Asma Barlas speaks of the liberatory promise of Islam that gives us a story of dream interpretations and individual autonomy rath er than obedience and faith. Barlas writes,

> "If it is true, as Derrida (1995: 41) says, that death is 'the one thing in the world that no one else can either give or take: therein reside freedom and responsibility,' then it is only by assuming his own death that the son can make his sacrifice a morally purposive and self-determining act rather than one of treachery or betrayal on his father's part. This is partly why I believe the Qur'an gives him a voice in his sacrifice; else, it could have made him like Isaac in the Bible, unaware of his fate" (2011).

Hari Aziz arrives to us through an Islamic imaginary as the voice which brings us the story and the witness to his own death.

The film is replete with nostalgia for a nation that never existed: nostalgia of the father for an India where entire communities stood together to save their Muslim neighbors during communal riots, or a secular India that made room for all faiths. Right alongside the nostalgia for the loss of a Nehruvian secular ideal is also the greater nostalgia that has funded the rise of Hindutva, the nostalgia for a lost and glorious past of oneness where the entire nation was putatively one rashtra, a pure Hindu nation of endless unity and advaita, a nostalgia for a fictional *pitrubhoomi* (fatherland). Perhaps the film ultimately signifies that in narratives where a son sacrifices for the father's cause, loss is the ultimate arbiter of reality. In line with the ideologies of Hindutva that simultaneously valorize and disappear women as quiet corollaries to the patriarch, the film refuses to unsettle hegemonic notions of the heteropatriarchal socio-religious family and nation. The film coexists rather than dislodges the Hinducentric mythogeography replete with maps, sites, and markers for belonging, legitimacy, and authority.

The toxicity of nostalgia, as measured in the rise of Hindutva as an ideology grounded in an illusion of an antiquity founded on a monolithic religious identity that never existed, can be repurposed by grounding it in historical, materialist, scholarly labors on the ground. The question looms large: can a child's direct message lift a collective out of extreme appropriations mired in ideologies of religious majoritarianism? The film seeks to redress the wrongs of Babri, Godhri, Dadri and more, but it remains uneven, hanging in abeyance as the narrative moves forward with resolution toward the clarity offered by a viral video that is shared and funded by millions. After the film's release, the degradation visited upon the dispossessed and marginalized continue unabated as executive decisions such as CAA, detention centers, and state-sponsored killings of journalists and other outspoken intellectuals continue. The film's key female characters are locked in place as inspirational foil for the male figures - the young Sophia who immediately proceeds to fall in love with the boy, Hari as the wife; Parvathi performs the part of loyal companion to Imran Aziz, the father. Neither step out of character or trouble gender roles, existing as inspirations but not actors, in their own rights. Even as female voice rises in decibel, the feminist point of view remains muted.

The film, idealistic in its overture and dedication to changing minds, remains short of making room for the possibilities emerging from youth politics of grassroots work. Since 2014, the resistance against the oppressive policies of BJP government has been emblematized by youth across struggles waged across the subcontinent – disenfranchised migrants in the Northeast, military crackdown and internet crackdown in Kashmir, journalists, intellectuals, farmers from Punjab, to mention some of the many movements that boiled over in early 2020. The student movement,[18] often referred to as 'Tukde Tukde' (pieces) symbolizes the spectral rising of masses against the ubiquitous omnipresent fist of the state. In a recent parody of Arijit Singh's Bollywood song, "Pachtaoge," a young protester sings, "*Tum students se jo takraoge/bada pachtaoge/Laathiyon se haunsla tum todd na sake/tear gas se iraada modd na sake/kalam se laathi tum jab laddwaoge/bada pachtaoge, bada pachtaoge*" (When you confront students/you will regret, you will regret it a lot/ you were not able to break our spirit with your sticks/ you could not deter us with tear gas/ when you set out to make us fight your sticks with our pens/ you will regret it)."[19] The film refuses to name the zeitgeist of the moment into which it writes itself. In its desire to right historical wrongs, the film fails to call out the ideology of Hindutva that has accorded itself the place of moral and vigilante police of vulnerable lives. The film speaks of extremisms, pointing to fault everywhere, rather than calling out the ideology that is working in tandem with the political system to oust dissent and resistance in India today. Tethered on a capitalist individualist vision of reform, Padmakumar's film is not revolutionary. The film falls victim to the tired binary that imagines a false unity in a distant past that could have saved us all. Meanwhile, the dead keep dying and the living keep failing at moving forward into light.

In conclusion, in the idealistic longings and foreclosures presented by Padmakumar's cinema, the film seeks a revolution it fails to imagine. The director, in hoping to influence his spectators away from dogmatic position that wall Hindus from Muslims and create further divisions in a nation that he hopes retains the radical inclusion imagined at inception, augurs the centuries-long spirit of Sufism. Those were the poets and intellectuals who refused to abide by the religious doctrines of their times and radically loved producing a transgressive and syncretic corpus of poetry that stands the test of time and bears witness against the rising fundamentalisms of Hindutva and orthodox strains of Islam. I quote from one of the great poets of that tradition, Maulana whose verses follow. As a Haji and devout Muslim who also was a complex being, a Sufi who praised the vision of Bal Gangadhar Tilak and Aurobindo Ghosh, he repeatedly traveled to Mathura to celebrate Janamashtami, and wrote poems in Bhasha in the Bhakti vein celebrating God Krishna. His mysticism that emerges from Islam but is at home in Hindu piety points the way to a syncretism that is lost to our times. Prof. C. M. Naim's translations remind us of this lost discursive space generated by the great Maulana Hasrat, 1878-1951.

> áñkhoñ meñ nür-i-jalva-i-be-kaif-o kam hai khās/ jab se nazarpe unki nigāh-karam hai khās/ kuch ham ko bhi'ató hoki ai hazrat-i-kirishn/ iqlim-i-'ishq dp ke zer-i-qadam hai khās/ Hasrat kl bhi qubül ho mathurā men hāzirī/ sunte haiñ ashiqoñ pe tumhā rā karam hai khās

> When he cast at me a special, benevolent glance, / My eye lit up with a boundless, unending vision. / Revered Krishna, bestow something on me too, / For under your feet lies the entire realm of love. / May you accept Hasrat's attendance at Mathura - / I hear you are especially kind to all lovers (p. 39).

In conjuring the great Maulana here and his syncretic poems written in the school of Surdas, Tulsidas and Kabir, and the many great Sufis like Shah Latif, Bulleh Shah, Lallan Faqir in whose genealogy he arrives, my article connects the earlier syncretic Sufi order to the film's discursivity, the lover looking upon the nation as a beloved. The Sufi and bhakti tradition of medieval South Asian mysticism involved iconoclasts who preached questioning prevailing ideas of piety, brought about spaces of religious syncretism, and spoke often of reaching the divine from within the self. As the Sufi looks upon God, the film looks at the nation through a lover's eye. Like the mystic, this eye is at once adoring, irreverent and defiant of existing practices. Padmakumar's film centers a syncretic 'looking', an oppositional gaze of the curious and questioning child, a product of transgressive love. In pushing against the prevailing hegemonies of existing patriarchies, religious ideologies and film industrial complexes such as Bollywood and Hollywood, the gaze here reconstitutes that of the besotted devotee at Krishna's feet, a deity who figures large in tales of love, and who makes room for licit and/or illicit love. But in making room for loving intensely, fearlessly, and transgressively, the film fails to nod at the histories of contemporary resistance, popular uprisings and youth-led 'looking' to point at the revolutions in making. The struggle of Imran Aziz is not a solo performance, but rather a concert, a litany and a cacophony. In refusing to point out the crimes of Hindutva and the multiplicity rising against it, the film fails to legitimize the 'looking' that rights the gaze of rightwing ideologies and at all costs, raises the fundamental right to love, pray, and live that the merging of a billion colors can begin to promise.

REFERENCES

Anderson, Edward & Arkotong Longkumer. (2018). 'Neo-Hindutva': evolving forms, spaces, and expressions of Hindu nationalism, Contemporary South Asia, 26:4, 371-377, DOI: 10.1080/09584935.2018.1548576.

Arondekar, A. (2021, September 10-12). *Gender and Sexual Politics of Hindutva* [Conference Presentation]. Dismantling Global Hindutva: Multidisciplinary Perspectives Conference, United States. https://dismantling-hindutva.com/.

Arondekar, A. (2021). "Difference" in Lisa Bjorkman's *Bombay Brokers*. Durham: Duke University Press, 233-252.

Bacchetta, Paola. (2019). "Queer Presence in/and Hindu Nationalism" in Chatterji, Angana P., Hansen, T. B. & Jaffrelot, C. Eds. *Majoritarian State: How Hindu Nationalism is Changing India*. New York: Oxford University Press, 375-396.

Balagopal, K. (2002). Reflections on "Gujarat Pradesh" of "Hindu Rashtra." *Economic and Political Weekly*, *37*(22), 2117–2119. http://www.jstor.org/stable/4412183.

Banerjee, Mukulika. (2000). "Partition and the North West Frontier: Memories of Some Khudai Khitmatgars" in Suvir Kaul's *The Partition of Memory: The Afterlife of the Division of India*. Bloomington: Indiana University Press.

Barlas, Asma. (2011). *Abraham's Sacrifice in the Qur'an: Beyond the Body* [Conference presentation]. Religion and the Body Conference, Finland.

Benjamin, W., Zohn, H., & Arendt, H. (2019). *Illuminations : essays and reflections* (First Mariner Books edition.). Mariner Books, Houghton Mifflin Harcourt.

Bhat, M. Mohsin Alam, (2019). The Constitutional Case Against the Citizenship Amendment Bill (January 19, 2019). Economic and Political Weekly Vol. lIV No. 3 , Available at SSRN: https://ssrn.com/abstract=3367310.

Chatterji, A. P. (2019). "Remaking the Hindu/Nation: Terror and Impunity in Uttar Pradesh" in Chatterji, Angana P., Hansen, T. B. & Jaffrelot, C. Eds. *Majoritarian State: How Hindu Nationalism is Changing India*. New York: Oxford University Press, 397-418.

Citron, M. (2012). Women's Film Production: Going Mainstream. In Mary Celeste Kearney, (Ed.). *The Gender and Media Reader* (pp. 170-181). New York: Routledge.

Das, V. (2006). *Life and Words: Violence and the Descent into the Ordinary* (1st ed.). University of California Press. https://doi.org/10.1525/j.ctt1pprtk

Deb, Siddhartha. (2021). "They are Manufacturing Foreigners." New York Times Weekend Magazine. Sept. 19, 2021. Page 51.

Deb, S. (2019). Killing Press Freedom in India. In Tina Burrett and Jeffrey Kingston (Eds.). *Press Freedom in Contemporary Asia* (Ch. 18). New York: Routledge.

Faiz, Faiz Ahmad. (2019). "Hum Dekhenge: Faiz's Iconic Song Defines the Anti-CAA Protests." The Quint. Dec. 27, 2019. Video, 1:55. https://www.youtube.com/watch?v=bIWbO-6I7r4.

Faruqui, Munawar. (2020). "Nawab, Nehru, and Gujarat 2002." Ed. Anand Vijaykar. Mar. 21, 2020. Video, 10:43. https://www.youtube.com/watch?v=sfMCHRzaO0g.

Ghosh, A. (2010). Performing Change/Changing Performance: An Exploration of the Life of a Street Play by the Jana Natya Manch. *Asian Theatre Journal*, *27*(1), 76–99. http://www.jstor.org/stable/40982906.

Glissant, E. (1989). *Caribbean Discourse: Selected Essays*. Trans. J. Michael Dash. Charlottesville: University Press of Virginia.

Gowri, S. (2018). "Sunandha Raghunathan's "Bad Hindu" is Caught Between Two Worlds." The Theatre Times. Dec. 11.

Graff, V., & Galonnier, J. (2012). Hindu-Muslim Communal Riots in India II (1986-2011). *Online Encyclopedia of Mass Violence, Paris, Sciences Po, CERI.*

Grover, Varun. (2019). "Hum Kagaz Nahi Dikhayenge." Opia Films, Mumbai Protests. Dec. 28, 2019. Video, 3:36. https://www.youtube.com/watch?v=zbCuBp1cjkk.

Habib, S. Irfan. (2018). *Inquilab: Bhagat Singh on Religion & Revolution*. Delhi: Sage.

Hameed, U. (2020). Footprints of Fascism in India: Implications for Local Muslims. *Policy Perspectives, 17*(2), 27–46. https://doi.org/10.13169/polipers.17.2.0027

Hammond, J. (2021). 'Conference fuels growing US debate over Hindu Nationalism'. Religion News Service. https://www.washingtonpost.com/religion/conference-fuels-growing-us-debate-over-hindu-nationalism/2021/09/08/dc3d3a6a-10ed-11ec-baca-86b144fc8a2d_story.html.

Hasson, Michal. (2018). Crazy in Love: The Story of Laila and Majnun in Early Modern South Asia. Doctoral dissertation, Harvard University, Graduate School of Arts & Sciences.

Hess, Linda and Shukdev Singh. (1983). *The Bījak of Kabir*. Delhi: Motilal Banarsidas.

Human Rights Watch. 2019. "India: Government Policies, Actions Target Minorities," Feb. 19, 2019. Accessed Feb. 1, 2022. https://www.hrw.org/news/2021/02/19/india-government-policies-actions-target-minorities.

Jaffrelot, C. (2012). Gujarat 2002: What Justice for the Victims? The Supreme Court, the SIT, the Police and the State Judiciary. *Economic and Political Weekly, 47*(8), 77–89. http://www.jstor.org/stable/41419907.

Kamal, Neel. (Dec. 17, 2020). "BJP Real 'Tukde Tukde Gang', Says Sukhbir Singh Badal." *The Times of India*.

Kaul, Suvir, Ed. (2000). *The Partition of Memory: The Afterlife of the Division of India*. Bloomington: Indiana University Press.

Kumar, Nikhil. (Feb. 25, 2016). "The Arrest of a Student Leader Spotlights India's Battle for Free Speech." *Time*, https://time.com/4237319/the-arrest-of-a-student-leader-spotlights-indias-battle-for-free-speech/.

MacFarlane, Steve. (April 21, 2021). https://hyperallergic.com/639235/anand-patwardhan-interview/.

Mashal, Mujib, Suhasini Raj & Hari Kumar. (Feb. 8, 2022). As Officials Look Away, Hate Speech in India Nears Dangerous Levels. *The New York Times*, https://www.nytimes.com/2022/02/08/world/asia/india-hate-speech-muslims.html.

Mehta, D. (Director). (1998). *Earth* [Film]. Cracking the Earth Films Inc., Jhamu Sughand Productions.

Muralidharan, S. (1994). Patriotism without People: Milestones in the Evolution of the Hindu Nationalist Ideology. *Social Scientist*, 22(5/6), 3–38. https://doi.org/10.2307/3517900.

Naim, C. M. (2013). The Maulana Who Loved Krishna. *Economic and Political Weekly, 48*(17), 37–44. http://www.jstor.org/stable/23527186.

Narasimhamurthy, P. (Director). (2016). *A Billion Colour Story* [Film]. The Satish Kaushik Entertainment.

Prashad, V. (2001). *The Karma of Brown Folk*. Minneapolis: University of Minnesota Press.

Pritam, Amrita. (1948). "Ajj Aakhaan Waris Shah Nu." https://panjpedia.org/en/wiki/english-ajj-aakhan-waris-shah-nu.

Ramachandran, S. (2020). Hindutva Violence in India: Trends and Implications. *Counter Terrorist Trends and Analyses, 12*(4), 15–20. https://www.jstor.org/stable/26918077.

Ramanujan, A. K. (2004). Three Hundred Ramayanas: Five Examples and Three Thoughts on Translation. In Vinay Dharwadker (Ed.). *The Collected Essays of A. K. Ramanujan.* Oxford: Oxford University Press.

Redden, E. (2016). The Religious War Against American Scholars of India. *Inside Higher Ed*, https://www.insidehighered.com/news/2016/ 04/12/scholars-who-study-hinduism-and-india-face-hostile-climate#.Yf8oR-5ay1N0.link

Reddy, Deepa. (2018). What is Neo- about Neo- About Neo-Hindutva?. Contemporary South Asia, 26 (4): 483-490. doi:10.1080/09584935.2018.1548009.

Roy, Kumkum. (2011). Beyond Ramanujan and the Ramayana. *Economic & Political Weekly*, Nov. 12. Retrieved from https://bi-gale-com.libproxy.uhcl.edu/global/article/GALE%7CA272560961?u=txshracd2589.

Rubin, R. (2017). 'A Billion Colour Story' Wins Top Prize at London Indian Film Festival'. In *Variety*, https://variety.com/2017/film/news/a-billion-colour-story-wins-top-prize-london-indian-film-festival-1202484465/.

Sahil, Poojan. (2020). "Tum Students se Jo Takraoge." Parody of Arijit Singh's song, "Pachtaoge." Jan. 2, 2020. Video, 4:39. https://www.youtube.com/watch?v=5ze2UBSDJfM.

Sarkar, Tanika. (2019). "How the Sangh Parivar Writes and Teaches History." In Chatterji, Angana P., Hansen, T. B. & Jaffrelot, C. Eds. *Majoritarian State: How Hindu Nationalism is Changing India*. New York: Oxford University Press, 151-173.

Sen, M. (2019). 'Durga did not kill Mahishasur': Hindus, Adivasis and Hindutva. In P. Rollier, K. Frøystad, & A. E. Ruud (Eds.), *Outrage: The Rise of Religious Offence in Contemporary South Asia* (pp. 149–177). UCL Press. https://doi.org/10.2307/j.ctvh1dx8q.13.

Sidhwa, B. (1991). *Cracking India*: A Novel. Minneapolis, MN: Milkweed Editions.

Subramanian, Shreerekha Pillai. 2011. "Malayalee Diaspora in the Age of Satellite Television". *M/C Journal* 14 (2). https://doi.org/10.5204/mcj.351.

Subramanian, Shreerekha (2013). *Women Writing Violence: The Novel and Radical Feminist Imaginaries.* Delhi, India: Sage.

Sundar, N. (2021, September 10-12). *Contours of the Nation* [Conference Presentation]. Dismantling Global Hindutva: Multidisciplinary Perspectives Conference, United States. https://dismantlinghindutva.com/.

Thapar, Romila. (2013). *The Past Before Us: Historical Traditions of Early North India.* Boston: Harvard University Press.

Thomas, P. (2015). Contested Religion, Media, and Culture in India: Explorations, Old and New. *Economic and Political Weekly, 50*(18), 32–39. http://www.jstor.org/stable/24481909.

Truschke, A. (2020). Hindutva's Dangerous Rewriting of History. South Asia Multidisciplinary Academic Journal, 24/25. https://doi.org/10.4000/samaj.6636.

Upadhyay, S. P., & Robinson, R. (2012). Revisiting Communalism and Fundamentalism in India. *Economic and Political Weekly, 47*(36), 35–57. http://www.jstor.org/stable/41720111.

Valiani, A. A. (2010). Physical Training, Ethical Discipline, and Creative Violence: Zones of Self-Mastery in the Hindu Nationalist Movement. *Cultural Anthropology, 25*(1), 73–99. http://www.jstor.org/stable/25619814.

Waikar, P. (2018). Reading Islamophobia in Hindutva: An Analysis of Narendra Modi's Political Discourse. *Islamophobia Studies Journal, 4*(2), 161–180.

Yaadav, Arman. (2019). "Saffron Ablaze." Prod. Shaayak. Dec. 30., 2019. Music video, 2:59. https://www.youtube.com/watch?v=T-tWVHHBZOY.

ENDNOTES

1 Shreerekha Pillai Subramanian is Professor of Humanities at University of Houston-Clear Lake. She was the first recipient of the Marilyn Mieszkuc Professorship in Women's Studies established at her university and published the monograph, *Women Writing Violence: The Novel and Radical Feminist Imaginaries* (Sage India 2013). She works on feminist and postcolonial novels, film, and media from South Asian, African and diasporic traditions. At present, she is publishing an edited volume on carcerality through the Dissident Feminisms Series at University of Illinois Press (*forthcoming* 2023).

2 Hindutva, the right-wing Hindu ideology permeating and framing the current political order, disseminates its own toxic untruths in vocabulary that is circulated through social media and other easy forms of online dissemination. "... Love Jihad" and "Land Jihad," the manifesto stated, using the Hindu Right's catchphrases for the supposed menace posed by Muslim men marrying Hindu women and by Muslims occupying land – acts intended, according to the Hindu Right, to engineer a demographic shift" (For more, read Deb, 2021.

3 Mujib Mashal's (2022) latest reportage from Haridwar shares the call to "kill two million of them (Muslims)" from the Hindu holy city of Haridwar by one of the Gurus of a current strain of Hindutva, Yati Narasinghanand.

4 Reports on the anti-dissent policies of the BJP government led by Prime Minister Narendra Modi includes the arrest of student union leaders at JNU, Kanhaiya Kumar and Umar Khalid, after they led student protests on the third anniversary of the hanging on Muhammad Afzal Guru. Accused of anti-nationalism and sedition, a crime left in place by the British colonial machinery, set in place to arrest the nationalists of the day, it is ironic that the same laws are now used to target youth and critics of the government under work considered anti-nationalist. For more, read Nikhil Kumar 2016.

5 Youth fighting against violence faced by Dalit groups formed the Birsa Ambedkar Phule Students' Association in 2014. Young women fighting conservate gender policing formed the Pinjra Tod (Break the Cage) movement in 2015. JNU student union leaders and youth across dozens of universities and colleges in India were targeted for protesting in solidarity with minoritized subjects such as Muslim, Dalit, and other vulnerable people. Kausalya Shankar, a young woman who witnessed her own husband being hacked to death as punishment for having married above his caste by his wife's family in an honor killing on Mar. 12, 2016, survives and continues to fight anti-caste violence and discrimination.

6 Suvir Kaul's theoretical interventions are of use in unpacking the point here. Kaul writes, "... in the subcontinent, national identities are not affirmed by erasing non-national affinities, but often by invoking them. The domestic politics that results allows less and less space for the articulation of minority voices or of divergent cultural and social practices: authoritarian and military priorities become acceptable political currency, in times of war and in times of peace" (p. 8).

7 Anti-India sentiments become code words for Hinduphobia, a sublimation that Audrey Truschke warns us to be aware of, and thus, the work of this article along with others is urgently required. In her article on "Hindutva's Dangerous Rewriting of History," she writes, "As Hindutva ideology exerts increasing influence within both popular and academic spheres, it becomes more pressing for academics to describe, document, and analyze harmful Hindutva approaches to remolding Indian history and distinguish these political uses of the past from academic approaches to history."

8 Sarkar p. 152.

9 Armaan Yadav, "Saffron Ablaze," poetry of protest from the Delhi streets, YouTube, Dec. 30, 2019, https://www.youtube.com/watch?v =T-tWVHHBZOY.

10 The mother's family, from the South, worry about the tension they see in their grandson, signs of a child who is lost and at sea betwixt the faiths, with the 'paati', his maternal grandma, changing the child out of his green kurta because it is too Muslim in order to appease her own anxieties of where the child will belong, and which faith will claim him. The father's Muslim family, North Indian, speak about Hari's complexion as too dark, signifying he is looking 'southern' and not authentic enough as part of their lights-skinned lineage.

11 The father's manhood is questioned by men in power who deem him 'unmanly' for being unable to look after his family or afford his son's schooling. His mother is questioned around her gender performance when she walks out in cutoff shorts and a sleeveless blouse by Salimbhai who has assigned himself the role of modesty police for women in the building.

12 "The BJP's embrace of the Hindu majority at the expense of minorities has seeped into government institutions, undermining equal protection of the law without discrimination," said Meenakshi Ganguly, South Asia director at Human Rights Watch. "The government has not only failed to protect Muslims and other minorities from attacks but is providing political patronage and cover for bigotry."

13 Borrowing from the CFP for this special joint issue focused on youth activisms.

14 For more, view Munawar Faruqui comedy.

15 For more, view Varun Grover's poetry performance.

16 For more, read Amrita Pritam, poem, https://panjpedia.org/en/wiki/english-ajj-aakhan-waris-shah-nu.

17 For more, view "Protest Song" inspired by Faiz, sung by students first at IIT Kanpur, Dec. 17, 2019, https://www.youtube.com/watch?v=bIWbO-6I7r4

18 For more, read Neel Kamal's report in *The Times of India*.

19 For more, view Poojan Sahil, Jan. 2, 2020, "Pachtaoge" (translation mine), https://www.youtube.com/watch?v=5ze2UBSDJfM.

CHAPTER 14

Double Bind of Muslim Women's Activism in Pakistan: Case of Malala Yousafzai and Sharmeen Obaid-Chinoy

Naila Sahar[1]

ABSTRACT

A majority of Western[2] feminist studies has dealt with women from the third world as a homogenous entity of poor and passive victims without agency, who need saving and thus need to be spoken for. Chandra Talpade Mohanty and Gayatri Chakravorty Spivak have both underscored the urgency of seeing and dealing with third world feminism in terms of a genre that is different in socio-cultural background from Western dynamics, and they emphasize the importance of being wary of the ways in which Western feminism creates the 'discursive homogenization and systematization of the oppression of women in the Third World' (Mohanty, 1991). In this paper, I am going to investigate Pakistani Muslim women activism and the ways in which these women emerge from being a benign presence in a masculinist culture to occupying spaces of resistance, challenging patriarchal notions and stereotypical images of women, and thus becoming a guiding force for other women. I argue that even when Muslim women activists struggle in their respective domains to bring the voices of women into light, they are kept imprisoned in the double bind where they are judged by patriarchy at home and are perceived as victims who need saving in the western hegemonic discourses. Malala Yousafzai and Sharmeen Obaid Chinnoy are globally celebrated yet are extremely controversial in their home country. Both are accused by their fellow Pakistanis of being complicit with the Western agenda of maligning Pakistan and defaming their country. This reaction points to the double bind (Spivak) that this paper aims at highlighting, namely the ways in which women's resistance to patriarchy at home is then taken up by Western media and public as a justification for imperialist surveillance and stereotypical images of these women as victims and objects to be 'saved'.

Introduction

Narratives relating to the representation of Muslim women are marked by discourses of oppression and subjugation that indicate that Muslim women are victims that need saving from radical Islam/ Muslim men. While one cannot deny that such postulations about Muslim societies are partly true, most assumptions about Islam as oppressive religion are propaganda based as well. Patriarchy and misogyny in Muslim countries do run deep, but many of these discursive practices regarding gender discrimination pertain to power dynamics and are the consequence of cultural perceptions rather than religious injunction[3]. This paper investigates instances of two Pakistani women activists, Malala Yousafzai and Sharmeen Obaid-Chinoy, and will attempt to unravel ways in which these women emerge from being a benign presence in a masculinist culture to occupying spaces of resistance, challenging patriarchal notions and stereotypical images of women, and thus becoming a guiding force for other women. I also argue that even when these Pakistani women activists struggle in their respective domains to bring the voices of women into light, they are kept imprisoned in the double bind (Spivak 2011) where they are judged by patriarchy at home and are perceived as victims who need saving in the western hegemonic discourses. Seen through this lens, these two women are caught in a war of discourses which imprisons them in a double bind where their burden of decision-making remains indispensably tied with 'burden of responsibility'[4] for the whole nation's honor and shame. Contesting these power structures that tie these women with 'burden of responsibility', this paper outlines struggles of Yousafzai and Obaid-Chinoy that help them emerge as empowered. As PM Ryder (2015) puts it, both these women rely on Western media to circulate their message as they persistently disrupt its dominant messages (176). This paper outlines the way these both women use the hegemonic power of western media to disrupt orthodox religious discourses regarding women's empowerment and offer alternative readings of the Quran that are progressive on women's issues.

Women activists are varied and diverse in both their experience and in terms of numerous other markers of their identity such as ethnicity, geographical location, immigration status, and marital status. Pakistani women activists are doubly trapped in the limiting sexist discourse of gender exclusivity and religious patriarchy and yet existing in different locales make their experiences of resistance distinct and diverse. Applying Gayatri Spivak's theory of the double bind to the condition of these women, I contend that these women are constantly imprisoned in the double bind where 'the burden of decision making is also the burden of responsibility' (Spivak 104-105) for them, which includes the responsibility of keeping intact the honor of their family, society, nation, and the whole Muslim community. The double bind becomes that existential crisis for Muslim women where despite all efforts of liberation the Muslim woman constantly finds herself struggling with the expectations and stereotypes of what it is to be a Muslim woman. This double bind imprisons them simultaneously in the Eurocentric discourse for being 'oppressed Muslim women', and in patriarchal and religious discourses at 'home,' mostly for being brash and unashamed libertines and not being Muslim 'enough'. This paper looks at the ways in which Yousafzai and Obaid-Chinoy have endeavored to reoccupy the hegemonic discourse, utilizing the liminal spaces and interstices open to them by virtue of existing in unique milieus in which to construct their identity.

Malala Yousafzai and Sharmeen Obaid-Chinoy are both famous worldwide for their activism and for securing prestigious awards and accolades. Where Yousafzai is the youngest Nobel prize winner, Obeid-Chinoy secured Academy awards twice for her two documentaries, *Saving Face* (2012) and *A Girl in the River: The Price of Forgiveness* (2015). Yousafzai became globally famous when she was shot in Swat, which is in northern Pakistan, after she continued her efforts to keep going to school and advocating the need for girls' education while the Taliban were against it. After getting shot in the head, she was taken to the UK for her treatment, and she has continued living there after recently having graduated from Oxford University.

While Yousafzai was born and bred in a humble household, Obeid-Chinoy grew up in more privileged circumstances in Karachi, which allowed her to attend some of the best elite educational institutions both there and abroad, including Stanford University in the United States. Where Yousafzai has been constantly struggling for girls' education on a global level, Obeid-Chinoy's award-winning documentaries talk about violence against women in Pakistan as a result of cultural and structural inequalities that are inbred in Pakistani society. Her first documentary that won the Academy award was *Saving Face,* which talks about the under-reporting of violent acid attacks against women. Her second award-winning documentary was *A Girl in the River: The Price of Forgiveness,* which broaches the subject of honor killings in Pakistan. It is about the case of nineteen-year-old girl who survived an attempted honor killing by her father and uncle, and who has solid reasons not to forgive the perpetrators in the court room, yet she has to succumb to the public and societal pressures to forgive them, so the attackers are set free to return home without any repercussions for their crimes.

As has been observed in many accounts[5] with the fall of the twin towers in September 2001, it became a challenge for Muslims around the globe to rethink their identity in relation to a world that was antagonistic to their religious affiliations. The events of 9/11 brought an unmatched amount of attention to Islam and Muslims and there was an unprecedented increase in the hatred directed toward them. In this scenario, no one suffered as much as women from Muslim countries, who were already living with the stigma and stereotype of being a veiled, docile, home bound victim. Women in countries like Iran, Afghanistan, and Pakistan, are challenging and questioning the religious influences within their culture as the determinants of their identity and in the post 9/11 era, they are further frozen in the Eurocentric and hegemonic discourse as subjugated, repressed, and tyrannized by restrictive religious laws and Muslim patriarchy and in need of being 'saved'. Such a discourse about them is further problematic because it is based mainly on the notion of difference from a mainstream Western logic and usually ignores what these women have to say about themselves. The dilemma faced by Pakistani women is that they are either silenced by the Muslim patriarchy and restrictive laws/policies concerning women's rights in the locales they inhabit or when they dare break the silence and speak, the mainstream western media tries to distort and manipulate this discourse for their own ends. Thus, whether at home or abroad, these women have to contend with double standards that leave them with no other choice but to adapt and develop ways of expressing themselves from within a system that persists in objectifying them in every way.

Feminist debates and Women activism in Pakistan

Before dwelling on the politics and ideology of two women activists chosen for discussion here, I want to investigate why these women need to be studied in a way that is different from other Western female activists, and what the potential differences are between Islamic feminist activism and Western feminist social movements. First, the Pakistani women activists who are actively pursuing change in their home countries have lived in a distinctive position that is significantly different from situations in which women in the rest of the world, especially Western women, live. For a long time, mainstream Western feminism has avoided engaging with the difficult conditions and situations in which religious women strive to thrive and survive. Religion is seen as patriarchal and oppressive for women, and though there has been much written about women, religion, and resistance, there has been much less attention given to women, religion, and autonomy. It is important to learn how women from Muslim countries, especially those who identify as religious and do not see the dynamics of religion in relation to resistance to religion but instead feel part of the religious structure] in terms of female authority, fight for their rights. The basic difference between Muslim women's activism and Western feminist movements lies in secularizing the feminist narratives in the West that constitutes Muslim women's struggle as a site of exclusion from mainstream feminist deliberation.

Many Western feminist studies has dealt with women from the third world as a homogenous entity of poor and passive victims without agency, who need saving and thus need to be spoken for. Chandra Talpade Mohanty and Gayatri Chakravorty Spivak have both underscored the urgency of seeing and dealing with third world feminism in terms of a genre that is different in socio-cultural background from Western dynamics, and they emphasize the importance of being wary of the ways in which Western feminism creates the 'discursive homogenization and systematization of the oppression of women in the Third World' (Mohanty, 1991). Mohanty writes in *Under Western Eyes: Feminist Scholarship and Colonial Discourses*: 'I argue that assumptions of privilege and ethnocentric universality, on the one hand, and inadequate self-consciousness about the effect of Western scholarship on the "third world" in the context of a world system dominated by the West, on the other, characterize a sizable extent of Western feminist work on women in the third world' (55). Western feminist narratives' disregard for or attempt to 'recover' or 'interpret' the perspectives of third world and Islamic feminism also constitutes a commodification and fetishizing of all signifiers signifying Islam as a religion. In 'Three Women's Texts and a Critique of Imperialism' Spivak writes about the commodification and 'worlding' of the Third World in Western imperialist critiques of the Third world, wherein the Third world emerges 'as a signifier that allows us to forget that "worlding", even as it expands the empire of the literary discipline' (269). The third world thus emerges as a distant culture, exploited but with 'rich intact literary heritages' waiting to be explored. The same trope is often applied to Muslim women and their narratives. Where Muslim women activists have been trying to repudiate and renounce traditional and stereotypical images of women of Islam at home and around the world as weapons against their patriarchal oppression, similar images have been recreated and taken up by Western scholarship as a justification to intervene in a space that is supposedly unclaimed and need saving.

It is against this background that I will analyze Yousafzai and Obaid-Chinoy's unique position. While in Western Eurocentric narratives both these women are seen as victims who exposed depravities of patriarchal atrocities in Muslim countries, in their own country they are seen as wicked women who repudiate and renounce traditional Pakistani image of women around the world. As a result, these women are trapped in a double bind where not only are they mis-seen or un-seen by western media, but also, they are subjected to oppression and coercion by the patriarchy at home. I argue that because of such challenges at home, Yousafzai and Obaid-Chinoy's activism consists of challenging dominant religious, nationalist, and patriarchal ideologies and contesting local power structures. I will build on this argument further below.

Activism and cultural baggage

Where Yousafzai and Obaid-Chinoy have some hard-core fans in Pakistan, a majority has been accusing them of supporting the hegemonic discourses about Muslim women's victimhood that encourage the stereotypical perception of Pakistan being a regressive country. They are accused of having perpetuated Orientalist discourses about the systematic oppression of women in the Third World.

In Pakistan, Malala has become a one-word trigger for vitriolic anger and malicious suspicion. Pakistanis are split in groups where one group that supports her has the tendency to dismiss criticism of her as an example of cultural backwardness, patriarchal misogyny, religious imbecility, and tribal barbarism that is prevalent especially in Northwestern Pakistan, the other group consists of vocal critics of Malala and many of them are from her hometown. This group also consists of people who Malala symbolically championed; fathers who bore the wrath of the Taliban by allowing their daughters to attend schools, mothers who nursed injured girls beaten by the Taliban and grandparents who buried granddaughters that were blown apart on their way to school. Why is it then that they are vociferous critics of Malala? In his article *Malala: Why so many in Pakistan hate what she symbolizes* Saeed Afridi writes that after talking to such people, one realizes that their criticism may be directed at her but is seldom about her. For them Malala is not a single entity, but rather an unfortunate phenomenon and a naïve pawn in a sinister conspiracy of the West against Muslim countries and their ideology.

Gendered activism and nationalism in Pakistan have been marked by religious discourses and cultural baggage. As a result, Pakistani women end up existing in a double bind where their burden of decision-making remains indispensably tied with burden of responsibility for the whole nation's honor and shame (Spivak 2012). In Pakistan, there is general resentment against Western Eurocentric scholarship that has dealt with women from the third world as a homogenous entity of poor and passive victims without agency, who need saving and thus need to be spoken for. In post 9/11 scenario, when Muslim women are reduced to distorted caricatures of voiceless *hijabis/ niqabis* and are depicted in media as a resource in the politics of fear to encourage distrust, western narrative about Malala seemed another conspiracy theory against Pakistan. It was largely believed that attack on Malala was manipulated by her father for social mobility and was exploited by the West to support their stance about redeeming the Muslim women from religiously radicalized and oppressed Third World. Malala's father is famous for his anti-military sentiments and politically liberal ideas, and soon after Malala was shot, the Pakistani media saw the injured daughter as a pawn of her father to foster his personal ambitions.

Malala's plight fitted well with the narrative promoted by the United States and its ideological allies within Pakistan, and those who opposed promotion of liberal values saw propagation of Malala's narrative in the West as yet another US conspiracy to Westernize Pakistan. 'They cherry picked the names of Brand-Malala's advocates to highlight those with anti-Pakistan, anti-Muslim and xenophobic histories to demonstrate the validity of their suspicions' (Afridi 2018). Many in Pakistan felt that Malala's PR team was further reducing her as a puppet to the Western world by heightening public interest and media frenzy surrounding Malala and propagating brand Malala that implied carefully curated image of hers as a symbol of West's benevolence towards women who are oppressed by despotic Muslim countries. A spokesman from Edelman, which is an American public relations and marketing consultancy firm, said 'a team of five publicists were dedicated to managing the massive media and public interest in Malala's campaign. They have already issued of a two-month waiting list for an interview with her.' [6]

We can look for reasons of such dichotomous perceptions in history of Pakistani macho-nationalist ideals which regard home and the domestic sphere for women as the best guardian of the traditional values, culture, and identity. In Pakistan, women and modernity have come to be regarded as antithetical entities, with the result that the goal of national emancipation involve a betrayal of all prospect of progressive change for women (Young 2001)[7]. According to Young (2003), 'This has also meant that while women struggle with the legacies of colonialism in the postcolonial era, they are repeatedly accused of importing western ideas' (97). Moreover, development of religious nationalism in postcolonial Pakistan has actually placed women in a state comparable to that in which they found themselves during colonialism, thus putting them in a situation where while women struggle with the legacies of colonialism in the postcolonial era, they are repeatedly accused of importing western ideas. Question of women, their rights, their position and status in public and private spaces has always been an issue of concern in the state-building and Islamization of Muslim countries. Women in Pakistan have therefore become markers of political goals and sign of cultural identity during the processes of political revolutions. Where women's empowerment is becoming a focus of more significant debate, their liberation in Pakistan is seen as inimical to the nation's cultural identity. In the introduction to the book 'Gender and National Identity',

Valentine M Moghadam writes that nationalism, revolution and Islamization are gendered processes. To unravel the dynamics that intertwine the project of state-building with the question of women, Moghadam suggests we unpack the relationship between nationalism and images of women and examine the role that the 'Woman Question' (Moghadam 35) play in the discourses and programs of revolutionaries. According to her, there is a link between the consolidation of power by new states and laws about women and the question of women is integral to projects of Islamization.

Talking in the South Asian and specifically in Pakistani context, women have always been regarded as the caretaker of the domestic sphere (Samarasinghe 2000). Her primary responsibility is viewed as nurturing of children and taking care of the household chores while the men have always confined themselves to the area of dominance. Seen through this lens, Yousafzai and Obaid-Chinoy have negotiated their way through the culturally dominant ideas of femininity, and this has earned them adversaries as well.

Human rights discourses, Islamization and narrative consumerism

A general perception in Pakistan is that the Western media pounced on Malala's memoir and Sharmeen's documentaries for the emotional appeal of such narratives, and then fashioned these stories to their ultimate advantage to legitimize Western savior complex. In *Manufacturing Consent: The Political Economy of the Mass Media*, Noam Chomsky proposes that the mass communication media of the U.S. 'are effective and powerful ideological institutions that carry out a system-supportive propaganda function, by reliance on market forces, internalized assumptions, ... and without overt coercion' (96). The trope of uneducated Muslim men is thus evoked through the media as a set of othered bodies, frozen and Orientalized in the discourses that support the myth of the 'white man's burden'.[8] Such dichotomized narratives of liberation and victimhood are then inextricably tied with dynamics of social and political economies of power and privilege or the lack thereof, and this is why the Western media's propagation of Malala's narrative and the Academy award given to Sharmeen for exposing the ills of Pakistani society are perceived by many Pakistanis as reinforcement of Western notions regarding the need for Third World emancipation, and the re-inscription of neocolonial power relations.

The reproduction and perception of the figure of the Third World woman, who leads "an essentially truncated life based on her feminine gender (read sexually constrained) and being 'Third World' (read: ignorant, poor, uneducated, tradition-bound, domestic, family oriented, victimized, etc.)" (Mohanty 1991, 56), in the narratives of Malala and Sharmeen, has put both women at the crossroads of topographies of power relations where their identity construction is being controlled either by the Western media or by patriarchy at home. They are perceived as not Muslim enough for being blatant, not women enough for being more daring than is acceptable in Pakistani culture, and they are not liberated enough for they are from the Third World.

Malala was the center of attention throughout the world after she was shot, and now she is seen as a global symbol of resistance and a proponent of girls' education. But this is not the case in her own country. In Pakistan, she is seen as someone who aided the political agenda of the West by putting Pakistan in the limelight again for being a dangerous country that is plagued by terrorists. However, one needs to question the extent to which this perception is intensified by the Western media and not by Malala herself. Just as postcolonial critics, such as Edward Said, have seen problems and limitations in Western representations of Islam and the East, feminist scholars perceive problems in condescending and patronizing representations of women from Third World countries as objects of victimization. The construction of silent, voiceless, victimized Muslim women has its roots in a time when British colonizers and missionaries were called to 'save' Muslim women from cultural and religious practices of purdah (veil) and polygamy. In *Orientalism*, Edward Said writes: "Orientalism is premised upon exteriority, that is, on the fact that the Orientalist, poet or scholar, makes the Orient speak, describes the Orient, renders its mysteries plain for and to the West" (21). The Orient thus represented is not real because, not being able to represent itself for the lack of subject position, the Orient is thus politically and linguistically represented by the West.

Applying Said's analysis in the context of Malala, the use of the hashtag '#IamMalala' that was initiated by Gordon Brown and then eventually used by the whole West, is a version of Malala's case being taken over by the 'savior'. In 'Hash tagging girlhood: #IAmMalala, #BringBackOurGirls and gendering representations of global politics' (2016), Helen Berents writes about the ways in which social media activism, condensed into hashtags and tweets, reproduces problematic and limited concepts of girlhood in the Global South that serve to reinforce ideas about girlhood in the Global North. Through the implications of modern science and technology that empower some individuals more than others depending on the dynamics of the locales they inhabit; the internet thus situates hegemony in itself by accentuating the dichotomy between the notions of the developed North and underdeveloped South. Brenets writes that as Twitter users in the Global North repeat the hashtags, they reproduce problematic relations of power 'that are intimately bound up within simplistic conceptions of girlhood. Although generous readings would say the use of the hashtag and related activism in both cases engages in solidarity and "awareness raising," there is an element of co-option within the campaigns through the use of the claims that "I Am Malala"' (514). Seen from this perspective, it feels like subject construction of Muslim women from Pakistan is a result of Eurocentric savior complex and perpetuation of victimhood narratives about Muslim communities' inability to thrive independently. The cartoonist representations of Malala in the *New York Times* for instance, that render her walking while some disheveled, long bearded Taliban are trying to stop her[9] can be seen as a part of a Western agenda that seeks to reduce the 'other' as regressive. Such representations become problematic since they portray a homogenous mass of Muslim bearded men in stark contrast to Malala, signifying a rift between those who cherish the ideals of civilization/ progress, and those who lack them and are signified by a particular dress code. Shelina Khoja- Moolji (2017) writes: 'The reproduction of the Muslim world/ Orient as antagonistic to the rights of women and embroiled in premodern sensibilities is made possible through an invocation of the binary of vulnerable Muslim women and threatening Muslim men' (384).

Eurocentric discourses around brown Muslim bodies are discriminatory as their empowerment is viewed as individualized action against local cultures. According to Moolji, the research she conducted in Pakistan's villages indicates that there is a heightened sense of complementarity and interdependency in people that is employed to achieve individual as well as collective well-being. 'When living that is experienced in such complex ways is reduced to a list of rights, or to legal and state-defined definitions of what constitutes freedom, which close off other emancipatory projects, it can be read as a form of violence' (378). So, the universal language that surrounds the discourse of human rights is inadequate to explore the dynamics of lives that people are living in different parts of world, and therefore Moolji calls for 'reconstructing the human rights discourse such that it acknowledges multiple and diverse conceptualizations of what it means to be human (378). Referring to Wendy Brown's (2004) arguments on humanitarian intervention, suggesting that the state's intervention in crisis events is probably more about a 'particular form of political power carrying a particular image of justice', Moolji insists that we 'interrogate the self-articulation of human rights as an anti-political project' (380) and ask questions about the political functioning and processes of politicization of a certain event.

Fawzia Afzal-Khan also conveys the same kind of doubt concerning Eurocentric conceptualizations of narratives from third world countries, as she explains in her paper *The politics of pity and the individual heroine syndrome: Mukhtaran Mai and Malala Yousafzai of Pakistan,* when she says that, 'The reformist drama continues to be enacted on world stages... which allows audiences to both pity and then admire the objects of their pity, as long as the latter can be (re)constructed in the image of the 'ideal' citizens for our neoliberal times' (168). She questions western liberal feminism's complicity in solidifying and endorsing false universalisms and cultural essentialisms of dominant human rights debates. Feminists from the Global South have been challenging the homogenous applicability of international human rights discourses and politicization of 'women's empowerment' narratives and are asking to remain attentive to the local social contexts which reveal the tension between the universal and the particular in human rights debates. Being mindful of Elizabeth Philipose's (2008) assertion, 'It is not a question of working within the parameters of the existing systems, but of revolutionizing those systems through our advocacy and activism and creating analytics that refuse to be complicit in recolonizing the world' (114).

In her article, *The making of Humans and their Others in and through Transnational Human Rights Advocacy* (2017), Shenila Khoja-Moolji advocates decolonizing and pulverizing human rights discourse by pointing to alternative notions that are prevalent in Pakistan regarding what it means to lead a meaningful life. McDowell and Sharp argue that "gender relations are both affected and reflected in the spatial structure of societies" (1997:4). Language of international human rights discourses cannot be applied to Malala's narrative because there are contradictory views prevalent in Pakistan about her and her case needs to be resituated and contextualized within Pakistani socio-cultural and religious framework.

Muslim male preachers have been using the Islamic discourses of 'modesty' to limit women's domain to the private spaces of home. Modesty is then clearly a gendered notion, and female modesty is a tool for the Pakistani Muslim patriarchy to control women. Debates over the Islamization of public space started in Pakistan when Zia-ul-Haq, the military dictator who ruled Pakistan for eleven years till his death, made alliances with *Jamaa't-e-Islami,* a religious Right Islamist political party, and started radically Islamizing Pakistan in the 1980s by introducing the concept of '*chador aur chaardevari*' (veil and home) regarding women.[10] Moral regulation exclusive to women became a seminal part of the law in Pakistan after Zia meddled with law making and introduced policies to strengthen his illegitimate rule in Pakistan by seeking the favor of Islamists. In *The Great Arch*, Philip Corrigan and Derek Sayer write that: 'Moral regulation is coextensive with state formation, and state forms are always animated and legitimated by a particular moral ethos' (4). As in all Muslim countries, ideas and projects of moral regulation and modesty have been interpellated in Pakistan to regard women as repositories of culture and Islamic tradition. By considering women objects that belong to '*chador and chaardevari*', women are thus rendered a property of state and patriarchy that need to be morally regulated by keeping them in boundaries and restrictions and thus making them a part of the system and processes of hegemony.

Such dynamics of hegemony in Pakistan disclose the tension between gender politics and moral regulation, which shape the subjectivities of women through the discourses of Islam and nationalism. Malala and Sharmeen are very much aware of the positioning of the feminine as the property of patriarchy and have been resisting and responding to such discourses in different ways. To underscore the legitimacy of her visibility and contest her perception as a headstrong girl, Malala has constantly brought her father's presence alongside her to public knowledge. Malala writes that her father tells her to stop relying on mullah for Qur'anic interpretations and has encouraged her to critically think: "We don't have any option. We are dependent on these mullahs to learn the Quran," he said. "But you just use him to learn the literal meanings of the words; don't follow his explanations and interpretations. Only learn what God says. His words are divine messages, which you are free and independent to interpret" (70); thus, Malala grew up knowing that patriarchal interpretations of Quran have exploited the ignorance of the common masses.

Sharmeen, like Malala, doesn't blame religion but the wrong interpretations and cultural pressures that reinforce a pattern of moral and normative regulation of women. According to her, 'Islam had given power to women, which could be gauged from the fact that a girl was asked three times during the nikah whether she wanted to get married to that man with whom her nikah was being solemnized' (2016). Regarding the allegations of defaming Pakistan, Sharmeen has always retorted that she is showing the true face of society and her documentaries are an attempt at holding up a mirror to Pakistani men. 'If you don't like your reflection in the mirror, don't shoot the messenger. Grow up. Confront your issues. Bring about change' (2017), she reasons in her interview. Sharmeen has been accused of selling Pakistani women's miseries to a foreign audience to augment her personal wealth and fame, and it is said that the topics she chose for her documentaries were driven by sexy appeal for west, commercial oriented agendas, instead of paying attention to urgent human rights crises in Pakistan[11]. Going through the articles written about Sharmeen by Pakistani journalists, one realizes that for mainstream Pakistanis, her Oscar award does not hold much importance. For them, her upscale upbringing and elite background almost nullify the subjects she addressed in her documentaries, since for most Pakistanis her elitist links with powerful lobbies in the US media just strengthened her image as someone who exploits sufferings the of poor. The blog post about Sharmeen titled, *Sharmeen Obaid-Chinoy and her Oscar do not mean much for Pakistan* has listed several suppositions about Sharmeen, and positions her as a part of powerful mafia in the Pakistani and international media while criticizing her use of English language in her documentaries as a ploy to malign Pakistan's reputation in the world. According to the writer, if Sharmeen's aim was to create awareness and bring reform within Pakistan, she would have chosen to make her documentaries in Urdu, or any other regional language of Pakistan so to expand the outreach of her constructive message to her fellow citizens. 'Compare Sharmeen Chinoy's made for English speaking audience movie to Iranian Oscar-award winner movie (A Separation) which was made in Farsi (Persian) and was made available to Iranian domestic viewers.'[12] The article also criticizes her as an elitist show off, stating that when she was asked in an interview about the dress she would wear at Oscars, she named all the top designers for her jewelry and clothing, which would be affordable only to the richest of rich in Pakistan. Because of her personal indulgences, Sharmeen is regarded as an invalid spokesperson for those women to whom she has tried to give a voice in her documentaries who mostly come from very poor families.

Conclusion

Resisting or not, women are always seen through the prism of power relations that judges their agency as subliminal. The position and situation of these two Pakistani women activists is complicated, since their speaking and breaking silence is seen as fraught with contradictions and complications. The set of challenges these women activists face and their responses to these difficulties vary, so binding them together in a single definition that delineates them within religious/liberal, progressive/radical, fundamentalism/ feminism, or victim/abuser binary is a partial and fragmentary strategy. Yousafzai and Chinoy have endeavored to reoccupy the hegemonic discourse, utilizing the liminal spaces and interstices open to them by virtue of existing in unique milieus in which to construct their identity. However, they are constantly challenged by the double bind that imprisons them simultaneously in the Eurocentric discourse for being 'oppressed Muslim women', and in patriarchal and religious discourses at 'home,' mostly for being brash and unashamed libertines and not being Muslim 'enough'. In "The Double Bind Starts to Kick In" (2012), Spivak talks of the 'double bind' as a productive space only when people are willing to remain awkwardly within it as opposed to exiting quickly. Seen through this framework, the experience of double bind for Yousafzai and Chinoy contains the possibility of taking agency and assuming the burden of responsibility by creating a space where they can dare to defy the pressures to confirm to the stereotypes and venture to challenge the double binds. Both these women reject the discourses of Islamic exceptionalism and are not only drawing upon but also reshaping women's rights discourses in accordance with their lived experiences and distinct visions for the future.

The debate around religion and feminism is usually framed in terms of women's agency, autonomy, and power to make choices, which become a signifier of women emancipation. In her book *Do Muslim Women Need Saving?*, Lila Abu-Lughod asks readers to take time to listen to Muslim women instead of assuming through the noise of familiar stories. According to her, the familiar stories of Muslim women's oppression have been made convincing through their association with the 'purity' of the language of universal rights. Malala and Sharmeen's redemption out of the double bind of identity, in which they are caught as a result of being positioned in dualistic ideologies of Islam and secular politics, is possible only if their critique comes from well-informed sources that are contextualized within broader and more complex frameworks that address a constant increasing pressure on women regarding safeguarding their nation's honor due to social, cultural, and political anxieties (Toor 2014, 140). Also, such a critique needs to consider the diverse nature of the challenges that are fueled by economic and cultural globalization and require women activists to adapt varying strategies of resistance from different histories and cultures, ideas and philosophies surrounding the concepts of emancipation, freedom, and liberation.

REFRERENCE

"Sharmeen Obaid-Chinoy and Her Oscar Do Not Mean Much for Pakistan." *Pakistan Blogzine*, 2 Mar. 2012, pakistanblogzine.wordpress.com/2012/02/27/sharmeen-obaid-chinoy-and-her-oscar-do-not-mean-much-for-pakistan/

Abu-Lughod, Lila. *Do Muslim Women Need Saving?* Harvard University Press, Cambridge, MA, 2013.

Afridi, Saeed. "Malala: Why so Many in Pakistan Hate What She Symbolizes?" *Global Village Space*, 30 Mar. 2018, www.globalvillagespace.com/malala-why-so-many-in-pakistan-hate-what-she-symbolises/

Afzal-Khan, Fawzia. "The Politics of Pity and the Individual Heroine Syndrome: Mukhtaran Mai and Malala Yousafzai of Pakistan." *Performing Islam*, vol. 4, no. 2, 2015, pp. 151-171.

Berents, Helen. "Hashtagging girlhood: # IAmMalala#, BringBackOurGirls and gendering representations of global politics." *International Feminist Journal of Politics* 18.4 (2016): 513-527.

Brown, Wendy. "" The Most We Can Hope For...": Human Rights and the Politics of Fatalism." *The South Atlantic Quarterly* 103.2 (2004): 451-463.

Chinoy, Sharmeen Obaid, and Daniel Junge. "Saving Face." (2012).

Corrigan, Philip R. D., and Derek Sayer. *The Great Arch: English State Formation as Cultural Revolution.* Basil Blackwell, Oxford [Oxfordshire]; New York, NY; 1985.

Herman, Edward S., and Noam Chomsky. *Manufacturing Consent: The Political Economy of the Mass Media / Edward S. Herman and Noam Chomsky.*, 2008.

Khoja-Moolji, Shenila S. "The Making of Humans and their Others in and through Transnational Human Rights Advocacy: Exploring the Cases of Mukhtar Mai and Malala Yousafzai." *Signs,* vol. 42, no. 2, 2017, pp. 377-402.

Khaleeli, Homa. "Sharmeen Obaid-Chinoy: 'I Know There Will Be an Attempt to Silence Me'." *The Guardian,* Guardian News and Media, 27 June 2017, www.theguardian.com/artanddesign/2017/jun/27/sharmeen-obaid-chinoy-home-1947-installation-manchester-international-festival-pakistan

Lockett, Dee. "Meryl Streep, Ava DuVernay, and Sharmeen Obaid-Chinoy School Jon Stewart About the 'Radical Act' of Being a Woman in Hollywood." *Vulture,* 23 Apr. 2015, www.vulture.com/2015/04/streep-duvernay-talk-activism-with-jon-stewart.html.

Mack, Phyllis. "Religion, Feminism, and the Problem of Agency: Reflections on Eighteenth-Century Quakerism." *Signs,* vol. 29, no. 1, 2003, pp. 149-177.

Ryder, Phyllis Mentzell. "Beyond critique: Global activism and the case of malala yousafzai." *Literacy in Composition Studies* 3.1 (2015): 175-187.

Said, Edward. *"Introduction," from Orientalism.* ARC, Amsterdam University Press, 2018.

Sadaf, Shazia. "I am Malala: Human rights and the politics of production, marketing and reception of the post-9/11 memoir." *Interventions* 19.6 (2017): 855-871.

Salman, Peerzada. "Oscar Double Winner Sharmeen Obaid-Chinoy Rejects Criticism of Documentary." *DAWN.COM,* 6 Mar. 2016, https://www.dawn.com/news/1243768.

Toor, Saadia , "The Political Economy of Moral Regulation in Pakistan". *Routledge Handbook of Gender in South Asia* ed. Leela Fernandes. Abingdon, Routledge, 18 Feb 2014

Yousafzai, Malala. *I am Malala: The girl who stood up for education and was shot by the Taliban.* Little Brown, 2013.

ENDNOTES

1 Naila Sahar is AAUW International Postdoctoral Fellow at Department of Global Gender and Sexuality Studies, University at Buffalo where she is researching the social and religious activism of Muslim women migrants and refugees in the Middle East and South Asia. She did her PhD as a Fulbright scholar in the department of English, University at Buffalo. The topic of her PhD dissertation is *Reimagining Muslim women: Gendered Religious Life and Resistance in the age of Islamophobia.* Her research interests include feminist studies, gender studies, gendered religious nationalism, South Asian studies and postcolonial studies. Her work has appeared in edited volumes with Routledge, South Asian Review, Journal of Commonwealth and Postcolonial Studies and South Asian Voices.

2 Acknowledging the diversity of feminist theoretical and geographical backgrounds in the West, this paper uses the term 'western' as a shorthand for the unabashedly exclusionary "white, middle class, liberal/neo-liberal feminism" that reinforces existing structures of power by only seeking to "add women and stir" into those structures thus rendering them as absent or missing in action as agents in the history of feminist struggle.

3 Read: Shaheed, Farida. "Contested identities: Gendered politics, gendered religion in Pakistan." *Third World Quarterly* 31.6 (2010): 851-867. According to Shaheed, in Pakistani context, a vigorous cultural agenda prescribing everyday norms is a hallmark of all politico-religious projects, in which gender-normative regulations are most visible as dress codes, women's seclusion and restricted activities (851).

4 Spivak 2012, p104-05.

5 Read: *Kumar, Deepa. Islamophobia and the Politics of Empire: Twenty years after 9/11. Verso Books, 2021,* and *Zine, Jasmin. Under Siege: Islamophobia and the 9/11 generation. McGill-Queen's Press-MQUP, 2022.*

6 https://www.vuelio.com/uk/blog/brand-malala/

7 According to Robert Young, this was spectacularly dramatized in India and Africa on the occasions when the colonial government attempted to outlaw practices such as child marriage, widow- burning, and female genital mutilation. The preservation of these practices became celebrated causes for nationalist resistance (2003, p. 97).

8 In February 1899, British novelist and poet Rudyard Kipling wrote a poem entitled "The White Man's Burden: The United States and The Philippine Islands." In this poem, Kipling urged the U.S. to take up the "burden" of empire, as had Britain and other European nations.

9 http://www.nytimes.com/2012/10/13/opinion/heng-cartoon-malala-yousafzai-shot-by-taliban.html

10 The Islamic laws of Zia also included laws for women. Zia put forward the theory of "Chadfear Aur Chaar Devari" and this was to be applied to women. Thus, for the first time, a woman could be flogged for adultery. If a rape was reported, four witnesses were to be provided otherwise, legally, the rape could be termed adultery. Another law, The Law of Evidence, under the Shariah laws proposed that the testimony of a woman was not equal to that of a man. In legal matters, two women would have to stand witness against the testimony of one man. The status of women was thus arbitrarily cut in half by Zia. http://storyofpakistan.com/islamization-under-general-zia-ul-haq

11 https://pakistanblogzine.wordpress.com/2012/02/27/sharmeen-obaid-chinoy-and-her-oscar-do-not-mean-much-for-pakistan/

12 https://pakistanblogzine.wordpress.com/2012/02/27/sharmeen-obaid-chinoy-and-her-oscar-do-not-mean-much-for-pakistan/

CHAPTER 15

Feminists as Cultural 'Assassinators' of Pakistan

Afiya Shehrbano Zia[1]

ABSTRACT

Pakistan's annual Aurat March (Women's March) signifies a milestone in the culture of feminist protest, but a tense impasse follows a series of encounters between sexual and religious politics, and this has serious implications for rights-based activism in the Islamic Republic.

Introduction

The Aurat March movement in Pakistan has been inspired by the global #MeToo movements and is the spontaneous graduation of online call-outs against sexual harassment to full scale street-level protests. Since its debut in several cities across the country in 2018, it has become a cultural signifier for its supporters and critics alike (Saigol and Chaudhry 2020, A.S. Zia 2020a). The provocative slogans and performative activism of these events have attracted misogynist and conservative backlash that have escalated with each successive year. Four years on, the tail-winds of pent up misogynies have now unleashed their full fury on this feminist festival, with a forecast of potentially dangerous consequences. These reveal the sinister palate of Pakistani patriarchy that comprises the collusion of men, military and *mulla* (clerics) politics in the Islamic Republic.

In the days following the 2021 Aurat March events, legal petitions were filed against the organisers in different cities. Some charges were for lesser offenses, like the nationalistic claims that the organisers are 'cultural assassinators,'[2] but far more malicious attempts included the framing of false charges of blasphemy against some members, despite efforts to peremptorily quash the complaints (Shah 2021). The unfolding of these reactionary hostilities exposed the limits of resistance politics which denies or avoids the core contradictions of the Pakistan state's arterial patriarchies which are, religious politics and military nationalism. The Aurat March organisers' lack of conceptual or political preparation has landed them in a predictable religio-patriarchal trap that could have been avoided, if they had cultivated ideological and strategic clarity in equal measure to their creative performative politics.

Unplanned sex

In 2018, a new wave of younger feminists took their rage against patriarchy, male violence, moral policing of women's bodies, and suppression of sexual choices for women and marginalised genders to the streets of Pakistan. Since then, International Women's Day on March 8th has been reclaimed from what had become a mundane, NGO-led, celebratory, cake-cutting event of former years. There was nothing subtle about the core focus on sexuality in these Aurat March events in the main cities which even included some fringe demands for LGBTQ rights that did not exist on the map of resistance politics prior to these events (*The News* 2019, Khatri 2020). The provocative slogans and performative activism of these marches predictably drew misogynist reaction and conservative backlash in mainstream media, and death threats over unregulated social media platforms (Mohydin 2019). The sources of patriarchal vitriol included, the disapproving garden variety conservatives, several women's pietist collectives (Minhaj ul Quran 2019, Ali 2020) and even, some embedded foreign 'influencers' sponsored by the state to promote Pakistaniat (Shackle 2020).

Despite these warning signs, the Aurat March organisers showed admirable determination to continue their events the following year but ignored (and sometimes, rubbished) the cautions cited by other feminist collectives on the need to develop a clear ideological position and strategy for dealing with state and religious political opposition. Some younger members were especially defensive about the prognosis that it was only a matter of time before the 'docile agency' (Mahmood 2005) of pietist Muslim women would spill into a politics that would directly challenge feminist activism and agendas (A.S. Zia 2018). This is precisely what happened immediately after the first year's events. Jolted by the feminist audacity to sex the streets and ignite *fitna* (socio-sexual chaos), in 2019, the right-wing and pietist organisations held oppositional marches that were purposefully titled, the 'Haya March' (Modesty March). These pious women are organised, dedicated, and attract many women supporters who would not qualify as 'extremist' or even Islamist. Their commitment defies the argument that it is only the far-right who are chauvinistic, or that it is 'toxic masculinity' that drives misogyny. Sexual freedoms are unanimously perceived as western and in contradiction to Islamic morality and Muslim gender norms.

Between theory and practice

Historically, direct clashes between the religious and the rights-based women's events have been rare, since ideological boundaries have always been mutually respected. For decades, women of the right-wing political parties have observed International Women's Day and participated in United Nations conferences (A.S. Zia 2013). Their events are always clearly thematically framed around the political and social agenda of the religious party or movement – usually on 'the family' and women's roles as dutiful mothers, wives and daughters within the private realm, and in service of Islam.

The rise of a new movement of pietist women has been the subject of a generation of Pakistani postsecular scholars writing in the 'War on Terror' years. They have been influenced by the post 9/11, postsecular turn in the humanities in western academia that is critical of 'liberal-secularism' and has flirted with Islamism as a reassertion of some authentic tradition (see Mufti 2013, Abbas 2014, A.S. Zia 2018). Some of these scholars were convinced by Saba Mahmood's (2005) influential tract that argues for the 'docile agency' of women of mosque movements as an alternative to emancipatory liberal desires, and applied it to movements in Pakistan, such as, the Al-Huda (Iqtidar 2011, Mushtaq 2010, Shaikh 2013). Interestingly, it is not just young Pakistani women but even many men who are very defensive and claim that they get 'triggered' by any critique or disagreement of the works of 'giant scholars' who work on Muslim subjectivities (exclusively in western academia) and who have been critical of the 'hegemony of secularism'. Both sets of scholars are either silent about or extend their criticism to secular resistance movements in Muslim contexts, including feminist ones.[3]

This academic turn that made a case for a recognition and valuing of the virtuous subjectivities of pietist subjects was even applied to the women disciples of the Jamia Hafsa – the women's madrasa associated with the controversial Lal Masjid in Islamabad and which has ties to jihadist causes and ideologically sympathises with the Taliban, ISIS, and murderers who kill to avenge perceived blasphemy (Babar 2017, A.S Zia 2020). The Shuhuda Foundation of the Lal Masjid (that was subject of a state siege in 2007 for its suspected terrorist links) had attempted to file a case for the ban of the Aurat March (see note i).

Masooda Bano (2012) has urged that the women of Jamia Hafsa associated with the Lal Masjid derived empowerment in their roles as mothers, sisters, wives and daughters as they spread their Islamic learnings, and that this madrasa education and learned piety empowers the girls to deal with material scarcity and cope with peer pressure against observing Valentine's Day and fashion trends. Such sanitised analysis allows such scholars to advocate support for Islamic female leadership as a viable alternative to 'Western feminism.' Several young women who support or participate in the Aurat March and identify as 'radical left feminists' in a bid to distinguish themselves from 'liberal' feminists, have similarly pleaded for understanding the complex relationship between pietist women's bodily practices and interior meanings in order to devise better feminist strategies. In view of the pietist women's affront and opposition to the Aurat March, it is puzzling why this advice to empathise, engage, and be sensitive to pious women's virtuosity was not followed by the younger activists who had pleaded the case of pietist agency -- before or even after, taking to the streets to demand sexual liberties?

The insistence for women's sexual freedoms directly offends the very core of pious women's subjectivities and is the antithetical to the central tenets of modesty and virtuosity prescribed for Muslim womanhood. After the second year's March, the backlash was notably vicious across the country. Hussain (2019) observes the irony; "Aurat March slogans were met with howls of outrage, anger, accusations of vulgarity, immodesty and much more and the *'bahaya'* [immodest] slogans of the Minhaj al Quran women's counter-march that calls the Aurat March women *'gali ki kutiya'* [bitches on the streets] accepted as civilised expression."

Some of the provocative posters and slogans stated that, "Our rights are not up for grabs and neither are we," "Girls just wanna have fundamental human rights," "Transwomen are women; shut up!", "Tu kare tou Stud, Mai Karun tou slut" ("If you do it, you're a stud, but if I do it, I'm a slut"), "Safe-street program for women," "Stop being menstrual -phobic", "Consent ki Tasbeeh Rozana Parhen" ("Respect the Rosary of Consent") and "Paratha rolls, not gender roles." The core slogan and poster of "Mera Jisam Meri Marzi," ("My Body My Choice")however, provoked the most reaction and was received as most (sexually) subversive along with, the ones that mocked the domestic roles of good women such as, "Apna khana khud garam karo! ("Heat your food yourself"), "Mujhe kia maaloom tumhara mauza kahaan hai!" ("How should I know where your socks are?"). The organisers staged an Urdu version of the Chilean protest song, "A Rapist in Your Path," that assails rape culture and victim-shaming and pride colours speckled some city marches. The optics and messaging clearly signaled a generational turn and the routine slogans and demands about equality in law, society and health were overshadowed by the bold and colourful shock value of these posters. Moreover, since conservative anxieties are fixated on women, sex and religion, their homing devices found those posters offensive which demanded that men stop sexting women pictures of their genitalia (sexual harassment); to cook their own food and be responsible for domestic work (breaking gender stereotypes); to respect consent to sex even in marriage. This reaction exposed the double standards where men's conduct is not judged as vulgar or inappropriate but if women behave in similar ways, they are considered indecent and sexual deviants. Several feminists demystified the March demands in subsequent writings and events (Zia 2019) but it was clear from the start that the posters and slogans were going to be the litmus test in the tussle for pious propriety over feminist protest politics.

Conservatives, Islamists and pietist organisations guard the cause of female sexual purity closely, and moral policing is essential in maintaining an Islamic sexual and gendered order. Ironically, the Aurat March and those members who profess to be 'radical feminists' have deeply offended the pious sensibilities of believing women more than any secular feminist movement ever has.

Neither were the devout the only offended community. Even the political parties (who the Aurat March organisers decided to remain aloof from), were horrified by this sex talk on the streets. While the liberal-leaning Pakistan People's Party has consistently extended the Aurat Marchers its political support in the wake of abusive online threats, the provincial legislative Assembly of Khyber Pakhtunkhwa passed a resolution demanding an inquiry into the "foreign hands" behind the Aurat March as a plot to undermine Pakistan's social norms (Hayat and Akbar 2019). Members of Prime Minister, Imran Khan's government (2018-2022) accused the March of promoting 'western' values and advised members to modulate their language so as not to offend Muslim sensibilities. Even many older feminists were not convinced of the value of such demands in an ideological vacuum (Dawn 2019).

Generational grievances

Those of us who recruited feminist consciousness in the 1990s, witnessed an older generation of activists of the Women's Action Forum getting tear-gassed and beaten on the streets for protesting against a military dictatorship and discriminatory Islamic laws, and for demanding secular state laws and policies. State-sponsored backlash and threats – either of death or social-death - is not new to human rights defenders. This is how feminism has been shaped in Pakistan and matured to become a fairly influential political force today. For decades, these activists were framed as anti-Islamic, western or RAW agents, and fired or gate-kept from universities, and lived under death-threats and in some cases, witnessed sister-activists get punished or killed for their resistance to patriarchal powers. But they schooled us on the importance of a stable ideological vision that was committed to changing state institutions and policies and developing strategic engagement with political parties and laws.

There has been no work or dialogue on sexual politics in Pakistan, so it was not surprising that several from the older-generation of liberal progressives were uncomfortable over the impropriety of the sexually explicit language used in the Aurat Marches. For too long, they have fought against the discriminatory zina (adultery) laws and honor crimes under the strategic legal pretense that the victim is always and permanently innocent or framed, as if they never actually violate the Islamic laws prohibiting adultery and fornication (Khan 2006, Jahangir and Jilani 1990). Even when they acknowledged that some women willingly transgress sexual norms, they did not concede the strategic response for the larger demand for sexual freedoms. The privatisation of sexual autonomy has now become an internalised logic within women's rights activism.

For this older generation, and in some lesser metropolitan cities, sexual rights and sex positivity are considered a more limited expression of feminism, and they prioritise economic, social and democratic crises as ideological frames. But they did support the Aurat March and urged the organisers to connect protest marches on sexual freedoms and violence with women's bodily, health, and labour rights. Many remain uncomfortable with public discussions around sexual pleasures, desire, and the politics of sexually explicit language, which they consider sensationalist, even violent and a patriarchal tool.

The 'post'-alities that influence the politics of a younger generation of activists, and the alternative spaces of social media as a political forum have enabled wider spread, creativity and impressive mobilisation tactics, but this has also made collectivism more diffused. This is especially challenging since there are more ideological differences and more 'male allies' directly involved in new waves of women's movements, while the goals are more blurred and buried under disagreements over representation on panels, platforms and performances. Most of all, there is a millennial distrust and distancing from the state that rides on the back of a post-9/11 ambiguity which is convinced that secular political confrontation to Islamism is always 'western'. Many such scholar-activists are convinced that it is only their brand of some unspecified hybrid and fluid formula that can overcome false discursive binaries and rescue Islam simultaneously from Islamophobia and Islamic extremism, all the while observing liberal and secular lifestyles and sexual freedoms themselves. Apparently, the opponents to the Aurat March didn't get this memo.

Internal differences are also quite obvious in the collectives who organise and lead the Aurat Marches in different cities. There is no consensus on the place of religion and how to strategically relate to the state, including with political parties and the legal-judicial system. The Aurat March organising committees in Hyderabad and across Sindh, adhere very clearly to the vision of a secular Marxist feminism and have dealt with religious backlash deftly, defiantly and sometimes, strategically non-confrontationally.

The founder members of the left-associated Women's Democratic Front of Islamabad/Pindi are more ideologically clear but younger members of the Punjab collectives who have studied from western universities tend to be far more ambiguous about the place of women's pietist subjectivities and even over Islamic feminism, while others remain silent on these issues. They are caught in a double bind now -to deflect the motives of pious women's politics to 'toxic masculinity' is unhelpful – it undermines the pious women's voluntary and un-coerced 'docile agency' theory that they were insisting on for the past decade.

A 'middling' generation attempted to bridge this political distance by encouraging the older feminists to recognise the importance of challenging the sexual order on the one hand, and to encourage the Aurat March organisers to connect their performative activism with legal cases and state policies. Most of all, they urged the need to develop an ideological strategic framework for the rights that Aurat Marchers were demanding. This was critical, since the spirit of the Aurat March clearly transgressed and contradicted the Islamic gendered and sexual orders that define an Islamic Republic. Initially, the younger feminists did not take the critique or warnings well. Several reacted to these as rebuffs and turned to social media to express their resentment against such cautioning with support from the growing phenomenon of online 'male allies'. Four years on, the organisers of the Marches found themselves facing very serious charges, which have affected internal dynamics, as well as having implications regarding strategic methods for the wider women's movement.

Piety turns political

In order to reclaim the public from the 'vulgar' invitation represented in the Aurat March's leading slogan, "Mera Jisam Meri Marzi" (My Body, My Choice), and to rescue Muslim women's collective modesties from such anti-Islamic causes, several pietist organisations led oppositional marches in 2019 under their rebuttal slogan, "Mera jisam Allah ki Marzi" (My Body, Allah's Choice). In 2020, conservative critics of the March actively filed legal cases in an attempt to thwart the events. The Aurat March organisers were compelled to respond to these measures and while they managed to win relief, these judgements were no clear victories. In his order, Chief Justice of the Lahore High

Court, Mamoon Rashid Sheikh conceded that "under the law and Constitution of the country, the Aurat March cannot be stopped" but cautioned that the marchers should "refrain from hate speech and immorality" (Bilal 2020). Meanwhile, the Chief Justice of the Islamabad High Court, considered the most liberal of judges, dismissed a petition seeking a ban on the March with the reprimand that the petitioners should introspect on the range of abuses that women suffered in the country but he too, observed that the participants should ensure that 'their conduct was consistent with the norms of decency' (The Express Tribune 2020a). The state may have offered a conciliatory legal verdict, but the moral censure defined the expectant limits of freedoms and propriety related to women's rights.

In 2020, pietist movements were as determined as the Aurat March collectives to advocate their respective causes on the streets. The women of the Jamia Hafsa expressed their resistance by defacing a mural in Islamabad that had been prepared by the Aurat March organisers (Ali 2020). These conscientious objectors led their counter-rally to the Aurat March, which included men and pious veiled women carrying banners, appealing that 'only Islam gives rights to women'. There was some pelting of stones, shoes and sticks at the Aurat Marchers, but these were controlled by law enforcement, averting conflict temporarily.

By 2021, the country's growing political and economic discontent was worsening under pressure of the global Covid-19 pandemic. The Aurat March was determined to not lose momentum even though, there were pending issues on the matter of gaining No Objection Certificates (NOC) from the city authorities. This opened the debate over the viability of feminist protest that could be denied under excuses of impropriety – which is what happened to the Aurat March event of Islamabad in 2021. Without a NOC, the state easily shrugs responsibility for such events. Brewing also were internal disagreements over symbolism, representation of queer symbols and language, and who could speak for the events. It was clear that there were political, ideological and strategic differences that had developed amongst the Aurat March collectives across the different cities and these were all going to have repercussions.

The chilling effect

Under the Imran Khan 'Riyasat e Medina'4 government, a culture of abusive language overpowered the political discourse of Pakistan. In the past, threats to rape and murder women activists, journalists, and even parliamentarians were not uncommon but under Khan's government, these carried impunity because no leader or authority censured or even publicly disapproved of such behaviour (Gul 2020). On the contrary, after the controversies following the 2020 March, PM Khan had chimed in his opinion of the need to 'weed out foreign cultural influences such as those observed in the Aurat March' (Dawn 2020a). The climate of conservatism and censorship was a throwback to the oppressive era of General Zia ul Haq's 'Islamic' dictatorship (1977-1988). Universities issued directives for women to observe the Arabic dress code of the abaya for women students (Ali 2021), and the government sponsored and conferred national awards to the celebrity-singer and loyal Imran Khan supporter, Ali Zafar, even as he was in litigation in a high-profile and contentious case of sexual harassment (Dawn 2020d).

The chilling effects of all these developments and the paternalistic criticism that the Aurat March did not prioritise the 'real' issues of Pakistani women, took its toll on the organisers and supporters. In their 2021 Manifesto, the thematic stress on women's health clearly steers away from any mention of sexual autonomies or freedoms, and the banners of "Mera Jisam Meri Marzi" were not prominently featured at the March. Due to the persistent interrogation from the media about 'offensive' slogans and posters, some organisers offered mitigating interpretations or distanced themselves by reasoning that they cannot control what participants express at the events. They also made efforts to filter participation and media coverage of the event while others denied any allegations of promoting homosexuality.[5]Despite all these efforts, the critics and opponents were intent on chastising the underlying ethos and 'original sin' of the March, regardless of a non-controversial manifesto of 2021 (Ahmed 2021). Journalists descended at the events to grill the marchers on how they squared their demands with their religious beliefs as Muslim women. A bulk of this coverage betrays sexist anxieties on the part of the reporters and exaggeration of any contradictions or confusion expressed by participants,[6] but some of the organisers too, were clearly out of their depth or back-pedaling on the more radical tone of the original March (The Express Tribune 2020a).

Confrontation between religious and secular politics are inevitable. It has always been naïve and academic of those who pretend there should not be polarisation or binaries in strategic confrontations. This is delusional. How do you counter the religious right without a plan?

A red flag or herring?

As in previous years, obscenities trended in the aftermath of the 2021 March and the usual distorted and photo-shopped images were circulated on social media. Artwork and slogans were manipulated into pornographic renderings and even blasphemous content. Soon after the events, threats of charges of blasphemy against the organisers of Aurat March began circulating – an offense that carries the death penalty and has incited routine vigilante attacks and murders in the past, including that of the late Governor of Punjab, Salmaan Taseer, and several scholars and students (HRW 2019).

In Islamabad, the Women's Democratic Front that led the Aurat March was accused of promoting the agenda of the 'anti-Islamic' French state because they have a tricoloured (differently so) flag. A doctored audio that faked a blasphemous voice-over of the original slogans raised by the organisers at the Karachi event was broadcast by some mainstream media channels without verification (Farmer 2021). In Lahore, organisers had to issue a clarification about a multimedia blanket of shame that carried the testimony of sexual abuse of a minor by a religious teacher and which was deliberately misinterpreted to allege that this was mocking the tradition of divine prophetic personalities (Samaa online 2021). Even the militant Tehreeq e Taliban Pakistan - responsible for the murders of hundreds of thousands of citizens - issued its disapproval of the March (The Express Tribune 2021b).

Such deceptive propaganda required pre-determined effort and political motivation. Underlying the anti-March campaign is an interesting twist of logic – the actual Aurat March messages were not offensive enough, it seems, so the pious nationalists decided to create excessive content by doctoring footage, instigating lies and spreading misinformation to smear the event but in the process were actually producing blasphemy themselves. The irony in all of this punitive pietist politics is that this fetishisation of female sexuality, production of erotica, prevalence of male obscenities, and distortions that lead to blasphemy accusation, were the exact premise that feminist "cultural assassinators" were protesting. The distorters simply indicted themselves and proved that what the Aurat March women are opposing is a legitimate cause.

Despite efforts to quash the First Information Reports in the aftermath of the Aurat March 2021, an orchestrated campaign of disinformation and pressure has succeeded in at least, two petitions of blasphemy registered in the High Courts of Peshawar and Sindh. These charges identify the names of some organisers and is a trend that for vigilantes, translates into targets on the backs of the accused.

Sex and secularism – the banes of blasphemy

The Aurat March participants were understandably nervous – some deleted their social media accounts and erased their timelines. Others reportedly considered leaving the country. The attack was blatantly malafide but revealed what activists have been saying for years – that the blasphemy laws are not only weaponised for settling personal or political vendettas through false allegations, but they are tools for those faithful who claim genuine religious injury and offense. Any perceived secular demand can qualify as blasphemy.

Postsecularists insist that blasphemy accusations are always cynical and politically motivated – as if, no one in Pakistan could ever 'commit blasphemy' or for that matter, be genuinely offended by the commission of such an offense (but they would consider claims of moral injury by Muslims in western contexts as credible). One view even argues that blasphemy accusations are exercised to enable powerful Muslim mobs to extend the right to protection to dependent minorities. This is contrary to feminist analyses that argue that the intent of those deploying the blasphemy laws is to protect Islam from the offense of minority beliefs (including, the declared-heretic, Ahmediya sect). Yet another speculation is that blasphemy allegations are primarily levelled at minorities and progressives even though, the majority of cases involve other Muslims who are often from the same class or community (NCHR 2018).

For all their academic acrobatics, a younger generation of activists does not advocate for the repeal of the blasphemy laws as a previous generation did within a secular dispensation. At this point, everyone has simply reconciled with the need to diffuse the misuse of the law by amending the procedures to file cases, rather than confronting the rage of those who weaponise it with impunity.

Meanwhile, after the 2021 March, confusion and lack of clarity preoccupied the Aurat March organisers, as different feminist collectives rallied on how to respond to the legal

Banality of binaries

The three obvious antidotes to the patriarchal trinity of military-mullah-men are quite obvious: complete civilian supremacy, institutional and societal secular options, and sexual autonomies for all genders equally. Curative treatment of just one symptom simply activates the brotherly cells into rescue mode. At the outset, the Aurat March collectives were neither invested in the politics of 'changing the state', nor did they strategise how to counter religious backlash, despite a history of three decades of feminist struggle built on the bedrock of these principles. The Aurat March members centralised their advocacy for sexual freedoms around male behaviour and patriarchal practices but without addressing the core contradictions of Islamic laws that prohibit these, or by directing their demands for equal legal rights on matters of sexuality. For these reasons, the Aurat March soon found itself stranded ideologically and politically.

Their demands have expanded and been more politicised over the years, but the manifesto still does not specify an ideological framing for its demands – are these to be within Islamic reasonings and limits, or aligned with secular, universal human rights? Are they addressing the state directly, or lobbying the political parties to fulfil the demands? What makes them radical or even different from other more experienced pressure groups? Organisationally, the Aurat March members of each city follow their own direction but organically, it is neither a political movement, nor a purely celebratory event or performative protest (Saigol and Chaudhry 2020).

The Aurat March may host members from the sexually marginalised communities but the platform has lost its radical edge and is unlikely to be able to foreground the theme of sexual autonomies meaningfully in the future. In 2022, in view of the backlash and falsified blasphemy allegations from the previous year, the organisers of the Aurat Azadi March in Islamabad decided to hold a jalsa (public meeting) in a park instead of a street protest or March. Several older activists in Islamabad felt this amounted to retreat and would be taken as a sign of concession and right-wing vindication, so they hurriedly organised a token street protest. Despite the pledge to the slogan of 'Mera Jisam Meri Marzi' and other provocative and satirical agitprops, the original claim of Aurat March about undisciplined bodies, defiant language and free expression has been successively invalidated over the years, as these have become schooled and policed, evident in the diluted slogans, posters and pragmatic manifesto demands. The external pressures are a constant on every rights-based movement in Pakistan but snarky defensiveness on social media, petulant cancelling of unfavourable analysis, internal differences, and no collective theoretical framing or plan on how to confront religious patriarchy or farms of nationalist trolls, puts this movement at risk of ending up as a collective of cultural mitigators, rather than some radical 'assassinators'.

REFERENCES

Abbas, Sadia. *At Freedom's Limit: Islam and the Postcolonial Predicament*. New York: Fordham University Press, 2014

Ahmed, Umaima R. "Aurat March' 2021 presents feminist healthcare manifesto in Pakistan." *Global Voices*. 14 Mar. 2020 https://globalvoices.org/2021/03/14/aurat-march-2021-presents-feminist-healthcare-manifesto-in-pakistan/.

Ali, Farman Shakeel. "University in Kohat imposes dress code for students, faculty members." *The News*, 9 Mar. 2021 https://www.thenews.com.pk/latest/801569-university-in-kohat-imposes-dress-code-for-students-faculty-members.

Ali, Kalbe. "Jamia Hafsa students claim responsibility for defacing feminist mural in Islamabad." *Dawn*, 5 Mar. 2020. https://www.dawn.com/news/1538478/jamia-hafsa-students-claim-responsibility-for-defacing-feminist-mural-in-islamabad.

"Aurat March posters ignite feminist firestorm in Pakistan." *The News*, 5 Apr. 2019 https://www.thenews.com.pk/latest/453835-aurat-march-posters-ignite-feminist-firestorm-in-pakistan.

Babar, Aneela. *We are all revolutionaries here: Militarism, Political Islam and Gender in Pakistan*,. SAGE Publications, Inc. 2017, pp. 134-167

Bano, Masooda. *The Rational Believer: Choices and Decisions in the Madrasas of Pakistan*. Ithaca: Cornell University Press, 2012

Bilal, Rana. "Aurat March can't be stopped under Constitution': LHC directs govt to speed up decision on clearance." *Dawn*, 3 Mar. 2020 https://www.dawn.com/news/1538075.

Farmer, Ben. "Online blasphemy smear campaign threatens Pakistan's Women's Day marchers." *The Telegraph*, 12 Mar. 2021. https://www.telegraph.co.uk/global-health/women-and-girls/online-blasphemy-smear-campaign-threatens-pakistans-womens-day/.

"'Fix your ways': Taliban threaten organisers of Aurat March." *The Express Tribune*, 13 Mar. 2021 https://tribune.com.pk/story/2289084/fix-your-ways-taliban-threaten-organisers-of-aurat-march.

- - - "IHC rejects petition seeking ban on Aurat March." 6 Mar. 2020. https://tribune.com.pk/story/2170450/1-ihc-reserves-verdict-maintainability-petition-aurat-march.

- - - "Tribune Fact Check: A flag, two viral videos and Pakistan's Aurat March." 11 Mar. 2020. https://tribune.com.pk/story/2288842/tribune-fact-check-a-flag-two-viral-videos-and-pakistans-aurat-march.

Gul, Ayaz. "In Rare Testimony, Female Pakistani Journalists Describe Social Media Attacks to Lawmakers." *Voice of America*, 18 Aug. 2020. https://www.voanews.com/press-freedom/rare-testimony-female-pakistani-journalistsdescribe-social-media-attacks-lawmakers .

Hussain, Neelam. "Aurat March and its discontents." *The News on Sunday*, 24 Mar. 2019 https://www.thenews.com.pk/tns/detail/567460-aurat-march-discontents/

Iqtidar, Humeira. *Secularizing Islamists? Jamaat-i-Islami and Jama`at-ud-Da`wa in Urban Pakistan*. Chicago: Chicago University Press, 2011

Jahangir, Asma and Hina Jilani. *The Hudood Ordinances: A Divine Sanction?*. Lahore: Rohtas Books, 1990 "Journalists, activists condemn anti-Aurat March campaign." *Samaa TV* (online), 12 Mar. 2021 https://www.samaa.tv/news/2021/03/journalists-activists-condemn-anti-aurat-march-campaign/.

Khan, Shahnaz. *Zina, Transnational Feminism, and the Moral Regulation of Pakistani Women*. Vancouver, CA: UBC Press, 2006

Khatri, Sadia. "Should feminists claim Aurat March's 'vulgar' posters? Yes, absolutely." *Prism*. 22 Jan. 2020. https://www.dawn.com/news/1469815.

Mohydin, Rimmel. "Let Me Womansplain the Aurat March to You." *Prism*. 13 Mar. 2019 https://www.dawn.com/news/1469183.

Mufti, Aamir R. "Why I Am Not a Postsecularist." *Boundary 2*, vol. 40, no. 1, 2013, pp. 7-19.

Mushtaq, Faiza. "A Controversial Role Model for Pakistani Women." *South Asia Multidisciplinary Academic Journal* [Online] 4, 2010

"MWL Holds a Peaceful March to Decry Anti-women Agenda." *Minhaj-ul-Quran*, 14 Mar. 2019 https://www.minhaj.org/english/tid/46325/MWL-holds-a-peaceful-march-to-decry-antiwomen-agenda.html.

"National Commission of Justice and Peace: Human Rights Monitor 2019: a report on the religious minorities of Pakistan." http://www.ncjp-pk.org/wp-content/uploads/2019/09/HRM19-final.pdf.

"Pakistan: End Ordeal for 'Blasphemy' Defendants." *Human Rights Watch*, 6 Oct. 2019 https://www.hrw.org/news/2019/10/06/pakistan-end-ordeal-blasphemy-defendants.

"Poet Kishwar Naheed slammed the Aurat March, and then Twitter slammed her." *Dawn*, 13 Mar. 2019. https://images.dawn.com/news/1182047/poet-kishwar-naheed-slammed-the-aurat-march-and-then-twitter-slammed-her.

"PM Imran Khan says Aurat March is a result of cultural differences like it's a bad thing." *Dawn* 14 Mar. 2020 https://images.dawn.com/news/1184828.

Saigol, Rubina and Nida Usma Chaudhry. *Contradictions and Ambiguities of Feminism in Pakistan; Exploring the Fourth Wave*. Pakistan: Friedrich-Ebert-Stiftung (FES), 2020

Shackle, Samira. "How western travel influencers got tangled up in Pakistan's politics." *The Guardian*, 12 Nov. 2020 https://www.theguardian.com/news/2020/nov/12/western-travel-influencers-social-media-pakistan-politics.

Shah, Waseem Ahmad. "Court orders registration of FIR against Aurat March organisers." *Dawn*, 27 Mar. 2020. https://www.dawn.com/news/1614833/court-orders-registration-of-fir-against-aurat-march-organisers.

Sheikh, Khanum. "Gender, Religious Agency, and the Subject of *Al-Huda* International." *Meridians*, vol. 11, no. 2, 2013, pp. 62–90.

"Women's rights activists urge govt to rethink Ali Zafar's Pride of Performance Award." *Dawn*, 20 Aug. 2020 https://www.dawn.com/news/1575475

Zia, Afiya Shehrbano. "Who's Afraid of Pakistan's Aurat March?" *Economic and Political Weekly*, vol. 55, no. 8, 22. Feb 2020.

--- "Drivers or decoys? Women and the narrative of extremist violence in Pakistan." In, in *Encountering extremism: Theoretical issues and local challenges*, Ed. Alice Martini, Kieran Ford and Richard Jackson, Manchester: Manchester University Press, 2020

--- "Engendering The Sovereignty Of The Islamic Republic Of Pakistan." *Kafila*, 10 Jan. 2013 https://kafila.online/2013/01/10/engendering-the-sovereignty-of-the-islamic-republic-of-pakistan-afiya-shehrbano-zia/.

--- *Faith and Feminism in Pakistan: Religious Agency or Sexual Autonomy?* Brighton: Sussex Academic Press, 2018

--- "Propriety and protest." *The News on Sunday*, 17 Mar. 2019, https://www.thenews.com.pk/tns/detail/567418-propriety-protest/

ENDNOTES

1 Dr. Afiya Shehrbano Zia is the Frank B Weeks, Visiting Assistant Professor of Feminist, Gender and Sexualities Studies at Wesleyan university. She is author of *Faith and Feminism in Pakistan; Religious Agency or Secular Autonomy?* (SAP 2018) and has authored over a dozen peer-reviewed essays for scholarly journals and contributed chapters for over 10 edited volumes, including an award-winning Routledge publication on Human Rights. Afiya is an active member of the Women's Action Forum; has served as a board member of the Trust for Democratic Education and Accountability and is an advisory member of the Centre for Secular Space, UK. Email: azia@wesleyan.edu

2 This petition was filed by the Shuhuda Foundation of the Lal Masjid (Red Mosque) against the Islamabad authorities for permitting the Aurat March event to be held in 2021. It argues that the "gangster" organisers and alleged funders are a "third force or class... which Lord Macaulay had planned to introduce [and] has grown up [sic] which is Pakistani in blood and colour, but English in taste, in opinion, in morals and in intellect. This class is trying to swamp the culture and values of Islam and hence the ideology of Pakistan under the auspices and policy and instructions of West. They have been advised by their imperialist masters that religion i.e. Islam is anti-civilization as in their opinion Westernization or modernization means civilization. Thus under the given policy and agenda they are trying to change the culture of Pakistan by celebrating walks and talks like VALENTINE DAY and AURAT MARCH etc. The religion is being humiliated and ridiculed indirectly by maneuvering campaign against Mullaism, freedom of women's rights."

The petition reasons that the Aurat March threatens the "Muslims of Pakistan [who have] been under the danger of two intellectual and cultural assassinators [sic]. West and Hindus both played a vital role to imbibe the culture, ideas and faith of the generation of Muslims of the subcontinent..."

The judge of the Islamabad High Court did not dismiss the petition but recused himself from hearing it on the grounds that his views on the March were widely known and a wider bench was formed by the next judge.

3 See Saba Mahmood's (2008) disdain for "the many heroes of the secular left [and] self-identified liberal Muslim reformers [who] share secular assumptions about enlightened religiosity with the U.S. State Department...." She goes on to explain that "My object of analysis, however, is not their motives and intentions but the discursive assumptions (about knowledge, history, language) that underpin their methods and programs of reform. Do we have to subscribe to a full-fledged theory of shared interests and motives to be able to see the common set of discursive presuppositions that cut across political projects? Might people be politically opposed and still share a set of epistemological and conceptual truths? Could one analyze this convergence critically without being accused of "belittling" the heroes of our stories?" ("Secular Imperatives," *Public Culture* 20:3, pg. 463).

This argument could be equally applicable to those of Pakistan's self-acclaimed left progressives who defended the 'docile agency' of women of the pietist movements in Pakistan.

4 A reference to the social welfare state of Medina in the 7th century.

5 Many talk shows and social media programmes fueled the backlash to the Aurat March too, with men and women TV anchors despairing equally about non-binary gender representation at the

events. In one programme on Bol TV, anchor Fiza Akbar objected to the "same-sex, gay wala concept" promoted at the Aurat March events and reasons that, gay and lesbian discussion is unacceptable in the Islamic Republic. On the panel was a more experienced feminist activist who attempted to defend this by explaining that the cause was not about homosexuality but 'queer' people who are 'not the same as gays'. The cleric on the panel then complained that he was not being given the opportunity to speak, to which the woman anchor joked that when women are on a panel there is bound to be more noise. Other than the usual moralistic objections to bay-hayaee (immodesty), the cleric raised an important argument on the subtext of the March slogan, 'My body, My choice'; he argued that if it requires repeated clarification then it's not simply an innocuous or unambiguous reference to safety from violence, as its defenders now attempt to dilute its inference to sexual freedoms. He questioned other contentious posters, including one which claimed pride for being 'Awara' (drifter) and a 'loafer' and admonished the absurdity of one poster that claimed women's right to sit with their legs apart. Bol News, 8th March. https://www.youtube.com/watch?v=YNNJupVVc4E.

6 There is less print content of such sensationalism but a youtube search reveal countless hours of coverage that are laden with sexual innuendo, lewd references and attempts to belittle March participants. For e.g., "Aurat March 2021 Mein Be Hayai Ka Bazar Garam, Gardan Par Kiss Ke Nishan - Hassaan Hashmi", https://www.youtube.com/watch?v=Cq1YHBGgvAg.

CHAPTER 16

The Fundamentalist Nexus of Neoliberalism, Rentier Capitalism, Religious and Secular Patriarchies, and South Asian Feminist Resistances

Fawzia Afzal-Khan[1]

ABSTRACT

In two case studies from Pakistan, which I then link to Afghanistan (under the Taliban before and after the Soviet/US proxy war there) as well as the Farmer's Movement in India—I wish to proffer an intersectional analysis of debates around the issue of women's rights in the global south. Feminist artivism (art-as-activism), can help build solidarities to mount resistances against globally-inflected state repression in our age of neoliberal economic and religious fundamentalisms, which, working in tandem, seek to roll back the rights of women and minorities in and across South Asia, as elsewhere.

Brief Overview of Neoliberal Economic Fundamentalism and its(neo)colonial underpinnings

> Many social scientific analyses of the global economy ... are ... willfully indifferent to... colonialism...[and] they ignore categories of gender and sexuality as integral to developing an intersectional analysis and understanding of our shared worlds.
>
> *(Zophia Edwards, Monthly Review*[2]*)*

In 1993, in a series of interviews with David Barsamian, Noam Chomsky traced the "the new global economy" of neoliberalism, back to Richard Nixon's dismantling of the Bretton Woods system in 1971, which, as he cogently argued,

> led to a deregulation of currencies, and which together with other changes, expanded the amount of unregulated capital in the world that accelerated the globalization or internationalization of the economy. It was a way to restore and continue US global dominance in finance, by increasing corporate profits through exporting jobs to low-wage areas of the world: the so called third world.[3]

This process, in turn, has also brought the "third world" home to Euro-America—by creating a two-tiered society of the extremely wealthy and privileged (white), and the extremely impoverished, often "superfluous" segment of the population (largely of color), with their expendable jobs, dubbed the "precariat"—members of what has been called the "gig" economy. Gutting of the social welfare net "at home" in western capitalist nations, and through structural adjustment programs (SAPS) abroad, neoliberal economic fundamentalism has led to the same deligitimation of "big" government at home in the US and Europe, and in the global south nations via its multinational corporations operating in "free trade" zones that protect the capital investments of the West by imposing austerity measures on developing nations as a prerequisite for high-interest "aid" packages delivered by western lending agencies such as the World Bank, IMF, and their trade agreements with ruling elites if global south nations such as GATT, NAFTA, and so on.

British economist Guy Standing, discussing the key themes from his book *The Corruption of Capitalism: Why Rentiers Thrive and Work Does Not Pay* in 2017, points out the corruption engendered by this neocolonial system of global governance, in what he names a system of "Rentier Capitalism":

> There is a lie at the heart of global capitalism. Politicians, financiers, and global bureaucrats claim to believe in free, competitive markets, but have constructed the most unfree market system ever made. It is corrupt because income is channeled to the owners of property–financial, physical and intellectual–at the expense of society. [4]

This book reveals how global capitalism is rigged in favor of what Standing calls "rentiers" (i.e. global elites/owners of capital), to the detriment of all of us, especially the precariat. A plutocracy and elite enrich itself, not through production of goods and services, but through ownership of assets, including intellectual property, aided by subsidies, tax breaks[5], debt mechanisms, revolving doors between politics and business, and the privatization of public services. Rentier capitalism is entrenched by the corruption of democracy, manipulated by the plutocracy and an elite-dominated media.

Feminist Artivist Interventions in South Asia

As a schol-art-ivist who has focused her work on a transnational feminism of the 99%[6]—I have always been alert and committed to learning and teaching a form of feminist theory and activism (through theatre and performance/gender performativities and performance in the global south, specifically Pakistani street theatre, and more recently, via study of land rights movements in Pakistan and India)—that is NOT about women "breaking the glass ceiling."[7] This is a counter-feminism to the "lean- in" variety preached by the likes of Sheryl Sandburg—who have popularized "individual empowerment" scripts that seem to be the most easily understood and popular forms of feminism here (arising out of liberal white feminist theory). Most of my students come in to my classes attached these "individual empowerment" scripts and my job as I see it, is to shift that perspective.

Because when we start paying attention to issues in the US such as unaffordable housing, poverty wages, inadequate health care, border policing, climate change which are coming to the fore of our collective consciousness now thanks to COVID—we see how these are actually issues that arise out of the phenomena of neoliberal capitalism that has the entire world, north and south, firmly in its grip. Such a vice-like grip of neoliberal capitalist oppression is visibilized clearly when we see people from the global south including pregnant women and children from Central and Latin American countries willing to brace the risks of trying to get to USA borders looking for asylum from the depredations unleashed by such a corrupt system. We now understand more clearly that they are fleeing the consequences of this neoliberal system that that benefits corporate America, but has worsened poverty, access to education and jobs, affordable child and healthcare in their home countries, thanks to the privatization doctrine the US and its lending agencies (World Bank, IMF) force governments in these countries to follow, which has led to the gutting of the welfare state. We see that same logic at work in our own country here in the USA, affecting our own internally marginalized populations in the same way.

Rentier Capitalism is Fostering Revolt: Case Study# 1, Artivism through the Alternative or Parallel Theatre Movement and the Women's Movement in Pakistan, 1980s-Present

In my scholarly work—citing one example —I wrote about a play written and performed by Ajoka Theatre of Pakistan—where the plot exposes the convergence of neoliberal capitalism (linked to Klein's "disaster/vulture" capitalism"[8])—with patriarchal repression and the rise of "Islamic fundamentalism" in Pakistan—and how theatre activism—artivism—especially around women's and minorities' rights issues, became a form of resistance in the face of fear and repression that such a dangerous nexus of forces/phenomena has resulted in. I have referred elsewhere to this convergence of forces as "the unholy alliance of [neoliberal or] postmodern capitalism, patriarchy and fundamentalism"[9], by which I mean both the economic fundamentalism practiced by the imperialist US and its acolytes, as well as the Islamist fundamentalism that such neoliberal ideology and practices has engendered as a regressive reaction.

The play in question, entitled *Dukhini (Suffering Woman)* by the *Ajoka* Theater Group, brings these issues (one of them being proprietorship over women's bodies-in the name of religion- exacerbated under neoliberal or postmodern capitalism), to light through the theme of the trafficking of women, who are smuggled from poverty-stricken Bangladesh, across India, and into Pakistan under the false promise of a "better life," only to find themselves sold into prostitution to the highest bidder. These women become victims not only of some sort of "Muslim fundamentalist religious patriarchy," but also of a capitalist consumerist ideology unleashed by a neoliberal economic "fundamentalism" that treats women's bodies as commodities to be bought and sold in the market-place. Thus, the Islamist/traditionalist/patriarchal ideologies that work to keep these trafficked women oppressed by convincing them of their "fallen nature," (they cannot "go back" to families, for instance, because of the 'dishonor' associated with being trafficked in the sex trade), work in tandem with/feed into, globalized neoliberal/rentier capitalism, linked to European colonialism of yesterday, and its cousin US imperialism of today. Indeed, the colonialist interventions of yesteryear that link to the imperial hegemonic nexus of our times represented during the Cold War by the US and USSR power blocs, the reigns of which today are held solely by the USA and is western/NATO allies (chief among them the biggest colonial power of its day, Great Britain) in our unipolar world—this colonial-imperial nexus has boosted the rise of regressive Islamist movements everywhere.

Figure 1: Poster of Ajoka's play, Dukhini

Dukhini is a play that exposes what I call, this unholy alliance of fundamentalisms. Agnes Khoo, a labor activist and researcher of South and South-East Asia underscores the ways in which a strengthening of patriarchy (in its so-called Islamist variant in Pakistan), feeds into and upholds the neoliberal (colonial/imperial) economic model that rules our world today. She writes,

> the re-structured economies in most parts of Asia have resulted in a permanent pool of no small number of reserve labour force, the majority of whom are women. This reserve labour pool will ensure that labour cost is kept the lowest, at all times, in favour of International Capitalist Production and Capital Accumulation. Thus, in this new millenium, labour, especially women's labour, will be kept insecure, unprotected and flexible… creat[ing], ultimately, a class of impoverished, 'globalized' workers that are not protected by their State nor by the governments in the countries/areas where they are working.[10]

This statelessness of migrant labor—particularly involving women's labor (including sex labor) in a Neoliberal Globalized Unipolar New World Order—serves the needs both of imperialist capitalism, as well as of the militarized postcolonial third-world state, dependent on imperialist aid for its own legitimization—all at the expense of a democratic and secular polity. In turn, in order to secure legitimacy for its own illegitimate seizure of power and suspension of democratic civilian rule, the past two military dictatorships in Pakistan (in the 1980s, and again the 2000s), have strengthened the military-mullah alliance[11]. Thus, the women sold into sexual slavery, such as the protagonists of *Dukhini,* become victims also of the Zina Ordinance passed by Gen. Zia's regime into Law back in 1980s, when he was simultaneously the CIA's darling and heavily funded by the US state dept as well as the Saudi government, to create religious madrassahs that could become breeding grounds for jihadists to fight against the Soviet Union in neighboring Afghanistan.

The Deadly Nexus and Women's Oppression in/as the Precariat Class. Artivism's Positive Effects

This same ideology of globalized neoliberalism, that works in tandem with the military-mullah nexus in countries like Pakistan, shapes the experiences of victimization of the trafficked women of the Pakistani play, *Dukhini*. For example, when one of the women in the play *Dukhini,* refuses to leave the gravesite she visits in Karachi regularly (to pay her respects to a woman like herself who rebelled by immolating herself in a public square in Karachi)—in order to service a client, her pimp arrives to threaten her in no uncertain terms that he has the military state's Law on his side, and therefore she must comply with his commands. That is, if she refuses to listen to him, he will bring a policeman to the scene and get her booked under the Hudood Ordinance—specifically, the law of "zina" passed by General Zia's government in the late 70's according to which a single woman, could, with impunity, be labelled a "whore" or an "adulteress" by her husband or even an unrelated man—and because of the law of Evidence (also passed under the Hudood Ordinance), according to which her testimony is regarded as equal to only half of a man's—she would be unable to prove her innocence, and therefore be automatically thrown into jail, there to be further abused by male police officers and wardens.

What is important to note here is that "militablishments" such as that of General Zia, and others like the one that was headed by another army general, Pervez Musharraf who declared Martial Law in 1999 and then ruled as President from 2000-2008, either passed or went along with the pursuit of anti-women's and minority rights agendas. Despite such contraventions of human rights and democratic rights, these illegitimate governments were aided and abetted by US imperialist forces and their neoliberal economic policies, under the guise of a seemingly benign discourse of globalization.

Even civilian elected governments (such as the Pakistan Tehrik Insaf (Pakistan Justice Movement) government in power today led by former cricketer Imran Khan), is controlled and beholden to the power behind the throne—the Pakistan Army, which, which, as the de facto state, continues to follow the diktat of the IMF, World Bank and other multinational corporations. These agencies acting on behalf of international capital, force the governments of countries like Pakistan to enact structural adjustment programs that take money away from public services and funnel them into private hands/ private industry. At the same time, such governments have strengthened the power of religious extremist parties in order to maintain legitimacy of their martial as well as civilian-backed regimes in the Islamic Republic of Pakistan, by claiming the support of religious leaders.

Despite the chokehold of this nexus of forces on the lives of ordinary citizens, thanks to the theatre activism promoted by plays such as *Dukhini* that surely aided women's rights lobbyists in their fight against the military state-mandated draconian laws against women,[12] the next military dictator of Pakistan, General Musharraf (1999-2008), under pressure by civil society/women's rights/feminist groups such as WAF (The Women's Action Forum), was forced to pass the Women's Protection Bill in November 2006.[13]

The annual women's rights marches that have been organized across major urban centers in Pakistan since 2018, called Aurat March, (*aurat* means woman in Urdu), have carried on the tradition of resistance against continuing repression and anti-women legislation. Protesting citizens enact their iterative (i.e., performative) demands as cultural activists, for many different rights that are taken up during these events, when thousands of women and their male supporters, as well as transgender activists, labor rights activists and so on, take to the streets every March 8, despite threats of bodily harm and accusations of being western stooges levelled against them by members of various extremist groups, including state-sponsored ones.[14]

Even a cursory glance at some of the demands carried on placards and repeated as chants and performed through skits on the streets during these marches, demonstrate how these activists point to the nexus of forces I have been alluding to in this paper. For instance, the Aurat March in Lahore described the 2021 rallies as a protest against the "patriarchy pandemic," in which they linked domestic violence with sexual harassment in the workplace (connecting private with public space), and injustice toward women in these interlinked spheres, with lack of a robust welfare state that is needed to protect the health and safety of ALL its citizens. Thus, protesters held signs and shouted out demands for an increase in the health care allocation in the following year's fiscal budget, as well as demanding transparency on how this increase would reach women and transgender communities. They also called for access to Covid vaccination regardless of gender or ethnic background, and, importantly, for putting an end to privatization of the health care system.[15]

Figure 2: Aurat March 2021

Case Study #2: Okara Peasant Movement in Pakistani Punjab, 2000-2007, Women's Roles and Activism:

Historical Background

Colonial roots of the late 20th and 21st century struggles of tenant farmers in the region of Okara, Pakistani Punjab, expose the links between colonial extractive labor policies and the later continuation under a neocolonial "neoliberal" discourse, utilized by the Pakistani Army to control these lands and marginalize the farmers from the rights promised them by the departing colonists during the time of Independence.

Around the beginning of the twentieth century, the British rulers of then undivided British India had encouraged thousands of migrants, mainly Muslims and Christians from the Eastern Punjab, now part of India, to migrate to the region which, at the time, was unproductive dry jungle and wasteland[16]. The goal of the British was to make the region agriculturally productive by developing intensive irrigated agriculture drawing upon waters from the Ravi and Sutlej rivers, through an extensive network of canals. As part of the incentive to encourage migration to the barren region, the British promised the farmer settlers, proprietary rights to the land as soon as it came under cultivation[17] (Akhtar 2006). Okara very soon became one of the most fertile regions in British India, but the promise by the British to give the peasants legal title to the land was never kept.

Jumping ahead almost a century later to 2000, the Pakistani military decided to change the share-cropping system under which landless peasant farmers at least had some control over their crops and usually kept a 50% share in the output. The Army rationale for the attempt to introduce the new cash rent system was that it would make the collection of rents more efficient (the usual neoliberal mantra). To the tenants, however, this new system would not only threaten their existence as cultivators, but their very economic survival, as, if they were forced to leave the farms for being unable to pay fixed amount of "rent" as cash (rentier capitalism), they would have no means of earning a living. Farmers claimed that the hidden agenda of the military was that it wanted to hand over the fertile land to retired officers for stud farming—on lands it didn't own! These lands had *de facto,* if not *de jure,* belonged to the Punjab provincial government even during the time of the British. Indeed, the land was owned by the Imperial Government of Punjab and leased to British Army who paid rent till 1943. After Partition, the land was transferred to the Pakistani army.

Farmers' and Peasant Women's Resistance

The landless farmers of Okara's military-owned farms (numbering approx. 200,000 in 2016)[18]-- have had a long history of resistance against the military and land-owning classes after the creation of Pakistan in 1947. The tenants (mazareen), who had been tilling the land for over a hundred years, were angered into an almost decade-long battle of collective action during the early 2000s, when, under the dictatorship of General Musharraf, attempts were made to change the extant system under which they had some rights to the land as well as a share in the profits, into a contract-based system, rendering it easier to evict the peasants with very little notice. During Musharraf's rule, laws were passed to further corporatize agriculture (including passing on the control of the Military Dairy Farm from tenant farmers to the multinational company, Nestle). The new contract enforced on the farmers thus further eroded their rights/ control over their lives and livelihood, made their working conditions worse, and decreased wages.

In response to these repressive measures, a farmers' organization, *Anjuman-e-Mazareen Punjab* (Punjab Farmers Collective) was formed to resist and defend their livelihood, with the powerful slogan making clear they would rather die than submit to these unjust changes, *Maliki Ya Maut! (trans:Death or Ownership!).* The slogan spelt out unequivocally, that nothing less than the century-old promise of land ownership be now fulfilled, as the Army was in fact, not the legal owner of these lands. As Rizvi points out, "the AMP enlarged tenants' objection to cash contract farming into a discussion of land reform, citizenship rights, democracy, and human rights in Pakistan" (2019, p. 99).

With the increasing suppression by the state in response to the farmers' rights movement, which led to massive confrontations between the army and farmers and subsequent beatings, tear-gassing, arrests, injuries and even deaths of the protestors (including women) [19]--, it was women who rose to the fore-front of the movement. As more and more of the AMP leaders got arrested, the women received messages from these imprisoned male leaders, asking them to, team up, go from village to village, and motivate the families to gather in protest. They were afraid that if people went into hiding, it would be very difficult to ever mobilise them again. The vacuum of power was filled by the women who went from one village to another rallying all the women, gathering in a public space or an intersection, and making moving speeches to rouse their spirits [20]

Thaapa (a bat used for beating clothes while washing) became their symbol of resistance, and '*Thaapa rakh tayyar kurray*' became the slogan used by the women peasants in Okara, meaning, '*Keep your washing bat ready girl!*' . When the army rangers attempted to prevent the harvest from taking place, for example, these women would show up with their *thaapas* and bar vehicles from entering the villages. Further, their movement became a truly intersectional example of feminist solidarity, bridging sectarian, religious and class divides. As Saeed points out, nearly half the population of landless peasants is Christian (p.70), and as women in the movement began acquiring leadership status, they started forging relationships with urban feminists of different class and educational backgrounds. National and international organizations linked to the Christian community started offering material and media support strengthen and publicize the movement, as did various urban-based women's rights NGOs, which helped to forge facilitative bonds of solidarity in the face of extreme repression targeting the peasants' rights movement by the powerful Army state apparatus (Saeed, p. 70). While the peasants have not been able to obtain full ownership of the land so far, they have managed not to give their crop to the land managers for over eleven years now (Saeed, p 73).

Figure 3: Book Cover Image, *On Their Own Terms*, By Fouzia Saeed

Over time, splits in the movement have occurred, with women now organized as a separate faction called the Peasant Women's Society, and some women leaders within the AMP exhibiting different leadership strategies/approaches than what they started out with. Yet, the overall mission and goal has remained the same and because of solidarity building across different groups, the movement has succeeded in ending violent confrontations between the state and the peasant farmers, and "the landless, powerless families who had considered abuse and humiliation their fate for generations now control their own lives" (Saeed p 72).

Women labor activists from the AMP, such as an Okara-based leader named Badrunnisah, who has been arrested several times over the course of this struggle for land rights, made a speech at an evening event that featured performances of skits, songs, motivational speeches and poetry in Lahore marking International Women's Day in 2018. It was organized by the newly-formed Feminist Collective composed largely of younger-generation feminists and LGBTQ activists. I was in attendance there and witnessed a variety of performances that became performatives of the remarkable solidarity across different groups and movements for social justice unfolding in contemporary Pakistan.

Here are Badrunissah's words to me, which encapsulate the feminist movement-building through performances of cross-class solidarity across urban-rural divides I have chronicled here:

> I had approximately 13-14 FIR's [First Information reports that start official police and legal proceedings against accused persons) -- on me when I first came to Lahore, and I didn't think I would be with my kids, in fact I thought I would be behind bars. But before I was jailed for my activism, these feminist groups [the urban-base Women's Action Forum, and the Feminist Collective] got to me, and they have provided such incredible support to me that even if I quoted their example all my life, it wouldn't be enough. And now my kids are in Lahore, I am in Lahore, I go to Okara, I come back and handle my issues there and here. My daughter is now doing an MA in history and Law at Government College, and my son is doing his BA and has a job, thanks to support and guidance from these women's organizations who have helped us in our fight.' (Baddrunisah, interview with author, March 8th, 2018, Lahore Alhamra).

Figure 4: Photo of BaddrunisahW taken by the author

In the Pakistani province of Sind, women farmers inspired by their sisters' struggle in the Punjab, have won land tenancy for the first time; 1214 landless women farmers and sharecroppers have received land tenancy rights for the first time in their lives as of 2016

Figure 5: Women farmers/sharecroppers show off their Land Tenancy Agreements from their Landlords in Mirpur Khas District, Sindh Province, Pakistan. Photo: UN Women/Faria Salma

Before concluding this section, I want to draw attention briefly to how, across Pakistan's border with India, Indian women farmers contributed prominently to the challenge issued by the Indian Farmers Movement, against the neoliberalist, Hindu fundamentalist and rentier capitalist ideological agenda of PM Narendra Modi's government. That such was the character of the Indian Farmers Movement as a whole, was recognized as a shared experience of oppression across South Asia's borders by the Pakistani wing of Farm Workers organizations. Farooq Tariq, the general secretary of the Pakistan Kissan Rabita (Farmers' Contact) Committee (PKRC), in an interview with The Diplomat, for instance, called out the common struggle thus:

> The Indian farmers' movement is against the neoliberal agenda that [Indian Prime Minister Narendra] Modi has been trying to impose there – privatize everything, give everything to big companies, end the **mandi** [market] system, end the minimum support price, and let the market dictate everything. Those realities already exist in Pakistan[21]

However, as Pramila Venkateswaran argues cogently[22], it is important for the Indian farmers' protest movement that recently took New Delhi, India, and the world at large by storm, to be seen as an intersectional feminist issue, with women activists who are part of the long arc of farmer activism in Indian history, protesting not only the Indian state with its development model, but also patriarchy and capitalism.

Figure 6: The Economic Times: India's 'invisible' women hope for recognition at farmers' protests

Thus, referencing the environmental feminist philosopher and activist Vandana Shiva, Venkateswaran claims that Shiva's brand of ecological activism is based on understanding that the exploitation of the earth and our ecology is "both intersectional and transnational" and that the oppression of the most vulnerable, that includes Mother Earth, women, and the poor, has its roots in the neoliberal world order that yokes together colonialism and capitalism to create an undending cycle of deprivation for the many and profits for the few.

Drawing attention to grassroots movements such as Fatima Burnad's Society for Rural Education and Development (SRED), which lists support of women farmers as part of the intersectional model it uses to challenge the oppression of Dalit and women in a spirit of solidarity, that brings " religious, caste, communal, and gender perspectives into the fight for farmers' rights," Venkateswaran concludes.

> As Shiva and other feminist activists see, a stitching together of agricultural activism across borders can impact governments subservient to corporate interests. In the current farmers' protest, Sikh women in the U.S., Canada, Amsterdam, are taking to the streets, bringing attention to their farming families spread over the diaspora. (Venkateswaran, "Farmers' Protest)

Drawing lessons of hope from this wave of farmers' protests, Vijay Prashad concludes,

The cycle of farmer agitations and the linkage with the main trade union federations suggests the possibility of the future growth of progressive forces.[23]

Afghanistan: The Nexus and its Deadly Effects on Women and their Resistance

Vera Mackie, in an article entitled "Faces of Feminism in Transnational Media Space,", delineates the continuing colonialist significations of the trope of the veil as it has been used to justify the imperialist US-NATO war in Afghanistan following 9/11. Pointing to several cover images of Afghan women photographed in their seemingly ubiquitous blue burqas, Mackie observes how,

> ...the way that the veiled woman is deployed in a series of metonymical associations... [she stands in] for the people of Afghanistan, the land of Afghanistan, and by extension the nation-state of Afghanistan. The deployment of a female figure as metonym for the nation, however, means that any narratives of the invasion of the nation, attacks on the nation, defeat of the nation, and what has been termed the 'liberation' of the nation, are also expressed in terms of gendered metaphors.[24]

Thus, the desire expressed by western photographers, painters, writers, occupiers of Muslim lands and the white women who support these ideological efforts to "unveil the woman" of the undifferentiated "Middle East"-- stands in for the desire to achieve full knowledge of this or that nation[25] and the unveiling of the woman in the case of Afghanistan, became both metaphor and metonym for 'saving' the nation from the oppressive Taliban regime by the armed forces of the United States and its allies. But as many scholars have pointed out, this "saving of the brown women from brown men,"[26] has provided convenient cover (pun intended)—for the US/West's continuing colonial/imperial economic and hegemonic agendas.

> Mackie has termed the support by Laura Bush and the Feminist Majority Foundation of the Global War on Terror (GWOT) unleashed for 20 years in Afghanistan by the USA and its western/NATO allies, as "Imperial Feminism on Display." Ann Russo, another scholar writing on this war of occupation, reminds us how the justification for the US invasion of Afghanistan is connected to the arguments of the Feminist Majority Foundation's campaign to 'Stop Gender Apartheid in Afghanistan.' Indeed, shortly after the decision to bomb Afghanistan had been made following the attacks on the Twin Towers on 9/11, in which NO Afghans had been involved--the figure of the veiled and oppressed Afghan woman was invoked, and 'First Lady' Laura Bush emerged from her own domestic space to make what was then a rare public speech calling for support for the 'war against terrorism' in the name of 'saving' Afghan women. In this "**mission civilisatrice**" First Lady Bush was backed up by feminist organizations in US such as the Feminist Majority Foundation. And while the Feminist Majority Foundations's campaign did bring public attention to some of the realities of women's lives

> under the Taliban since the mid-1990s, it did so, argues Russo, from a framework of 'imperial feminism' that ultimately continues to bolster US world hegemony and empire.[27]

This 'imperial feminist' awareness, as Russo and others point out[28], has circulated within US and European feminisms since the colonial era during the nineteenth century and on into the present, in service to different forms of empire building[29]. It is a feminism that focuses exclusively on the gender-based oppression of 'third world' women and does so 'without acknowledging the role of racism, colonialism and economic exploitation' (Russo, 558).

This imperial feminism is, indeed, part and parcel of a neoliberal global economic agenda to turn every society into a "free market" for US goods and services, as seen in the trillions of dollars spent on "development" projects in Afghanistan over the past 20 years that have benefitted a few at the expense of the many. Such a feminist project 'claims solidarity with Third World women and women of color, but in actuality contributes to the stereotyping of Third World cultures as "barbaric" and "uncivilized"', which then justifies imperialist intervention (Russo, 558). And, Russo further underlines,

> the campaign is mostly silent with respect to a history of US global geopolitical involvement in, and contributions to, the rise of the Taliban and fundamentalism in Afghanistan. Even in its current critique of the US military's failure to provide adequate security forces and lack of follow through in supporting women's rights in Afghanistan, the Feminist Majority Foundation never questions the underlying premises of the US invasion and the right to control the future of Afghanistan (Russo, 559).

And this "right to control" has, as I have also been arguing, has everything to do with maintaining the economic advantage of capitalist neoliberalism for US Empire in our own day and age. Michael Schwartz also draws attention to this nexus of US military neoliberalism/ neoliberal US-backed enterprise of state-building that has occurred through a displacement of the Afghan state itself when he claims that Republican President George W. Bush's National Security Strategy of 2006, which was the predecessor of Democratic President Barak Obama's NSS four years later,

> included nine 'essential tasks' assigned to the United States military, many of them having nothing to do with the military. Prominent among these tasks: **'Ignite a new era of global economic growth through free markets and free trade'**[30]

Indeed, the Afghanistan National Development Strategy (ANDS, 2008- 2013), which was written for the neoliberal transnational corporate interests represented by the World Bank and the International Monetary Fund (IMF), listed as the third goal of its Prioritization and Implementation Plan (PIP) from mid-2010 to mid-2013, that poverty reduction and development will be based on a *"private-sector-led market economy,"* without noting the growing economic gap between the poor and the rich and the resentment this gap has created within and among and between different sectors within, societies.[31] Such neoliberal-driven state-building enterprises working in tandem with an ongoing occupation and bombing campaign orchestrated by the US, have created resentment among the majority of rural based poor Afghans (including women)—against this intervention that led to corruption and worsening conditions for them and contributed to the rise back into power of the Taliban. [32]

RAWA, Revolutionary Association of Women of Afghanistan–and Women's Resistance

For many years before the so-called global 'war against terrorism' (GWOT), non-governmental organizations, including The Revolutionary Association of Women in Afghanistan (RAWA), had been circulating information to the West and around the world about the oppressive conditions suffered by women under the regimes of the Mujahideen (who the US supported)—and their successors, the Taliban. Women and girl children were being prevented from receiving an education or working outside the home and their freedom and mobility were severely restricted. Regular reports and petitions were circulated by e-mail for several years before the so-called 'war against terrorism' commenced. However, in those years, there was no move to intervene in this situation from the United States, its allies, or the United Nations.

RAWA was formed in Afghanistan by Meena Keshwar Kamal in 1977, decades prior to the unfolding of GWOT, as an indigenous resistance movement of Afghan women against ongoing repression of their fundamental human rights under various regimes backed in those years by either the Soviet Union or the USA. Later, once the Taliban took office for the first time in 1996 following the defeat of the Soviet forces by US-armed mujahideen fighters, RAWA protested against the misogynistic religious fundamentalist beliefs being propagated to further curb Afghan women's rights and access to education and employment. Meena eventually moved and based her RAWA organization in Quetta, Pakistan, as it became too dangerous for her to continue living in Afghanistan. Both she and her husband were assassinated in Pakistan by suspected agents of KHAD, the Afghan Secret Service, and men in the employ of Gulbeddin Hekmatyar, an Afghan warlord, respectively, a few months apart in 1986/87.

According to its website, RAWA has continued its activities in Pakistan over the many decades since Meena's death, focusing on women's rights, human rights and exposition of the barbaric actions of Taliban extremists. Despite lack of funding and political support from neoliberal regimes, RAWA maintained its social work activities on behalf of Afghan women from refugee camps in Quetta and Peshawar. As scholar and community psychologist Anne Brodsky who has written a book about RAWA points out admiringly in a recent interview,

> On both sides of the Durand Line – the British-drawn boundary between Afghanistan and what is now Pakistan – RAWA established schools and orphanages for Afghan boys and girls, literacy programmes for older women, health clinics and income-generating programmes.[33]

RAWA's website also states that as part of their cultural activism (artivism), they have produced cassettes of songs usually with anti-fundamentalist content and containing educational content, they have staged dramas and skits; held "Nights of poetry" and "Nights of story"; published posters, brochures, booklets, "Payam-e-Zan" (both online and printed editions) in Pashtu, Persian and Urdu and the non-periodical "The Burst of The 'Islamic Government' Bubble in Afghanistan" in English.[34]

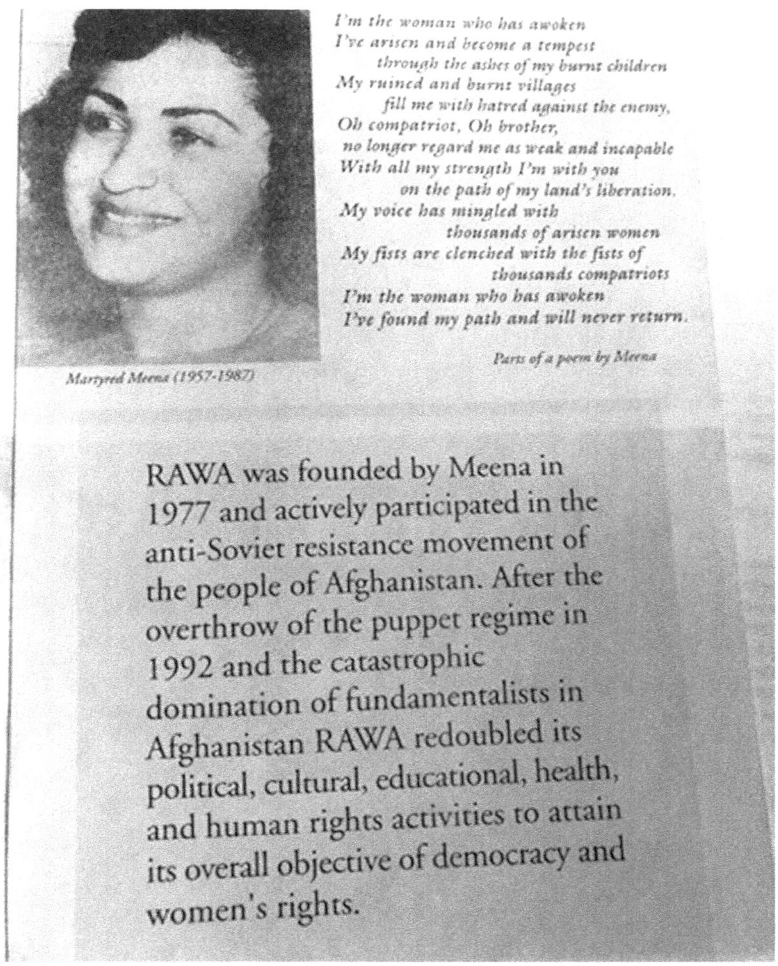

Figure 7: Poem by and Photo of Meena, Founder of RAWA- Revolutionary Association of Women of Afghanistan, circa 1986

However, RAWA has always raised awareness around the situation in Afghanistan being a result of many forces, including unwelcome foreign interventions buoyed up a neoliberal economic world system that keeps all manner of "fundamentalisms" in play and power at the expense of peoples' rights and security. Indeed, RAWA from its inception, saw/called out the nexus of fundamentalist patriarchy working in tandem with forces of neoliberal/postmodern capitalism and imperialism to keep the entire citizenry of Afghanistan impoverished. For instance, on the first days of the US occupation of Afghanistan in 2001, RAWA had declared in a public statement published on the internet dated October 11, 2001:

> The continuation of US attacks and the increase in the number of innocent civilian victims not only gives an excuse to the Taliban, but also will cause the empowering of the fundamentalist forces in the region and even in the world. [35]

And, later, during the era of the Obama administration, RAWA had this to say:

> The so-called 'new' strategy of Obama's administration and the surge of troops in Afghanistan have already dragged our ill-fated people in the danger zone and his 100-day old government proved itself as much more war-mongering than Bush and his only gifts to our people is hiking killings and ever-horrifying oppression. This administration is bombarding our country and tearing our women and children into pieces and from the other side, is lending a friendly hand towards the terrorist Gulbuddinis and Taliban -- the dirty, bloody enemies of our people-- and holding secret negotiations and talks with such brutal groups.[36]

Here is RAWA's statement on the 20-year US-NATO occupation of Afghanistan and its economically disastrous effects that have in fact, strengthened the hand of the Taliban:

> It is worth mentioning that the United States and the West have tried for 20 years to keep Afghanistan a consumer country and have hindered the growth of industry. This situation created a wave of unemployment and poverty, paving the way for the recruitments of the puppet government, the Taliban and growth of opium production.

Alongside this strong indictment of US economic "underdevelopment" in Afghanistan, RAWA also provided a broader overview of this terrible war and its consequences for women:

> In the past 20 years, one of our demands was an end to the US/NATO occupation and even better if they take their Islamic fundamentalists and technocrats with them and let our people decide their own fate. This occupation only resulted in bloodshed, destruction and chaos. They turned our country into the most corrupt, insecure, drug-mafia and dangerous place especially for women...from the very beginning we could predict such an outcome.

Indeed, the only logical conclusion to the ongoing destruction visited not just on Afghanistan, but the planet, has led RAWA to issue a clarion call for transnational solidarity among progressive forces, led by women, around the globe. On International Women's Day 2022, RAWA declared, in a clear-eyed statement, the need to recognize, and thence to continue "our fight against, the tyrannical ideological nexus of patriarchal religion, neoliberal capitalism, and imperialism"[37]

Figure 8: RAWA statement on the International Women's Day, 2022:

The women of Afghanistan, who have been held captive by the most misogynist and inhuman group in the history of our country, due to the 20-year betrayal and crimes of the US/NATO and their Afghan mercenaries, are living in cruelly odious times. The ongoing conditions proves that the world has once again completely forgotten them. On the eve of the International Women's Day, a large-scale campaign in support of Afghan women was expected around the world, but due to the Ukraine crisis and the conflict between the opposing militarist superpowers, the case of Afghanistan, and especially its women, has once again become completely indifferent.... the fight against terrorism would be incomplete without the fight against imperialism and its ideologies. Forty years betrayal of the White House and its fundamentalist and non-fundamentalist mercenaries proved to Afghan people by experience that a homeland can't be saved by relying on any external power and its puppets. Only with the slogan of death to fundamentalism and imperialism under the banner of secular democracy, can we overcome the catastrophic disaster and open the way to full political and economic independence, freedom and social justice. Afghan women must be at the forefront of this great struggle because they have shown in practice that they have the potential and the determination for such a great cause. Now that imperialist states and deadly arms traders have turned the planet into a gunpowder depot on the eve of another world war, it is the

responsibility of every conscious human being to seek to revive the international anti-war and anti-imperialist movement. If especially the people of the great imperialist countries do not perform this task, the super-capitalists will lead the world to complete destruction of human future for their own benefit.
(http://www.rawa.org/rawa/2022/03/08/afghan-women-will-never-surrender-to-the-most-misogynist-and-inhumane-group.html)

A Conclusion That is Ongoing: Progressive Solidarities

Vijay Prashad, in his inspiring book about earlier anticolonial movements (as exemplified in the Bandung Conference and the Non-Aligned Movement) and how their political insights and solidarities need to be revived in our own times, offers the following conclusion that is ongoing:

> The third world may be in distress, where the will of the national liberation movements has put the tendency to anti-imperialism in crisis, and where the Third World within the United States has often been overrun by the dynamic of the color blind and of the desire to make small, individual gains over social transformation. Nevertheless, the struggle is on, in places like Kerala and Vietnam, but also within the USA as the Black Radical Congress greets the Asian Left Forum, the Forum of Indian Leftists, the League of Filipino Students...and all of them join together in the fight against imperialism, against racism. **History is made in the struggle and past memories of solidarity are inspiration for that struggle**[38].

Indeed, the women activists of RAWA are a prime instantiation of Prashad's contention that the "struggle is on," for their statement on International Women's Day 2022 is a clarion call for all progressive forces to join and participate in this movement for solidarity against the deadly nexus:

> While we do not expect the slightest from the warring Western governments and the rulers of the neighbors involved in Afghanistan, we call on the progressive forces, women's rights organizations, progressive figures and peace activists to side with the miserable women and people of Afghanistan and to disclose and condemn the interventions of their policy-makers.

An important component of what I'm calling an ongoing "conclusion", is our recognition that we clearly haven't yet reached it and may never do so, but which therefore requires us to recommit to the struggle at every stage and in our own era, such a recognition demands that we acknowledge a worldwide debt to Black Feminism.

Black feminism provides us with the possibility of a coalitional model of politics that can help us re-commit to the goals of progressive solidarity to end the chokehold (pun unintended) of the nexus of neoliberal capitalism, imperialism and religious as well as secular patriarchies. Therefore, now is a perfect time to enunciate clearly, the meaning of Black feminist identity politics that requires us to recognize it as a maneuver of strategic essentialism, en route to building affiliative coalitions across race, class, gender, sexuality and nation.[39] Black feminism has produced an influential analysis and approach to combating all forms of oppression — particularly patriarchy, white supremacy, and capitalism—within a common struggle that has come to be known as identity politics, but one that calls for broad (re) conception of "identity" that can—nay, must—move from essentialist understandings of identity to identity-as-affiliation, arising out of shared political visions and affiliations. This is a form of politics that can be called feminist, anti-racist, socialist, and I would add, also anti-imperialist.[1]

Today, the most progressive forms of Black feminism embrace the notion that solidarity means to fight for someone you don't know but whose vision for social change you share. This Black feminist call for solidarity whilst based in ideas of difference-in-identity, moves beyond it to notions of affiliation leading to a coalitional politics (an idea also at the root of Jesse Jackson's rallying cry in the 1980s for a Rainbow Coaltion)—and in so doing invites us to look at hierarchies of class, gender, sexuality and race, and to grasp how these hierarchies impact both individuals and collectives. A Black model of feminism thus has the power to foster solidarity and make our movements stronger. Solidarity doesn't mean we are all the same or always in agreement; but it does open up the space for collective action toward political goals that are interlinked in a struggle to create a better, more equitable and just world. Therefore, solidarity requires that we not subscribe to a narrowly conceived idea of "identity"—but rather, embrace a global and transnational affiliative politics, that is rooted in the recognition of identity as intersectional, allowing us to work together to ensure a world for generations that follow, that will be based on social justice ideals. That is the reward of a transnational feminist commitment to end the injustices perpetuated by the intertwined nexus of neoliberal capitalism, patriarchy, and imperialism.[40]

REFERENCE

Afzal-Khan, Fawzia. "Exposed by Pakistani Theatre: the Unholy Alliance of Postmodern Capitalism, Patriarchy, and Fundamentalism." *Social Text*. Vol 19, number 4 (69), 2001, 67-91.

A Critical Stage: the Role of Secular Alternative Theatre in Pakistan. Seagull Press, 2005.

Abu-Lughod, Lila. "Do Muslim Women Really Need Saving? Anthropological Reflections on Cultural Relativism and its Others." *American Anthropologist*, vol. 104, No. 3 (Sep 2002), 783-790.

Akhtar, Aasim Sajjad. "Reading between the lines: the *mullah* – military alliance in Pakistan." *Contemporary South Asia*. Volume 15, issue 4: 2006, 383-397.

The state as landlord in Pakistani Punjab: Peasant struggles on the Okara military farms," *Journal of Peasant Studies*, July 2006, 33(3):479-501. July 2006.

Ali, Imran. *The Punjab Under Imperialism, 1885-1947*. Princeton, NJ: Princeton University Press.

Alloula, Malek. *The Colonial Harem*, University of Minnesota Press, 1986.

Amos, V. and Parmar, P. 'Challenging Imperial Feminism', *Feminist Review* 17: 3–19, 1984.

"Battling the 'patriarchy pandemic" https://www.dw.com/en/pakistani-women-protest-patriarchy-pandemic /a-56808462

Chomsky, Noam and David Barsamian. *The Prosperous Few and the Restless Many*. Odonian Press,1994

Combahee River Collective Statement, 1973. https://www.reed.edu/cres/assets/Combahee-River-Collective,-Black-Feminist-Statement,-How-We-Get-Free---Taylor.pdf

Fraser, Nancy, Cinzia Arruza and Tithi Bhattacharya, *Feminism for the 99%: A Manifesto*. Verso Books, 2019.

Gopal, Anand. "The Other Afghan Women," *The New Yorker,* Sept 6, 2021. https://www.newyorker.com/magazine/2021/09/13/the-other-afghan-women

Klasra, Kaswar. "Threatened by Violence and Intimidation, Pakistani Women Still Vow to March," NBC News, March 7, 2022. https://www.nbcnews.com/news/world/pakistani-international-womens-day-marchers-face-threats-rcna18938

Klein, Naomi. *The Shock Doctrine: The Rise of Disaster Capitalism*. Holt and Company, 2007.

Mackie, Vera. "Faces of Feminism in Transnational Media Space." http://www.igs.ocha.ac.jp/igs/IGS_publication/journal/6/journal06001.pdf

Mallick, Ayyaz. "Okara Military Farms: Ownership or Death." *Fair Observer,* March 15, 2013. https://www.fairobserver.com/region/central_south_asia/okara-military-farms-ownership-or-death/

Popalzai, Zubair. "Neo-liberal State-building and Displacement of the Afghan State." https://www.files.ethz.ch/isn/167203/Neoliberal_St_(BMC)_FINAL.pdf

Prashad, Vijay. "India's Farmers' Protests Could upend the Political Landscape." *The Peoples' Dispatch,* March 02, 2021. https://peoplesdispatch.org/2021/03/03/how-indias-farmers-protests-could-upend-the-political-landscape/

Everybody Was Kung Fu Fighting: Afro-Asian Connections and the Myth of Cultural Purity. Boston: Beacon Press, 2001.

Revolutionary Association of the Women of Afghanistan (RAWA) 1997-2022. www.rawa.org And http://www.rawa.org/rawa/2022/03/08/afghan-women-will-never-surrender-to-the-most-misogynist-and-inhumane-group.html

Rizvi, Mubbashir A. *The Ethics of Staying: Social Movements and Land Rights Politics in Pakistan,* Stanford: Stanford University Press, 2019.

Russo, Ann. "The Intersections of Feminism and Imperialism in the United States" in *International Feminist Journal of Politics,* 8:4 December 2006, 557– 580 http://www.csun.edu/~sm60012/GRCS-Files/Readings/Russo-Feminist_Majority.pdf

Saeed, Fouzia . *On Their Own Terms: Early 21st Century Women's Movements in Pakistan*. Karachi: Oxford University Press, 2020.

Schwartz, Michael. "Military Neoliberalism: Endless War and Humanitarian Crisis in the Twenty-First Century." *Societies Without Borders* 6 (3): 2011, 190-303. https://scholarlycommons.law.case.edu/swb/vol6/iss3/3)

Shahid, Kunwar Khuldune. *Newsbeat National,* 2016. https://newslinemagazine.com/magazine/land-land-peasants-okara-fight-rights/

"Pakistani Farmers Are Gearing Up For India-Like Protests," in *The Diplomat,* Feb 25, 2021. https://thediplomat.com/2021/02/pakistani-farmers-are-gearing-up-for-india-like-protests/

Spivak, Gayatri C. "Can the Subaltern Speak?" in *Colonial Discourse and Post-Colonial Theory: A Reader* eds. Patrick Williams and Laura Chrisman. Hemel Hempstead: Harvester, 1993.

Deconstructing Historiography." *Selected Subaltern Studies*. New Delhi: Oxford University Press, 1988, 3-32.

ENDNOTES

1 Fawzia Afzal-Khan is Professor of English, a University Distinguished Scholar (2009-10), and former Director of the Women and Gender Studies Program at Montclair State University, NJ (2009-2015). In addition to having published numerous scholarly and journalistic essays, poems, plays and a memoir *Lahore with Love: Growing Up With Girlfriends Pakistani Style* (Syracuse University Press, 2010), she has authored three books of scholarly criticism, *Cultural Imperialism: Genre and Ideology in the Indo-English Novel* (Penn State Press 1993), *A Critical Stage: The Role of Secular Alternative Theatre in Pakistan* (Seagull Press, 2005), and *Siren Song: Understanding Pakistan Through its Women Singers* (OUP: 2020), and edited two scholarly anthologies, *The PreOccupation of Postcolonial Studies* (Duke University Press, 2000), and *Shattering the Stereotypes: Muslim Women Speak* Out (Interlink Books 2005).

Fellowships awarded include most recently, the Fulbright-Hays Visiting Specialist award (2016-2022), and the National Endowment for the Humanities Bridging Cultures Through Film award (2011). She has also held a W.E.B Dubois Fellowship at Harvard University and been a Rotary International and AIPS (American Institute of Pakistan Studies) Fellow and won an NJCH (NJ Council of the Humanities) grant for a symposium on Women's Cross-Cultural Prison Memoirs. She was also Writer-in-Residence at Chateau de Lavigny in Switzerland 2005 which enabled her to complete her memoir.

Afzal-Khan is a trained vocalist in North Indian Classical music, a published playwright, actor and poet, whose scholarly, journalistic and creative writing focuses on issues of gender and social justice from a postcolonial perspective.

She is also producer and director of the award-winning short documentary film, *Siren Song*, about Pakistani women singers, which has several different versions including an earlier one called *The Nightingales of Pakistan: from the Melody Queen to the Muslim Madonna.* She is a regular contributor to *Counterpunch.org*, and currently serves on the Editorial and/or Advisory Boards of *TDR (The Drama Review)* and *Arab Stages* and has served in the past on the boards of *SAR (South Asian Review)*, *Transformations*, and *International Solidarity (Journal of Pakistani English Literature)*. She is a member of the NY chapter of NOW (National Organization of Women), the Modern Language Association and NWSA, where she is founding chair of the South Asian Feminist Caucus. She is a long-time member of IFTR (International Federation of Theatre Research) where she has belonged to the Feminist Research Working Group for over 20 years. She maintains a blog called www.travelingfeminista.com and her website can be accessed at www.fawziaafzalkhan.com

2 https://monthlyreview.org/2021/03/01/racial-capitalism-and-covid-19/

3 Noam Chomsky, interviewed by David Barsamian, in *The Prosperous Few and the Restless Many*, Odonian Press,1994, p 5.

4 https://www.ids.ac.uk/events/the-corruption-of-capitalism-why-rentiers-thrive-and-work-does-not-pay/

5 Zoom, for instance, made 660 million$ in 2020, but paid 0 federal income tax on profits which increased over the previous year by 4000%. According to the Institute on Taxation and Economic Policy, at least 55 of the largest US corporations paid zero$ in Federal taxes on 2020 profits.

6 Nancy Fraser, Cinzia Arruza and Tithi Bhattacharya, *Feminism for the 99%: A Manifesto*, Verso Books, 2019.

7 "breaking the glass ceiling" can be seen as akin to liberal mainstreaming of gender—by simply incorporating women (add and stir) into existing structures, rather than transforming the structures themselves.

8 See Naomi Klein, *The Shock Doctrine: The Rise of Disaster Capitalism*. Holt and Company, 2007.

9 See Fawzia Afzal-Khan, "Exposed by Pakistani Theatre: the Unholy Alliance of Postmodern Capitalism, Patriarchy, and Fundamentalism," in *Social Text*. Vol 19, number 4 (69), 2001. P. 67-91. https://doi.org/10.1215/01642472-19-4_69-67

10 Agnes Khoo, "Women's Rights and Migrant Workers' Rights: Subverting Globalization and Reaffirming internationalism." Cited in Afzal-Khan, Fawzia, "Exposed by Pakistani Theatre: The Unholy Alliance of Postmodern Capitalism, Patriarchy, and Fundamentalism," in *Social Text*. Vol 19, number 4 (69), 2001, p. 77.

11 Aasim Sajjad Akhtar et al point out, and I agree: "there is evidence that the emergence of the religious right as a political force in Pakistan is an outcome of state patronage. Following the 'War on Terror', corporate media and official western representations of revivalist trends in Pakistan have been almost completely de-contextualised. This representation has provided both the dominant military state oligarchy and the religious right an ideal opportunity to reinforce an old alliance previously supported by western imperialism, while eroding the organising capacity of progressive social and political forces in Pakistan." "Reading between the lines: the *mullah* – military alliance in Pakistan," in Contemporary South Asia, Vol 15, Issue 4: 2006 (383-397). https://doi.org/10.1080/09584930701329982

12 For further elaboration of the coming together of women's rights and theatre activists especially during the 1980s and 90s, see Fawzia Afzal-Khan, *A Critical Stage: The Role of Secular Alternative Theatre in Pakistan* (Seagull Press, 2005).

13 "The object of the WPB [Women's Protection Bill] was to 'bring the laws relating to zina (sex outside of marriage) and qazf (perjury), in particular, in conformity with the stated objectives of the Islamic Republic of Pakistan and...in particular to provide relief and protection to women against misuse and abuse of law.' The most important feature of the WPB is that it breaks the link between the offenses of rape and zina, so that a woman who brings a charge of rape is no longer in jeopardy of being prosecuted for zina." https://www.dawn.com/news/630865/2006-political-drama-of-womensprotection-bill

14 Kaswar Klasra, "Threatened by Violence and Intimidation, Pakistani Women Still Vow to March," NBC News, March 7, 2022. Accessed: https://www.nbcnews.com/news/world/pakistani-international-womens-day-marchers-face-threats-rcna18938

15 'Battling the 'patriarchy pandemic' https://www.dw.com/en/pakistani-women-protest-patriarchy-pandemic/a-56808462

16 See Imran Ali, *The Punjab Under Imperialism, 1885-1947*. Princeton, NJ: Princeton University Press. Also, Ayyaz Mallick, "Okara Military Farms: Ownership or Death," in *Fair Observer*, March 15, 2013. Accessed https://www.fairobserver.com/region/central_south_asia/okara-military-farms-ownership-or-death/. And Mubbashir A. Rizvi, *The Ethics of Staying: Social Movements and Land Rights Politics in Pakistan*, Stanford: Stanford University Press, 2019.

17 Aasim Sajjad Akhtar, "The state as landlord in Pakistani Punjab: Peasant struggles on the Okara military farms," *Journal of Peasant Studies*, July 2006, 33(3):479-501. July 2006. DOI:10.1080/03066150601063058

18 Statistics reported in https://newslinemagazine.com/magazine/land-land-peasants-okara-fight-rights/

19 "Peasant women were confronted by the military officials at Okara Military Farms while protesting against the arrest of Mehr Abdul Sattar [one of the leaders of the resistance movement]," says Asim Raza Dogar a local resident and activist. "The army surpassed all limits of brutality when they sent tanks and guns to target their own citizens, many of whom were injured." Kunwar Khuldune Shahid, *Newsbeat National*, 2016. https://newslinemagazine.com/magazine/land-land-peasants-okara-fight-rights/

20 Fouzia Saeed, *On Their Own Terms: Early 21st Century Women's Movements in Pakistan*. Karachi: Oxford University Press, 2020, p. 44.

21 Kunwar Khuldune Shahid, "Pakistani Farmers Are Gearing Up For India-Like Protests," in *The Diplomat*, Feb 25, 2021. https://thediplomat.com/2021/02/pakistani-farmers-are-gearing-up-for-india-like-protests/

22 Pramila Venkateshwaran, "Farmers' Protest in India Is An Intersectional Feminist Issue," in Women in and Beyond the Global, Dec 27, 2020. Accessed at http://www.womeninandbeyond.org/?p=24548

23 Vijay Prashad, "India's Farmers' Protests Could upend the Political Landscape," in The Peoples' Dispatch, March 02, 2021. Accessed https://peoplesdispatch.org/2021/03/03/how-indias-farmers-protests-could-upend-the- political-landscape/

24 Vera Mackie, "Faces of Feminism in Transnational Media Space," http://www.igs.ocha.ac.jp/igs/IGS_publication/journal/6/journal06001.pdf (accessed Jan 9th, 2022).

25 One of the earliest such studies is of French photographers in Algeria, documented and analyzed at length by Malek Alloula in *The Colonial Harem*, University of Minnesota Press, 1986.

26 This phrase was popularized by postcolonial feminist critic and scholar G.C. Spivak in "Can the Subaltern Speak?" in *Colonial Discourse and Post-Colonial Theory: A Reader* eds. Patrick Williams and Laura Chrisman. Hemel Hempstead: Harvester, 1993, p. 93.

27 "The Intersections of Feminism and Imperialism in the United States" in *International Feminist Journal of Politics*, 8:4 December 2006, 557– 580. Can be accessed at http://www.csun.edu/~sm60012/GRCS-Files/Readings/Russo-Feminist_Majority.pdf

28 Russo, citing Amos, V. and Parmar, P. 1984. 'Challenging Imperial Feminism', *Feminist Review* 17: 3–19.

29 See for example, Lila Abu-Lughod's now iconic essay on the topic, "Do Muslim Women Really Need Saving? Anthropological Reflections on Cultural Relativism and its Others" in *American Anthropologist*, vol. 104, No. 3 (Sep 2002), pp. 783-790.

30 Michael Schwartz, "Military Neoliberalism: Endless War and Humanitarian Crisis in the Twenty-First Century." *Societies Without Borders* 6 (3): 190-303, 2011, my emphasis. Available at: https://scholarlycommons.law.case.edu/swb/vol6/iss3/3)

31 Zubair Popalzai, "Neo-liberal State-building and Displacement of the Afghan State" (p. 1) https://www.files.ethz.ch/isn/167203/Neoliberal_St_(BMC)_FINAL.pdf)

32 See Anand Gopal, "The Other Afghan Women," in The New Yorker, Sept 6, 2021. https://www.newyorker.com/magazine/2021/09/13/the-other-afghan-women.

33 https://www.aljazeera.com/features/2022/3/1/the-afghan-revolutionary-who-took-on-the-soviets-and-patriarchy

34 Revolutionary Association of the Women of Afghanistan (RAWA) 1997-2022. www.rawa.org

35 http://www.rawa.org/us-strikes.htm

36 http://www.rawa.org/rawa/2009/05/07/lets-rise-against-the-war-crimes-of-us-and-its-fundamentalist-lackeys.html

37 Standing, Guy. *The Corruption of Capitalism: Why Rentiers Thrive and Work Does Not Pay*. Biteback Publishing, 2018.

38 Vijay Prashad, *Everybody Was Kung Fu Fighting: Afro-Asian Connections and the Myth of Cultural Purity*. Boston: Beacon Press, 2001, p 148-9, my emphasis

39 Strategic essentialism is a concept coined by postcolonial feminist theorist Gayatri Spivak, that advocates a provisional acceptance of essentialist foundations for categories of identity such as those of gender, race, class etc, mobilizing such identitarian notions as a strategy for shaping broader collective affiliations in order to pursue shared political goals. See Gayatri C. Spivak, "Deconstructing Historiography," in *Selected Subaltern Studies*. New Delhi: Oxford University Press, 1988. pp. 3-32.

40 This intersectional understanding of Black Feminism was promulgated very clearly in the manifesto of the Combahee River Collective in 1973. It can be accessed her https://www.reed.edu/cres/assets/Combahee-River-Collective,-Black-Feminist-Statement,-How-We-Get-Free---Taylor.pdf

CPSIA information can be obtained
at www.ICGtesting.com
Printed in the USA
LVHW070720210323
742130LV00007B/121

9 781952 356025